CINÉFRANCO
2004

Thank you sponsors
for your invaluable support.

Thank you audience
for making the 7th annual celebration
a great success.

See you in 2005!

www.cinefranco.com <http://www.cinefranco.com>

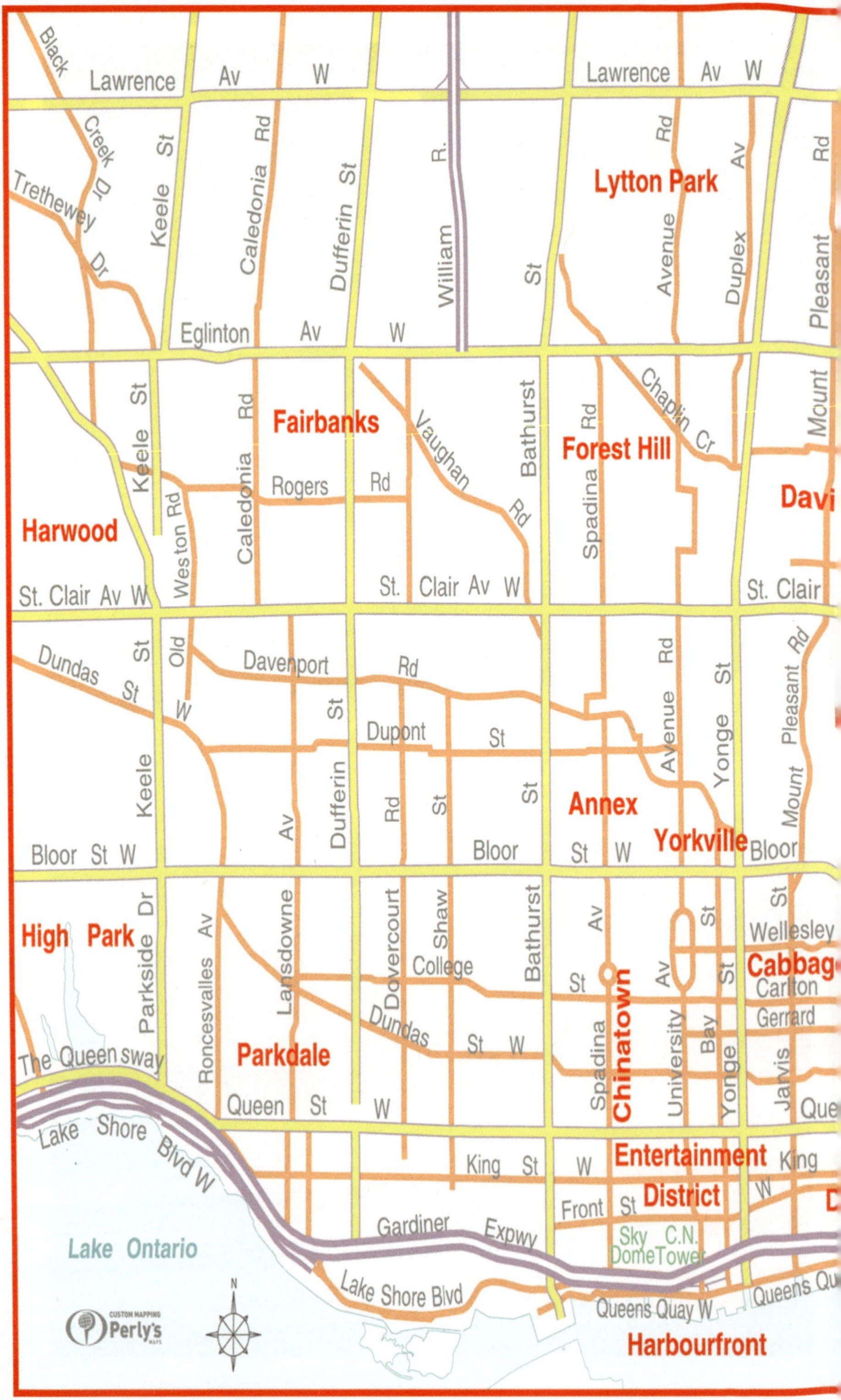
Lawrence Av W
Black Creek Dr
Trethewey Dr
Keele St
Caledonia Rd
Dufferin St
William R.
St
Lytton Park
Avenue Rd
Duplex Av
Mount Pleasant Rd
Eglinton Av W
Fairbanks
Vaughan Rd
Bathurst
Forest Hill
Spadina Rd
Chaplin Cr
Rogers Rd
Harwood
Weston Rd
Davi
St. Clair Av W
Old Weston Rd
Dundas St W
Davenport Rd
Dupont St
Annex
Yorkville
Lansdowne Av
Dovercourt Rd
Shaw St
Bloor St W
High Park
Parkside Dr
Roncesvalles Av
College St
Wellesley St
Cabbag
Carlton
Gerrard
Spadina Av
Chinatown
University Av
Bay St
Yonge St
Jarvis St
The Queensway
Parkdale
Queen St W
Que
Lake Shore Blvd W
King St W
Entertainment District
King W
Front St
Gardiner Expwy
Sky Dome
C.N. Tower
Lake Ontario
Lake Shore Blvd
Queens Quay W
Queens Qu
Harbourfront
N
CUSTOM MAPPING
Perly's
MAPS

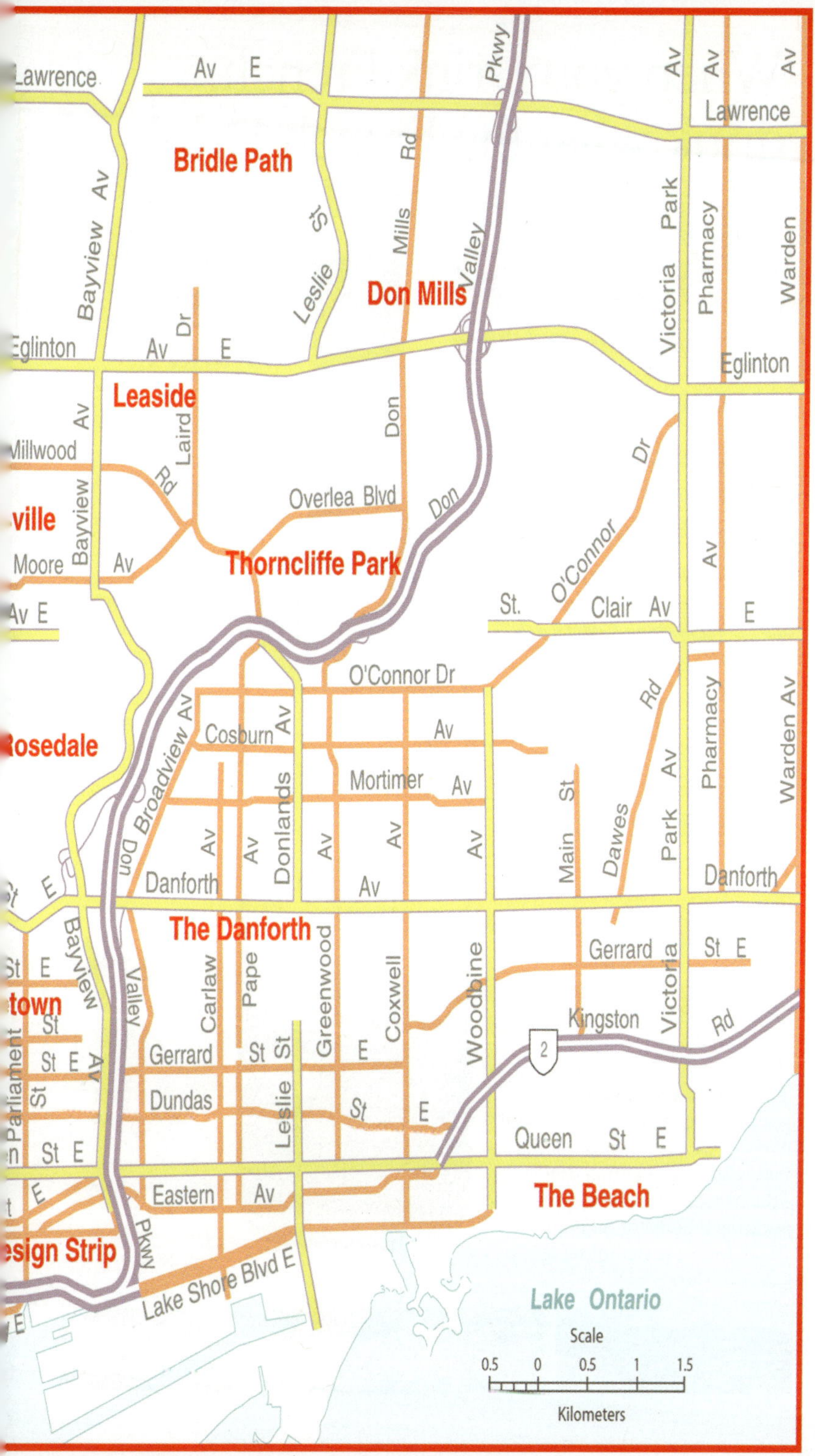
Bridle Path
Don Mills
Leaside
Thorncliffe Park
Rosedale
The Danforth
The Beach
Design Strip
Lake Ontario
Lawrence Av E
Eglinton Av E
Millwood Rd
Moore Av
St. Clair Av E
O'Connor Dr
Cosburn Av
Mortimer Av
Danforth Av
Gerrard St E
Dundas St E
Queen St E
Eastern Av
Lake Shore Blvd E
Kingston Rd
Overlea Blvd
Bayview Av
Leslie St
Don Mills Rd
Don Valley Pkwy
Laird Dr
Broadview Av
Donlands Av
Pape Av
Carlaw Av
Greenwood Av
Coxwell Av
Woodbine Av
Main St
Dawes Rd
Victoria Park Av
Pharmacy Av
Warden Av
Parliament St
2
Scale
0.5
0
0.5
1
1.5
Kilometers

the french side of toronto

The essential 2004 guide to French food and culture in Toronto.

franco **toronto**

FRANCO TORONTO MEDIA & PUBLISHING

ISBN: 0–9733020–1–1

All information is correct and accurate at the time of publishing and is subject to change at any moment. Changes may occur at any time between the research and printing stage. We apologize in advance for any discrepencies and recommend that readers contact merchants directly when absolute confirmations are needed.

Published by:	Franco Toronto Media & Publishing
Ordering:	contact@franco–toronto.ca
Advertising inquires:	ads@franco–toronto.ca
Special Sales:	Bulk purchases are available to corporations, organizations, mail-order catalogues, institutions and charities at special discounts.
Printed and bound in Canada by:	AGMV Marquis
Maps of Toronto provided by:	Perly's Maps, www.perlys.com

Visit our web site at **www.franco–toronto.ca**

contents

Testimonials 9

Acknowledgements 10

The French Side of Toronto Team 10

Foreword 11

Finding the Right Words 12

A Culinary Adventure

FRENCH FOOD SHOPPING

Breads, Pâtisseries & French Sweets 13

Chocolatiers 29

Cheese Shops and Crème Fraîche 43

Meats, Pâtés & Terrines 51

Fishmongers & Oyster Specialists 61

Other French Specialties 69

DINING OUT

Bistros 87

Fine Dining 105

Brunch 107

COOKING IN FRENCH

French Cooking Courses & Schools 117

A Cultural Adventure

INFORMATION & ENTERTAINMENT

Newspapers 122

Books & Magazines 122

Music 125

Film 126

Art Galleries 129

Theatre 130

Radio & Television 130

FRANCOPHONE & FRANCOPHILE GATHERINGS

French Cultural Events in Toronto 131

Evening Entertainment & Social Gatherings 132

Cultural Associations 133

Business Associations 134

Artists Associations 135

OTHER CULTURAL RESOURCES

The French Side of Toronto by Neighbourhood 136

Index 140

Here's what readers had to say about our first edition:

"Not only is The French Side of Toronto *replete with essential information for a Francophile like me, it is written in a delightful, very French style. It's an adventure in every sense of the word."*

— JEREMY PALMER, TORONTO

"As a French food lover, The French Side of Toronto *is my new bible! Fabulous work!"*

— NATASHA JONES, WHITBY

"This is a unique and useful guide which everyone visiting or living in Toronto should have."

— KARIN GENTON-L'EPÉE, PRAGUE

"One can really appreciate the multiculturalism of Toronto through this guide. It is a treasure for those who love anything French!"

— SANDRA SKAIRJEH, MISSISSAUGA

"I love The French Side of Toronto *because it's concise, yet packed full of useful information. I'm not French but this book makes me wish I was."*

— LYNN SHULMAN, TORONTO

"My seemingly endless search for a reliable source of fleur de sel is finally over thanks to your book. Fantastique!"

— IAN, TORONTO

"The authors dig out Toronto's French hideaways tucked through-out the city in this 100-page bilingual guidebook. The flavours of Paris-inspired cuisine are highlighted, including where to go for a relaxing brunch or find a fine French bistro full of mouth–watering dishes, rich sauces and scrumptious desserts. This is a no-frills guide. The French Side of Toronto *has no photographs or fancy design, but it has Toronto's French connections well covered, from where to find French newspapers, books, theatre and films, to locating the best brie cheese around."*

— TANYA ENBERG, *METRO TORONTO*, APRIL 8, 2003

acknowledgements

The following individuals have been instrumental in the pursuit of this dream. Thank you all for your support and guidance:

Dominic Canazzi, Thomas Chanzy, Alexandre Colliex, Tony di Pede, Randy Garrett, Marcelle Lean, Dan Mozersky, Lulu Phongmany, Christopher Tuner, Darren Weeks, Dan White.

The French Side of Toronto team

Head Writer & Editor-in-Chief: Krizia de Verdier

Translator: Krizia de Verdier

English guide & web site Copy Editor & Writer: Fionna Boyle

English Marketing Copy Editor: Nicholas Palmer

French guide & web site Copy Editor & Writer: Aude Lemoine

Creative Director: Debi De Santis

Research: Krizia de Verdier, Fionna Boyle, Mark De Shaw, Derek Lowe, Franck Nanguy, Nicholas Palmer, Lulu Phongmany, Franco Taverna and Hilda Toh

Fact Checker: Faith Gill

Advertising Layout: Steve Jenkinson

Web site: Helios Lab Design

Publishing Consultant: Dan Mozersky

Advertising: ads@franco–toronto.ca

Publisher: Franco Toronto Media & Publishing

Visit our web site at **www.franco–toronto.ca**

foreword

The multicultural flair of Toronto is unparalleled anywhere else in the world, and it is this unique cosmopolitan diversity that makes me love this city so much. So many Canadians of different ethnic backgrounds live here, side by side ... *vive la différence!*, as the French would say.

The city's French cultural scene is thriving, and continues to develop a little more each year. However, unlike other cultural groups, Francophones and Francophiles don't have their own distinct neighbourhood within Toronto. The places that cater to their needs are scattered not only throughout the city but the Greater Toronto Area. The absence of a central region or location can often make it challenging to locate the essentials of French cuisine and culture. Ater all, to fully appreciate the complex richness of France and many French-speaking countries and regions, one must dive wholeheartedly into the food, the wine and the cultural activities.

The long search to gather the information in this guide is always the most exciting part of the whole project. Once again, it was enlightening to meet so many devotees of good food and culture, whether it was owners of French shops and businesses, readers who enthusiastically shared their stories or the many Francophiles we encountered at gatherings throughout the city.

Many calories were ingested in the process of sampling the food mentioned in this guide, but such is the sacrifice we were willing to make for our readers. Our quest for French food and culture has been meticulously recorded in this second edition of our guide. The sections and listings are more robust than before, because so much more is offered to us Torontonians. An additional benefit in this edition is the inclusion of many addresses in the Greater Toronto Area.

The core philosophy of *The French Side of Toronto* is to give you easy local access to some of the finest French addresses in Toronto. Some listings seem as if they have been transported straight from France, others have more of a Quebec influence and the rest are little gems that will satisfy the most ardent Francophile living in Toronto. All appear in this guide for one purpose: to celebrate authentic French gastronomic and cultural experiences in our city.

Enjoy and *au plaisir!*

Krizia de Verdier
Head Writer & Editor–in–Chief

finding the right words

In an attempt to keep *The French Side of Toronto* as authentic as possible, we've kept many of the French names for products and dishes. To brush up on your French culinary language, visit our site at **www.franco-toronto.ca** and order your FREE e–book *Glossary of French Food* for English translations.

What's the difference between a Francophone and a Francophile?

The most commonly-asked question we encounter is: "What is the difference between a Francophone and a Francophile?"

The simplest explanation is this: A Francophone is a person of French decent, or a person that originates from any French-speaking country or region (such as Calgary, New Brunswick, New Orleans, Northern Ontario and Quebec).

A Francophile is a person who is not of French descent, but who has a passion for all things French. A Francophile can also be a Francophone if s/he speaks French fluently.

breads, pâtisseries and french sweets

One might think a North American Francophile living outside Quebec would have a difficult time locating many of the French delights easily found in Paris, Belgium, Switzerland or Montreal. After all, once you've tasted exquisite breads, croissants, sweets and chocolates you can never go back to the mundane! (Ask any self-professed Francophile to live without French or Quebecois cheese and it's just like asking him or her to stop breathing.)

Francophiles living in Toronto never have to compromise when it comes to French food, nor do we have to take a trip abroad to enjoy French culinary pleasures. There is an extensive range of products at our disposal from Franco-European countries, as well as *la belle Province.* This first section might well be the one you use the most – happy shopping!

Ace Bakery

1 Hafis Road (South of Lawrence Avenue, East of Keele Street) ☎ 416 241-3600 (office); 416 241-8433 (Ace Café)

Monday–Friday 10–4, Saturday 10–3, closed Sunday (Ace Café)

Subway: LAWRENCE WEST + bus

www.acebakery.com

GOOD BREAD Without a doubt, Ace makes one of Toronto's best baguettes – crusty on the outside and chewy on the inside. The popularity of the Ace baguette is such that it is the baguette of choice on Air France's flights from Toronto to Paris. No wonder Ace Bakery has been a thriving business since 1993. While nothing beats buying fresh from the oven at the bakery, you can also find Ace products in over 700 stores, restaurants and hotels in Canada and the U.S. (Ontario, Quebec, Michigan and New York).

Ace also specializes in a variety of sumptuous breads that should not be missed, including wholewheat and multigrain sandwich breads, a fig-and-nut round loaf, cranberry and rosemary foccacias and a terrific organic sunflower-seed bread. During the Christmas and Easter holidays, Ace offers a selection of breads that are almost too cute to eat: a fig-and-nut large flower and a wholewheat or multigrain bear. They also have a large flower version available in wholewheat or multigrain.

All the Best Fine Foods

1099 Yonge Street ☎ 416 928-3330

Monday–Wednesday 8:30–6:30, Thursday–Friday 8:30–7, Saturday 8:30–6, Sunday 10–5

Subway: SUMMERHILL

www.allthebestfinefoods.com

Did you know?

The baguette is perhaps the second-strongest visual symbol of France (the Eiffel Tower being the first). A day without a baguette is simply inconceivable for the true Francophile, so it's fortunate there are no shortage of these delicious baked goods here in Toronto. The French baguette evolved from the need to create a product to satisfy the demands of French consumers on the eve of World War I. At the beginning of the last century, French consumers could only buy two types of breads – *la miche ronde* (a round bread) and *le pain long* (a fairly long bread). Very much like today's baguette, *le pain long* had a crusty exterior, but unlike our current baguette, it had a very dense and coarse texture inside. Most consumers liked the outer crust, but were not so keen on the rest of the baguette. Bread makers of the time saw this dissatisfaction as a challenge to come up with a better product. Many failed attempts finally led to the creation of the baguette we know and love – crusty on the outside, while moist and soft on the inside. If you want to know more about the origins of bread, consider a visit to the following museums devoted to the craft of bread-making on your next trip to Switzerland: Musée de la boulangerie Ismseng and La Maison du blé & du pain à Echallens.

FRENCH DELIGHTS All the Best Fine Foods sells *pains au chocolat* (chocolate croissants), butter croissants, *croissants aux amandes* (almond croissants) and a few other selections from premier French pastry shops in the city.

GOOD BREAD The in-house artisan baker makes many types of country-style breads. The *pain au levain* (sourdough bread) and rustic baguettes are only a few of the tasty selections you'll find at All the Best Fine Foods. Of course, you'll be able to buy bagels from St. Urbain Bagel Bakery here, as well.

Arz Bakery

1909 Lawrence Avenue East (between Warden Avenue and Pharmacy Avenue)
☎ 416 755-5084

Monday–Saturday 8–9, Sunday 8–7:30, statutory holidays 8–5 (Arz Bakery is always open)

Subway: LAWRENCE + bus

www.arzbakery.com

FRENCH DELIGHTS Lebanese brothers Jack and Armand Boyadjian run Arz Bakery – Jack is the owner, whilst Armand is the Pastry Chef. A good indication of the quality of pastries found at Arz can be found in the experience and education of its staff – French-trained Armand heads a kitchen full of pastry chefs who have also been through rigorous French training, including a graduate of the prestigious Lenôtre culinary school. At Arz, you'll discover large counters filled with scrumptious French pastries and Lebanese-style baklavas. The baklava counter in particular promises a sweet treat. Visually, the presentation of these light caramel-coloured desserts sprinkled with ground pistachio nuts and laid out on large metallic wheels is stupendous. Take your selections home to end a good dinner, or take a break at the café adjacent to the store and enjoy them on the spot.

FRENCH SWEETS Arz Bakery also has a large selection of French and Lebanese cookies. Those on the lookout for the popular European sugar-coated almond candy known as *dragées* need look no further – Arz Bakery sells varieties from France and Spain.

Balzac's Coffee House

55 Mills Street (Distillery District)
☎ 416 207-1709

Monday–Saturday 7–8, Sunday 8–8

Subway: KING + streetcar; PAPE + bus

www.thedistillerydistrict.com

FRENCH DELIGHTS Located in the artistic Distillery District, Balzac's Coffee House is not a pâtisserie but a coffee shop. Luckily for patrons, the owners rely on Clafouti and Daniel et Daniel to satisfy the need of their clientele. Clafouti's popular selections include butter croissants, sandwiches, apple turnovers, *pains au chocolat* and *amandines.* From Daniel et Daniel, you can savour croissants, *amandines, pains au chocolat, croissants au fromage* (cheese croissants) and fruit danishes. Although Daniel et Daniel pastries are only available on Mondays, this is surely a reason to look forward to the beginning of the week!

Bonjour Brioche

812 Queen Street East (East of Broadview)
☎ 416 406-1250

Closed Monday, Tuesday–Friday 8–5,
Saturday 8–4, Sunday 8–3

Subway: **QUEEN** + streetcar

FRENCH DELIGHTS You need only to open the doors at Bonjour Brioche to be greeted with the warm, delicious scent of sugar and butter. Croissants and brioches of every conceivable variation await you. The almond croissants and sugar brioches are undoubtedly delicious, but without a doubt, the star is the royal brioche, filled with *crème pâtissière* (custard) and lemon. This is also the perfect pâtisserie for fans of the lemon tart, though the pear and almond variety is also mouth-watering. You'll also want to try their decadent and superb flourless chocolate cake. Not only are Bonjour Brioche's desserts a great way to end a delicious brunch, they make wonderful little surprises to offer your dinner guests and make at-home entertaining a little more remarkable.

GOOD BREAD If you are on a low- or no-carbohydrate diet, this may not be the best place for you. Few can resist the seduction of Bonjour Brioche's wonderful baguettes – they simply melt in your mouth, and when combined with a little butter and jam, you can almost hear the angels sing. This is the ideal version for those who like their baguette soft on the inside and out. Bonjour Brioche also sells a nice selection of multigrain and wholewheat breads. Another specialty is their olive and rosemary loaf – simply *magnifique!* – which, unfortunately, is only available on weekends. New on the menu is the foccacia, equally as tempting and memorable as Bonjour Brioche's other breads.

FRENCH SWEETS Bonjour Brioche sells a variety of delicious homemade cookies individually or in small packs, including shortbreads, macarons, *tuiles* (thin cookies) and a few other French-inspired varieties.

Casa Açareana

235 Augusta Avenue (inside Kensington Market) ☎ 416 593-9717

Monday–Saturday 8:30–6:30,
closed Sunday

Subway: **SPADINA** + streetcar;
QUEEN'S PARK + streetcar

FRENCH SWEETS If you've ever been to Casa Açareana, you'll know they have a wide variety of French treats to suit palates of all ages – including the hard-to-find sugar-coated almond candy known as *dragées.*

Clafouti

915 Queen Street West (East of Strachan Avenue, across from Trinity Bellwoods Park) ☎ 416 603-1935

Closed Monday; Tuesday–Saturday 8–6,
Sunday 9–5

Subway: **OSGOODE** + streetcar

FRENCH DELIGHTS When Clafouti opened in the middle of a brutal winter in January 2003, owners and brothers Boris Dosne and Olivier Jansen-Reynaud wondered if anyone would notice their little pâtisserie. They needn't have worried. Patrons patiently wait in queues that regularly reach the door for fear of

Glossary of French sweets

Sweets may be the one common global food item amongst all cultural groups, and the French are no exception. Fortunately, there's no shortage of shops in Toronto that sell goodies from France to satisfy all varieties of sweet tooths. If you haven't already done so, make a point of trying one (or all!) of the French sweets listed below – sheer decadance with every bite! Sweets are listed by their French brand names.

Bonbon Anis de L'abbaye de Flavigny: flavoured candy drops made with anise

Bonbon Barnier: flavoured lollipops

Bonbon La Vie de la Vosgienne: small flavoured candy drops

Pastilles Vichy: candy that is not overly sweet, made with water from Vichy Falls

Cachou La Jaunie: liquorice drops

Carambar: caramel sticks

Gâteau Brossard: small, flavoured butter cakes sold in boxes

Langues de chat: Translated as "cat's tongues", this delicate oval-shaped vanilla-flavoured cookie is an ideal accompaniment to ice cream, but is equally delicious by itself.

Madeleines Gaillard: small coffee-like cakes flavoured with orange blossom water

Macaron: light shells, filled with different flavours

Quatre-quarts: pound cake *à la française*

Sirop William/William Syrup: fruit-flavoured syrups that can be added to drinks or desserts

Nougats aux amandes Chabert et Guillot: almond nougat

Réglisses Haribo: liquorice

Pâte de fruits de Provence: fruit paste

Sucettes Pierrot Gourmand: lollipops

Where to find these French sweets

1. All the Best Fine Foods
2. Arz Bakery
3. Brandt Meat Packers Supermarket
4. Cheese Boutique
5. Clafouti
6. Comptoir de Célestin
7. Daniel et Daniel
8. Dinah's Cupboard
9. La Cigogne
10. Le Gourmand
11. Max Market
12. Mercatto
13. Pâtisserie d'Or
14. Rahier
15. Scheffler's Delicatessen & Cheese

not making it to the counter before their favourite croissant vanishes. Indeed, when it comes to croissants, Clafouti reigns supreme – after being open less than six months, Clafouti received the "best croissant in T.O." distinction from *NOW* magazine. Pastry Chef Boris Dosne is a genius at work. Not only are his croissants delicious, but the flavours, including fig and brown sugar, can be found in no other pâtisserie in town. If Clafouti runs out of these two favourites, we recommend the *pain au chocolat* or *pain au raisins* (raisin danish), both of which are mouth-watering. Apricot, cherry and *crème pâtissière* (custard) brioches are also some of the other tempting treats Boris whips up in his kitchen. Clafouti's dessert selections are both delicious and original. Choose from coconut and apple, chocolate, lychee and caramel, lemon and caramelized chocolate tarts, *baba au rhum* (rum cake) and their signature offering, Dominus (chocolate mousse cake topped with caramelized apples). A rare treat in Toronto: during the first two weeks of January, Boris makes *galettes des rois* – flaky little pastries filled with frangipane and traditionally eaten in France on January 6 to celebrate *l'Épiphanie* (visit www.franco-toronto.ca's glossary for more details). If you are lucky enough to live or work in the Queen and Bathurst area, Clafouti will undoubtedly become a favourite. Come early to avoid disappointments.

GOOD BREAD Clafouti's French charm shines through in their fine details, like the wooden wine boxes used to present their homemade breads, including olive, rosemary foccacia, spinach foccacia and muesli. Clafouti is also a hot spot for St. Urbain's Montreal-style bagels in the Queen West area.

FRENCH SWEETS Cookie connaisseurs won't be disappointed – bergamot, Grand Marnier, and vanilla and hazelnut are amongst some of the more exotic varieties found at Clafouti, as well as more traditional French favourites such as *madeleines, quatre-quarts* (pound cake), and *langues de chat.*

Comptoir de Célestin

623 Mount Pleasant Road (corner of Manor Road) ☎ 416 544-1733

Closed Monday–Tuesday; Wednesday–Saturday 7:30–7, Sunday 8:30–5

Subway: EGLINTON + bus

FRENCH DELIGHTS Adjacent to Célestin restaurant, this little *pâtisserie* is owned by brothers Martial and Pascal Ribreau, innovators in bringing the French concept of restaurant and *comptoir* (upscale food counter) to Toronto. Comptoir de Célestin offers an array of classic French pastries such as amandines, pains au chocolat, pains au raisin, apple turnovers and brioches. Pastry chef Martial Ribreau also introduces Torontonians to some very French selections such as *la viennoise* (a brioche-like baguette), *la viennoise chocolat, bostock* brioche (brioche with almond syrup and cream) and *le diplomate* (a brioche with candied fruit, *crème anglaise* (cream) and Grand Marnier). The *croissant aux amandes* (almond croissant) is delicious, and if you're fortunate enough to try one straight out of the oven, it's almost sinful. When it comes to desserts, Comptoir de Célestin's list is long and very French. Tried-and-true classics include *tarte tatin* (double *feuilletage* of caramelized apples), *tarte au citron* (sugared vanilla biscuit and lemon cream) and an assortment of pastries that were, until now, only found in France, such as *gland* (cream puff filled with kirsch pastry cream), *paris brest* (cream puff with hazelnut cream) and *religieuse* (cream puff with coffee pastry cream or chocolate ganache). However, Comptoir de Célestin's *pièce de résistance* is surely its *millefeuille* – so exquisite, it is only available by special order.

GOOD BREAD Comptoir de Célestin's baguettes are the best artisan breads in Toronto. Available in regular or wholewheat, they are best enjoyed in the simplest fashion, with only a little butter and jam. Other breads include rye and honey, sourdough, and a black bread made with seven grains and bursting with complex flavours. A rare find is the traditional French *viennoise* – shaped like a baguette, but very close to a brioche in taste. Comptoir de Célestin's viennoises come in plain or chocolate. If you thought a croissant was the only way to start your weekend, now you know better!

FRENCH SWEETS The delectable pastries at Comptoir de Célestin more than make up for the small selection of sweets and treats. You will, however, find a dozen or so flavours of French *macarons* (light-weight shell, filled with different flavours).

Daniel et Daniel – Food Shop

248 Carlton Street (corner of Parliament Street) ☎ 416 968-9275

Closed Sunday; Monday–Saturday 7:30–6

Subway: CASTLE FRANK + bus;
COLLEGE + streetcar

www.danieletdaniel.ca

FRENCH DELIGHTS In addition to their reputation as one of Toronto's finest caterers, Daniel et Daniel's Cabbagetown headquarters offer French temptations such as *croissant aux amandes, pain au chocolat* and *croissant au fromage.* Their selection of classic tarts are not only outstanding but ideally-priced for dinner parties. Speaking of dinner parties, you'll be sure to impress guests with Daniel et Daniel's signature crème brûlée, sold in little ceramic containers that make it easy to achieve a perfect burnt sugary crust at home.

Dinah's Cupboard

50 Cumberland Street ☎ 416 921-8112

Monday–Friday 9–7, Saturday 9–6; closed Sunday (open Sundays in December)

Subway: YONGE or BAY

FRENCH DELIGHTS This charming little store is hidden on Cumberland Street, just behind the Holt Renfrew Centre, and features brioches and croissants from Patachou.

Fred's Bakery

45 Brisbane Road, Units 13–14
☎ 416 736-3733

Note: Bakery not open for public shopping

GOOD BREAD Andrea Damon-Gibson

and husband Steve Gibson are the artists behind Fred's Bakery, and have been making artisan-inspired breads since 1995. Of all the bakers listed in this guide, Fred's has an assortment of flavours that would make carbohydrate junkies out of the most sensible of us, including: sourdough, raisin, walnut, green and black olive, cheese, herb and onion, ancient grain and wild honey, three types of foccacia (potato, rosemary and tomato), an extra-crunchy baguette, a brioche-like bread and a sweet black bread (a mixture of chocolate, espresso, molasses and honey). Fred's breads are available across Toronto at The Big Carrot, All the Best Fine Foods, Pusateri's, Holt Renfrew, Max Market, Le Gourmand, the Royal York Deli and IGA in the the Beach.

Holt Renfrew – Epicure Shop

50 Bloor Street West (corner of Bay Street) ☎ 416 922-2333

Monday–Wednesday 10–6, Thursday–Friday 10–8, Saturday 10–6, Sunday 12–6

Subway: **YONGE** or **BAY**

FRENCH DELIGHTS Holt Renfrew has a well-deserved reputation for serving only the best products, so it is no surprise this famous Canadian retailer has joined forces with Patachou to offer an array of croissants.

GOOD BREAD Every day, eager Parisian *gourmands* flock to *rue du Cherche-Midi* to buy a sourdough loaf from celebrity baker Lionel Poîlane's famous bakery. Luckily, Toronto Francophiles need not cross the Atlantic to buy their pain Poîlane – we can enjoy this designer bread right here at home, as Holt Renfrew specially flies the bread in every other day by FedEx. You can purchase the *boule* (round loaf) or quarter-boule at the Epicure Shop, located on the store's concourse level. If you've never tasted a Poîlane before, don't let the price deter you. Although France's most famous bread does not come cheaply, those who have had the pleasure of experiencing bread before can tell you it's worth every penny.

FRENCH SWEETS Holt Renfrew imports many higher-end sweets from France (complete with a higher-end price tag). That said, an occasional indulgence is well worth the splurge – particularly during Christmas, Valentine's Day and Easter, when the imported items are especially dazzling.

La Cigogne

(formely La Framboisine)

1626 Bayview Avenue (South of Eglinton Avenue) ☎ 416 487-1234

Monday–Friday 7:30–7, Saturday 8–7, Sunday 8–5:30

Subway: **EGLINTON** + bus

FRENCH DELIGHTS Residents of Bayview Avenue are incredibly blessed. New owner and Pastry Chef Thierry Schmitt is from Alsace, and brings with him some of the region's favourite dishes, including the house specialty *tarte flambée d'Alsace*. If it sounds like a mouthful, it is – this Alsatian-style thin crust pie is stuffed with bacon, chopped onions and cream cheese, and baked in a stone oven. It's a weekends-only feature, which is almost a blessing as it would prove to be too tempting to have such a dish available seven days a week! Once you've tried the house specialty, try sampling La Cigogne's numerous pastries, including *pain perdu* (French toast), crème brûlée, danishes, croissants, almond croissants, chocolate croissants and apple turnovers. During Christmas and Easter, Chef Schmitt prepares a special holiday menu featuring a variety of delectable desserts that will leave your guests wanting more. An annual favourite is the hard-to-find (in Toronto) *galette des rois,* consisting of puff dough filled with almond cream, traditionally served on January 6.

Did you know?

"Entre la baguette et le camembert, au panthéon des gloires supposées du patrimoine gastronomique français se trouve le croissant." –Le Monde, 2003.

Translated, this passage from the French newspaper *Le Monde* says: "in between the baguette and camembert cheese, at the top of the list of food honouring French heritage, one can find the glorious croissant." Well said! There is no doubt the French have perfected the *croissant* (which, translated, means 'crescent'); however, it might be surprising to discover the origins of the croissant are not, in fact, French! We can trace the origins of this rich, buttery pastry back to the time when the Turks were at war with Austria. By 1683, the Turks were planning to take over Vienna. In the middle of the night, a few local bakers heard the Turks tunnelling under their kitchens and quickly spread the alarm. Because of their bravery, Vienna was saved from the hands of the enemy. To reward the vigilant bakers, King Jean III Sobieski of Poland awarded them the privilege of creating a commemorative pastry, shaped like the crescent on the Turkish flag. This how the *Hörnchen* came to life ('little horn' in German).

Another story attributes the invention of the croissant to a man by the name of Kolschitski. This Austrian coffee shop owner lived in Vienna during the war between the Austrians and the Turks, and showed immense courage in protecting his country. He was given a large amount of coffee beans taken from the enemy as a reward, and came up with the idea of serving a crescent-shaped pastry with each cup of coffee.

It was only in 1770 when Marie-Antoinette, wife of King Louis XVI, introduced the croissant to French royalty. During a trip to Austria she was seduced by the charms of this pastry and brought some back with her to France. But it took until 1920 for bakers to start perfecting the recipe and give the croissant the distinctive buttery, flaky taste so well associated with France. Like any lover of good bread, lovers of good croissants will often travel far to find the best variety. The best Montreal-style croissants are treated with the same reverence as their siblings, the Montreal-style bagel – smuggled back into Toronto by expats and savoured as a special treat!

Must-try French pâtisserie *treats*

1. **almond croissants** from Le Comptoir Célestin
2. **Bostock** from Patachou
3. **Brioche Royale** from Bonjour Brioche
4. **chocolate croissants** from La Cigogne
5. **fig croissants** and **cinnamon croissants** from Clafouti
6. **Financiers** from Zane
7. **fruit danishes** and **raisin danishes** from Pâtisserie d'Or
8. **Gâteau Basque** from Pain Perdu
9. Lebanese **baklavas** from Arz Bakery
10. **pistachio danishes** from Rahier

GOOD BREAD La Cigogne is known for their signature baguettes and sourdough bread.

FRENCH SWEETS The following French treats will tempt you at La Cigogne –*madeleines* and *langues de chat.*

Le Gourmand

152 Spadina Avenue (corner of Queen Street) ☎ 416 504-4494

Monday–Friday 7–9, Saturday 9–6, Sunday 9–4

Subway: OSGOODE + streetcar; SPADINA + streetcar

FRENCH DELIGHTS Although Le Gourmand may not have a resident pastry chef, a selection of pastries and croissants from Rahier compensate nicely.

Le Petit Gourmet

1064 Yonge Street ☎ 416 966-3811

Monday–Friday 7:30–7, Saturday 7:30–6, closed Sunday

Subway: ROSEDALE

FRENCH DELIGHTS Rosedale residents are not shy in buying half a dozen croissants at a time from Le Petit Gourmet (it's no wonder they are usually sold out by 11 a.m.!) Croissants, almond and chocolate croissants, raisin and cinnamon danishes, and apple and fruit turnovers are just some of the baked goods prepared by owner Christian Bonito over the past 20 years. Other luscious offerings include 15 varieties of cakes and tarts including a *gâteau basque*, which you might recognise from the menu at L'Escargot Bistro. The chocolate, pear and cream tart is especially fantastic, but be sure to leave room for the ganache cake and the *tarte tatin.*

Magnolia Fine Foods

548 College Street (corner of Euclid Avenue) ☎ 416 920-9927

Monday–Friday 9–8, Saturday 9–6, Sunday 10–6

Subway: QUEEN'S PARK + streetcar

FRENCH DELIGHTS This small but discerning shop is the ideal place for residents of Little Italy to find French pastries, including a nice selection from famed Queen West *pâtisserie* Clafouti.

Mercatto

- 15 Toronto Street (East of Yonge, one street North of King Street) ☎ 416 366-4567

  Monday–Friday 7–6, closed Saturday–Sunday

  Subway: KING

• 330 Bay Street (North of Adelaide Street) ☎ 416 306-0467
Monday–Friday 7:30–8, closed Saturday–Sunday
Subway: KING

FRENCH DELIGHTS Don't let the name fool you – this Italian bistro café has a serious love affair with French goodies. Mercatto's croissants are from Clafouti, and like those found at the *pâtisserie* on Queen Street, they tend to disappear fast. Fortunately, the croissants are available five days a week at Mercatto – so if you come early, you won't be disappointed.

Pain Perdu

736 St Clair Avenue West (West of Christie Street) ☎ 416 656-7246
Closed Monday, Tuesday–Friday 7–7:30, Saturday 7–5, Sunday 8–4
Subway: ST CLAIR WEST + streecar

FRENCH DELIGHTS This *pâtisserie* is named after the house specialty – *pain perdu,* or French toast. Owners Yannick and Christophe Folgoas prepare theirs in the French tradition by using day-old baguettes and an old family recipe. Pain Perdu offers a wide variety of tempting delights to both start and end your daily meals. Breakfast treats include a selection of croissants, *pain aux raisins* and *brioche sucré* (brioche with a sugary top), whilst traditional desserts range from *religieuse, mille-feuille* and *marquise* to fruit tarts and *paris brest.* Pain Perdu's signature desserts include a delicious *tarte au citron* (lemon custard) and the best *gâteau Basque* in Toronto – an experience in itself that can only be fully appreciated when tasted. Pastry Chef Christophe Folgoas is constantly innovating, so be sure to drop by frequently to sample his latest creations, including the new *béret* Basque – a chocolate genoise cake topped with chocolate mousse, drizzled with rum syrup and sprinkled with chocolate flakes. *Fantastique!* Those watching their waistlines will be pleased to know most desserts come in small, medium and large sizes, so you can decide how decadent you want to be. Best of all, Pain Perdu might be one of the only *pâtisseries* in the city that doesn't run out of goods before 11 a.m. The reason is simple – Chef Folgoas bakes a continuous supply of fresh pastries and desserts throughout the day!

GOOD BREAD Good baguettes and mouth-watering sourdough bread have been hallmarks of Pain Perdu ever since it opened its doors in May 2003.

FRENCH SWEETS It simply never ends at Pain Perdu! The delicate little French cookies are equally as tempting as the desserts. Among the sweets offered you'll find chocolate-covered candied orange treats, shortbread, thin almond sheets and flaky sugar-coated *palmiers,* all strategically placed in baskets that are hard to ignore. You'll also find nougat, chocolate candies and blackcurrant and raspberry fruit paste.

Patachou

1095 Yonge Street ☎ 416 927-1105
Monday–Friday 8:30–7, Saturday 8:30–6, closed Sunday
Subway: SUMMERHILL

FRENCH DELIGHTS Patachou has offered

Rosedale and Summerhill residents bite after bite of pure pleasure since 1978. Their fabulous selection of pastries, desserts and cakes includes croissants, brioches, almond and chocolate croissants and raisin danishes. When it comes to desserts, the *gâteau Basque* and *tarte au citron* are must-trys. You'll also be delighted to discover a number of specialty holiday items for Christmas, New Year's, Easter and *l'Épiphanie* that will certainly impress your guests, including the house specialty – *petits fours glacés.* These miniature flavoured cakes are impossible to resist (you can easily eat four or five without realising it!). To enjoy Patachou's holiday desserts, you need only place an order. Patachou is also the place to find the proper pastry shells to make *bouchées à la reine* (pastries filled with chicken or shrimp in a *béchamel* sauce). Or, why not try one of Patachou's delicious prepared goods – quiches, sandwiches and salads? If you prefer to linger and savour your selections inside the pâtisserie, there is a little area at the back where you can sit and eat. During the summer months, you can also enjoy the food and the weather on Patachou's terrace. A word of warning, however: most desserts are gone by early afternoon on weekends, so don't sleep in too late on Saturday!

FRENCH SWEETS Patachou sells three flavours of *macarons,* as well as many flavours of homemade cookies.

PÂTISSERIE D'OR

301 Robinson Street, Oakville (South of Lakeshore Road) ☎ 905 815-8999

Closed Monday–Tuesday;
Wednesday–Friday 8–5:30, Saturday 8–6, Sunday 8–4

FRENCH DELIGHTS If you are looking for the best French pastries prepared by a master pastry chef, you must stop by this Oakville shop. Owners Jean-Luc Soulabaille and his wife Monica are both former chefs at Toronto's Four Seasons Hotel who decided to open their own *pâtisserie* in August 2000. One taste and you immediately know Chef Soulabaille is of classical French training – his pastries are so delicate, only a master pastry chef could create them. Pâtisserie d'Or features butter, almond and chocolate croissants and raisin danishes (made with a croissant

Did you know?

Lionel Poîlane's breads are sold in more than 600 locations and available in over 300 restaurants in the City of Lights. In addition, *pain* Poîlane is exported daily to points all around the globe, including Tokyo, New York and Chicago. Even though the king of Parisian bread-making passed away a few years ago, the tradition of the pain Poîlane has not changed. Each *boule* is still made with natural sourdough, French flour and sea salt, shaped by hand and cooked in a wood oven. This artisan way of making the breads guarantees that no two loaves will ever be identical. In fact, this built-in imperfection is what makes these breads so perfect.

dough and not a brioche dough) by the basketful. Fruit-filled danishes are prepared using seasonal fresh fruits only – you'll taste the difference from the very first bite – while all chocolate desserts are made with Switzerland's *Lindt* chocolate. Indeed, ingredients really do make the difference at Pâtisserie d'Or. When it comes to desserts, Pâtisserie d'Or's list is long and classically French. In fact, you'll find specialties here that are found in few other regional *pâtisseries,* including *paris brest,* chocolate *éclairs, saint-honoré* (layers of sweet puff dough filled with pastry and whipped cream, covered with caramel), *mille-feuille* and Black Forest cake. Be sure to consult our French Frozen Goods listing to see all the amazing goodies Chef Soulabaille keeps in his take-out freezer!

GOOD BREAD Pâtisserie d'Or's baguette is simple yet classic, and a favourite of Oakville residents.

FRENCH SWEETS Whether it's *macarons,* vanilla cigarettes, shortbread or perfectly-prepared *madeleines,* you're bound to succumb to the variety of tasty cookies prepared by Chef Soulabaille.

Pâtisserie Saint Honoré

2945 Bloor Street West (corner of Grenview Boulevard, East of Royal York Road) Note: no telephone is available

Closed Monday Tuesday–Thursday 8–7, Friday 8–9, Saturday 8–7, closed Sunday

Subway: ROYAL YORK

FRENCH DELIGHTS Jean-Jacques Carlier's *pâtisserie* features a scrumptious array of almond, chocolate, and plain croissants, fruit danishes and raisin brioches. Savoury (but equally appealing) croissant flavours include cheese and ham, as well as feta and spinach. Pâtisserie Saint Honoré also produces an impressive variety of cakes and tarts.

GOOD BREAD The staple French *pâtisserie* in Bloor West Village, Pâtisserie Saint Honoré makes a tasty baguette that can be enjoyed with or without garnishings.

Pusateri's Fine Foods

- 1539 Avenue Road (North of Lawrence Avenue) ☎ 416 785-9100

  Monday–Wednesday 8–8, Thursday–Friday 8–9, Saturday–Sunday 8–7

  Subway: LAWRENCE + bus
- 57 Yorkville Avenue (corner of Bay Street) ☎ 416 785-9100

  Monday–Wednesday 10–8, Thursday–Friday 10–9, Saturday 8–8, Sunday 10–7

  Subway: BAY

  www.pusateris.com

FRENCH DELIGHTS Pusateri's has a well-deserved reputation for both excellence and exclusivity. This is evident in the way they pamper their upscale clientele with selections of pastries, tarts and cakes from three renowned local French *pâtisseries* – Clafouti, Rahier and Patachou.

Rahier

1717 Bayview Avenue (South of Eglinton Avenue) ☎ 416 482-0917

Closed Monday–Tuesday, Wednesday–Friday 8–5, Saturday 8–4, Sunday 8–3

Subway: EGLINTON + bus

FRENCH DELIGHTS Some have dubbed Rahier the Rolls Royce of Toronto's *pâtisseries.* In fact, many of the newer French pastry shops attribute their existence to Rahier's success. Located in the heart of Bayview Village, Rahier has tickled our taste buds and tempted our tummies with its delectable and fragrant confections since 1996. This is a great place for croissants, cakes, pastries, fresh fruit tarts and plenty of other French sweet delicacies, all made on the premises. The pistachio danish and the almond croissants are highly recommended. During the holiday season, Rahier offers an impressive collection of specialty items your guests will be sure to love, including a classic Christmas log *(la bûche de Noël)* that is unparalleled by other pâtisseries in the city.

GOOD BREAD Rahier makes a traditional French baguette.

FRENCH SWEETS Rahier has the most plentiful selection of homemade French cookies in the city, available individually or in packs.

St. Urbain Bagel Bakery

Various locations across the Greater Toronto Area ☎ 416 787-6955

GOOD BREAD St. Urbain Bakery is an excellent source for Montreal-style bagels in Toronto. Although St. Urbain has three stores in the Greater Toronto Area, you can also purchase their bagels at the following locations: All the Best Fine Foods, Clafouti, Cheese Boutique and My Market Bakery (Kensington Market).

Senses

- 318 Wellington West (inside the SOHO Metropolitan Hotelcorner of Blue Jay Way) ☎ 416 961-0055

  Monday–Sunday 7–9

  Subway: ST ANDREW + streetcar

  www.senses.ca

- 2901 Bayview Avenue (inside Bayview Village) ☎ 416 227-9149

  Monday–Friday 8–9, Saturday 8–6, Sunday 9–5

  Subway: BAYVIEW

FRENCH DELIGHTS The location may have changed (formerly at 15 Bloor Street West), but the quality has remained intact. Senses has it all under one roof: catering services, a fine-dining restaurant and a take-out pastry store. While not a proper French *pâtisserie* per se, most of Senses's desserts are infused with a French influence. When it comes to French pastries, you can be assured you'll find the best of the best here – the assortments of croissants, fruit and chocolate tarts, fruit mousses and chocolate cakes is mind-boggling. You'll also find many unique local creations that should not be missed, such as a sublime chestnut cake. Everything looks so good that choosing is a near-impossible task – we recommend at least two goodies each visit!

FRENCH SWEETS The cookies at Senses truly are remarkable. Christmas, Valentine's Day and Easter are well-celebrated, with special limited-edition holiday cookies.

The Bagel House

- 1548 Bayview Avenue ☎ 416 481-8184

  Monday–Saturday 7–7, Sunday 7–6

Did you know?

While it is true the bagel doesn't have French roots, you'd be hard-pressed to find a Quebecker who hasn't embraced this dense, round, holed bread as much as the croissant. Originally derived from the culinary history of Russian and European Jews, the history of the bagel in Canada can be traced to 1919, when a Jewish immigrant by the name of Isadore Shlafman opened his first bagel shop in Montreal on St-Laurent Street. This was followed by a second shop in 1949 on Fairmount Street, a region that would become known as the bagel district. There are bagels, and then there are Montreal-style bagels. Their distinctive taste and texture is achieved by a process of hand-rolling, boiling and baking in a wood-burning oven. Montreal-style bagels are exactly what real bagels are meant to be – slightly chewy, a little sweet and perfectly sprinkled with sesame or poppy seeds.

For many years, the only hope Montreal expats living in Toronto had of satisfying their bagel cravings was to stock up by the dozen with each trip to *la belle Province,* then deep-freeze this manna from heaven, to be savoured on special occasions only. *Mais, enfin!* There is a small but steady supply of Montreal-style bagel shops right here in the city for your convenience and continuous enjoyment.

Where to find Montreal-style bagels

1. All the Best Fine Foods
2. Cheese Boutique
3. Clafouti
4. My Market Bakery (Kensington Market)
5. Pusateri's
6. St. Urbain Bagel Bakery
7. The Bagel House

Subway: EGLINTON + bus

- 1722 Avenue Road (corner of Fairlawn Avenue) ☎ 416 781-0032

Monday–Saturday 6:30–7, Sunday 6:30–6:30

Subway: LAWRENCE + bus

GOOD BREAD Montreal ex-pat Jessie Sahdra has 17 years' experience in some of the most popular bagel shops in Quebec, and it shows. There are only a handful of places in Toronto that make authentic Montreal-style bagels, with their distinctive texture, taste and preparation, and The Bagel House is one of them. Mr. Sahdra's mastery of his art is evident with every bagel he produces. The bagels at The Bagel House come in 12 or so flavours, although purists will likely stick to the sesame or poppy varieties!

Whole Foods Market

87 Avenue Road (North of Bloor Street) ☎ 416 944-0500

Monday–Friday 9–10, Saturday 9–9, Sunday 9–8

Subway: BAY or MUSEUM

www.wholefoodsmarket.com

FRENCH DELIGHTS Whole Food Market offers a respectable variety of pastries from Patachou. Although the selection might be a fraction of what you'll find at the Rosedale *pâtisserie,* the convenience makes up for the limited assortment.

GOOD BREAD Like everything else in the store, Whole Foods Market has a remarkable selection of breads that are baked on premise. Varieties include country-style, raisin and pecan, multigrain, olive and, of course, the famous baguette. You'll also find more unconventional choices, such as a roasted garlic loaf.

ZANE PÂTISSERIE & BOULANGERIE

1852 Queen Street East (West of Woodbine Avenue) ☎ 416 690-2813

Monday closed, Tuesday–Sunday 7:30–5:30

Subway: QUEEN + streetcar

FRENCH DELIGHTS The *grande dame* of French *pâtisseries* in the Beach, Zane Pâtisserie & Boulangerie is owned by Mo Zane, who also doubles as the Pastry Chef. Chef Zane felt obliged to extend his apologies for being covered in flour and sugar when we first met, but we found this a charming testament to his dedication to his craft. Where to begin? Classic French pastries can be found here in abundance. For starters, there are plain, almond and chocolate croissants, as well as lemon, apricot, blueberry and hazelnut danishes. For a different taste, consider the custard-filled twists and squares. A dozen cakes and close to a dozen tarts are also all very tempting, as is the *quatre-quarts* (poundcake) – with three flavours to choose from (lemon, vanilla/chocolate and hazelnut/chocolat), it is quite a popular item and tends to sell out on Saturday mornings within a few hours. If you're looking for bite-sized treats, Chef Zane prepares a wonderful assortment of *petits fours frais* (mini pastries), including mini fruit, chocolate and raspberry tarts, mini *tarte au citron,* mini *éclairs* and mini *choux* (cream puff filled pastries). And as if all that wasn't enough, you'll also find *financiers* (similar to *madeleines)* – little almond and hazelnut butter cakes that will seduce you.

GOOD BREAD All breads are made on the premises, naturellement! You'll be hard-pressed to choose between the great baguette, the fabulous nut loaf and the tasty multigrain, not to mention the delicious rosemary, black olive and sun-dried tomato varieties. The sun-dried tomato loaf in particular is simply sinful, and can easily be eaten on its own or as a perfect accompaniment to soups and salads.

FRENCH SWEETS Residents of the Beach can satisfy their sugar cravings with over 15 different varieties of cookies, all baked by Chef Zane himself.

chocolatiers

White? Dark? Milk? Bittersweet? Flavoured? The possibilities are endless. People the world over have a love affair with chocolate, and the French are no exception. Of course, it is only fitting for a country that celebrates both passion and food so intensely to take that love affair to another level.

In fact, the French are so serious about chocolate, they've created an exclusive club of connoisseurs who meet regularly to taste and critique the newest creations. When it comes to chocolate, le Club des Croqueurs du Chocolat (The Chocolate Lovers Club) is comprised of the crème de la crème of France's chocolatiers.

However, the French are not the only nation to master the art and technique of fine chocolate-making; Swiss and Belgian chocolate is of an equal calibre of refined quality and taste. In this section, we spotlight all three!

A lesson in chocolate

If all you know about chocolate is that it all tastes good, it's time to learn a thing or two. And who better than to explain some of the most common terms associated with chocolate-making than one of Toronto's top chocolatiers? Patricia Cohrs, from the Belgian Chocolate Shop in the Beach, explains how some of the most delicious chocolate treats are made:

Truffle: First, the centre of the truffle is created. After it hardens, the truffle is dipped in liquid chocolate and usually rolled in powdered chocolate. Powdered chocolate is the traditional way of covering truffles; however, you'll also find many truffles covered with shredded coconut or slivers of almond.

Ganache: Ganache is usually made from two-thirds chocolate and one-third boiling *crème fraîche* (fresh cream).

Praline: A praline describes any chocolate where the centre is made of roasted or caramelized hazelnuts that have been ground into a smooth paste and folded into chocolate.

Arz Bakery

1909 Lawrence Avenue East (between Warden Avenue and Pharmacy Avenue)
☎ 416 755-5084

Monday–Saturday 8–9, Sunday 8–7:30, statutory holidays 8–5 (Arz Bakery is always open)

Subway: LAWRENCE + bus

www.arzbakery.com

Chocoholics won't be able to tear their eyes away from the long counter of truffles and pralines, imported directly from France.

Belgian Chocolate Shop

2455 Queen Street East (West of Victoria Park Avenue) ☎ 416 691-1424

Closed Monday; Tuesday–Friday 11–7, Saturday–Sunday 11–5

Subway: QUEEN + streecar

www.belgianchocolateshop.ca

Just in case the name didn't give it away, owners Eric Smets and Patricia Cohrs proudly display two clocks behind the counter to hint at their heritage – one is set to local time; the other, Brussels. Since 1984, the duo have been making truffles, pralines and ganaches in the true artisan tradition, right on the premesis, using only the best quality ingredients and no preservatives. Unlike imported sweets, the chocolate confections in this shop never see a warehouse or airline container so they are guaranteed to be the freshest they can be. Classic and exotic flavours include crunchy almond nougat, poached pear in vodka, bergamot, lemon cream, caramel, Grand Marnier and champagne ... tempted yet?

Cheese Boutique

45 Ripley Avenue (South of South Kingsway & The Queensway) ☎ 416 762-6292

Monday–Friday 8–9, Saturday 8–8, Sunday 10–6

Subway: RUNNYMEDE + bus

www.cheeseboutique.com

Chocolate at a cheese shop? *Mais oui!* In fact, there is so much chocolate from France, Belgium and Switzerland here, "Chocolate Boutique" may be a better name for the shop. On the mezzanine level, you'll find everything from hot chocolate powder mix from *Poulain* to fondue chocolate from Lindt to chocolate butter from Côte d'Or to refrigerated Michel Cluizel truffles. In addition, Cheese Boutique carries an array of gift boxes for an elegant finishing touch to your gift-giving.

Chocolate Addict

185 Baldwin Street (inside Kensington Market) ☎ 416 979-5809

Monday–Friday 9–6:30, Sunday 10–6

Subway: SPADINA + streetcar;
QUEEN'S PARK + streetcar

www.911chocolate.com

Chocolate Addict is a great little find inside Kensington Market. Truffle fans will find over 20 flavours to choose from, all handmade with the finest Belgian chocolate. For the purist, there is an impressive assortment of nut, fruit and liqueur-filled truffles, while those with more exotic tastes might be tempted by the lavender, basil or Sambuca varieties.

Chocolates & Creams

207 Queen's Quay West (Queen's Quay Terminal) ☎ 416 368-6767

Monday–Sunday 10–6 (in the winter), Monday–Friday 10–8, Saturday–Sunday 10–6 (in the summer)

Subway: UNION + streetcar

www.chocolatesandcreams.com

Chocolates & Creams is the exclusive Canadian importer of Belgium's handmade Manon chocolates. Prepared in the artisan fashion by Christian Vanderkerken, Manon chocolates are well-known in Europe for their meticulous selection of quality ingredients and the many awards of excellence they've won, dating as far back as 1985. *Manon* exports over 25 tonnes of pralines every year. The pralines are made as orders arrive and contain no preservatives (the shelf life of a *crème fraîche* praline is only seven days!). Chocolates & Creams carries one of *Manon's* most sumptuous pralines – *le bouchon* (cap), part of the collection *Des créations de Christian Vanderkerken*. Each *bouchon* requires three days of preparation, and may involve up to 10 different fillings. Once finished, *bouchons* are hand-dipped in chocolate, then covered with 24-carat gold. Now that's some serious chocolate!

Chocolates by Bernard Callebaut

- 4242 Dundas Street West (East of Royal York Road) ☎ 416 234-0611

  Monday–Wednesday 9:30–7, Thursday–Friday 9:30–8, Saturday 9:30–6, Sunday 12–5

  Subway: ROYAL YORK + bus

- 194 Lakeshore Road East, Oakville

Simple pleasures!

Although chocolate is a pleasure that should be enjoyed as often as possible (daily!), some of the more exclusive Franco-European varieties tend to be priced out of range for regular indulgences. For everyday treats that will satisfy both your craving and your pocketbook, any of the following brands are sure to delight: *Alprose, Côte D'or, Dolfin, Jacques de Belgique, Galler de Belgique, Lindt, Marquise d'Angélis, Maxim's, Mazet, Michel Cluizel, Petite Périgord Gold, Pierre Ledent, Poulain, Révillon, Sarments, Suchard, Swiss Delic* and *Valrhona.*

WHERE TO FIND THESE FRANCO-EUROPEAN CHOCOLATES

1. Arz Bakery
2. Brandt Meat Packers Supermarket
3. Cheese Boutique
4. Chocolates & Creams
5. Comptoir de Célestin
6. Domino Foods Ltd.
7. Daniel et Daniel
8. La Cigogne
9. Le Gourmand
10. Leonidas
11. Loblaws
12. Max Market
13. Mercatto
14. Pâtisserie d'Or
15. Pusateri's Fine Foods
16. Rahier
17. Scheffler's Delicatessen & Cheese
18. Simone Marie Belgian Chocolate
19. Sobey's
20. Sun Valley Fruits & Grocery

(near Trafalgar Road) ☎ 905 339-2100

Monday–Thursday 10–6, Friday 10–8, Saturday 10–6

www.bernardc.ca

Bernard Callebaut chocolates are made with a perfect balance of modern flair and old world Belgian tradition, passed down from one generation to the next. Headquartered in Calgary, Callebaut's creations are inspired by different cultures and religions. This originality, coupled with ingredients of only the best quality, makes Callebaut chocolates truly stand out from the rest. Available in mostly traditional flavours, their distinctive, rich taste can be attributed to a reduction in the amount of sugar used during preparation, in favour of an increase in the amount of cocoa. Naturally, Callebaut chocolates are also prepared without preservatives – but when chocolate tastes this good, it doesn't last very long to begin with! Be sure to try the chocolate banana popsicles – whole bananas dipped in Callebaut chocolate, then frozen on sticks. Sinfully good!

CLAFOUTI

915 Queen Street West (East of Strachan Avenue, across from Trinity Bellwoods Park) ☎ 416 603-1935

Closed Monday; Tuesday–Saturday 8–6, Sunday 9–5

Subway: OSGOODE + streetcar

Clafouti has a good selection of well-known Franco-European brands of chocolates, as well as powdered chocolate from *Poulain* (you can even order a hot cup of *Poulain* cocoa to go!).

Daniel et Daniel Food Shop

248 Carlton Street (corner of Parliament Street) ☎ 416 968-9275

Monday–Saturday 7:30–6, closed Sunday

Subway: CASTLE FRANK + bus;
COLLEGE + streetcar

www.danieletdaniel.ca

Although Daniel et Daniel only carries a limited range of truffles, they are well worth a try. Choose from traditional favourites including hazelnut, white chocolate, nut and coconut, as well as champagne truffles from France.

Holt Renfrew Epicure Shop

50 Bloor Street West (corner of Bay Street) ☎ 416 922-2333

Monday–Wednesday 10–6, Thursday–Friday 10–8, Saturday 10–6, Sunday 12–6

Subway: YONGE or BAY

With their tantalizing display of *Neuhaus* and *Joseph Schmidt* chocolates, Holt Renfrew has mastered the art of silent seduction. You won't be able to resist these smooth, silky chocolates, available in a variety of classic and exotic flavours to tempt your palate (the orange and macerated cherry in Armagnac is simply divine!). Both Belgium's *Neuhaus* and America's *Joseph Schmidt* use Belgian chocolate in their creations, for a taste unlike any other. During the holidays, Holt Renfrew pulls out all the stops with numerous imported festive chocolates from France and Belgium. It's not easy to overshadow *Neuhaus* and *Joseph Schmidt* chocolates, but the chocolate-covered almonds from *Fauchon* are certainly worth your attention. You'll also find *Neuhaus* chocolate in bar sizes – a sinful pleasure at a simple price!

J. S. Bonbons

- 163 Dupont Street (corner of Davenport Road) ☎ 416 920-0274

  Closed Monday; Tuesday–Saturday 10–7, Sunday 11–5

Subway: DUPONT

- 811 Queen Street West (west of Bathurst Street) ☎ 416 703-7731

Closed Monday; Tuesday–Saturday 10–7, Sunday 11–5

Subway: OSGOODE + streetcar

www.jsbonbons.com

A visit to J. S. Bonbons is an assault on the senses. As you walk in the door, you are met by the sweet and intoxicating smell of chocolate. Then, feast your eyes on the antique-looking counter, which displays a multitude of preservative-free creations, including truffles (26 flavours!) that can be packaged in beautiful chocolate bowls and an assortment of sugar-coated, chocolate-dipped fruit. Finally, let your tastebuds succumb to the amazing variety of herbal, floral and tea-infused flavours, such as tarragon and black pepper, coriander and lime, lavender, chai tea, bergamot and rosemary. Although some of these blends may not sound like they would ordinarily be combined with chocolate, the end results are unique, impressive and, most of all, delicious.

Did you know?

Biting a praline is considered a sacrelige, as the only effective way to fully release all of the chocolate's intense flavours is to put the entire praline in your mouth at once.

La Cigogne

(formely La Framboisine)

1626 Bayview Avenue (South of Eglinton Avenue) ☎ 416 487-1234

Monday–Friday 7:30–7, Saturday 8–7, Sunday 8–5

Subway: EGLINTON + bus

On special occasions such as Christmas, Valentine's Day, Mother's Day and Easter, Pastry Chef Thierry Schmitt creates a delicious selection of 10 or so truffles, made with French chocolate, that should not be missed.

La Maison du Chocolat

☎ 1 800 988-5632
Monday–Saturday 10–7, Sunday 12–6

If you've had the privilege of indulging in chocolates from La Maison du Chocolat's shops in Paris or New York, you already know they taste simply sublime. To our detriment, La Maison du Chocolat does not have a Toronto location; however, their irresistable chocolates can be ordered by phone from the New York boutique and shipped directly to your home via air mail. At $100 (CDN) for a box of 77 pieces, this is an indulgence best saved for the most special of occasions!

Le Gourmand

152 Spadina Avenue (South of Queen Street) ☎ 416 504-4494

Monday–Friday 7–9, Saturday 9–6, Sunday 9–4

Subway: OSGOODE + streetcar; SPADINA + streetcar

Le Gourmand is a small bistro/ merchant located on the fringes of Toronto's Fashion District. Inside you'll find an impressive selection of chocolates from France. You can even order a cup of *Poulain's* decadent hot chocolate – *fantastique!*

Leonidas

- 50 Bloor Street West (corner of Bay, inside the Holt Renfrew Centre) ☎ 416 944-8822

  Monday–Thursday 10–6, Friday 10–7, Saturday 10–6, Sunday 12–5

  Subway: YONGE or BAY

- 176 Yonge Street (subway level of The Bay at Yonge Street and Queen Street) ☎ 416 861-6486

Monday–Friday 10–6

Subway: QUEEN

With over 2,000 stores around the globe, Leonidas is one of the world's largest chocolatiers. Their popularity can be attributed to the quality of their ingredients – butter, milk, cream and chocolate with 100 per cent cocoa butter is used in every Leonidas chocolate. Other fine ingredients used include Turkish hazelnuts, Morello cherries from Périgord and Italian almonds. The must-try at Leonidas is the *crème fraîche* (fresh cream) praline. It's almost too perfect to eat. The plain dark chocolate and cream is exquisite, but the other 11 varieties, in an assortment of milk, dark and white chocolate flavours, are equally dazzling. Needless to say, Leonidas does not use preservatives in the preparation of their chocolates. As a result, the *crème fraîche* pralines have a shelf life of only eight days, but it is highly unlikely anyone buying them will need this long to eat them!

Pain Perdu

736 St Clair Avenue West (West of Christie Street) ☎ 416 656-7246

Closed Monday; Tuesday–Friday 7–7:30, Saturday 7–5, Sunday 8–4

Subway: **ST CLAIR WEST** + streetcar

Truffles, truffles and more truffles! Pastry Chef Christophe Folgoas creates an assortment of superb truffles in mouth-watering flavours, such as white chocolate, bittersweet chocolate and rum and bittersweet chocolate and raspberry.

Pâtisserie d'Or

301 Robinson Street, Oakville (South of Lakeshore Road) ☎ 905 815-8999

Closed Monday–Tuesday; Wednesday–Friday 8–5:30, Saturday 8–6, Sunday 8–4

This gourmet pastry shop carries a few well-chosen Swiss chocolates, delicately and artistically displayed in a glass case at the back. Flavours are mostly traditional, yet never bland – orange, pistachio, violet, pecan, nut, coconut and white chocolate flavours are highly recommended!

Pusateri's Fine Foods

- 1539 Avenue Road (North of Lawrence Avenue) ☎ 416 785-9100

  Monday–Wednesday 8–8, Thursday–Friday 8–9, Saturday–Sunday 8–7

  Subway: **LAWRENCE** + bus

- 57 Yorkville Avenue (corner of Bay Street) ☎ 416 785-9100

  Monday–Wednesday 10–8, Thursday–Friday 10–9, Saturday 8–8, Sunday 10–7

  Subway: **BAY**

  www.pusateris.com

Tucked away in a little corner of this luxury grocery store you'll find a glass counter full of ganaches and pralines from Belgium's premier house of chocolates – *Neuhaus*.

Senses

- 318 Wellington West (inside the SOHO Metropolitan Hotelcorner of Blue Jay Way) ☎ 416 961-0055

  Monday–Sunday 7–9

  Subway: **ST ANDREW** + streetcar

  www.senses.ca

- 2901 Bayview Avenue (inside Bayview Village) ☎ 416 227-9149

  Monday–Friday 8–9, Saturday 8–6, Sunday 9–5

  Subway: **BAYVIEW**

Senses sells a variety of outstanding and unforgettable creations from Vancouver-based chocolatier Thomas Hass. Hass uses only Belgian chocolate in his truffles and pralines. For the most part, flavours are classic but they do include unique combinations such as champagne and espresso, white chocolate and rum and blackberry and honey.

Simone Marie Belgian Chocolate

126 Cumberland Street (corner of Bellair Street) ☎ Monday–Saturday 10:30–6:30, closed Sunday

Subway: BAY (Cumberland exit)

www.simonemarie.net

Simone Marie opened her Yorkville chocolate shop in 1993. Since then, it has become one of the city's most treasured spots for imported Belgian truffles and sweets. Unusual flavours include cinnamon, black chocolate orange and orange peel, dark chocolate and violet cream, lemon cream and orange cream. There's also a nice selection of liquor-filled truffles, including champagne, Cointreau and Amaretto. Be sure to enquire about the flavour of the month, which is always something especially exotic.

Swiss-Master Chocolatier

2538 Bayview Avenue (corner of York Mills Road, North of The Bridle Path/Post Road)
☎ 416 444-8802

Monday–Saturday 10–6, closed Sunday

Subway: YORK MILLS + bus

www.swissmaster.com

Swiss-Master chocolates are imported directly from the Swiss Alps to the shop's two locations in Toronto and Hong Kong. Although Chocolatier Ingrid Läderach opened her first shop in 1984, she chose to limit herself to just two locations in order to maintain strict control over quality and ensure it always remains a priority. For Läderach, chocolate is not only a love affair, it's also a family affair – an uncle living in Switzerland scouts out some of the best chocolate the country has to offer. One of Swiss-Master's signature pieces is the pastel chocolate. Available only during the summer months, these delicate white chocolate and fruit truffles come in orange, strawberry, lime, lemon and passionfruit flavours and simply must be tasted to be believed. Other truffle flavours are more traditional, yet no less satisfying. Be sure to try the rum and raisin, and the Grand Marnier, which comes in two varieties – *crème fraîche* and liqueur. Swiss-Master makes gift-giving simple. Those who traditionally 'say it with flowers' can now say it with chocolate instead – Swiss-Master has a line of sweet treats that literally say *I love you, For you* and *Thank you.* There is also an assortment of chocolate boxes, and, for children, a delightful selection of chocolatey insect-shaped critters, including ladybugs and bees. During the holidays, the shop is transformed into a small storybook castle filled with tonnes of chocolate specialties created exclusively for the occasion.

Teuscher Chocolates

55 Bloor Street West (corner of Bay Street, inside the Manulife Centre)
☎ 416 964-8200

Monday–Wednesday 10–6,
Thursday–Friday 10–7:30, Saturday 10–6, closed Sunday

Subway: YONGE or BAY

You know you're on to something good when *Bon Appétit* magazine declares Teuscher "the most meltingly marvellous of all chocolate creations." What a statement! For the past 65 years,

CLAFOUTI
PATISSERIE ET CAFÉ

Teuscher has developed a well-deserved reputation for excellence and quality based on their guarantee of freshness and commitment to using only the most refined ingredients. Teuscher's Zurich headquarters produces more than 100 different flavours (!) of chocolate, which are flown weekly to all parts of the world, including Toronto. With so many flavours to choose from it's hard to pick a favourite, however the orange, apricot, white chocolate, lemon, nougat and caramel are exceptional. Teuscher also offers a grown up version of a childhood favourite – the cherry blossom, which is macerated in Schnapps and coated with dark chocolate. Other noteworthy selections are the slices of crystallized orange dipped in milk, white or dark chocolate and the chocolate shooting stars. Don't miss the miniature chocolate animal kingdom, either – kids will get a kick out of the dog, cat, bee, butterfly and fish-shaped creations.

The Chocolate Messenger

1645 Bayview Avenue (South of Eglinton Avenue) ☎ 416 488-1414

Closed Sunday–Monday; Tuesday–Friday 10–6, Saturday 10–5

Subway: **EGLINTON** + bus

www.chocolatemessenger.com

This Swiss chocolatier uses *Lindt* chocolate to create a marvellous assortment of preservative-free pralines and truffles – over 20 different flavours of each. Fresh cream truffles are the specialty of the house. Be sure to try the port, green tea, peach and vodka and orange and vodka ... heavenly! During Valentine's Day, Christmas and Easter, this little shop is filled with boxes of truffles and chocolates treats. During the Christmas holidays, you can also find candied fruits and *marrons glacés* (sugar-coated chestnuts).

Toronto's most exotic chocolate flavours

1. Chocolate Addict's **lavender truffle**
2. Chocolates by Callebaut's **bitter dark chocolate and lavender oil truffle**
3. J. S. Bonbons's **masala chai, cinnamon and saffron truffle** and **white chocolate and lemon and thyme truffle**
4. Simone Marie Belgian Chocolate's **dark chocolate and cream of violet truffle**
5. Pâtisserie d'Or's **cream of violet truffle**
6. Teuscher's **jasmine truffle**
7. The Belgian Chocolate Shop's **poached pear in vodka ganache**
8. The Chocolate Mesenger's **port praline** and **green tea praline**
9. Truffle Treasures' **dark chocolate and macerated ginger in cognac truffle, mango and lime truffle** and **Veuve Clicquot champagne and strawberry truffle**

** the above list is in random order*

The Pie Shoppe

93 Front Street East (basement of St. Lawrence Market) ☎ 416 366-7957

Closed Sunday–Monday; Tuesday–Thursday 8–6, Friday 8–7, Saturday 5–5

Subway: **UNION**

Did you know?

Appointed by King Louis XIV, the first chocolatier in Paris was one of Queen Anne's officers, who opened his doors in 1659 on *la rue de l'Arbre* in *le 1er arrondissement.*

The Pie Shoppe carries a good selection of chocolates from The Chocolate Messenger, Bayview Avenue's favourite chocolatier.

Truffle Treasures

178 Reach Industrial Park Road, Unit 10, Port Perry (Reach Road and Highway 12)
☎ 905 982-0506 or 1-866-582-2773

Monday–Saturday 9–6:30

www.truffletreasures.com

There can be little doubt chocolatier Lara Vaarré is passionate about her craft. After apprenticing with a veteran chocolatier who had 70 years of experience, she perfected her craft at the renowned Lenôtre culinary school in Paris. The care and dedication Vaarré puts into her truffles are evident from the very first bite. With over 30 flavours ranging from the traditional to the original, there is a Truffle to be Treasured by every palate, including the ultimate in decadance – Veuve Clicquot champagne and strawberry. If travelling to Port Perry is a bit out of your way, fear not. You can also find Truffle Treasures at many Fortino grocery stores throughout Toronto, or you can stop by the Truffle Treasures booth at many of the food and wine shows in the Greater Toronto Area.

Whole Foods Market

87 Avenue Road (North of Bloor Street)
☎ 416 944-0500

Monday–Friday 9–10, Saturday 9–9, Sunday 9–8

Subway: BAY or MUSEUM

www.wholefoodsmarket.com

Whole Foods Market carries a small selection of *Callebaut* chocolates.

cheese shops & crème fraîche

Though France is as well-known for its creamy camembert as its crispy baguettes and good wine, it is not the only country that produces a wide variety of outstanding cheeses. Belgium, Switzerland and Quebec also export hundreds of kinds of cheese all over the world, from soft bries and chèvres to ripe roqueforts and okas. Let your taste buds be your guide as you enter the delicious world of cheese!

Did you know?

France's *Appellation d'Origine Contrôlée*/Appellation of Controlled Origin (AOC) designation guarantees a product has been produced within a specified region following established methods of production. Although the French AOC system can't guarantee quality, it can control most of the elements that go into making the product. The AOC designation applies to wines, eaux-de-vie, dairy and farm products, and is administered by Institut National des Appellations d'Origine (INAO). The French initiated the AOC system as a means of safeguarding the more quality-conscious winemakers, vineyards and certain areas in France from unethical producers who were taking advantage of better-known names. In the case of cheese, the AOC has established precise definitions for source milk, regions, methods of production and length of maturity. Some of the more well-known AOC cheeses include Cantal, Fourme d'Ambert and Roquefort (made exclusively with sheep milk). These cheeses have been made in the same tradition for centuries. To illustrate the strict controls and stringent approval needed to produce an AOC cheese, consider the following: there are over 2,000 different types of brie cheeses, but only two have earned the AOC distinction.

Alex Farm Products

Various locations across the Greater Toronto Area.

☎ 1 877 488-7778 (main number)

www.alexcheese.com

France produces close to 200 different varieties of cheese, and you would easily think Alex Farm Products imports them all. All the classics are covered, including brie, morbier, *Belle des Champs,* raclette, chèvre and camembert. Rarer selections like etorki, pouligny-saint-pierre, coulommiers, pont l'évêque, époisses de Bourgogne, saint-andré, fourme d'ambert, saint agur, rondin du Poitou, brique du Jussac and grain d'orge from Normandy are also available. Alex Farm Products even sells a small selection of AOC (see above) cheese – cantal lagioule, chaumes, abondance, chaource and vacherin Mont-d'Or de Badoz. The selection from Switzerland is more limited, but you'll be sure to find raclette, gruyère and three varieties each of emmenthal and appenzeller.

All the Best Fine Foods

1099 Yonge Street ☎ 416 928-3330

Monday–Wednesday 8:30–6:30, Thursday–Friday 8:30–7, Saturday 8:30–6, Sunday 10–5

Subway: SUMMERHILL

www.allthebestfinefoods.com

This Rosedale shop has an interesting selection of cheese from France, Switzerland and Quebec that cover everything from well-known classics to hard-to-find varieties. From France, you'll find a huge assortment of popular choices (époisses, comté, morbier, camembert Jort, livarot, mothais, selles-sur-cher, pouligny-saint-pierre and many varieties of brie) to specialized artisan varieties (chèvre chabichou of Poitou, fourgerus, colombier, Riblaire, champenois and édel de cléron). You'll also find saint-basile, saint-félicien, Lechevalier Mailloux, le pied-de-vent and ange cornu from Quebec, as well as several unpasterized varieties.

Cheese Boutique

45 Ripley Avenue (South of South Kingsway & The Queensway)
☎ 416 762-6292

Monday–Friday 8–9, Saturday 8–8, Sunday 10–6

Subway: **RUNNYMEDE** + bus

www.cheeseboutique.com

As you would expect, Cheese Boutique has an impressive and vast range of cheese from around the world, including 10 or so varieties from Switzerland, 30 from Quebec and more than 100 from France. It's also one of the only shops in Toronto to age imported cheese on the premises, including the hard-to-find French explorateur. Most cheesemongers only import explorateur for a short time during Christmastime – you'd be hard-pressed to find during the remainder of the year. Not only will you find it at Cheese Boutique year-round, you can choose between non-aged and aged-on-premises varieties – *magnifique!* Another item of note at Cheese Boutique are the many kinds of artisan cheese imported from Quebec.

Cheese Magic

182 Baldwin Street (inside Kensington Market) ☎ 416 593-9531

Monday–Saturday 8:30–7, Sunday 9–6

Subway: **SPADINA** + streetcar;
QUEEN'S PARK + streetcar

The smallest of the cheesemongers inside Kensington Market, Cheese Magic carries a nice selection of Swiss appenzeller, gruyère, emmenthal and raclette, French roquefort, morbier, bleu d'Auvergne, port-salut and raclette and Quebecois oka, saint-benoît bleu bénédictin, brie and chèvre.

Chris' Cheesemongers

93 Front Street East (St. Lawrence Market)
☎ 416 368-5273

Closed Sunday–Monday;
Tuesday–Thursday 8–6, Friday 8–7, Saturday 5–5

Subway: **UNION**

Chris' Cheesemongers is an affiliate of Alex Farm Products, but while the latter focuses on French cheese, Chris' Cheesemongers spotlights cheese from Quebec. In fact, the list of fromages found here from *la belle Province* is simply mind-boggling – over 60 varieties! To whet your appetite, here's a sampling of what Chris' Cheesemongers has to offer: chèvre noir (black chèvre), grand cru de Chaput, herb double-brie, double-brie au poivre, pied-de-vent from *Îles-de-la-Madeleine,* capra, freddo, jeune cœur from *Îles-de-la-Madeleine,* mi-careme from *Île aux Grues* (very similar to camembert from Normandy) and cendré de Warwick (the Quebecois version of morbier). There is also a respectable selection of cheese from France, including chaumes, saint-paulin, brie triple crème, port-salut, bresse bleu, camembert from Normandy, pont l'évêque, boursault, rouy and vacherin Mont-d'Or.

Did you know?

France produces over 160,000 tonnes of camembert every year – now, that's a lot of cheese!

Dinah's Cupboard

50 Cumberland Street ☎ 416 921-8112

Monday–Friday 9–7, Saturday 9–6, closed Sunday (open Sundays in December)

Subway: YONGE or BAY

Although Dinah's Cupboard only has a small selection of cheese, it includes about a half a dozen or so of some of the most popular varieties from France.

Global Cheese

76 Kensington Avenue ☎ 416 593-9251

Monday–Friday 8:30–7, Saturday 8–6, Sunday 9–5

Subway: SPADINA + streetcar; QUEEN'S PARK + streetcar

Vive le fromage! French cheese is well represented at Global Cheese – there are about 25 different types available, including staples like morbier, saint-agur, truffier, fourme d'ambert, champagne, chèvre, saint-andré, saint-paulin, pont l'évêque, bleu d'Auvergne and roquefort. Global Cheese also has a nice selection of cheese from Quebec including herb, pepper and regular varieties of brie, camembert and oka, while gruyère and emmenthal represent the shop's Swiss selection. The best part about shopping at Global Cheese – other than the very reasonable prices – are the free samples you can nibble on before you make your purchase!

Loblaws

Various locations across the Greater Toronto Area.

If you are pressed for time and cannot pop by your favourite cheese shop, you can always pick up the basic varieties of French cheese at Loblaws. While not at par with most of the other cheesemongers listed here, Loblaws's selection of cheese from France and Quebec is still quite respectable. You'll find brie, camembert, *Boursin, Caprice des Dieux,* emmenthal, coulommiers, comté, bleu d'Auvergne, oka, blue cheese and chèvre. Loblaws also imports raclette and gruyère from Switzerland.

Max Market

2299 Bloor Street West (West of Runnymede Road) ☎ 416 766-6362

Monday–Wednesday 9–7, Thursday 9–7:30, Friday 9–8, Saturday 9–7, Sunday 9–6

Subway: RUNNYMEDE

Max Market stocks a decent variety of cheese from France, Quebec and Switzerland including morbier, raclette, appenzeller, bleu d'Auvergne, fourme d'ambert, saint-agur, roquefort, chèvre Riblaire, oka and gruyère.

Mendel's Creamery n' Appetizer

72 Kensington Avenue (inside Kensington Market) ☎ 416 597-1784

Monday–Friday 8:30–7, Saturday 7:30–6, closed Sunday

Subway: SPADINA + streetcar; QUEEN'S PARK + streetcar

Though Mendel's Creamery n' Appetizer is small in size, the amount of French, Swiss and Quebecois cheese they import is huge! You'll find about 80 kinds from France, 10 from Quebec and half a dozen from Switzerland. Must-try French cheese includes morbier, roquefort, saint-paulin, saint-andré, chèvre from Corsica and brie bleu (a cross between brie and blue cheese). When it comes to Quebec, the oka, camblu (a cross between a camembert and blue cheese) and brie are noteworthy, while Swiss selections include gruyère, raclette, emmenthal, appenzeller and vacherin Mont-d'Or.

Where to buy AOC cheese year-round

1. Alex Farm Products
2. All the Best Fine Foods
3. Cheese Boutique
4. Chris' Cheesemongers
5. Global Cheese
6. Mendel's Creamery n' Appetizer (Christmastime only)
7. Olympic Cheese Mart
8. Pusateri's Fine Foods
9. Scheffler's Delicatessen & Cheese
10. Whole Foods Market

Olympic Cheese Mart

- 93 Front Street East (St. Lawrence Market) ☎ 416 363-7602

  Closed Sunday–Monday; Tuesday–Thursday 8–6, Friday 8–7, Saturday 5–5

  Subway: UNION

- 7780 Woodbine Avenue, Markham (near 14th Avenue) ☎ 905 944-8676

  Monday–Wednesday 10–6, Thursday–Friday 10–7, Saturday 9:30–6, closed Sunday

Talk about selection – more than 400 kinds of cheese under one roof! You're guaranteed to discover something new with every visit. Olympic Cheese Mart has over 100 types of French cheese alone. Among the more popular choices, you'll find camembert, brie *en brioche,* saint-morgon, saint-andré, raclette and chèvre. Lesser-known varieties include pepper camembert, gourmelin, époisses, roquefort, comté, beaufort and *p'tit reblo.* There's also an impressive selection of rare cheese from Quebec – mouton noir, saint-ambroise (a cheese made with beer), frère jacques, moine, le douanier, mamirolle, Sir Laurier d'Arthabaska, cantonnier and cheeses from the Plessisville and Saint-Benoît regions. If your tastes lean more towards cheese from Switzerland, you'll find varieties of gruyère, emmenthal, raclette, vacherin fribourgeois, vacherin Mont-d'Or, maréchal, mont vully, weinkäse, tête de moine and three types of appenzeller. Olympic Cheese Mart also imports many cheeses made with raw milk.

Pusateri's Fine Foods

- 1539 Avenue Road (North of Lawrence Avenue) ☎ 416 785-9100

  Monday–Wednesday 8–8, Thursday–Friday 8–9, Saturday–Sunday 8–7

  Subway: LAWRENCE + bus

- 57 Yorkville Avenue (corner of Bay Street) ☎ 416 785-9100

  Monday–Wednesday 10–8, Thursday–Friday 10–9, Saturday 8–8, Sunday 10–7

Did you know?

Oka – the oldest Canadian cheese of French origin – made its way to (Lower) Canada in 1893, when Brother Alphonse Juin, a Cistercian monk and cheesemaker in his own right, emigrated from Port-du-Salut Abbey in France. After joining a trappist monastery near Lac des Deux Montagnes, Quebec, Brother Alphonse used the skills he mastered in France to come up with this delicious new creation. Although the Cistercian monks are no longer behind the making of this great cheese, their recipe has been well-preserved – for over a century, each wheel of oka cheese has been turned and washed by hand. Quality has always remained a priority in the production of oka, making it an enduring favourite of Canadians.

Subway: BAY

www.pusateris.com

Pusateri's imports some of the best Franco-European and Quebecois cheese in Toronto. From France you'll find roquefort, époisses, bleu d'Auvergne, saint-agur, etorki, tomme de Savoie, morbier, saint-albray, chaumes and welsche, a rare aged cheese from Alsace. There's also chimay from Belgium and rebloch'art from Quebec.

QUALITY CHEESE

111 Jevlan Drive, Vaughan (corner of Highway 7 and Weston Road) ☎ 905 265-9991

Monday–Friday 8:30–6, Saturday 8:30–5, closed Sunday

This family-owned shop is renowned for its prize-winning cheese. Some of the winners include a rich and creamy French brie.

SCHEFFLER'S DELICATESSEN & CHEESE

93 Front Street East (St. Lawrence Market) ☎ 416 364-2806

Closed Sunday–Monday; Tuesday–Thursday 8–6, Friday 8–7, Saturday 5–5

Subway: UNION

The St. Lawrence Market has a number of excellent cheesemongers, and Scheffler's Delicatessen & Cheese is no exception. Imported from France you'll find saint-agur, camembert, saint-andré, l'ermite, chèvre and saint-paulin, as well as cheese made with sheep's milk. There's also Swiss gruyère and emmenthal, and camembert, brie, chèvre, oka, frère jacques and bleu bénédictin from Quebec.

SOBEY'S

81 St Clair Avenue East (East of Yonge Street) ☎ 416 413-0594

24 hours a day, 7 days a week

Subway: ST CLAIR

Sobey's new Yonge/St. Clair location satisfies the needs of neighbourhood Francophiles with a variety of French products, including cheese. French selections include saint-aubin, morbier, *p'tit reblo*, saint-paulin, emmenthal, brie, camembert and rustique from

Normandy, while closer to home, there is Quebec oka and chèvre.

Sun Valley Fruits & Grocery

583 Danforth Avenue (East of Pape Avenue) ☎ 416 469-5227

8–9, 7 days a week

Subway: PAPE

Because of its location in the heart of Toronto's Greektown, Sun Valley Fruits & Grocery has developed a reputation for good quality feta. But you probably didn't know it's also also developing a reputation as a purveyor of good quality Franco-European cheese. Although the selection is not extensive, there is gruyère and emmenthal from Switzerland, and about 15 varieties from France, including morbier, tomme de montagne, fourme d'ambert, saint-nectaire, roquefort and bleu d'Auvergne.

Whole Foods Market

87 Avenue Road (North of Bloor Street) ☎ 416 944-0500

Monday–Friday 9–10, Saturday 9–9, Sunday 9–8

Subway: BAY or MUSEUM

www.wholefoodsmarket.com

A trip down Whole Foods Market's cheese aisle reveals an incredible selection of Dutch, Italian and German cheese, as well as numerous French cheese that are almost impossible to find on this side of the Atlantic – fourme d'ambert, comté, tomme de savoie, chaumes, munster, cantal, l'ossau-iratry-brebis Pyrénées, crottin de chavignol, pont l'évêque, saint-aubin, explorateur, chaource, montagnou and petit livarot from Normandy, to name a few. Whole Foods Market also sells a number of AOC-labelled cheeses, a designation both familiar and important to the French. Most cheese shops in Toronto only import one variety of Swiss gruyère, but at Whole Foods Market, you'll find three different types! There's a gruyère made with raw milk, a high altitude gruyère (made from the milk of cows that live in mountaineous regions) and a cave-aged gruyère, which is saltier compared to the other varieties. All three gruyères have distinct tastes, so the best way to fully appreciate their differences is to try all three. Other Swiss imports include emmenthal, raclette, appenzeller, vigneron (made from sheep's milk and slightly aged) and mostkäse (hand washed with apple cider, giving it a liquor-like aftertaste). There is also cheese containing olives and mustard grains that are must-trys from Switzerland. Closer to home, Whole Foods Market offers an outstanding (and constantly growing) variety of rare cheese from Quebec. Currently, you'll find maroilles, geai bleu, tourelle de Richelieu, pont couvert, cantonnier (made with raw milk), le douanier and cendré de Warwick (both comparable to French morbier) and one of Quebec's oldest classics – oka. You may be surprised to discover a limited range of hard cheese from New Brunswick at Whole Foods Market – Sieur de Duplessis (made with sheep's milk) and tomme de champ doré, both of which are surprisingly good. There are numer-

Crème fraîche

Crème fraîche is a staple in any respectable French kitchen. Unlike the liquid, milky whipping cream readily found in local supermarkets, *crème fraîche* is thick in texture and sour in taste. It is also is indispensible in many French soups and desserts. *Crème fraîche* isn't easy to find in Toronto, but there are a few locations that stock it:

ALEX FARM PRODUCTS: Carries bona fide *crème fraîche* from Normandy.

ALL THE BEST FINE FOODS: Stocks a homemade variety of *crème fraîche.*

CHEESE BOUTIQUE: Carries *crème fraîche* imported from France.

CHRIS' CHEESEMONGERS: Located inside the St. Lawrence Market, Chris' Cheesemongers imports their *crème fraîche* from Normandy.

MAX MARKET: This Bloor West Village shop carries *crème fraîche* from Quebec.

OLYMPIC CHEESE MART: Stocks *crème fraîche* imported from Quebec.

PUSATERI'S FINE FOODS: Carries Quebecois *crème fraîche.*

SCHEFFLER'S DELICATESSEN & CHEESE: Stocks *crème fraîche* from both France and Quebec.

SOBEY'S: Due to repeated requests from customers, Sobey's now carries *crème fraîche* from Ontario.

SUN VALLEY FRUITS & GROCERY: Located on the Danforth, this is another great source for *crème fraîche* in Toronto.

WHOLE FOODS MARKET: This Yorkville shop carries Ontario-produced *crème fraîche.*

ous reasons for a French cheese lover to shop at Whole Foods Market, but perhaps the best one is the knowledgable employees. They will spend the necessary time to ensure you select the perfect cheese to match your palate, which makes a considerable difference when trying something new. (And contrary to what many may think, the cheese at Whole Foods Market is quite affordable!)

meats, pâtés & terrines

Most local butchers already offer the basics – beef, chicken, veal, lamb and pork – in a variety of cuts, so for our purposes, the focus of this section is strictly on the specialties of the house as well as the essential meats for many French dishes.

Bloor Meat Market

2283 Bloor Street West (west of Runnymede Road) ☎ 416 767-2105

Closed Monday; Tuesday–Friday 9:30–6:30, Saturday 8:30–6, Sunday 10–5

Subway: RUNNYMEDE

The majority of the meats and kebabs at Bloor Meat Market have been marinated in a tantalizing house blend of herbs and spices. Even plain chicken breasts are available in dressed up versions, such as Florentine, Kiev and Cordon Bleu. When it comes to Francophones dishes, Bloor Meat Market is the ideal place to find (frozen) Cornish hens and cuts of meat for Chinese (using beef bouillon instead of oil) and *bourguignonne* (using oil) fondues.

Brandt Meat Packers Supermarket

1878 Mattawa Avenue, Mississauga (Dundas Street & Dixie Road) ☎ 905 279-4460

Closed Sunday–Tuesday; Wednesday 8–6, Thursday–Friday 8–7, Saturday 7–2

Although Brandt Meat Packers caters mostly to German-Canadians, you'll still find many of the meats needed for French cuisine including veal sausages, tongue, kidney and liver, tripe, chicken liver, blood sausages, pheasant thighs, smoked pheasant thighs and whole smoked pheasant. In terms of frozen fare, Brandt Meat Packers offers goose, duck, Cornish hen, pheasant, veal liver and pork fat.

Brown Brothers Meats

93 Front Street East (St. Lawrence Market) ☎ 416 364-7469

Closed Sunday–Monday; Tuesday–Thursday 8–6, Friday 8–7, Saturday 5–5

Subway: UNION

Brown Brothers Meats sells veal liver, milk-fed veal, filet mignon, cuts of meat for Chinese and *bourguignonne* fondues, and "AA" and "AAA" cuts of beef from Ontario – perfect for your French culinary needs!

Cumbrae's Naturally Raised Fine Meats

481 Church Street (corner of Wellesley Street) ☎ 416 923-5600

Monday–Friday 9:30–7, Saturday 9–6, Sunday 11–5

Subway: WELLESLEY

Cumbrae's Naturally Raised Fine Meats offers an impressive selection of meats that would make any French dinner memorable – deer, rabbit, duck, quail, sweetbreads, blood sausages, *poussin* (chick), squab, goose, Guinea fowl and pheasant. Depending on the item, you may want to place a special order as many of Cumbrae's meats are imported from from Quebec. You're in good hands – the high level of service and knowledge of Cumbrae's staff is as oustanding as their products. Cumbrae's also sells duck confit, fat and breast (smoked and non-smoked), chicken and veal kidneys, cuts for fondues, lamb from Quebec and *merguez* sausages (Moroccan sausages). Cumbrae's is also well-known for their preseasoned and pre-marinated meats – a wonderful practical solution when you don't want to do all the work yourself!

Di Liso's Fine Meats

93 Front Street East (St. Lawrence Market)
☎ 416 601-9780

Closed Sunday–Monday;
Tuesday–Thursday 8–6, Friday 8–7,
Saturday 5–5

Subway: UNION

Delicious French dinners start at Di Liso's, where you'll find filet mignon, rabbit, many cuts of lamb and cuts of meat well-suited for fondues.

European Quality Meats & Sausages

- 176 Baldwin Street (inside Kensington Market) ☎ 416 596-8691

  Monday–Thursday 8–6:30, Friday 8–7,
  Saturday 7–6:30, closed Sunday

  Subway: SPADINA + streetcar;
  QUEEN'S PARK + streetcar

- 16 Jutland Road (Queensway/Kipling)
  ☎ 416 251-6193

  Monday–Wednesday 8–6,
  Thursday–Friday 8–7, Saturday 8–6,
  closed Sunday

  Subway: KIPLING

The house specialty – very reasonable prices. Cuts are simple, and easily adaptable to most types of cuisine. Unfortunately, in the best Kensington Market tradition, line-ups at European Quality Meats & Sausages are impressively long. An important criterion is patience, as the service-by-number system is in operation – but it's well worth the wait!

Grace Meat Market

644 College Street (corner of Grace Street)
☎ 416 534-7776

Monday–Wednesday 8–6, Thursday–Friday
8–7, Saturday 8–6, Sunday 10–4

Subway: QUEEN'S PARK + streetcar

This Little Italy butcher serves up beautiful cuts that will create spectacular Francophone dishes. You can buy rabbit, *poussin,* Guinea fowl and deer on special order, while readily-available selections include smoked turkey, filet mignon, Cornish hen, frozen quail, milk-fed veal, sweetbreads, lamb sausages, liver, kidney and cuts for fondues. Grace Meat Market also roasts chickens and sausages to go.

Greco Meat Packers Limited

93 Front Street East (St. Lawrence Market)
☎ 416 869-3251

Closed Sunday–Monday;
Tuesday–Thursday 8–6, Friday 8–7,
Saturday 5–5

Subway: UNION

Greco Meat Packers has a terrific selection of "AA", "AAA" and Black Angus beef from Ontario, as well as veal kidney, filet mignon, milk- and grain-fed veal, cuts of meat for Chinese and *bourguignonne* fondues and numerous cuts of lamb.

Highland Farms

4750 Dufferin Street (North of Finch Avenue) ☎ 416 736-6606

Monday–Saturday 7–10, Sunday 8–8

Subway: DOWNSVIEW + bus

Highland Farms offers a selection of meat that is incomparable to most supermarkets and rarely seen outside a butcher's shop, including rabbit, beef tripe, veal liver, capon and a multitude of cuts of veal and lamb.

Dried Meats, Pâtés and Terrines

Alex Farm Products This merchant imports a diverse selection of rich delicacies from France such as *foie gras* flavoured with truffles or Port wine, as well as duck breast, mousse, confit and *rillettes* (a coarse, highly-spiced cold spread made from meat or poultry). From Quebec, you'll find 15 or so flavours of pâté. You'll also find *foie gras* from La Ferme Périgord. It's available in mousse, *rillettes* or pâté.

All the Best Fine Foods An exotic assortment of pâtés, *terrines* and mousses from Quebec and Ontario awaits you at All the Best Fine Foods. Be sure to try the green pepper and quail or pepper pâté, the duck and pistachio *terrine* and the truffle or quail and truffle mousse. You'll also find La Ferme Périgord *foie gras* imported from France.

Brandt Meat Packers Supermarket Although this supermarket caters mostly to Canadians of German and Eastern European descent, it has an impressive counter of dried meats that is sure to please most Francophiles.

Caviar Direct In addition to caviar, Caviar Direct sells *foie gras* from Quebec that can be purchased by the block or in small portions, as well as blocks of sumptuous goose and truffle *foie gras* from France.

Cheese Boutique This cheese shop offers authentic French and Quebecois *foie gras*. There's also six flavours of pâté from Quebec's La Maison du Gibier, a Quebecois *mousse de foie gras* (which makes for a very acceptable substitute at a quarter the price of the French *foie gras)* and a decent selection of dried meats.

Chris' Cheesemongers Cheese isn't all Chris sells from *la belle province* – you'll also find pâtés and *terrines* from two very reputable houses – La Ferme Périgord and La Maison du Gibier, as well as a small assortment of duck breast and confit.

Cumbrae's Naturally Raised Fine Meats This is a great place to buy pâtés and *terrines* from Quebec, in the most delicious combination of flavours: pork from Toulouse, duck and green pepper, duck and pink peppercorn, pheasant and pistachio, *pâté de campagne* and wild mushrooms and duck *rillettes.* Cumbrea's Naturally Raised Fine Meats also sells dried sausages *comme les français,* and *foie gras.*

Daniel et Daniel – Food Shop There are only a few varieties, but the flavours are traditionally French: *pâté de campagne,* pepper and duck *rillettes.*

Dinah's Cupboard This charming gourmet boutique located on Cumberland Street stocks a dozen or so *rillettes,* pâtés and *terrines* from Quebec and a few that are made in Dinah's own kitchen. Choose from *rillettes du Mans,* duck *rillettes,* rabbit *terrine* with pistachios, venison *terrine,* boar *terrine* with apricots and *foie gras.*

Global Cheese In this world of cheeses, there's also room for a few pâtés and *foie gras* from Quebec and France!

Max Market This shop has an incredibly impressive selection of 15 or so pâtés and *terrines* from Quebec. There's something for every palate, from the traditional to the adventurous, but here's the short list of must-try pâtés: ostrich and blackcurrant, pork and truffle, duck and pistachio, quail, Grand Marnier and pink peppercorn.

Meat on the Beach This butcher's exotic flavours of *terrines* from France include pheasant and Corinthian raisin, deer and Cognac and hare – *ooh la la!*

Mendel's Creamery n' Appetizer A small selection of pâtés from France and Quebec is available at Mendel's, in rosemary and mushroom, Grand Marnier and pepper and Cognac flavours. There's also *foie gras* from Quebec and France.

Olympic Cheese Mart You'll find an assortment of pâtés and *cretons* (pork pâté) from Quebec. You'll also find *foie gras* from France.

Patachou This *pâtisserie* is becoming as well-known for their excellent homemade pâtés as its excellent homemade pastries! Choose from the chicken liver pâté, *pâté de campagne* or duck *foie gras* paté.

Pusateri's Fine Foods Upscale Pusateri's has a reputation for excellence that extends to their pâtés, *terrines* and *foie gras*. For the discerning gourmand, *fois gras* is sold in blocks, in a butter–like pâté spread, with truffles, as a mousse and as a jelly. The selection of pâtés is just as elaborate – you can find duck and orange, cranberry and pheasant, salmon and spinach, smoked trout, Florentine veal and, for traditionalists, pepper cognac.

Scheffler's Delicatessen & Cheese This merchant imports their pâtés and *terrines* from Quebec, their duck breast and duck confit from France, and their *foie gras* from both places. Their selection of pâtés includes about 10 or so exotic flavours such as rabbit and walnut, duck *rillettes*, quail and pear, duck and pistachio, rabbit, pork, blueberry and maple syrup, and caribou and fig.

Sobey's This supermarket imports exquisite Quebecois pâtés, *terrines* and *foie gras* in a variety of unusual flavours that will be sure to pique your curiosity. Be sure to try the ostrich and Corinthian raisins *terrine*, wild meat *terrine* (ostrich, deer, pheasant, bison and boar) and pork and cranberry pâtés.

The Butcher Block Café This butcher sells *foie gras* from Quebec.

The Butchers Quebecois *foie gras* and a small selection of pâtés – pheasant, duck and pistachio, deer and smoked trout – can be found at The Butchers.

Village Butcher This butcher carries several kinds of pâtés and *foie gras* mousses.

White House Meats In this butcher's shop, you'll find a small but respectable selection of pâté, including three different kinds of *foie gras* – mousse, *bloc* (denser textured) and *foie gras de canard entier* (whole pieces). You can also buy duck fat, fatty duck legs for confit, confit *de canard* and *magret* (duck breast).

Whole Foods Market This upscale supermarket sells a small assortment of domestic and wild meats preservative-free pâtés from Quebec that are absolutely divine. Whole Foods Market intends to increase the number of Quebecois pâtés they carry, but for now, you'll have to be content with caribou, pork and fig, pork and pistachio, and duck, pork and pistachio flavours.

Manos Meats

93 Front Street East (St. Lawrence Market) ☎ 416 364-2652

Closed Sunday–Monday; Tuesday–Thursday 8–6, Friday 8–7, Saturday 5–5

Subway: UNION

Manos Meats carries a small assortment of essentials for French cuisine including veal, liver, filet mignon and cuts of meat for Chinese and *bourguignonne* fondues.

Meat on the Beach

1860 Queen Street East (West of Rainsford Road) ☎ 416 690-1228

Monday–Thursday 7–7, Friday 7–8, Saturday–Sunday 7–6

Subway: QUEEN + streetcar

Although Meat on the Beach recently moved, nothing has changed about their excellent service, quality and selection. Many of the all-grain-fed meats you'll find here are perfect for Francophone dishes, including a good selection of game (duck, goose, and squab), smoked turkey, blood sausages, Guinea fowl and rabbit year-round (by special order). Unlike many other butchers in the city, Meat on the Beach carries a full range of offal (organ meats), considered to be a French delicacy. Meat on the Beach also carries *merguez* sausages, multiple cuts of lamb, an incredible assortment of homemade sausages, filet mignon and cuts of meat for Chinese and *bourguignonne* fondues. During the Christmas season, you'll even find pheasant and capon. If you are looking for a change from the everyday, try their bacon-stuffed specialties.

Nick's Wholesale Meats & Delicatessen

93 Front Street East (St. Lawrence Market) ☎ 416 364-2652

Closed Sunday–Monday; Tuesday–Thursday 8–6, Friday 8–7, Saturday 5–5

Subway: UNION

Nick's Wholesale Meats specialises in filet mignon, pork, beef and chicken kebobs.

Nicola's Choice Meats

298 Eglinton Avenue West (corner of Avenue Road) ☎ 416 485-4429

Sunday–Monday closed, Tuesday–Friday 7–7, Saturday 7–5

Subway: EGLINTON + bus

Nicola's is as discerning about their meats as their customers are. Many of their meats have received the coveted Honour for Excellence and Quality award from the Royal Agricultural Winter Fair. When it comes to meat for French cuisine, you can expect to find rabbit, blood sausages, veal liver, mutton, quail, pheasant, goose, duck and cuts of meats for Chinese and *bourguignonne* fondues, as well as a good selection of offal.

Olliffe

1097 Yonge Street ☎ 416 928-0296

Monday–Thursday 8:30–6:30, Friday 8:30–7, Saturday 8:30–6, Sunday 10–5

Subway: SUMMERHILL

The quality and the high standards at Olliffe are befitting of its Rosedale location. Choice cuts suited to compliment any Francophone dish include milk-fed veal, *merguez* sausages, duck breast, rabbit, blood sausages, veal liver, pheasant, squab, Cornish hen, *poussin,* Guinea fowl, fondue meats and quail (fresh during the winter months and frozen the remainder of the year). Some items are available through special order only. During the Christmas holiday season, Olliffe also imports duck *foie gras* and goose from France and Quebec. Olliffe sells a beautiful selection of well-cut meats, but be warned – this butcher is so upscale, prices are not even displayed. In fact, chances are if you have to ask, you probably can't afford it.

Pusateri's Fine Foods

- 1539 Avenue Road (North of Lawrence Avenue) ☎ 416 785-9100

  Monday–Wednesday 8–8, Thursday–Friday 8–9, Saturday–Sunday 8–7

  Subway: LAWRENCE + bus
- 57 Yorkville Avenue (corner of Bay Street) ☎ 416 785-9100

  Monday–Wednesday 10–8, Thursday–Friday 10–9, Saturday 8–8, Sunday 10–7

  Subway: BAY

  www.pusateris.com

Pusateri's offers an elegant selection of perfectly marinated and prepared meats. Selections that are sure to please Francophiles include cranberry and fig stuffed quail, Mediterranean quail (wrapped in bacon and stuffed with goat cheese, chipotles and arugula) and the Cornish hen with cranberries. It's never been so easy to serve a French-inspired meal with little or no effort on your part – you only need to choose whether to grill, bake or sauté! Pusateri's is also one of the rare places in Toronto where you'll find Guinea fowl.

Royal Beef

1968 Danforth Avenue (West of Woodbine Avenue) ☎ 416 421-1029

Closed Monday; Tuesday–Wednesday 9–5, Thursday–Friday 9–7, Saturday 9–7, Sunday 10–4

Subway: WOODBINE

Royal Beef meats are sold the same day they are cut – now that's fresh! Another fresh twist is their range of healthy offerings – herb-fed veal scallops and free-range chicken. When it comes to meats that most suit French dishes, you'll find rabbit, duck, pheasant, filet mignon, offal, quail, Cornish hen and cuts of meat for Chinese and *bourguignonne* fondues. Blood sausages and Guinea fowl are available by special order, while geese are available exclusively at Christmastime.

St. Lawrence Upper Cut

93 Front Street East (St. Lawrence Market) ☎ 416 364-2652

Closed Sunday–Monday; Tuesday–Thursday 8–6, Friday 8–7, Saturday 5–5

Subway: UNION

Rabbit, milk-fed veal, pheasant, Cornish hen, squab and great cuts of filet mignon are just some of the meats available at St. Lawrence Upper Cut. It's also an excellent place to buy cuts of meat for Chinese and *bourguignonne* fondues (by special order only).

Where to buy merguez *sausages*

Most of the places listed here import these spicy Moroccan sausages from Quebec.

1. Cumbrae's Naturally Raised Meats
2. Meat on the Beach
3. Olliffe
4. Scheffler's Delicatessen & Cheese
5. The Butchers
6. Village Butcher
7. White House Meats

Scheffler's Delicatessen & Cheese

93 Front Street East (St. Lawrence Market) ☎ 416 364-2806

Closed Sunday–Monday; Tuesday–Thursday 8–6, Friday 8–7, Saturday 5–5

Subway: UNION

Scheffler's is one of a handful of places in Toronto that sells Moroccan *merguez* sausages.

Sobey's

81 St. Clair Avenue East (East of Yonge Street) ☎ 416 413-0594

24 hours a day, 7 days a week

Subway: ST CLAIR

If you live in the Yonge/St. Clair neighbourhood, look to Sobey's for the following French favourites – rabbit, deer medallions, quail and Cornish hen. More game meats are promised to be available in the future.

The Butcher Block Café

3251 Yonge Street (North of Lawrence Avenue) ☎ 416 544-1729

Monday 10–6, Tuesday–Friday 9–7, Saturday 8–6, Sunday 11–6

Subway: LAWRENCE

www.thefriendlybutcher.com

The place for barbecue lovers! Not only can you buy the most succulent meats for the grill (including "AAA" Canadian Black Angus), you can buy the grill itself – The Butcher Block Café also sells top-range barbecues! A unique feature of The Butcher Block Café is its chef-for-hire service. Order a chef for an evening or just a few hours to come to your home and cook your meats to perfection. That's sure to impress your guests! Here's something else that's impressive – the selection of "AA" and "AAA" Black Angus cuts, rabbit, milk-fed veal, quail, Cornish hen, filet mignon and cuts of meat for Chinese and *bourguignonne* fondues. You'll also be able to find deer, offal and Guinea fowl (by special order). Horse meat is available through very special order (Health Canada has stringent regulations about the sale of horse meat where meat from cows is also sold due to potential blood contamination; as a result, ordering horse meat is an expensive and often laborious process).

The Butchers

2636 Yonge Street (North of Eglinton Avenue) ☎ 416 483-5777

Monday–Wednesday 9–6, Thursday–Friday 9–7, Saturday 9–6, Sunday 9–5

Subway: EGLINTON

The name is simple, but the selection is diverse! At The Butchers, you'll find organic "AA" and "AAA" lamb, pork and beef, all from Ontario's Beretta Farm, as well as several wild game and fowl including Canadian venison. You'll also find many meats that are sure to please Francophiles, such as duck confit, duck breast, Cornish hen, deer, rabbit, milk-fed veal and cuts of meat for Chinese and *bourguignonne* fondues. A variety of other meats can be purchased by special order, including squab, duck, goose, Guinea fowl, offal and quail – you can even order horse meat. *Merguez* sausages are another house specialty, for those who like to make Moroccan *tajine* (stew of veal, lamb, chicken or squab with vegetables).

Village Butcher

2914 Lakeshore Boulevard West (near Islington Avenue) ☎ 416 503-9555

Sunday–Monday closed, Tuesday–Friday 7:30–6:30, Saturday 7:30–5

Subway: **ISLINGTON** + bus

Here is a butcher who loves his job! Rupert, the Village Butcher himself, offers service that is as impeccable as his meats. His selection of French favourites is outstanding – superb cut of filet mignon, fresh rabbit, milk-fed veal, duck liver, quail, pheasant, deer, Cornish hen, buffalo, blood sausages, squab, liver, kidney (other offal can be bought by special order) and cuts of meat for Chinese and *bourguignonne* fondues. Rupert notes that certain game meats are only available by special order and advises ordering these meats up to three weeks in advance due to the long tenderization period needed. You'll also want to try Village Butcher's specialties of the house – organic chicken, and homemade pork, veal, turkey and lamb sausages. As if all this wasn't enough, when asked if he carried the hard-to-find *merguez* sausages, Rupert not only said he did, but that he made them himself!

White House Meats

- 93 Front Street East (St. Lawrence Market) ☎ 416 364-2652

  Closed Sunday–Monday; Tuesday–Thursday 8–6, Friday 8–7, Saturday 5–5

  Subway: **UNION**

- 1539 Bayview Avenue (South of Eglinton Avenue) ☎ 416 488-2004

  Closed Monday, Tuesday–Friday 9–7 (closed at 6 during the winter), Saturday 8–6, Sunday 11–5

  Subway: **EGLINTON** + bus

White House Meats is the ideal place for lovers of unusual meats, and it only takes one look at their large selection to understand why. House specialties include ostrich, buffalo and venison, while choices of poultry and fowl include *poussin,* Cornish hen, goose, Guinea fowl, duck breast, fresh and frozen pheasant and even squab. They are also one of the few butchers in Toronto to carry game bird (duck, pheasant, quail) and big game (venison, buffalo, elk) stocks. For French dishes, you'll find fabulous cuts of filet mignon and lamb, rabbit, milk-fed veal, sweetbreads and liver sausages (Bayview location only). White House Meats also carries the hard-to-find *merguez* sausages, imported from Quebec, as well as cuts of meats for Chinese and *bourguignonne* fondues and Quebecois black and white blood sausages (both by special order). Stanley and Leila, the brother/sister duo that run White House Meats, get high marks for customer service, and are happy to offer advice about cuts and selection.

fishmongers

Breaded, fried, poached, grilled, smoked or raw … there are almost as many ways to prepare fish as there are varieties. Although seafood is a staple ingredient in French cuisine, a good fishmonger can be as hard to come by as a good hairdresser. The following list should help tremendously.

Avenue Seafood

302 Eglinton Avenue West (corner of Avenue Road) ☎ 416 481-2288

Monday 12–7, Tuesday–Thursday 9:15–7, Friday–Saturday 9–7, Sunday 12–6

Subway: EGLINTON + bus

You'll find a good diversity of treasures from the sea at Avenue Seafood, including fresh tuna, trout, Alaskan crab legs, Cuban lobster tails, octopus, sardines (by special order) and a variety of salmon, including some from the West Coast.

Big Fish Market

765 The Queensway (West of Royal York Road) ☎ 416 259-1585

Closed Sunday–Monday; Tuesday–Wednesday 10 –6, Thursday–Friday 10–8, Saturday 9–6

Subway: ROYAL YORK + bus

Big Fish Market has a wonderful selection of fish, shrimp and exotic seafood, such as Peruvian scallops, lobsters from Nova Scotia, New Zealand green mussels and several kinds of oysters from Prince Edward Island and the United States. They also carry shrimp, crawfish and fresh cod and tuna.

Bill's Lobsters

599 Gerrard Street East (East of Broadview Avenue) ☎ 416 778-0943

Monday–Saturday 9:30–6

Subway: BROADVIEW + streetcar

Lobster may be Bill's main specialty, but it is not his only one! He also sells a wide variety of conventional and exotic seafood including frog's legs, sea urchins, clams, trout, crab, a variety of shrimp and oysters from Canada's East and West Coasts.

Brandt Meat Packers Supermarket

1878 Mattawa Avenue, Mississauga (Dundas Street & Dixie Road) ☎ 905 279-4460

Closed Sunday–Tuesday; Wednesday 8–6, Thursday–Friday 8–7, Saturday 7–2

Specialties from the sea include fresh eel, canned escargot, smoked fish and jarred or canned fish filets — Brandt Meat Packers Supermarket carries a wide variety, ranging from sardines to mackerel.

Caviar Centre

220 Duncan Mills Road (near Don Mills Road) ☎ 416 441-9788

Monday–Friday 11–6; closed Saturday–Sunday (will open Saturdays by special request)

Subway: SHEPPARD or DON MILLS

www.caviarcentre.com

Arguably, caviar is an acquired taste. But if you enjoy this delicacy of raw fish eggs, visit Caviar Centre for the most extensive selection in Toronto. In addition to French caviar, they also sell Beluga, Osetra and Sevruga varieties.

Caviar Direct

93 Front Street East (basement of St. Lawrence Market) ☎ 416 364-2652

Closed Sunday–Monday; Tuesday–Thursday 8–6, Friday 8–7, Saturday 5–5

Subway: UNION

www.caviarforsale.com

Here's a little shop where you'll dis-

Did you know?

Just like wine, oysters require breathing time — you should open oysters half an hour before eating them. It's also recommended that you drain the oysters once you have opened them, because they will secrete a new flow of water that is far more fragrant.

Just-bought oysters should not be put in the fridge; instead, place them on ice to keep them fresh. Putting them in the fridge will keep them at a temperature that is too low, and they will lose their flavour.

If you like your oysters raw, you can bring out their flavour by using white pepper. (Purists will tell you not to use shallot vinegar or lemon to flavour oysters, as this will change their true flavour.) Of course, the best accompaniment for oysters is a glass of chilled white wine — *magnifique!*

cover big surprises. Caviar Direct imports large quantities of Beluga, Osetra and Sevruga caviar, as well as a few "Black Label" selections from Iran. Caviar Direct also carries a good assortment of dried and smoked fish, including smoked salmon from Scotland and Canada, smoked trout and smoked mackerel.

Diana's Seafood

2101 Lawrence Avenue East (near Warden Avenue) ☎ 416 288-9286

Monday 9–6, Tuesday–Friday 9–7, Saturday 9–6, Sunday 10–5

Subway: LAWRENCE + bus; KENNEDY + bus

The best oysters from Canada's East and West Coasts await you at Diana's Seafood.

Domenic's Fish Market

93 Front Street East (St. Lawrence Market) ☎ 416 364-2652

Closed Sunday–Monday; Tuesday–Thursday 8–6, Friday 8–7, Saturday 5–5

Subway: UNION

The perfect choices for popular French fish dishes are available at Domenic's Fish Market, including octopus, clams, oysters, fresh tuna and cod and even fresh sardines.

Domino Foods

93 Front Street East (far end of the basement level of St. Lawrence Market) ☎ 416 364-2652

Closed Sunday–Monday; Tuesday–Thursday 8–6, Friday 8–7, Saturday 5–5

Subway: UNION

Domino Foods carries many varieties of canned and jarred fish.

Global Cheese

76 Kensington Avenue ☎ 416 593-9251

Monday–Friday 8:30–7, Saturday 8–6, Sunday 9–5

Subway: SPADINA + streetcar; QUEEN'S PARK + streetcar

Cheese isn't all you'll discover here – there's also several varieties of imported marinated fish, including herring, trout and mackerel.

Highland Farms

4750 Dufferin Street (North of Finch Avenue) ☎ 416 736-6606

Monday–Saturday 7–10, Sunday 8–8

Subway: DOWNSVIEW + bus

Tucked away in Highland Farms' freezers, you'll find salmon, tuna, trout, eel, swordfish and sprats.

Kensington Market's Fish Houses

Subway: SPADINA + streetcar;
QUEEN'S PARK + streetcar

▸ Coral Sea Fish Shop

198 Baldwin Street ☎ 416 593-9656

Monday–Saturday 8–6, closed Sunday

▸ Medeiros Fish Market

168 Baldwin Street ☎ 416 593-9738

Monday–Saturday 7:30–6, closed Sunday

▸ New Seaway

195 Baldwin Street ☎ 416 593-5192

Monday– Sunday 7–6

▸ Sea Kings

189 Baldwin Street ☎ 416 593-9949

Monday–Saturday 8–6, Sunday 9–4

Seven Seas Fish

196 Baldwin Street ☎ 416 593-9875

Monday–Sunday 8–5

These five neighbouring fishmongers receive their goods from the same supplier, so their prices are in the same (very reasonable) range. As a result, their stores are often incredibly busy and line-ups can be long, particularly on Saturday mornings. Impatient souls may want to consider waiting until the afternoon, Sundays or during the week to do their shopping. When it comes to finding the perfect catch for your French-inspired cooking, the fishmongers in Kensington Market offer scallops, red snapper, sole, crab, mussels, octopus, many varieties of shrimp, fresh and frozen sardines and fresh tuna and cod. Most varieties of fish are fresh; however, many of these shops also have large freezers with ample selections. Most of these shops also carry smoked and dried fish, as well as fresh eel during the winter months. Sea Kings and Coral Sea Fish Shop sell sea urchins during the Christmas season.

Lobster Island

27 Milliken Boulevard (East of Kennedy Road) ☎ 416 591-6488

Monday–Saturday 9–6, Sunday 9–12

Subway: FINCH + bus

Lobster Island sells an impressive array of lobsters and an equally impressive assortment of other treasures from the sea, including oysters from Canada's East and West Coasts.

Mendel's Creamery n'Appetizer

72 Kensington Avenue (inside Kensington Market) ☎ 416 597-1784

Monday–Friday 8:30–7, Saturday 7:30–6, closed Sunday

Subway: SPADINA + streetcar;
QUEEN'S PARK + streetcar

Mendel's carries a small selection of marinated seafood — herring, anchovies, mackerel in olive oil and smoked mackerel and oysters.

Mike's Fish Market

93 Front Street East (St. Lawrence Market)
☎ 416 364-2652

Closed Sunday–Monday;
Tuesday–Thursday 8–6, Friday 8–7,
Saturday 5–5

Subway: UNION

Mike's Fish Market imports many items that are sure to please Francophones and Francophiles. In addition to their large freezer containing many varieties of fish and seafood, there is also fresh tuna, octopus, mussels, red snapper, clams and oysters. Fresh sardine are available on a monthly basis. If you're looking for a quick and delicious meal, why not try one of Mike's Fish Market's varieties of marinated fish?

Newport Fish Importers & Wholesalers

1140 Dupont Street (corner of Dufferin Street) ☎ 416 537-1278

Monday–Wednesday 7–5, Thursday–Friday 7–7, Saturday 7–4, closed Sunday

Subway: DUFFERIN

If you can't find it at Newport Fish Importers & Wholesalers, it probably doesn't exist! Choose from about 50 different varieties of fish filets (!), and approximately 20 freezers crammed with every kind of seafood imaginable — shrimp, sole, giant scallops, lobster and crab are just a few items offered. You'll also find salted fish and canned clams. If you're planning a trip, come on a Tuesday. That's the day Newport Fish Importers & Wholesalers receives their weekly shipment of fresh fish and seafood, many of which are perfect for French-inspired cuisine. There's fresh cod, sardines and tuna, octopus, eel, crab, red snapper and shrimp that are generous in quantity and size. A rare French delicacy found here is the bucket of fresh escargot (escargot has been spotted in other fish shops in Toronto, however their only purpose was to keep the fish tanks clean — obviously those fishmongers were not *au courrant* in the ways of French seafood!).

Osler Fish Warehouse

16 Osler Street (corner of Dupont Street)
☎ 416 769-2010

Monday 10–5, Tuesday–Friday 8–7,
Saturday 8–5, closed Sunday

Subway: DUNDAS WEST

Osler is *the* expert when it comes to fish and seafood imported from Portugal. That said, Francophiles will find many items they'll need to prepare their favourite fish dishes, too. Fresh tuna, sardines and cod, octopus from Morocco, salted cod, red snapper, trout, eel and even sea urchins are just some of the things available.

Oyster Boy

872 Queen Street West ☎ 416 534-3432

Monday–Sunday after 5

Subway: QUEEN + streetcar

Depending on the season, Oyster Boy stocks up to six different varieties of oysters.

Pisces Gourmet

1103 Yonge Street ☎ 416 921-8888

Monday 9:30–6:30, Tuesday–Thursday

9–6:30, Friday 9–7, Saturday 9–6, closed Sunday

Subway: **SUMMERHILL**

Pisces Gourmet has beautiful cuts of fish. The variety is plentiful, the service incomparable and the prices reflect the high standards of the shop. Among the selections, you'll discover fresh cod, tuna and sardines, trout, clams, octopus, smoked trout and oyster meat (sold without the shells). If you don't want to spend a lot of time on meal preparation, Pisces's medley of marinated fish kebabs are a tasty alternative and can be ready in just a few minutes. There's also a pre-made, heat-and-serve bouillabaisse (traditional French fish soup). As a bonus, you'll receive a lemon to fragrance and flavour your dish with each purchase. *Génial!*

Pusateri's Fine Foods

- 1539 Avenue Road (North of Lawrence Avenue) ☎ 416 785-9100

  Monday–Wednesday 8–8, Thursday–Friday 8–9, Saturday–Sunday 8–7

  Subway: **LAWRENCE** + bus
- 57 Yorkville Avenue (corner of Bay Street) ☎ 416 785-9100

  Monday–Wednesday 10–8, Thursday–Friday 10–9, Saturday 8–8, Sunday 10–7

  Subway: **BAY**

  www.pusateris.com

Pusateri's offers fresh cod, red snapper, trout, scallops, octopus and many varieties of giant shrimp. The Avenue Road location also has a freezer full of crab, lobster, shrimp and scallops. You'll also find many varieties of canned fish filets, and Beluga, Osetra and Iranian Sevruga caviar.

Rodney's Oyster House

469 King West (corner of Spadina Avenue) ☎ 416 363-8105

Monday–Saturday 11:30–1 a.m., closed Sunday

Subway: **KING** + streetcar

www.rodneysoysterhouse.com

Rodney's imports many varieties of oysters from the four corners of the world — Europe, Japan, and Canada's East and West Coasts. Don't be surprised to find up to a dozen varieties at any given time, but as a general rule of thumb, you'll find eight or nine kinds in the summer and up to 20 (!) in the winter. Best of all, Rodney is open until 1 a.m. six nights a week to satisfy your late night cravings.

Seafront Fish Market

93 Front Street East (St. Lawrence Market) ☎ 416 364-2652

Closed Sunday–Monday; Tuesday–Thursday 8–6, Friday 8–7, Saturday 5–5

Subway: **UNION**

You'll find fresh tuna and cod, fresh sardines (on occasion), salmon, scallops, clams and mussels, among many other varieties of seafood, at Seafront Fish Market. Check their large freezer when your favourite fish or seafood item is no longer in season – you'll be surprised at what you can find!

Snappers Fish Market

263 Durie Street (corner of Bloor Street West) ☎ 416 767-4083

Monday–Friday 10–6:30, Saturday 9–6, Sunday 12–5

Subway: **RUNNYMEDE**

Snappers Fish Market is a haven for those looking for high-quality seafood in the High Park area. Among the varieties in stock are fresh tuna and cod, sole, haddock, red snapper and scallops. Frozen Alaskan crab, escargot, octopus, sardines and lobster tails are also available, as well as a large selection of canned fish filets. All varieties of fish are readily available at Snappers Fish Market, but if you have a penchant for something a little more out of the ordinary, simply place a special order.

Village Butcher

2914 Lakeshore Boulevard West (near Islington Avenue) ☎ 416 503-9555

Sunday–Monday closed, Tuesday–Friday 7:30–6:30, Saturday 7:30–5

Subway: ISLINGTON + bus

Seafood at a butcher's? Although you'll only find a small selection of fish at Village Butcher, it is delivered three times a week to guarantee freshness. Choices include salmon, halibut, scallops, shrimp and tilapia (an Oriental fish that lives off algae — ideal for *meunière* recipes). You can also purchase different kinds of seasonal fish throughout the year.

Oyster Specialists

If you're craving oysters, the following are some of Toronto's best suppliers. Most fishmongers sell only one kind of oysters; however, these merchants carry a wide variety of fresh fare straight from Canadian and many other international coasts.

1. Big Fish Market
2. Bill's Lobsters
3. Diana's Seafood
4. Lobster Island
5. Oyster Boy
6. Rodney's Oyster House

other french specialties

Though many epicureans and food enthusiasts prefer to buy their items fresh or make them from scratch whenever possible, today's frantic lifestyle doesn't always make this possible. In this section, you'll discover a multitude of shops throughout the Greater Toronto Area that stock the ultimate in convenience and quality – frozen, canned, jarred and ready-to-serve French foods. For added ease, shops that offer frozen French goods have been flagged to stand out at a glance. Take advantage of the wonderful shops and products mentioned here to make your life a little easier on those days where everything seems hectic.

Markets

The experience of market shopping is full of old-world nostalgia, and for convenience and selection, it can't be beat. Most of the products sold in Toronto markets are local or come from Ontario's interior. Frequent visits almost guarantee the vendors will become accustomed to not only your face, but your tastes. In terms of large-scale offerings, Toronto is doubly blessed with the sights, sounds, smells, tastes and textures of both St. Lawrence and Kensington Markets. During the summer months, the city and the Greater Toronto Area plays host to a variety of smaller specialty, farmers and organic markets (consult your local newspaper for further information).

Highland Farms

☎ (416) 736-6606
Subway: DOWNSVIEW + bus

Highland Farms is definitely a "super market" – the selection of breads, meats, fruits and vegetables (many from Ontario) is ample and diverse enough to rival the St. Lawrence or Kensington. Not to mention, Highland Farms carries a lot of seasonal fruits and vegetables that you simply won't find anywhere else (for example, yellow beets and red carrots during Christmastime). The abundance of fresh herbs available during the summer months is also impressive. Best of all, the prices at Highland Farms are more than reasonable, which makes it tempting to try many things that you might not try otherwise. Beyond fruit and vegetables, Highland Farms also carries several of the most common varieties of cheese from France and Quebec, as well as an assortment of breads from diverse ethnic origins. If you're an olive lover, Highland Farms has enough types in stock to make you feel like a kid in a candy store.

Kensington Market

Subway: SPADINA + streetcar;
QUEEN'S PARK + streetcar

Baldwin and Spadina marks the spot for this Toronto treasure that carries everything from meat to cheese to spices. Kensington Market has a dual attraction – not only are all the goods for French classical and nouvelle cuisine readily available, but the market is only steps away from Chinatown ... even the most ardent French food lover needs a little variety once in a while! Perhaps the only drawback to Kensington Market is Toronto's chilly winters – outdoor shopping in icy winds and snow definitely isn't for everyone!

St. Lawrence Market

Subway: UNION
www.stlawrencemarket.com

The St. Lawrence Market is an ideal one-stop shopping destination for essentials from France, Morocco and Quebec. Permanent vendors are located in the South building – here you can find butchers, cheese shops, fishmongers and bakers that will supply most of the staples for your next French, Moroccan or French Canadian meal. On Saturdays, the North building hosts a farmers' market, featuring local goods such as fruits, vegetables, honey, maple syrup, fruit tarts and cheese. The selection is always fresh and delicious, so it's no wonder regulars make the St. Lawrence Market a weekly pilgrimage!

Alex Farm Products

Various locations across the Greater Toronto Area.

☎ 1 877 488-7778 (main number)

www.alexcheese.com

Just a few of the things found on the shelves at Alex Farm Products – walnut, hazelnut, almond and white and black truffle oils, *Maille* vinegars, jarred *béarnaise* and hollandaise sauces from France's *Delouis Fils* and both natural and *herbes de Provence fleur de sel*, sold at very reasonable prices.

All the Best Fine Foods

1099 Yonge Street ☎ 416 928-3330

Monday–Wednesday 8:30–6:30, Thursday–Friday 8:30–7, Saturday 8:30–6, Sunday 10–5

Subway: **SUMMERHILL**

www.allthebestfinefoods.com

This Rosedale shop carries an abundance of gourmet French specialties, including chestnut purée, whole jarred chestnuts, hazelnut and olive oils, nut oil from Périgord, dried chanterelle mushrooms, *cornichons,* Niçoise olives, olives from Nyons, canned *flageolets, Meaux Pommery* mustard, *fleur de sel* from Guérande, *Vilux* and *A l'Olivier* vinegars, chestnut honey and lavender honey from Provence.

FROZEN FRENCH GOODS Finally, an alternative to the commercial frozen pastry found in grocery stores! All the Best Fine Foods carries exceptional *pâte feuilletée* (flaky pastry) from Rahier.

Arz Bakery

1909 Lawrence Avenue East (between Warden Avenue and Pharmacy Avenue)
☎ 416 755-5084

Monday–Saturday 8–9, Sunday 8–7:30, statutory holidays 8–5 (Arz Bakery is always open)

Subway: **LAWRENCE** + bus

www.arzbakery.com

The Lebanese and Middle Eastern goods at Arz Bakery make it a great place to discover a more exotic side to French culture. France's history with Lebanon in the nineteenth and twentieth centuries resulted in many aspects of French culture being integrated into Lebanese culture – including food. Regulars insist the pita bread at Arz Bakery is the best in the city. You'll also find many varieties of bulgur wheat and couscous, as well as *harissa* paste to flavour your Lebanese or Moroccan dishes and a diverse assortment of nuts and seeds. There's a generous olive counter, including Tunisian olives sold in packages, and a large selection of olive oils from Lebanon, Italy, Spain and Greece. The rose and orange blossom waters sold at Arz Bakery are rare finds in Toronto (orange flower water is one of the ingredients needed to make *madeleines).*

Bonjour Brioche

812 Queen Street East (East of Broadview)
☎ 416 406-1250

Closed Monday, Tuesday–Friday 8–5, Saturday 8–4, Sunday 8–3

Subway: **QUEEN** + streetcar

Bonjour Brioche's signature vinaigrettes and homemade jams – the very same ones that accompany their salads and baguettes – are now available to take home!

Brandt Meat Packers Supermarket

1878 Mattawa Avenue, Mississauga (Dundas Street & Dixie Road)
☎ 905 279-4460

Closed Sunday–Tuesday; Wednesday 8–6, Thursday–Friday 8–7, Saturday 7–2

Diverse treasures from around the world await you at Brandt Meat Packers Supermarket. Look no further for hard-to-find whole and puréed chestnuts, several varieties of French mustard, jarred sauerkraut, dried and canned mushrooms, whole jarred cherries in syrup, *pain d'épices* (ginger bread) and – *quelle surprise!* – canned bouillabaise (traditional French fish soup). Flavoured syrups are another specialty of Brandt Meat Packers Supermarket. Choose from the well-known French brand, *William*, or brands from Eastern Europe, available in manyy flavours.

Clafouti

915 Queen Street West (East of Strachan Avenue, across from Trinity Bellwoods Park) ☎ 416 603-1935

Closed Monday; Tuesday–Saturday 8–6, Sunday 9–5

Subway: OSGOODE + streetcar

Clafouti carries a few essential French specialties, including whole jarred and canned chestnuts, canned *flageolets*, jarred white asparagus, jams from France and Belgium, *William* syrups and *fleur de sel*. You'll also find many French specialties prepared by Pastry Chef Boris Dosne such as savoury ham, cheese or asparagus croissants, sandwiches served on baguettes or croissants, quiches and a traditional favourite, *croque monsieur* (open-face

Did you know?

Many gourmands refer to *fleur de sel* crystals as "little specks of white gold". Others call it "diamonds of the sea" or "the caviar of all salts". But whatever the nickname, one thing's for certain – a little *fleur de sel* satisfies the palate and brings out the flavour in almost every food.

A gift from nature, *fleur de sel* is the result of a perfect combination of ocean, sun and wind, and has a unique, incomparable taste. Unprocessed and unrefined, these delicate granules of creamy-white sea salt are traditionally hand-harvested by skimming the surface of the water of the salt marshes of Guérande, France (off the Northwest coast).

Fleur de sel is ideal with *crudités*, salads, grilled meats and vegetables. It can be enjoyed *au naturel* or combined with other spices to create a heavenly and customized blend of tastes and flavours – sprinkle a little on *foie gras* or add it to pure vanilla extract to flavour homemade *pâtisseries* and see what a big difference just a little makes. Try it once and adopt it for life!

toasted sandwich made with egg, cheese and ham). Clafouti also sells one of Toronto's best-kept (and most delicious) secrets – authentic Belgium waffles! You can only find them on the weekends and like everything else at Clafouti, they tend to disappear quickly.

Cheese Boutique

45 Ripley Avenue (South of South Kingsway & The Queensway)
☎ 416 762-6292

Monday–Friday 8–9, Saturday 8–8, Sunday 10–6

Subway: RUNNYMEDE + bus

www.cheeseboutique.com

There's more to Cheese Boutique than just cheese! *William* syrups, canned flageolets, multiple brands of canned fish and French mustard, AOC oils from Provence, *Herbes de Provence,* truffles, nut and hazelnut oils, *fleur de sel* from Guérande, fresh chanterelle mushrooms, numerous flavours of vinegar from *Vilux* and vinegar and vinaigrettes from *Maille* are just some of the French fare offered here. Prices may be slightly higher than elsewhere in the city, but the quality and selection more than compensates.

Chris' Cheesemongers

93 Front Street East (St. Lawrence Market)
☎ 416 368-5273

Closed Sunday–Monday; Tuesday–Thursday 8–6, Friday 8–7, Saturday 5–5

Subway: UNION

Chris' Cheesemongers sells nut oils from the French *huilerie Lapalisse,* jarred truffles, French mustard, almond oil and imported champagne vinegar.

Daniel et Daniel – Food Shop

248 Carlton Street (corner of Parliament Street) ☎ 416 968-9275

Closed Sunday; Monday–Saturday 7:30–6

Subway: CASTLE FRANK + bus;
COLLEGE + streetcar

www.danieletdaniel.ca

The wide selection of gourmet and imported French food items found at Daniel et Daniel include rose and violet petal confit, packaged chestnuts, several varieties of vinegar and a large assortment of flavoured *William* syrups.

Dinah's Cupboard

50 Cumberland Street ☎ 416 921-8112

Monday–Friday 9–7, Saturday 9–6; closed Sunday (open Sundays in December)

Subway: YONGE or BAY

Dinah stocks her Cupboard with these specialty items from France – *Vilux* vinegars, *Meaux Pommery* mustards, *fleur de sel* from Guérande, jarred truffles and truffle oil.

Domino Foods

93 Front Street East (far end of the basement level of St. Lawrence Market) ☎ 416 364-2652

Closed Sunday–Monday; Tuesday–Thursday 8–6, Friday 8–7, Saturday 5–5

Subway: UNION

Domino Foods is one of the city's hidden gems. This tiny, out-of-the-way shop is a treasure trove of rare and exclusive French gourmet products. For starters, you'll find what is likely the most complete selection of *St Dalfour* jams in Toronto. Domino Foods also stocks wine vinegar from the Champagne region, canned chestnut purée, vanilla oil from Tahiti, *fleur de sel* and many flavours of *William* syrups. Rarer finds include cognac and violet mustards, walnut vinegar and about 16 kinds of dried mushrooms, such as chanterelles, morels, porcini, portobello and white truffles.

Great Cooks

176 Yonge Street (The Bay Queen Street, concourse level) ☎ 416 861-4727

Monday–Friday 10–6, Saturday 10–5, Sunday closed

Subway: QUEEN

www.greatcooks.ca

Forfeit boring and tasteless food courts for the delicious and satisfying fare at Great Cooks. Although Great Cooks is a cooking school, the chefs also prepare a variety of diverse dishes from around the world. French specialties prepared by Chef Jean-Pierre Challet of Bouchon restaurant include goat cheese tart and poached salmon. Quality and freshness are evident with every bite, and prices are quite reasonable – although if you don't get there before 2 p.m, you may be out of luck.

Harvest Wagon

- 1133 Yonge Street ☎ 416 923-7542
  Monday–Wednesday 8–6:30, Thursday and Friday 8–7, Saturday and Sunday 8–6

Subway: SUMMERHILL

- 546 Eglinton Avenue West
  ☎ 416 487-0388

Monday–Friday 8–7, Saturday and Sunday 8–6

Subway: EGLINTON + bus

Harvest Wagon is one of the few places in Toronto that sells chanterelle and morel mushrooms. They also have a nice selection of fresh herbs, canned *flageolets* and *fleur de sel.*

Holt Renfrew – Epicure Shop

50 Bloor Street West (corner of Bay Street) ☎ 416 922-2333

Monday–Wednesday 10–6, Thursday–Friday 10–8, Saturday 10–6, Sunday 12–6

Subway: YONGE or BAY

This luxury Canadian retailer has a French soul, judging by the many Franco-European gourmet goods it carries from brands like *Fauchon, Neuhaus* and *Mariage Frères.* When it comes to luxury food items, *Fauchon* raises the standards. Holt Renfrew offers a tempting array of their prod-

Where to find fleur de sel

1. Alex Farm
2. All the Best Fine Foods
3. Cheese Boutique
4. Clafouti
5. Dinah's Cupboard
6. Domino Foods
7. Harvest Wagon
8. Holt Renfrew
9. Pusateri's
10. Scheffler's Delicatessen & Cheese
11. Whole Foods

ucts, like candied chestnuts, vinegars, *fleur de sel,* mustards, cookies and teas, not to mention a selection of jams in some of the most exotic and original flavours – apricot with jasmine flowers, Calvados apple, Cavaillon melon, clementine, mango and peach, Morello cherry, and pear and vanilla bean. You'll also find other decadent items such as a spreadable hazelnut paste from *Neuhaus* and *Mariage Frères* teas. For tea conoisseurs, Holt Renfrew carries a recipe book from the famous French house of tea *Éloge de la cuisine au thé.*

K.I.S. Global Flavors

☎ 905 477-0024

www.kisglobalflavors.com

K.I.S. Global Flavors' web site is a visual avalanche of upscale food items from France, Switzerland and Italy. Among the French products you'll find are olive-shaped chocolates, *marrons glacés* (sugar-coated chestnuts), candied fruits, candied oranges, chocolate-covered lemons, *calissons* (almond treats) from Aix en Provence, nougat, truffles, flower-based jellies and Provence flower honey. K.I.S. Global Flavors' also carries many attractive gift baskets – the perfect solution for elegant gift-giving. Just a few clicks and you're all set!

Le Gourmand

152 Spadina Avenue (South of Queen Street) ☎ 416 504-4494

Monday-Friday 7–9, Saturday 9–6, Sunday 9–4

Subway: **OSGOODE** + streetcar; **SPADINA** + streetcar

Le Gourmand lives up to its name by stocking only the finest French foods, such as white truffle olive oil, grapeseed oil from *Vilux, Meaux Pommery* mustard, walnut oil and vinegar from the house of *Clovis.*

Loblaws

Various locations across the Greater Toronto Area

This national chain imports many French specialty items like *Maille, Meaux Pommery Vilux* mustards, *Vilux* vinegars (including cognac and champagne flavours) and an impressive assortment of *St Dalfour* jams in flavours that are not easily found elsewhere – black raspberry, fig Royal, mirabelle, orange and ginger and pineapple and mango.

FROZEN FRENCH GOODS True, nothing compares to the real thing, but Loblaws sells a surprisingly good assortment of French-inspired hors d'œuvres, desserts, breakfast and dinner items in their *President's Choice*® line, including butter croissants, mini chocolate éclairs, profiteroles, *cassoulet* (casserole of white and several kinds of meat and poultry) and quiche Lorraine.

Max Market

2299 Bloor Street West (West of Runnymede Road) ☎ 416 766-6362

Monday–Wednesday 9–7, Thursday 9–7:30, Friday 9–8, Saturday 9–7, Sunday 9–6

Subway: **RUNNYMEDE**

Max Market has a huge counter of ready-to-serve meals. Particularly of note are the dozen or so varieties of rich stuffed crêpes – choose from chicken and pesto, ham and cheese, mushroom and salmon and seafood. Max Market also sells a dozen flavours of *Vilux* vinegar.

Mercatto

- 15 Toronto Street (East of Yonge, one street North of King Street) ☎ 416 366-4567

  Monday–Friday 7–6, closed Saturday–Sunday

  Subway: KING

- 330 Bay Street (North of Adelaide Street) ☎ 416 306-0467

  Monday–Friday 7:30–8, closed Saturday–Sunday

  Subway: KING

This Italian merchant has a small but satisfying assortment of French products, such as walnut and olive oils from Provence and *Herbes de Provence.*

Olympic Cheese Mart

- 93 Front Street East (St. Lawrence Market) ☎ 416 363-7602

  Closed Sunday–Monday; Tuesday–Thursday 8–6, Friday 8–7, Saturday 5–5

  Subway: UNION

- 7780 Woodbine Avenue, Markham (near 14th Avenue) ☎ 905 944-8676

  Monday–Wednesday 10–6, Thursday–Friday 10–7, Saturday 9:30–6, closed Sunday

Truffles, specialty olive oils, vinegars and vinaigrettes from *Maille* are just some of the French goods found at Olympic Cheese Mart. You'll also find a rarity in Toronto – *Kressi* Swiss vinegar, the ideal seasoning for hollandaise sauce. Rarer still – Olympic Cheese Mart has a *girolle* machine (machine that shaves cheese from big wheels)! If you've looking for the perfect item to bring to a pot luck, shower or party, consider a French cheese tray from Olympic Cheese Mart. Ask the staff about this easy, elegant and tasty solution.

Pain Perdu

736 St Clair Avenue West (West of Christie Street) ☎ 416 656-7246

Closed Monday, Tuesday–Friday 7–7:30, Saturday 7–5, Sunday 8–4

Subway: ST CLAIR WEST + streecar

When quiches look, smell and taste as good as the ones at Pain Perdu, why bother going anywhere else? Or, if you're after something savoury, try the onion tart. Hungry regulars line up for the terrific quiche and salad or tart and salad specials. Other popular French specialties include homemade mayonnaise, vinaigrettes and jams, and an organic maple syrup from Lake Erie (the same syrup served with the *pain perdu).*

Patachou

1095 Yonge Street ☎ 416 927-1105

Monday–Friday 8:30–7, Saturday 8:30–6, closed Sunday

Subway: SUMMERHILL

In addition to their signature vinaigrettes and homemade jams, Patachou sells flavoured olive oils from France. Choose from the following fragrant blends – chili, basil, *Herbes de Provence* and lemon. Recently, Patachou introduced their new take-out menu and weekend take-out menu. The take-out menu includes *confit de canard* (duck

Where to find flageolets

1. All the Best Fine Foods (canned)
2. Casa Açareana (dried)
3. Cheese Boutique (canned)
4. Clafouti (canned)
5. Harvest Wagon (canned)
6. Scheffler's Delicatessen & Cheese (canned)

confit served with braised red cabbage and polenta), *bœuf bourguignonne* (French beef stew) *agneau navarin* (lamb stew with zucchini, white turnips, carrots, fresh rosemary and thyme), *portobello farcis* (portobello mushrooms stuffed with ratatouille and goat cheese), Israeli couscous (couscous with roasted peppers, black olives, capers and almonds) and *pissaladière* (a French pizza-like dish made with caramelized onions, tomatoes and black olives). The weekend take-out menu offers many delicious dishes that are ideal for a dinner *à deux* enjoyed at home.

PÂTISSERIE D'OR

301 Robinson Street, Oakville (South of Lakeshore Road) ☎ 905 815-8999

Closed Monday–Tuesday; Wednesday–Friday 8–5:30, Saturday 8–6, Sunday 8–4

Chef Jean-Luc Soulabaille makes one of the best quiches in the Greater Toronto Area – delicate, silky and lighter than air.

FROZEN FRENCH GOODS Ingeniously, Chef Soulabaille has created frozen, bake-and-serve versions of many of his most popular items, so you can enjoy them whenever you want! Simply slip these French goodies in your oven and *voilà!* Before you know it, you'll be able to enjoy hot, fresh and delicious pastries and more in the comfort of your home. Choose from baguettes, buns, chocolate croissants, croissants, cookie dough, raisin danishes, *vol-au-vent* (pastry shells) and the house specialty – quiche. Another tempting frozen treat at Pâtisserie d'Or is the extraordinary homemade ice cream, made with fresh ingredients and no preservatives. Flavours are classic and bursting with taste – blackcurrant, caramel, chocolate, coffee, green apple, lemon, pistachio, raspberry, strawberry and, of course, vanilla.

PÂTISSERIE SAINT HONORÉ

2945 Bloor Street West (corner of Grenview Boulevard, East of Royal York Road) Note: no telephone is available

Closed Monday Tuesday–Thursday 8–7, Friday 8–9, Saturday 8–7, closed Sunday

Subway: ROYAL YORK

Pâtisserie Saint Honoré's house specialties shoud not be missed – quiche, French onion soup, pâté sandwiches and a mouth-watering *pissaladière*.

PETIT GÂTEAU

2365-B Lakeshore Road, Oakville (West of Bronte Road) ☎ 905 847-1888

Cosed Sunday–Monday; Tuesday–Saturday 9–6

Tourtière is a traditional Quebecois meat pie that tastes even more delicious when someone else has prepared it! Luckily, *tourtières* are a specialty of Petit

Gâteau. In addition to the traditional beef and pork variety, Petit Gâteau also offers salmon and chicken *tourtières*. Be sure to order in advance to avoid disappointment!

Pusateri's Fine Foods

- 1539 Avenue Road (North of Lawrence Avenue) ☎ 416 785-9100

  Monday–Wednesday 8–8,
  Thursday–Friday 8–9,
  Saturday–Sunday 8–7

  Subway: LAWRENCE + bus
- 57 Yorkville Avenue (corner of Bay Street) ☎ 416 785-9100

  Monday–Wednesday 10–8,
  Thursday–Friday 10–9, Saturday 8–8,
  Sunday 10–7

  Subway: BAY

  www.pusateris.com

Pusateri's upscale products (with prices to match) may not be suitable for everyday meals, but if you are celebrating a special occasion and willing to splurge a little, this is a shop you simply must visit. Among the French favourites you'll find – sugar-coated and packaged chestnuts, jarred truffles, *fleur de sel,* olive, walnut and almond oils and fresh chanterelle mushrooms (elusive at the best of times!). Pusateri's tempting ready-to-serve dishes are the perfect solution for harried (and hungry) Francophiles. French-inspired selections include grilled Cornish hen, *gratin dauphinois* (layered baked potato dish) made with real butter and *salade Niçoise.*

FROZEN FRENCH GOODS Pusateri's Fine Foods carries frozen porcini mushrooms.

Qualifirst Foods

☎ 416 244-1177
www.qualifirst.com

Since 1957, Qualifirst has been importing fine foods from around the world to discerning epicureans who value quality above price. Visit their web site for their full range of culinary creations, including a diverse and impressive collection of gourmet French goods sure to delight even the most discriminating Francophile – Qualifirst carries everything from mustards to black winter truffles.

Rahier

1717 Bayview Avenue (South of Eglinton Avenue) ☎ 416 482-0917

Closed Monday–Tuesday,
Wednesday–Friday 8–5, Saturday 8–4,
Sunday 8–3

Subway: EGLINTON + bus

On weekends, Rahier bakes several flavours of their delicious quiche, such as goat cheese and red pepper, broccoli and cheddar, smoked salmon and asparagus, eggplant and leek and quiche Lorraine (with ham).

FROZEN FRENCH GOODS Frozen goods that can be found at Rahier include homemade sherbets and ice creams, pastry shells, raspberry coulis, chocolate sauce, a few cakes and *pâte feuilletée.*

Scheffler's Delicatessen & Cheese

93 Front Street East (St. Lawrence Market)
☎ 416 364-2806

Closed Sunday–Monday;
Tuesday–Thursday 8–6, Friday 8–7,
Saturday 5–5

Spices

Variety is the spice of life, and variety in spices is the key to French cuisine. Most stores in the city cover the basic garden variety of herbs and spices, but when you're in need of something specific, nothing but an expert will do. Here are few locations that offer a more than impressive selection:

Casa Açareana

Kensington Market ☎ 416 593-9717

Casa Açareana boasts a plentiful range of spices sold in bulk. It's a perfect place to visit if you are introducing a new spice to your collection or trying out a recipe for the first time. You'll find everything you need for most of your French-inspired dishes such as honeysuckle, marjoram, sage, tarragon and thyme, as well as Provence herb mix and saffron at very reasonable prices. Casa Açareana is also a great place to find dried juniper berries – elusive until now! You'll also find yellow and black mustard grains, dried lavender, dried *flageolets* (small, pale green kidney-shaped beans), four types of lentils and pure vanilla bean extract and vanilla beans imported from Madagascar.

Domino Foods

St. Lawrence Market ☎ 416 366-2178

Domino sells many herbs essential for French cuisine in bulk including anise, chives, honeysuckle, laurel leaves, marjoram, Provence herb mix, rosemary, saffron, sage, tarragon, thyme and vanilla beans.

House of Spices

Kensington Market ☎ 416 593-9724

This little shop imports spices from all corners of the globe – laurel leaves, Provence herb mix, saffron, tarragon, thyme and yellow and black mustard grains are just a few of the staples you'll find for French dishes. You'll also find vanilla beans from Madagascar and liquorice roots. If you're looking for spices for North African dishes, House of Spices is the perfect place to find *harissa, zaatar* and *razahanut.*

Perola's

Kensington Market ☎ 416 593-9728

Although Hispanic and Brazilian specialties are the order of the house, French cuisine enthusiasts will be impressed to learn Perola's also dries their own bouquets of herbs, including basil, rosemary, sage and savoury.

Strictly Bulk

Various locations across the Greater Toronto Area ☎ 416 766-3319

A veritable Mecca for bulk spices! Variety and selection abound, and the prices are extremely affordable – you can even find notoriously expensive saffron and pure vanilla extract at a reasonable cost.

Subway: UNION

Scheffler's carries fleur de sel, saffron, canned *flageolets,* cream of chestnut dessert spread, jarred morel mushrooms, truffles, Maille vinegars, bottled vinaigrettes and Moroccan and French *cornichons* (unsweeted pickles that are much smaller in size than their North American equivalents).

SÉRÉNITÉ

87 Yorkville Avenue (corner of Bellair Street) ☎ 416 924-6398

Monday–Wednesday 10–6, Thursday–Friday 10–8, Saturday 10–6, Sunday 12–6

Subway: BAY

This chic little Yorkville boutique imports several high-end French brands including *Mariage Frères, Prince Jardinier, Clément Bruno* and *Alain Ducasse.* French tea connoisseurs insist *Mariage Frères* is the epitome of what tea should be – perfect as is, with no need to add sugar, milk or even lemon. Good thing, then, that Sérénité is the biggest importer of *Mariage Frères* teas in North America. *Mariage Frères* also produces many other products and food items found at Sérénité, including tablewear and accessories for tea time, jams, pure vanilla beans, crystallized sugar and tea bags for ice tea. The story of the *Prince Jardinier* (Prince of Gardens) brand almost sounds like something out of a fairy tale – it was founded by a real prince (Prince Louis Albert de Broglie) who happens to have a passion for gardening and the fruits of his labour. Among *Prince Jardinier*'s wares are a most unusual selection of jams. The most well-known flavours are the ones made with tomatoes – green tomato and lemon, green tomato and nuts, red tomato and orange confit and red tomato and ginger. If your tastes are more traditional, indulge in the rhubarb and wild strawberry preserve, the bitter orange with cinnamon preserve or the *Louise Bonne d'Avranche* pear preserve. *Clément Bruno* carries an assortment of exotic jarred delicacies such as truffle oil, black olive tapenade with truffles, spreadable cream of porcini mushrooms, tomato sauce with truffles, confit of tomato with summer truffles and a fondue of white truffles. You'll also find a few cookbooks and kitchen utensils. Sérénité also carries a line of products and cookbooks from famed French chef Alain Ducasse. If you are looking for fresh truffles, Sérénité can also import them for you by special order.

VILLAGE BUTCHER

2914 Lakeshore Boulevard West (near Islington Avenue) ☎ 416 503-9555

Sunday–Monday closed, Tuesday–Friday 7:30–6:30, Saturday 7:30–5

Subway: ISLINGTON + bus

During the Christmas season, Village Butcher sells traditional French Canadian *tourtières.* But be warned – this is not a last-minute purchase. You'll have to put your order in ahead of time as they go like hot cakes!

Whole Foods Market

87 Avenue Road (North of Bloor Street)
☎ 416 944-0500

Monday–Friday 9–10, Saturday 9–9, Sunday 9–8

Subway: BAY or MUSEUM

www.wholefoodsmarket.com

Whole Foods Market has a large selection of French specialty items in stock. Add the finishing touches to your French cuisine with olives from Nyons, *Meaux de Pommery* mustard, *Delouis Fils* hollandaise sauce, *béarnaise* sauce, garlic and Caesar mayonnaises, a small selection of jarred truffles and dried mushrooms (morel, trumpets and porcini). This is one of the few places in Toronto where you'll find AOC olive oils from Provence. You'll also find AOC olive oils that have won many gold and silver awards of excellence, and *fleur de sel* in two flavours – natural and *herbes de Provence.*

Zane Pâtisserie & Boulangerie

1852 Queen Street East (West of Woodbine Avenue) ☎ 416 690-2813

Monday closed, Tuesday–Sunday 7:30–5:30

Subway: QUEEN + streetcar

Every weekend, owner and Pastry Chef Mo Zane prepares half-a-dozen scrumptious quiches, including ham and bacon, vegetarian and smoked salmon.

Did you know?

In April 2004, the prestigious *Food & Wine* magazine declared the 200+ year old St. Lawrence Market one of the world's best markets, along with 24 others from cities such as Paris, Milan and Tokyo.

bistros & fine dining

The chefs and restauranteurs who practice the art of French cuisine do so out of love. You can taste it in the food they make and feel it in the way they greet and serve you. Perhaps that is why, for Francophiles, few things compare to the joy of indulging in a good French meal. Many Torontonians don't realize how fortunate we are to have such a diversity of French dining establishments on our doorstep; the number of bistros, casual eateries and upscale restaurants in the city is very impressive indeed. Hopefully the following list will not only reacquaint you with some old favourites, but create some new ones, too.

Bon appétit!

Savouring Toronto's French wine!

The story of Toronto's French wine begins with Mr. Laurent Quetton St. George (1771–1821). This French Royalist exile fought against the Republicans during the French Revolution, and fled to England at the end of the eighteenth century. He added the name 'St. George' to his French name because he arrived in his new country on April 23 – St. George's Day.

In those days, it was common practice for the British government to offer land grants to French exiles who were willing to move to Upper Canada and develop the North American lands of the British Crown. Quetton St. George landed in Quebec City in 1798 and made his way to Toronto the following year.

Laurent Quetton St. George started his career as a businessman in the fur trade with Native Canadian tribes. His trading operation allowed him to do business with merchants in New York and Montreal. After moving to York from his trading post in Orillia, Quetton St. George opened his first store, followed by others in Queenston, Fort Erie, Dundas and other areas, selling everything from furs to knickknacks. Although he sold local goods, he also imported many goods from Europe and was one of the first merchants to deal directly with Europe without going through Montreal.

Even though Quetton St. George was extremely successful, he was never fully accepted by the Anglophone community of York. However, this did not prevent him from developing a reputation as a force to be reckoned with in the business and trading world. His colossal success led to the building of his mansion in 1809, on the corner of King and Frederick Streets in today's downtown Toronto. His home is recorded in the city archives as the first brick home in York (the bricks were imported from the United States).

Quetton St. George was a close friend of Dr. William Warren Baldwin, who named one of his sons after him. Dr. Baldwin also gave the name 'St. George Street' to one of the streets that surrounded his massive property on Upper Spadina Street in 1836. Few are aware of the Francophone roots of one of Toronto's best-known streets, which cuts through the University of Toronto campus.

After the return of King Louis XVIII to the throne in 1815, Quetton St. George returned to France and was knighted as a reward his for his undying loyalty. He settled back in his homeland, buying a piece of land in Montpellier known as 'Le Château de l'Engarran', purchased with the fortune accumulated through his lucrative business dealings in Toronto.

Le Château de l'Engarran is located on slopes on the terroir of Saint Georges d'Orques, the oldest Coteaux du Languedoc appellation, and began producing wines in 1632 (almost 200 years before Quetton St George purchased the estate). After Quetton St. George passed away at age 50, his son Henry returned to Toronto in 1847 to claim his inheritance and start importing the château's wine.

Almost 160 years later, the winery purchased by Quetton St George still produces wine and it is still imported to Canada. A smooth blend of history and wine, the château has been classified as an historic monument and draws crowds of visitors on *journées du patrimoine* (Inheritance Days, celebrated in France).

Today, the wine produced by Le Château de l'Engarran is matriarchal in nature – in a profession dominated largely by men, sisters Constance Rerolle and Diane Losfelt are breaking ground by managing this old winery. They produce a little over 200,000 bottles of wine every year, including the unofficial French wine of Toronto, named in memory of Quetton St. George – *Le Château de l'Engarran, Coteaux du Languedoc,* and *Cuvée Quetton Saint Georges.* After all, this winery's continued existence is largely thanks to Quetton St. George's fortune amassed in Toronto.

The *Cuvée Quetton Saint-Georges* is an award-winning AOC red wine that has been acclaimed by oeneophiles from France, Quebec, Germany and the United States. It received the gold medal at the 2001 Concours Général Agricole in France. Critics rave about the *Cuvée Quetton Saint-Georges:*

"This is a marvelous little treasure."
– Jérôme-Henri Dejardin (Québec)

"Part of the top 50 picks."
– *Terre de Vins* (France)

"This is a domain worth discovering."
– *Sud Vin* (France)

Southern Impact magazine described the 1998 vintage: **GRAPE VARIETIES:** 75 per cent Syrah, 25 per cent Grenache. **VINIFICATION:** Selected parcels. Separate vinification of each variety. Three-week fermentation. Delestage and manual crushing. Fifty per cent oak-aged. **TASTING NOTES:** Vanilla and liquorice notes, melted with rich blackberry scents, well-structured palate with matter, concentrated with ripe notes and an attractive final spicy structure. Lengthy with firm but velvet tannins.

In Canada, Cuvée Quetton Saint-Georges is available through the Société des alcools du Québec (SAQ)/Quebec liquor board. Regrettably, the unofficial French wine of Toronto is not yet available through the LCBO, but there is hope that one day soon, you may be able to sip a glass of this fine red from Château de l'Engarran. *Santé!*

– *This story is courtesy of Mr. Pierre Fortier of La Société d'histoire de Toronto.*

AGORA

317 Dundas Street West (inside the Art Gallery of Ontario) ☎ 416 979-6612

Closed Monday–Tuesday; Wednesday–Sunday for lunch only

Subway: ST PATRICK

From the creative menu to the picturesque location, AGORA is undoubtedly one of the best spots in Toronto for lunch. Enjoy a meal that will tantalize your senses amid a breathtaking view of the Art Gallery of Ontario's Tanenbaum Sculpture Atrium.

The AGO's ingenuity, style and cultural richness is reflected harmoniously in AGORA. One of the restaurant's key strengths is its changing menu – Chef Anne Yarymowich creates menus that complement the AGO's major exhibitions. For example, during the Sculptures of Degas exhibit, Chef Yarymowich conceived a "Café Parisian" menu to extend the experience of French food and culture. French classics on the menu included oysters, Armagnac pâté, duck confit, *steak frites, tarte tatin* served with a honey and lavender ice cream, lemon tart served on a blackcurrant coulis and blackberries macerated in brandy. – *bilingual menu*

The best wine lists

1. Auberge du Pommier
2. Bistro 1603
3. Bistro 990
4. Bouchon
5. Brasserie Aix
6. Café Brussels
7. Café Margaux
8. Célestin
9. L'Escargot Bistro
10. La Brasserie.ca
11. La Petite France
12. Le Paradis
13. Le Trou Normand
14. Provence
15. Sélect Bistro

ARLEQUIN

134 Avenue Road (corner of Davenport Road) ☎ 416 964-8686

Monday–Saturday for lunch and dinner; closed Sunday

Subway: MUSEUM

Arlequin may have new management, new décor and a new chef, but the cosy and welcoming atmosphere of this neighbourhood bistro has not changed. Chef (and owner) Scott Saunderson's menu is pure Parisian bistro – bouillabaisse (traditional fish soup), duck confit, *gratin dauphinois* (layered baked potato dish), *cassoulet* and classic *steak frites* served with homemade aioli are just some of the choices you'll discover here. The *prix fixe* menu is a steal, and a great way to discover dishes from different regions of France. For dessert, a velvety crème brûlée, exquisite chocolate cake and tangy lemon tart are worth a look. Wines from many different regions of France are well-represented, notably Burgundy and Alsace.

AVANT-GOÛT

8 Birch Avenue (corner of Yonge Street, on a side street across from the Summerhill LCBO) ☎ 416 975-9150

Tuesday–Friday for lunch, Monday–Saturday for dinner;

closed Sunday
Subway: SUMMERHILL

The combination of French and Moroccan flavours, a retro, kitschy décor and warm, friendly service has made this small Rosedale bistro a hit with locals and out-of-towners alike since it opened in the summer of 2002. Chef and owner Kamal Hani's Moroccan heritage can be tasted in his cuisine. Dishes are savoury and spiced to perfection. Avant-Goût's lunch specialties include soup of the day, duck confit salad served on French lentils and mixed greens, grilled chicken baguette sandwich, Moroccan beef stew, and grilled Moroccan *kofta* (lamb or beef sausages) served with mixed greens and saffron rice in a roasted shallot and garlic jus. For dinner, Chef Hani pulls out all the stops with choices such as smoked duck, calf's liver, Moroccan stew served on a bed of basmati rice and grilled Black Angus steak in a mustard-seed sauce. The dessert menu changes regularly, but one staple is an excellent crème brûlée that will leave you wanting more. Avant-Goût's wine list offers a good selection of whites and reds from various regions in France. – *service in French*

Bistro 990

990 Bay Street ☎ 416 921-9990
Monday–Friday for lunch, Monday–Sunday for dinner
Subway: WELLESLEY

Bistro 990 has a well-deserved reputation as one of Toronto's most elegant and exclusive restaurants. Ingredients, preparation and presentation are all of the highest quality, in the best classic French style. This dedication to excellence is reflected in the price, but if you're looking for the perfect place to celebrate a special occasion or seal an important deal, Bistro 990 is it. You may even find yourself rubbing shoulders with one of the many Hollywood celebrities who dine here. House specialties include veal liver, grilled salmon infused with Grand Marnier, fresh tuna steak in an oriental sauce, *steak frites* served with a roquefort sauce, and filet mignon served with stilton and Port. Desserts are divine, and fittingly, Bistro 990 has a very good French wine list. Their cellar counts approximately 150 bottles, of which half are French. Over 30 French wines are served by the glass.

Did you know?

Feedback from the first edition of *The French Side of Toronto* included an oft-heard comment from Franco-Europeans and French Canadians – many were not thoroughly fluent in English, and found it quite challenging to locate restaurants that offered bilingual menus or service in French. In the second edition of the guide, you'll notice two new additions in the listings. Where applicable, restaurants listed in this section have been flagged to indicate special services available for Francophones. Menus in English and French have been identified with the caption ***bilingual menu***, whereas ***service in French*** means either the chef or a staff member can assist a patron in French.

– bilingual menu and service in French

Bistro Matisse

1710 Lakeshore Road West, Mississauga (Clarkson Village, between Port Credit & Oakville) ☎ 905 822-2222

Monday closed; Tuesday–Friday for lunch, Tuesday–Sunday for dinner

Since November 2002, Bistro Matisse's delicious menu and reasonable prices have made this small restaurant a hit. Chef and owner Jean Jacques Lemesle is no stranger to French cuisine. A former co-owner and chef at La Maison Benoît, Chef Lemesle's simple aesthetics and artistic presentation only enhance the flavours and textures of his food. The dinner menu offers such tempting specialties as baked chicken stuffed with proscuitto and emmenthal, calf liver coated with Parisian sauce, Black Angus steak with black peppercorn served in a cognac sauce, roasted duck, bouillabaisse and *merguez* sausages (Moroccan lamb sausages) with couscous. Bistro Matisse's best value is its *prix fixe* menu – enjoy a three-course meal for a little over $20. Chef Lemesle also makes homemade *andouillettes* (thin French style sausages) and *foie gras.* A small but constantly changing repertoire of desserts (including a silky crème brûlée) round out the menu. Bistro Matisse's wine list is balanced, and represents many regions and varietals. You'll find a few well-chosen reds and whites from France, as well as a pleasant surprise – the inclusion of several kinds of French beer! *– bilingual menu and service in French*

French restaurants with a patio

1. Bloor Street Diner
2. Bodega
3. Café Margaux
4. Épicure Café
5. La Brasserie.ca
6. La Maison Benoît
7. La Palette
8. Le Saint Tropez
9. Le Trou Normand
10. Merlot
11. Pourquoi pas
12. Provence

Bloor Street Diner

(La Rotisserie – L'Express)

Various locations across the Greater Toronto Area

www.eatertainment.com

The Bloor Street Diner has a genuine bistro feel, thanks in part to the selection of French classics on the menu – *croque-monsieur, salade niçoise,* French onion soup, numerous kinds of quiche, mussels, *steak frites* and roasted chicken served with dried tomato aïoli – the reasonable *prix fixe* menu, and the restaurant's signature touch – a warm half-baguette.

Boujadi

999 Eglinton Avenue West
☎ 416 440-0258

Closed Monday–Tuesday; Wednesday–Sunday for dinner

Subway: EGLINTON WEST

www.boujadi.com

Marhaba (welcome) to Morocco! Since 1992, Boujadi's chef and owner Charles Obadia has been serving traditional Moroccan dishes, many of which are prepared from recipes passed down by a long line of ancestors. Boujadi serves up three *tajine* dishes, six coucous dishes and half a dozen vegetarian selections. The dessert menu is short, but typically Moroccan. Drinks include the traditional sweet mint tea and a signature lemonade made with rosewater. Boujadi's warm and relaxing ambiance, décor and music is the ideal place to break away from the super-trendy "it" spots and fusion fare found around Bathurst and King. If you stop by on weekends, you may even be lucky enough to watch a performance by authentic belly dancers. Boujadi also offers food to go. – *service in French*

Brasserie Aix

584 College Street (near Palmerston Boulevard) ☎ 416 588-7377

Monday–Saturday for dinner, Sundays for brunch and dinner

Subway: COLLEGE + streetcar

www.brasserieaix.com

Located on the hot College Street strip, Brasserie Aix lives up to its surroundings – young, edgy, modern, full of energy and über-cool (definitely not the ideal spot for a romantic candlelit dinner!). The menu is full of old favourites with new twists – appetizers include poached cod mashed with potato and *sel gris* (grey salt), salmon tartare with smoked salmon and apple, escargot in Vidal garlic butter and sweetbreads with rosemary and bacon. For mains, there's roasted chicken supreme, *coq au vin,* grilled calf's liver, duck confit and *steak frites,* as well as a cheese plate and a cold meat plate. Or, try the *plat du jour* for the chef's latest creation. No matter what you choose, you'll be delighted by the rich flavours and beautiful presentation. Brasserie Aix's wine list is sure to please all palates, but if you're more inclined towards martinis, there's a colourful list of favourites to choose from. – *service in French*

Café Margaux

796 College Street (West of Ossington, on the corner of Roxton Road)
☎ 416 588-7490

Closed Monday; (open Mondays from April to August), Tuesday–Saturday for dinner, open Monday–Friday in the summer for lunch

Subway: QUEEN'S PARK + streetcar

Since October 2003, owner Pascal Barron and Chef Rob Briden have been dazzling the College Street crowd with a winning formula – great ambiance, mellow music, a menu that bursts with flavour from every dish, a remarkable wine list and reasonable prices. No strangers to the restaurant business, Barron's parents are former owners of La Maison Benoît, while Briden is a former chef at two of Toronto's best French eateries, Pastis and Quartier. The menu offers a variety of classic dishes that have been ever so slightly updated, creating a perfect balance of flavours, spices and herbs. Or, choose from the *menu du jour,* which features bold creative tastes such as the *foie gras* ravioli served with braised Belgian endives in an ice wine and quince

Did you know?

A March 2004 survey by *Elle à Table* (a popular French food magazine) revealed the top three favourite dishes in France: 1) *moules à la marinière* (mussels in white wine and garlic), 2) *blanquette de veau* (veal stew) and 3) *pot-au-feu* (boiled beef). Surprisingly – perhaps shockingly! – with all the scrumptious and legendary desserts France has to offer, the locals chose a simple fruit salad as their favourite!

It comes as no surprise, however, that the French still favour their own cuisine at home and when travelling abroad. A staggering 77 per cent picked French cuisine as *tête de peloton* (head and shoulders above the rest). When it comes to international cuisine, the French prefer the North African dish of coucous and a classic Italian favourite – pizza. Luckily for Franco-Torontonians, there is no shortage of fantastic French restaurants that offer their top three picks as well as many other local favourites!

sauce. For dessert, choose from a decadant chocolate marquise, classic crème brûlée, exotic Armagnac profiteroles or, if you can't decide, the *assiette gourmande* (selections vary). If you prefer savoury to sweet, finish your meal with a cheese plate comprised of bleu d'Auvergne, chèvre and brie. Café Margaux's wine list boasts an impressive 125 labels. There are about 75 reds and 50 or so whites, many of which are French. Spoiled for choice patrons can consult the wine encyclopedia found at the bar for suggestions and guidance. *– bilingual menu and service in French*

Café Moroc

49 Front Street East (West of Church Street) ☎ 416 961-0601

Monday–Thursday 11:30–11,
Friday–Saturday 11:30–1 a.m., Sunday 4–10

Subway: UNION

www.thesultanstent.com

Nestled in the downtown core, Café Moroc is an exotic oasis of tastes and aromas. Two large Moroccan lanterns flank the entrance, while inside, the décor is reminiscent of the home of a well-travelled friend – ceramic tiles, mirrors, lanterns, rich coloured woods, ebony-coloured round tables, movie-like posters and bamboo ceiling fans. The menu complements the décor and offers many traditional and not so traditional Moroccan dishes, such as *merguez* sausages on baguette, a Moroc hamburger (lamb burger served with signature *frites*) and *Keskesu Casablanca* (a couscous *tajine* with vegetables, fruits and nuts). Be sure to end your meal with a traditional Moroccan tea. Café Moroc's wine list reveals many interesting signature drinks that complement the menu. *– service in French*

Café Nicole

45 The Esplanade (between Yonge Street and Church Street) ☎ 416 367-8900

Monday–Sunday for lunch and dinner

Subway: UNION

Café Nicole is located inside the

Novotel hotel. Choose from an impressive and well-prepared selection of French specialties, including *steak frites,* rack of lamb with a fresh herb crust, seared duck breast accompanied by *gratin dauphinois* and beef tenderloin with ragout of wild mushrooms in a port wine sauce. Dessert lovers will be torn between a spectacular Grand Marnier cake, crème brûlée and crêpes. For theatregoers, Café Nicole's "theatre menu" is an ideal way to enjoy a delicious meal before the curtain rises. *– bilingual menu and service in French*

Chez Laurent

4965 Yonge Street (north of Sheppard Avenue) ☎ 416 590-0909

Monday–Saturday for dinner; closed Sunday

Subway: **NORTH YORK CENTRE** or **SHEPPARD**

Located in a little house, the unpretentious, welcoming atmosphere makes you feel like you've been invited to a friend's home for a casual meal. Hosts and proprietors the Ferrari family go out of their way to ensure your dining experience is enjoyable. Chez Laurent's menu is part French and part Italian, but steers clear of fusion; instead, each cuisine is celebrated in its own right. Presentation is simple, without theatrics but with lots of taste. On the French side, starters include *moules marinière* (mussels), escargots, French onion soup and *salade niçoise.* For mains, choose from *veau au citron* (veal in lemon sauce), *suprême de poulet* (chicken breast in creamy paprika sauce), *poulet chasseur* (chicken breast in rose sauce) and *poulet basquez* (chicken breast in tomato sauce), as well as three variations of steak. A simple dessert menu includes the twin staples of *crème caramel* and crème brûlée, both sure bets. *– bilingual menu*

Crêpes À Gogo

244 Bloor Street West (Northeast corner of Bedford Road, North of Bloor Street) ☎ 416 922-6765

Closed Monday (open Mondays in the summer); Tuesday–Saturday 10:30–8, Sunday 9:30–5

Subway: **ST GEORGE** (Bedford exit)

Considered by many to be the best *crêperie* in Toronto, Crêpes À Gogo has been creating quite a stir since it opened in May 2003. Regulars swear the crêpes here are as good as their French counterparts, and often stop by daily to get their fix! Crêpes À Gogo makes both sweet and savoury versions. Some of the most popular savoury varieties include *La Campagnarde* (eggs, tomatoes, mozzarella, mushrooms, red onions and parsley) and *La Niçoise* (tuna, cheese, basil and tomatoes). On the sweet side, you'll find Nutella and banana, *La Juliatella* (Nutella and raspberry jam), *La Big Ben* (mozzarella and jam), or, for purists, *La Simple* (raw sugar and cinnamon). Crêpes À Gogo also makes a variety of delicious baguette sandwiches. Although Crêpes À Gogo has a Bloor Street address, the entrance is actually located on Bedford Road – look for a sandwich board with a little man sporting a béret, or listen for the sound of the French melodies coming from the speakerphones. Or, just follow your nose! *– bilingual menu and service in French*

A category of its own!

Café la Gaffe

24 Baldwin Street ☎ (416) 596-2397

Monday–Friday 12–11,
Saturday–Sunday 11–11 (closed between 4–6 on Saturday–Sunday)

Subway: ST PATRICK

Neither a truly French café nor a bistro, Café la Gaffe offers a very eclectic menu with influences from many international cuisines. Particularly of note is the crème brûlée, which is a work of art – literally! Café la Gaffe's version of this traditional dessert is taken from the original 1885 recipe by none other than the master of French impressionism, Claude Monet.

Crêpes Café

246 Queen Street West ☎ 416 260-1611

Monday–Saturday 9–midnight,
Sunday 10–10

Subway: OSGOODE

No visit to the city of lights is complete without sampling the delicious crêpes sold on virtually every street corner. Parisian crêpes are made fresh before your eyes. You wait in mouth-watering anticipation as the heavenly aroma from the special spherical hot plate drifts up towards you, changing your mind at least three times as you contemplate the list of fillings. Perhaps the best part of the ritual is eating your crêpe on the go, savouring every delicious bite while strolling alongside the Eiffel Tower and the banks of the Seine. While the CN Tower and the shores of Lake Ontario may not exude quite the same atmosphere as their Parisian counterparts, Torontonians are now able to enjoy the experience of eating one of France's favourite foods *à emporter* (to go), thanks to Crêpes Café. Sweet and savoury menus offer typical Parisian classics, but there are also many flavours created exclusively for Canadian tastebuds. Egg and cheese, chicken and mushrooms, emmenthal cheese and maple syrup and tuna and mayonnaise are just some of the options on the savoury menu, while sweet crêpes include Nutella and banana, honey and coconut, ice cream and rum, coconut and banana. Crêpes Café has a comfortable seating area, or you can choose to take your crêpe to go, *comme les français* for a truly Parisian experience right here in our city. You can also enjoy one of Crêpes Café's delicious sandwiches. To ensure freshness, Crêpes Café prepares only a certain quantity of sandwiches per day, so when they're gone, they're gone.

Épicure Café

512 Queen Street West (West of Spadina Avenue, on the corner of Portland Street)
☎ 416 504-8942

Monday–Friday for lunch and dinner,
Saturday–Sunday for dinner

Subway: OSGOODE + streetcar

This unpretentious bistro serves a simple menu including French, Italian and Mediterranean dishes, but there's no fusion to be found here – when it's French, it's all French. Most of the menu features classic comfort food, such as rosemary lamb served in red wine jus, bouillabaisse, duck confit, calf liver and fresh tuna Provençal. The Épicure Café has also been known to feature a quintessential Francophile favourite on the menu – *moules* (mussels).

Holt's Café

50 Bloor Street West (corner of Bay Street; second floor) ☎ 416 922-2333

Monday–Wednesday 10–6, Thursday–Friday 10–8, Saturday 10–6, Sunday 12–6

Subway: **BLOOR** or **BAY**

The perfect blend of style and substance, Holt's Café is as much a feast for the eyes as the palate. This newly revamped luxurious café features décor that is very modern, very spacious and very upscale, and could easily be mistaken for the lobby of one of Toronto's new international boutique hotels. But the opulence, aesthetics and good taste extend to the cuisine as well as the atmosphere; indeed, Holt's Café really seduces by conquering your tastebuds. The menu, created by Chef Corbin Tomaszeski, is a local version of what can be found in the finest Parisian bistros. Exquisite avocado and chicken soup and salad topped with fried endive, lentil and fennel are just some of the choices sure to please even the most discriminating gourmand. But the real jewels in the crown at Holt's Café are the dozen or *tartines* (open face sandwiches), including a heavenly prosciutto and St. Marcellin cheese version, served on bread from Paris's Poîlane bakery – a Toronto exclusive. For dessert, the *tarte au citron* (lemon tart), ginger crème brûlée and bread pudding (also made with Poîlane bread) are all outstanding – and don't forget to treat yourself to one of Holt's Café's fabulous cappuccinos to round out your meal. Wine is also available, including a few selections from France. Menus change with the seasons and often highlight certain special events in the city – for instance, Chef Tomaszeski created dishes exclusively for the Toronto International Film Festival. Of course, the service is as exceptional as the food, but one would expect nothing less from Holt Renfrew.

Jacques Bistro du Parc

126-A Cumberland Street
☎ 416 961-1893

Monday–Saturday for lunch and dinner; closed Sunday

Subway: **BAY**

Jacques Bistro du Parc is a small bistro that offers huge value; the type of place where regulars return to frequently because the price is as outstanding as the quality. Owner and chef Jacques Sorin takes great pride in his menu. Dinners are available à la carte or *prix fixe.* Selections include rack of lamb, *entrecôte* with green peppercorns, house *terrine* and rabbit with baby onions served in a white wine sauce. With so many appetizing choices, it's easy to forget to leave room for a sweet treat, but just one look at the mousses, profiteroles and fruit tarts, and you'll remember to pace your efforts. For lighter lunchtime fare, be sure to try Chef Sorin's house speciality – a delicious variety of omelettes. – *bilingual menu and service in French*

L'Escargot Bistro

3185 Yonge Street (North of Lawrence Avenue) ☎ 416 485-8338

Monday–Saturday for dinner; closed Sunday

Subway: LAWRENCE

www.lescargot.ca

From the wine-coloured walls and banquettes covered in wide checked fabric to the old French posters and black and white photography to the quaint piano bar, owner Max Ballin has gone to great lengths to create an authentic French atmosphere at L'Escargot Bistro, even bringing in chanteuse Lauren Ingle to perform several French classics every other Sunday evening. L'Escargot Bistro's authenticity also extends to its menu. Dishes are simply prepared and presented, but full of delightful flavours and fragrances. One could almost dine on the appetizers alone. There is in fact three variations of escargot – garlic butter, tomato with herbs from Provence and phyllo pastry with julienne of vegetables in a cream of garlic sauce. If you can summon enough willpower to refrain from ordering more than one appetizer, there are a number of outstanding mains to choose from, including three fish dishes, chicken in a white wine sauce with mushrooms, onions and bacon, two variations of *steak frites,* pork tenderloin with maple syrup, calf liver, rack of lamb and veal medallions with blue cheese sauce. Dessert selections are limited, but include a few choices seldom seen elsewhere in Toronto, such as a magnificent *gâteau Basque,* and poached pears with English custard. (For traditionalists, there's also a satisfying crème brûlée and an excellent cheese plate.). L'Escargot Bistro's wine cellar boasts over 1,000 bottles, many of which are French. With a selection this extensive, it's easy to find something to suit every palate and price range. – *bilingual menu and service in French*

La Brasserie.ca

162 Cumberland Street (Renaissance Court, near the Four Seasons hotel) ☎ 416 944-1504

Monday–Friday for lunch and dinner, Saturday for dinner; closed Sunday (closed Mondays in winter)

Subway: MUSEUM or BAY

www.labrasserie.ca

Tucked away from the hustle and bustle of Yorkville, La Brasserie.ca is a typical French bistro, offering hearty food and good drinks in a relaxed atmosphere. Inside, the décor echoes France right down to the wiring on the wall, which is reminiscent of the base of the Eiffel Tower. La Brasserie.ca offers live entertainment on Friday and Saturday evenings, when you can dine to the sounds of jazz, R&B and occasionally, a few Francophone artists. Cornish hen, *salade niçoise* with fresh tuna, *cassoulet Toulousain,* duck confit, *bœuf bourguignon,* sweetbreads, stuffed quail and a *foie gras* special are just some of the creations from Chef Philippe Coeurdassier. There's also a *très* French wine and cheese menu (served with a delicious baguette, of course!) and weekly beer samplings, with a special menu to match. – *bilingual menu and service in French*

La Maison Benoît

1921 Avenue Road (North of Brooke Avenue) ☎ 416 782-9934

Monday–Saturday for lunch and dinner, Sunday for dinner

Subway: LAWRENCE + bus

Chef Jean Luc Mole adds his own creative flair to many traditional French dishes, and the results are dazzling – scallops in anise sauce, half-roasted duck with port and orange sauce, port pâté, escargot with Roquefort cheese and a well-prepared *steak frites.* La Maison Benoît also offers a *plat du jour* and a variety of daily specials that complement the regular menu. La Maison Benoît's charming atmosphere has just the right amount of retro chic. Reservations are highly recommended. – *bilingual menu and service in French*

La Palette

256 Augusta Avenue ☎ 416 929-4900

Monday–Sunday for dinner

Subway: SPADINA + streetcar;
QUEEN'S PARK + streetcar

This unpretentious little bistro in Kensington Market offers a selection of classic, well-prepared dishes at reasonable prices. The décor is simple (colourful tablecloths and French posters on the walls) and the service is easy-going, making La Palette a great choice for a casual meal. – *service in French*

La Petite France

3317 Bloor Street West (East of Islington Avenue) ☎ 416 234-8783

Monday–Friday for lunch and dinner, Saturday for dinner; closed Sunday (will open Sundays for large groups)

Subway: ISLINGTON

Chef Gilbert Letort prepares simple classics that are rich with flavour, and to keep things fresh, the seasonally-themed menu is changed every six months. Selections from the winter menu may include *bœuf bourguignon,* veal *blanquette, cassoulet,* Moroccan leg of lamb or port *foie gras,* while the lighter summer menu might offer escargots, *timbales,* smoked trout, duck confit with rum and raisins, rack of lamb with mint, *cuisses de grenouilles* (frog legs) and filet of *sole meunière.* There is also a nightly *prix fixe* menu. Desserts include apple pie, profiteroles, crêpes, *galette bretonne* (a Brittany-style flat cake), *Marjolaine* cake (made with chocolate, almond and hazelnut) and a vanilla crème brûlée that can only be described as a masterpiece. La Petite France's wine list comprises 60 or so bottles, including a generous selection

The best places for frites

1. Arlequin
2. Bloor Street Diner
3. Bouchon
4. Brasserie Aix
5. Café Brussels
6. Café Margaux
7. Café Moroc
8. La Maison Benoît
9. Le Paradis
10. Le Saint Tropez
11. Le Sélect Bistro
12. Marcel's Bistro
13. Matignon
14. Midi Bistro
15. Provence

of French reds, with a different wine region being celebrated each month. In fact, La Petite France regularly hosts numerous food and wine events, including a spectacular *fête de la Bastille* (Bastille Day, July 14) that should not be missed! – *bilingual menu and service in French*

Le Papillon

16 Church Street ☎ 416 363-3773

Closed Monday; Tuesday–Sunday for lunch and dinner

Subway: UNION

Brittany meets Quebec at Le Papillon, where rustic comfort food is served in a charming, warm atmosphere. A large brick fireplace makes for a cozy and relaxing setting for winter dinners. More than a mere specialty, the house trademark is a succulent collection of two dozen varieties of crêpes *bretonnes – superbe! – service in French*

Le Paradis

166 Bedford Road (North of Davenport Road) ☎ 416 921-0995

Tuesday–Friday for lunch and dinner, Saturday–Monday for dinner

Subway: MUSEUM or ST GEORGE

www.leparadis.com

Le Paradis offers a stellar mix of originality, flavour and value (not to mention one of the best *prix fixe* menus in the city) that can't be beat. *Flageolets* (French beans) feature prominently as a side dish on the ever-changing mains menu, which subtly blends flavours from Morocco and France. *Tajines*, lamb, *merguez* sausages and couscous are featured side by side with *blanquette au sauvignon* (mixed fish in sauvignon sauce), *bavette* (marinated beef flank), *entrecôte chasseur* (rib eye steak) and *lapin à la provençale* (rabbit). *Cassoulet* is made from a recipe that was literally imported from France – during a trip there, Le Paradis's owner, David Currie, found the perfect version of this white bean ragout at a restaurant in Castelnaudary, and had the restaurant's chef send a frozen container to Toronto, where it evolved into Le Paradis's house specialty. Although Le Paradis's dessert menu is fairly short, you'll still find it difficult to make a choice. Crème brûlée is eschewed in favour of a splendid *crème caramel.* The restaurant's rich cuisine lends itself to a wine list that is equally robust. Offerings include a variety of full-bodied reds and whites from most regions of France, as well as a number of French beers. – *bilingual menu and service in French*

You heard it here first!

According to Patrice Barron, owner of Café Margaux, *crème caramel* seems to be making a comeback in popularity in Toronto. Although many cultures have their own variations (such as the flans found in the Portuguese and Hispanic communities), nothing quite compares to the delicate refinement of a well-made French *crème caramel.*

Le Petit Gourmet

1064 Yonge Street ☎ 416 966-3811

Monday–Friday 7:30–7, Saturday 7:30–6;

closed Sunday

Subway: ROSEDALE

Le Petit Gourmet is all about comfort food. This Rosedale diner is a great spot to eat simple yet hearty French fare such as quiches, roasted chicken, *bœuf bourguignon* (beef ragout), *coq au vin* (chicken in red wine) and chicken pie. Typical *plats du jour* (daily specials) include duck with apples, roast lamb and pork roast. Best of all, Le Petit Gourmet offers a catering service so you can enjoy their homestyle dishes at any time. – *service in French*

Le Saint Tropez

315 King Street West (corner of John Street) ☎ 416 591-3600

Monday–Sunday for lunch and dinner

Subway: ST ANDREW

www.lesainttropez.com

Le Saint Tropez's casual, Mediterranean-style ambiance is a favourite with many French Torontonians, who traditionally gather here to celebrate Bastille Day or cheer on the French national football team during European or World Cup matches. Dine to the sounds of jazz on Monday and Tuesday, while accomplished pianist and vocalist Andrée Bernard performs folk, blues and jazz-inspired songs from Wednesday through Sunday. Le Saint Tropez's menu features many influences from the South of France, such as Toulouse sausages served with *frites,* sautéed shrimp with a twist from Marseille and veal scaloppini with port. For dessert, choose from traditional favourites such as crème brûlée, *tarte au citron* and *millefeuille.* Naturally, France also has a strong presence on the wine list. – *bilingual menu and service in French*

Le Sélect Bistro

328 Queen Street West ☎ 416 596-6406

Monday–Friday for lunch and dinner, Saturday–Sunday for dinner

Subway: OSGOODE

www.leselect.com

The décor is very *rive gauche;* the menu oh-so-French. The experience perfectly charming. If it's hearty French cuisine you are after, Le Sélect Bistro is where you'll find it. *Cassoulet, foie gras* and escargot are only a few of the favourites on the elaborate menu, although the *prix fixe* options are also worth a look for their outstanding value. If choosing what to eat isn't difficult enough, it may be even harder to select an accompanying wine – Le Sélect Bistro's cellar consists of more than 800 bottles. – *bilingual menu*

Merlot

2994 Bloor Street West ☎ 416 236-0081

Monday–Friday for lunch and dinner, Saturday–Sunday for dinner

Subway: ROYAL YORK

Located in the Bloor West Village, Merlot's cuisine is an interesting hybrid of French classics and more exotic fare, such as Alsatian-style sauerkraut. Meat features prominently on the menu – everything from the *steak frites* to the lamb is not only well-cooked but very affordable, making it possible to try something new that may be considerably more expensive elsewhere. No meal at Merlot is complete without one of their delicious desserts or selections from their affordable wine list. – *service in French*

Midi Bistro

168-A McCaul Street (between College Street and Dundas Street) ☎ 416 977-2929

Monday–Friday for lunch, Tuesday–Saturday for dinner

Subway: ST PATRICK

Another small bistro that is big on taste, Midi Bistro is one of those restaurants you'll go back to again and again for the good food, warm hospitality and relaxing ambiance. Midi Bistro's menu is a pleasant surprise in terms of both price and variety. Some of the more unusual starters include *Farçous Claudine* (Southern French spinach crêpes with onions and bacon), an intensely flavourful goat cheese and vegetable *terrine,* grilled goat cheese on toast and, of course, *moules.* Mains are also full of surprises – pan-seared salmon with a cinnamon crust and lime sauce, roasted duck confit leg with a light *Pommery* mustard sauce, oven-roasted Cornish hen with bacon, pine nuts and red grape reduction, striploin streak with bone marrow and red wine sauce and *moules frites.* Desserts are ever-changing, but consistently incredible. Selections might include home-made ice cream, *tarte tatin,* profiteroles filled with vanilla ice cream, crème brûlée and a warm chocolate cake (there's a preparation time of 20 minutes, but it's worth every second of the wait!) – *bilingual menu and service in French*

Restaurants that serve merguez sausages

1. Bistro Matisse
2. Bouchon
3. Boujadi
4. Café Moroc
5. Le Paradis
6. John and King hot dog stand
7. Monitz
8. Pourquoi Pas
9. The Sultan's Tent

Monitz

352 Melrose Avenue (corner of Avenue Road) ☎ 416 781-3764

Monday–Friday for lunch and dinner, Saturday–Sunday for dinner

Subway: EGLINTON + bus

Monitz blends the best of Northern Africa and Southern France in its diverse menu, which includes *mignon de bœuf* (beef medallions with three peppercorns), duck with Chambord Royal (blackberry) sauce, medallions of lamb with minted wine sauce, pork with *cassis* sauce (blackcurrant), duck breast with maple syrup and a variety of chicken, fish and couscous dishes. (*Merguez* sausages are also available by special request, although they do not appear on the menu.) These mouth-watering dishes are nicely complemented by an impressive variety of French wines. A very reasonable *prix fixe* menu is also available. – *bilingual menu and service in French*

Pourquoi Pas

63 Sheppard Avenue West (West of Yonge Street) ☎ 416 226-9071

Monday–Friday for lunch and dinner, Saturday–Sunday for dinner

Subway: **SHEPPARD**

www.toronto.com/pourquoipas

Located in a small house, Pourquoi Pas has a comfortable charm that feels more like a favourite aunt's living room than a restaurant. Egyptian owner Sherif Elkei first opened his doors in 1975, and has since perfected a winning combination of laid-back ambiance, attentive service and terrific French cuisine that has made Pourquoi Pas a favourite among locals. The menu offers an assortment of simple, interesting and reasonably priced selections such as *merguez* sausages, *cassoulet,* calf liver sautéed in red wine and shallots, pork medallions served with Calvados and roasted apples, braised lamb shank with a light tomato sauce, *canard à l'orange* (duck with an orange sauce), sweetbreads and a melt-in-your-mouth filet mignon. Desserts include several tried-and-true French staples like *crème caramel, saint-honoré* and crêpes Suzette. – *bilingual menu and service in French*

Quartier

2112 Yonge Street (between Davisville Avenue and Eglinton Avenue) ☎ 416 545-0505

Monday for dinner, Tuesday–Friday for lunch and dinner, Saturday for dinner; closed Sunday

Subway: **DAVISVILLE** or **EGLINTON**

This elegant neighbourhood bistro combines classic French flavours with international influences. Among the specialties you'll find a perfectly-prepared leg of lamb, shallot-flavoured rabbit served on a bed of truffle risotto, duck confit with Sardalaise apples and chicken with Morel mushrooms. The *steak frites* and fish dishes are also not to be missed, nor is the Monday evening *table d'hôte* dinner menu, which offers an interesting and eclectic selection of mains. Chocolate lovers will want to indulge in Quartier's velvety chocolate cake, which is more than worth the 20 minute preparation time. There's also a gratifying cheese plate to finish off your meal – the perfect accompani-

A category of its own!

John & King
Hot Dog Stand

(Corner of John Street and King Street West, across from the Princess of Wales Theatre)

Open year-round for lunch, dinner and late night

Subway: **ST ANDREW**

It's hard enough to find places in Toronto to enjoy Moroccan *merguez* sausages, let alone places where you can enjoy them to go – until now! Purely by chance, *The French Side of Toronto* discovered one of Toronto's best-kept secrets – the hot dog stand at the corner of John and King Streets, in the midst of the theatre district. Moïse, the owner, is a jovial man of North African descent who will be happy to serve you and chat in either English or French. – *Service in French*

French lunches worth a mention

Arlequin Arlequin is the perfect location for an intimate business lunch.

Bistro 1603 Business types in Mississauga already know Bistro 1603 offers an excellent French lunch without leaving the 905 area code.

Bistro Matisse Another Mississauga find, Bistro Matisse serves up one of the most reasonable lunch menus in town.

Bodega Bodega's lunches are superb, but did you know they cater, too? Catering by Bodega is an ingenious way to mesh business with pleasure, without setting foot outside the boardroom. A catered lunch from Bodega is sure to impress your business associates and clients.

Café Moroc and **The Sultan's Tent** A business lunch set amid enchanting Moroccan decor? *Pourquoi pas!* Stop by Café Moroc or The Sultan's Tent for a zesty meal that will surely "spice" up any negotiations.

Holt's Café For a simple yet satisfying lunch, try Holt's *tartines* (open-faced sandwiches) on Poîlane bread.

La Maison Benoît This uptown restaurant is located near the highway, making it the ideal place to wine and dine out-of-town business associates.

Midi Bistro The ambiance of this little bistro is a welcome haven for those in the University/St. Patrick's area.

Provence Enjoy a business lunch in one of Toronto's most charming restaurants.

ment to something from Quartier's wine list, which leans towards French varietals, especially when it comes to whites. – *bilingual menu and service in French*

Restaurant Jules

147 Spadina Avenue ☎ 416 348-8886

Monday–Friday 11:30–9, Saturday 12–5; closed Sunday (closed Saturdays in July and August)

Subway: SPADINA + streetcar;
OSGOODE + streetcar

Located in the heart of the condo district, Restaurant Jules is popular with the lunchtime crowd who want a delicious yet affordable alternative to the abundance of fast-food chains in the area. The standard here is excellence, in both food and value for money. Chef Eric Strippoli has created a French bistro menu which offers an impressive list of classics such as French onion soup, quiches, *bavette steak* (striploin), homemade mayonnaise and ratatouille – and don't forget to treat yourself to one of his delicious signature crêpes! – *bilingual menu and service in French*

fine dining

Auberge du Pommier

4150 Yonge Street (North of York Mills Road) ☎ 416 222-2220

Monday–Friday for lunch and dinner, Saturday for dinner; closed Sunday

Subway: YORK MILLS

Auberge du Pommier is fine dinning at its best. A perennial favourite on multiple Top 10 lists, this charmingly elegant restaurant has been honoured with numerous accolades from a variety of organizations, ranging from *Where Magazine (Most Memorable Meal Award)* to CAA *(Four Diamond Award).* The interior resembles the type of cozy country inn found in the French countryside and is the perfect setting for a refined and elegantly presented meal, from a menu that mixes flavours from the South of France with Parisian classics and a twist of nouvelle cuisine. Artistic desserts almost look too good to eat, or choose to finish your meal with a satisfying cheese plate paired with a selection from the exhaustive wine list. Auberge du Pommier's reputation for excellence is reflected in its prices; however, the combination of impeccable service, haute cuisine and charming décor puts this restaurant on the absolute must-try list, even if it's only once a year or for special occasions. – *service in French*

Bistro 1603

1603 Clarkson Road, Mississauga
☎ 905 822-5262

Monday–Tuesday for dinner, Wednesday–Friday for lunch and dinner, Saturday for dinner; closed Sunday

Mississauga's Bistro 1603 masters the art of blending traditional French dishes with local ingredients to create an outstanding and original haute cuisine menu. Selections include bouillabaisse with an Asian twist, a trio of duck breast, *foie* and confit, calf's liver and *steak frites.* Classic crème brûlée and a chocolate and raspberry mousse with *Lindt* chocolate ice cream are both exquisite. Possibly the only thing more impressive than the menu is the wine list – Bistro 1603's 250 vintages received the *Wine Spectator* Award of Excellence in 2002 and 2003. – *service in French*

Bodega

(formely La Bodega)

30 Baldwin Street ☎ 416 977-1287

Monday–Sunday for lunch and dinner

Subway: ST PATRICK

www.bodegarestaurant.com

Since our last edition, so much has changed at one of Toronto's oldest French restaurants, and yet so much remains the same. Bodega has a new owner, new decor and a new ambiance (not to mention a newer name!) but the restaurant's reputation for excellence in cuisine and service is as steadfast as ever. This new face lift has brought in a younger crowd looking for sophistication and creativity, and at Bodega, there's plenty of both. Bouillabaisse, *foie gras terrine,* escargots, kidney served in a flaky pastry shell, grilled duck liver and trout served on a bed of lentils are just some of the delectable mains

The best places to eat the Editor-in-Chief's favourite French dessert : tarte au citron

1. Arlequin
2. Bonjour Brioche
3. Bouchon
4. Café Margaux
5. Clafouti
6. Daniel et Daniel
7. Gamelle
8. Holt's Café
9. La Cigogne
10. Le Paradis
11. Le Saint Tropez
12. Marcel's Bistro
13. Patachou
14. Pâtisserie d'Or
15. Rahier

offered. Desserts are a combination of the classic and the exotic, including crème brûlée, profiteroles with figs served with port ice cream and warm chocolate sauce and a white chocolate and Grand Marnier mousse with three sauces. The daily *prix fixe* is an excellent way to sample excellent cuisine at a reasonable price.

Bouchon

38 Wellington Street East ☎ 416 862-2675

Monday for dinner, Tuesday–Friday for lunch and dinner, Saturday for dinner; closed Sunday

Subway: **KING** or **UNION**

www.bouchon.ca

One of the best things about Bouchon is its endless ability to reinvent itself – each time you visit, you'll find a menu bursting with new, fresh and original creations. Chef Jean-Pierre Challet adds his own unique flair to Gallic nouvelle cuisine, resulting in a rich mix of spices, flavours and scents that is nothing short of genius. The best of Morocco and Quebec are combined in an out-of-this-world *merguez poutine,* topped with St. Nectaire cheese and served with *frites* (not fries). Other dishes of note include *foie gras* in cranberry and rhubarb sauce with white asparagus, *bœuf bourguignon* and a *poutine* of *foie gras* topped with goat cheese and duck jus. Desserts are dazzling and change daily, but always include a fantastic *tarte au citron,* crème brûlée and an assortment of chocolate-based treasures. Wines are well-chosen and balance the menu well. – *bilingual menu and service in French*

Café Brussels

124 Danforth Avenue ☎ 416 465-7363

Monday closed; Tuesday–Sunday for dinner

Subway: **BROADVIEW**

Only in Toronto will you find a restaurant located in the heart of Greektown that features dozens of varieties of *moules* (mussels) prepared in the best Belgian tradition! Café Brussels is one of Toronto's hidden treasures. The luxe, spacious Art Deco décor provides an almost theatrical backdrop for a menu that is bold, colourful and dramatic – over 30 (!) kinds of *moules frites,* an award-winning wine list and a superlative assortment of meat dishes. Lamb, *steak frites,* filet mignon and *bœuf bour-*

Brunch

For many Torontonians, brunch is a weekend ritual. Meeting up with friends for a late breakfast/early lunch on weekends is an ideal way to combine the best of both worlds – good food, and good company. Granted, brunch is not a French concept, which explains why only a handful of French restaurants have a specific brunch menu. Many of the other places listed in this guide are still open during brunch hours, but serve a regular lunch menu instead.

Bloor Street Diner/Bloor Street Diner Bistros The *prix fixe* menu for brunch is a little more expensive than most other places, but the large selection more than makes up for it.

Bodega Brunch Bodega-style is an experience not to be missed! The menu is simple and delicious, consisting of a few traditionally French items and a few Torontonian favourites with a French twist – *pain perdu* (French toast), eggs Benedictine and smoked salmon omelettes. The regular lunch menu is also available.

Bonjour Brioche Not only is brunch is available both Saturday and Sunday, but Bonjour Brioche lets patrons enjoy their meal at a leisurely pace and doesn't hurry them out the door. Choose from either the special of the day or the regular lunch menu, which is full of other tasty options including mainstays like quiche, pizzas and vegetable tarts. Don't forget to finish your meal with one of their fantastic pastries or desserts!

Brasserie Aix Brasserie Aix now offers a reasonably-priced brunch on Sunday mornings. Selections include steak and egg, eggs Benedictine, omelette of the day, French toast served with fruit compote and eggs served with smoked salmon.

Épicure Café Épicure Café serves brunch all afternoon on weekends. You'll find mostly classic staples here, including many variations of omelettes and egg dishes.

Jacques Bistro du Parc Jacques Bistro serves up a simple but delicious brunch on Saturdays only, consisting of lighter fare such as omelettes, quiches and salads.

La Cigogne La Cigogne serves a nice assortment of French classics for brunch. On the menu you'll find many kinds of quiche, crêpes *fourrées* (stuffed crêpes), *croque-madame* (like a croque-monsieur, but topped with a fried egg and Béchamel sauce) and omelettes. Don't forget to try the house specialty – *tarte flambée* (Alsatian-style thin-crust pie with bacon, chopped onion and cream cheese), which is only made on weekends. For dessert, La Cigogne offers an enticing array of crêpes!

La Palette Arrive early, because this small Kensington restaurant fills up quickly for weekend brunch. The main attraction? Crêpes! La Palette also offers omelettes, *salade niçoise, salade basques* and *steak frites.*

Le Sélect Bistro Brunch at Le Sélect Bistro is a feast of tastes. Omelettes, French toast, various egg dishes and, of course, crêpes are just some of the items offered. The regular weekend menu is also available.

Provence Provence offers a tasty *prix fixe* brunch menu including salads and numerous egg dishes, with a side order of perfectly fried and seasoned *frites* accompaning every dish. Be sure to try the heavenly crème brûlée for dessert!

guignon are all exceptional, but the *moules* are the real *pièce de résistance* here, not just in terms of variety, but quantity – each portion is equivalent to one full kilogram (2.2 lbs). The remarkable vintages found at Café Brussels are sure to delight wine aficionados. It's easy to see why *Wine Spectator* magazine awarded the restaurant their "Top restaurant wine list Award of Excellence" for seven consecutive years. Impeccable service only adds to the pleasure of dining at Café Brussels. The staff take your enjoyment seriously and truly do everything they can to make your dining experience as perfect as possible. – *bilingual menu and service in French*

CÉLESTIN

623 Mount Pleasant Road (corner of Manor Road) ☎ 416 544-9035

Closed Sunday–Monday;
Tuesday–Saturday for dinner

Subway: EGLINTON + bus

Located in a former branch of a big-five bank, Célestin has definitely raised the rate of interest in French food in the Mount Pleasant neighbourhood. Chef Pascal Ribreau (formerly of Provence) combines traditional French cuisine, quality ingredients and abundant creativity for a result that is nothing short of spectacular. Even the bread is outstanding! Appetizers are a triumph, while main are simply seductive – pig ragoût, braised rabbit, garlic blood sausage, duck breast, pork loin and saffron lamb served with Provençal clams are just some of the more intriguing choices. For dessert, Chef Pascal collaborates with his brother Martial on creations such as a *millefeuille* that looks too good to eat. A cheese plate is also available. Célestin's 20-page wine list is uncommonly good and includes many noted labels from various regions of France. – *service in French*

GAMELLE

468 College Street (corner of Markham Street, West of Bathurst Street)
☎ 416 923-6254

Monday for dinner, Tuesday–Friday for lunch and dinner, Saturday for dinner; closed Sunday

Subway: OSGOODE + streetcar

www.gamelle.com

Gamelle's diminutive size may mistakenly give the impression of a bistro, but just one bite of the superb cuisine quickly underscores the restaurant's gourmet status. Amid a casual yet chic ambiance, Gamelle offers a menu full of subtle flavours and exquisite choices. Owner Jean Pierre Centeno is from the South of France, so you know the *foie gras* is guaranteed to be first-rate. Other specialties include pheasant, *magret* of duck, escargot, vegetable *millefeuille,* sirloin with brandy, French Canadian leg of lamb and a variety of savoury fish dishes. This is another restaurant where you'll definitely want to leave room for dessert. The *tarte au citron,* crème brûlée and chocolate cake are not to be missed. France is well-represented on Gamelle's extensive wine list. – *service in French*

FRENCH COUNTRY
french romance
for town and country
Linens, faience, hotel flatware, gifts
& decorative accessories for the home
6 ROXBOROUGH ST. W. TORONTO ONT. / 416-944-2204

Vinifera
Finest French wines, accessories
and service since 1988
RIEDEL
SPIEGELAU
Echtkristall
L'esprit & le vin
CAVAVIN
VINTAGE KEEPER
LAGUIOLE
Screwpull
1055 Yonge Street ◦ Suite 306
416 924-4004 ◦ vinifera.com

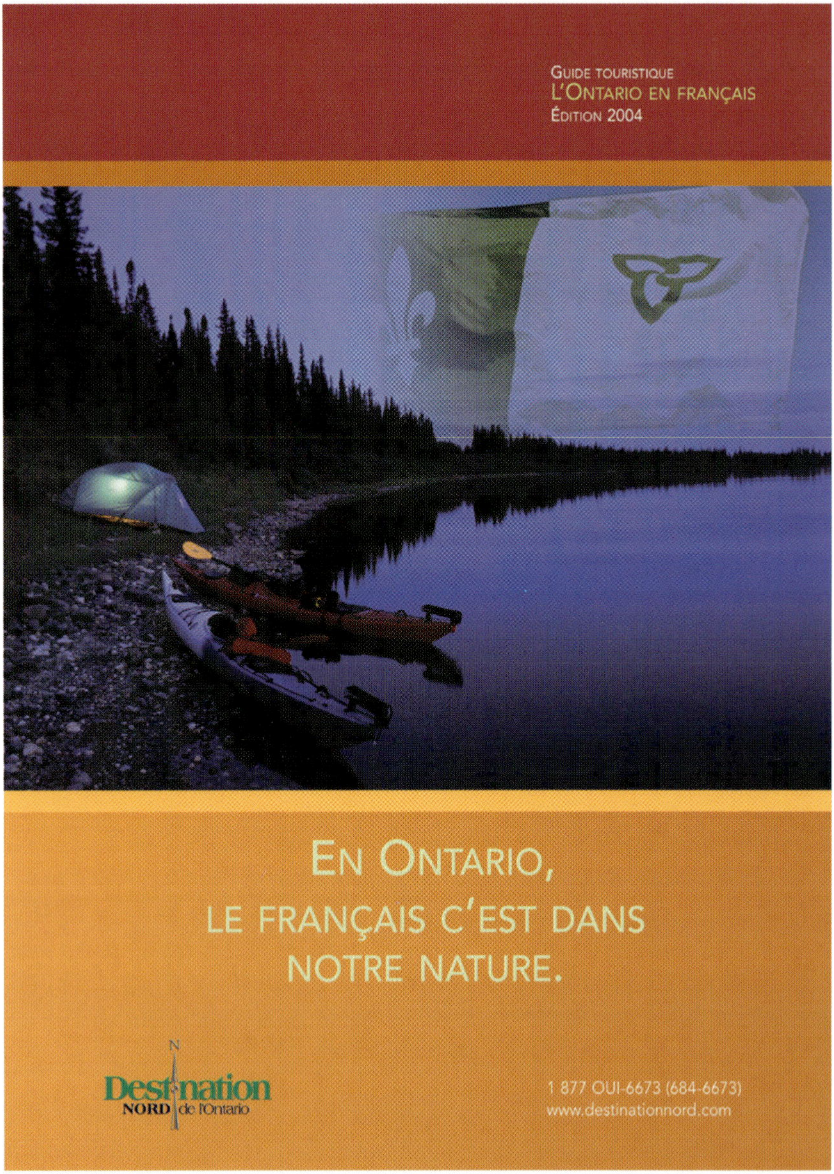
GUIDE TOURISTIQUE
L'ONTARIO EN FRANÇAIS
ÉDITION 2004
EN ONTARIO,
LE FRANÇAIS C'EST DANS
NOTRE NATURE.
N
Destination
NORD de l'Ontario
1 877 OUI-6673 (684-6673)
www.destinationnord.com

ONTARIO

Le Montmartre

911 Sheppard Avenue West
☎ 416 630-3804

Monday–Friday for lunch and dinner, Saturday for dinner; closed Sunday

Subway: DOWNSVIEW

www.toronto.com/lemontmartre

The wonderfully French ambiance at Le Montmartre can be heard through the music of Edith Piaf playing in the background, seen in the Van Gogh and Renoir paintings on the wall (which pay homage to the restaurant's namesake, the 19th century Artists' Quarter in Paris) and tasted in their authentic and delicious gourmet cuisine. Standouts on the menu include mouth-watering cuts of beef, *canard à l'orange* (duck in orange sauce), frog legs and *escargots bourguignon* (snails in a bourguignon sauce). For a perfect ending to a perfect meal, opt for the profiteroles filled with cold custard and served with ice cream. Wines include many fine selections from all over the world, including several interesting choices from France. Don't forget to inquire about Le Montmartre's *prix fixe* menu!
– bilingual menu and service in French

Le Trou Normand

90 Yorkville Avenue ☎ 416 967-5956

Monday–Saturday for lunch and dinner; closed Sunday

Subway: BAY

www.letrounormand.com

Le Trou Normand gets its name from the old Normandy custom of drinking a glass of calvados (apple brandy) in the middle of a meal, which slows digestion and allows the remaining courses to be tackled with great gusto. It's a tradition that would be well-served at this touristy Yorkville restaurant, where the *terroir* (from the earth) cooking is a joy meant to be savoured. Renowned for its strict adherence to authentic French cuisine, Le Trou Normand's Normandy-inspired menu (Northern region of France) features a number of seafood-based dishes, with most mains served with potatoes and cream. *Foie gras*, veal medallions *à la Normande* and scallops and shrimp in a lobster

The French Side of Toronto's *Favourite Desserts*

1. All tarts from Bouchon
2. All tarts from Daniel et Daniel
3. Dominus and the caramelized apple and chocolate pie from Clafouti
4. Chestnut cake from Senses
5. Chocolate cake from Gamelle
6. *Crème caramel* from Le Paradis
7. Fig and ice cream profiteroles served with Port from Bodega
8. Ice cream profiteroles from Midi Bistro
9. *L'assiette gourmande* from Café Margaux
10. *L'assiette gourmande* from Pastis
11. *Millefeuille* from Célestin
12. *Pain perdu* made with Poîlane bread, peaches and cinnamon from Holt's Café
13. Pear and almond pie from Bonjour Brioche
14. *Petits fours* from Patachou
15. Profiteroles from Jacques Bistro du Parc

The best places to eat Toronto's favourite French dessert: crème brûlée

1. Auberge du Pommier
2. Bistro 1603
3. Bodega
4. Café la Gaffe
5. Café Margaux
6. Café Moroc/The Sultan's Tent
7. Célestin
8. Gamelle
9. Holt's Café
10. La Petite France
11. Le Saint Tropez
12. Marcel's Bistro
13. Midi Bistro
14. Pastis
15. Provence

sauce with Grand Marnier are among the selections, while desserts include crème brûlée and other French classics. An extensive wine list, comprised mostly of French vintages, is priced to accommodate every budget. – *bilingual menu*

Marcel's Bistro

315 King Street West (corner of John Street) ☎ 416 591-8600

Closed Sunday–Monday; Tuesday–Friday for lunch and dinner, Saturday for dinner

Subway: ST ANDREW

www.marcels.com

With its low-key ambiance, refined menu and incredible service, it's easy to see why Marcel's Bistro has been a favourite of Toronto Francophiles since 1984. Marcel's celebrates the fresh, light and pure 'cuisine of the sun' found in the South of France, but also spotlights a different region of the country each month to truly reflect France's culinary diversity. The restaurant's philosophy that cooking is a 'living art' is echoed in the creative selections on their menu – *moules poulettes,* pheasant *terrine,* spinach salad with oyster mushrooms, grilled apples and Roquefort cheese, *steak frites,* roasted lamb served with pesto mashed potatoes and grilled Alberta beef tenderloin with *gratin Auvergnat.* For dessert, choose from traditional French fare such as crème brûlée, *millefeuille,* profiteroles and *tarte au citron.* Marcel's Bistro takes their wines as seriously as their cuisine, and offers an extensive range of French-centric vintages, as well as aperitifs like *kir, pineau des charentes* and *pastis.*
– *bilingual menu and service in French*

Matignon

51 St. Nicholas Street ☎ 416 921-9226

Monday–Friday for lunch and dinner, Saturday for dinner; closed Sunday (will open Sundays for large private functions)

Subway: YONGE

www.matignon.ca

Tucked away from the hustle and bustle of nearby Yonge and Bay Streets, Matignon is located in a lovely little brick house in a residential neighbourhood, making it the ideal place for an intimate *tête-à-tête* dinner. Charming maître d'hotel and owner Mustapha Amrani sets the standard for service *par excellence,* and with its elegantly-appointed dining rooms and a fantastic *prix fixe* menu, Matignon is sure to be a restaurant you'll return to again and again. *Prix fixe* choices include chicken with basil and cream sauce and a braised lamb shank with sauce provençale, while the regular menu offers *steak frites*, peppered Black Angus steak flambéd with cognac and rack of lamb with mustard, honey and mint. To finish your meal, the wonderful orange-flavoured *crème caramel* is highly recommended. Matignon's wine list is both diverse and reasonably-priced, and any selection would be sure to complement your meal. – *service in French*

Pastis Express

1158 Yonge Street ☎ 416 928-2212

Closed Sunday–Monday;
Tuesday–Saturday for dinner

Subway: SUMMERHILL

A cross between a bistro and a fine dining restaurant, Rosedale's Pastis serves delicious French cuisine in a warm and inviting atmosphere. A delightful find is the *Châteaubriand* for two – a rarity in Toronto, beautifully done here. The *foie gras poelé aux poires caramélisées* (pan-seared *foie gras* served on caramelized pears) is another must-try. Desserts at Pastis are outstanding. The crème brûlée is rumoured to be one of the best in the city, but the caramel-filled profiteroles with raspberry coulis is equally tempting. Courageous diners may want to tackle Pastis' almost celestial *assiette gourmande – crème brûlée* accompanied by a wedge of dark chocolate cake and raspberry purée, topped with a delicate *tuile* cookie – *fantastique!* The wine list is succinct, but the bottles have been well chosen. – *service in French*

Provence

12 Amelia Street (corner of Parliament Street, close to Wellesley Street)
☎ 416 924-9901

Monday–Sunday for lunch and dinner

Subway: COLLEGE + streetcar or
CASTLE FRANK + bus

www.provencerestaurant.com

Cabbagetown's Provence pays great attention to detail in everything from the service to the charming décor to the cuisine itself, to ensure you enjoy every moment of your dining experience. Prices are a little higher than average, but Provence is hard to resist (not to mention, the lunch and dinner *prix fixe* menus are outstanding). Provence delivers a menu that is simple and classic, with a rich and complex mixture of fragrances and tastes. Appetizers include duck terrine, escargot and even Sevruga caviar, while a refined selection of mains offers bouillabaisse, duck confit and calf's liver. Grand Marnier crème brûlée is the central attraction on the dessert menu, but for those who prefer a more savoury end to their meal, Provence offers not one, but two cheese plates. Provence's sophisticated wine list has been honoured by *Wine Spectator* magazine from 1999 to 2003 with the "Wine Spectator Award of Excellence". – *service in French*

The Sultan's Tent

49 Front Street East (West of Church Street) ☎ 416 961-0601

Monday–Saturday for lunch and dinner,
Sunday for dinner

Subway: UNION

www.thesultanstent.com

Looking for a change of scenery? Dining at The Sultan's Tent combines the best of Moroccan culture and cuisine for an unforgettable experience. Located at the rear of Café Moroc, an evening at The Sultan's Tent's pleases not only the palate, but the senses. Dim lights, billowing tents made of luminous, luxurious fabrics and large, plush banquettes create an enchanting, relaxing atmosphere that makes diners feel like they have been transported to Marrakesh. Best of all, sensual belly dancers perform nightly to the rhythms of exotic Arabic music. The food is as beguiling as the décor – the four-course menu, including appetizers and desserts, is a simple yet excellent way to savour many authentic Moroccan dishes. Be sure to finish your meal with a cup of sweet mint tea. – *service in French*

french cooking

courses & schools

Now that you know the best places in the city to buy the ingredients you'll need for French cooking, it's time to step into the kitchen and start creating a few sensational dishes of your own. Don't know where to begin? The following schools and courses should help unleash the amateur French chef in you!

Academy of Artisans

490 Eglinton Avenue West (West of Avenue Road) ☎ 416 322-9997

Classes: evenings only

Subway: **EGLINTON** + bus

www.academyofartisans.com

Grab your apron and head to this Forest Hill cooking school to learn a few new skills and techniques in French and Moroccan cuisine.

Calphalon Culinary Center

425 King Street West (corner of Spadina Avenue) ☎ 416 847-2212

Classes: evenings and Saturdays

Subway: **ST ANDREW**

www.calphalonculinarycenter.com

Calphalon Culinary Center offers six different introductory classes that cater to all levels of culinary expertise, from beginners to advanced students looking to update their skills. Once you have mastered the basics, you can choose from classes pairing fine food and wine, pairing food and Belgium beer, French cooking and even creating the perfect French crêpe.

Cooking at the Harvest Kitchen

134 Thomas Street, Oakville
☎ 416 346-4236 (administration office is located in Toronto)

Classes: evenings only

www.epicureanexpeditions.com

Call Cooking at the Harvest Kitchen to be added to their electronic newsletter, which will keep you abreast of the dates for their French cooking class, held twice a year.

Cook Gourmet

1204 Clarkson Road, Mississauga (near the QEW and Highway 10)
☎ 905 403-0059

Classes: evenings only

www.cookgourmet.ca

This Mississaugua-based cooking school offers French cooking classes.

Dish Cooking Studio

390 Dupont Street ☎ 416 920-5559

Classes: evenings and Saturdays

Subway: **DUPONT**

www.dishcookingstudio.com

Dish Cooking Studio is a fun and welcoming place to learn the basics of French and Moroccan cuisine. Classes include *A French Market Tour of the St. Lawrence Market, Great Bistro Cooking at Home, French Flair, In A French Kitchen, Chez Paris, Wine Country Casual* and *A Taste of Morocco.*

George Brown College

300 Adelaide Street East ☎ 416 415-5000

Classes: evenings and Saturday mornings

Subway: **KING**

www.gbrownc.on.ca

You'll find an array of choices here that can take your cooking to another level in the span of a school semester. French cooking classes include *French Cuisine Classic, French Cuisine Contemporary* and *Crêpes* (sweet and savoury). You'll even find a *French Farmhouse* class that will teach all you need to know about *terroir* (from the earth) cooking. Another option is the *Wine and Dine at Our Table series,* which focuses on a specific cuisine each class, including one evening dedicated to French cooking. For more information, visit the Hospitality & Tourism section of George Brown College's web site.

Give it a Stir

1560 Yonge Street (Delisle Court)
☎ 416 920-7447

Classes: during lunchtime, Tuesday evenings

Subway: ST CLAIR

www.giveitastir.com

Give is a Stir is first and foremost a kitchen store that just happens to contain a well-equipped area for learning purposes. Debbie Diamente teaches students the rudiments of Moroccan and French cuisine in private and group classes. Now, there's a theme for your next event — French or Moroccan cooking parties!

Great Cooks

176 Yonge Street (inside The Bay Queen Street, concourse level) ☎ 416 861-4727

Classes: evenings and Saturdays during the winter

Subway: QUEEN

www.greatcooks.ca

Great Cooks has been changing the way Torontonians cooks since 1989. Owners Esther Benaim and Maggie McKeown offer students unforgettable culinary learning experiences taught by instructors who are "great cooks" in their own right — Chef Bouchra Sidali teaches Moroccan cuisine classes while French cuisine is taught by Chef Jean-Pierre Challet from Bouchon restaurant. Chef Challet even offers a few classes in French. Now that is a *grand coup* in Toronto! Great Cooks was one of the first private cooking schools in Toronto, and has since opened a second location in Mississauga. The school also offers cooking classes as a team-building activity for large corporations and can easily accommodate groups of up to 70 people. – *some French cooking classes are offered in French*

J. S. Bonbons

163 Dupont Street (near Davenport Road)
☎ 416 920-0274

Classes: evenings

Subway: DUPONT

www.jsbonbons.com

If the thought of J. S. Bonbons's chocolates mentioned in the chocolatiers section of this guide made your mouth water, you'll be delighted to know you can learn how to make these sinful treasures yourself, at the hands of the master no less! Chocolatier Jenn Stone demonstrates the joys of chocolate-making in the back of her shop. Apart from spending an evening talking, looking and playing with chocolate, participants get to eat everything in sight once the class is finished —*fantastique!*

LCBO

Various locations across the
Greater Toronto Area ☎ 1 800 668-5226

Classes: evenings

www.lcbo.com

Wines from Alsace, Belgium beers and *Whites from the Burgundy Region* are just some of the classes you can take at the LCBO to learn more about wines, spirits and beer from French-speaking countries. The LCBO also offers a few French cooking courses, as well as a free cheese sampling class conducted by Ektor Stroutzas, Managing Director of Alex Farm Products.

Le Cordon Bleu Paris

453 Laurier Avenue East, Ottawa
☎ 1 888 289-6302

Classes: evenings, weekends and weekdays

www.lcbottawa.edu

Although Ottawa might be a little far away for an evening cooking class, it makes the ideal location for a weekend getaway. Le Cordon Bleu Paris teaches amateurs the basics of French cooking, including a wine-pairing class, and has also produced many top-calibre chefs who have mastered French cuisine perfectly.

Loblaws

Various locations across the
Greater Toronto Area

Classes: evening and Saturdays

About 20 Loblaws across the Greater Toronto Area offer cooking classes, usually located in culinary labs on the second floor. Several aspects of French cuisine are covered in various classes. Learn how to make the perfect *pâté feuilleté* (puff pastry), or discover new Moroccan and French cuisine techniques. Chef Jean-Pierre Challet of Bouchon restaurant even teaches a class in oyster sampling!

Richmond Hill Culinary Arts Centre

1550 16th Avenue (in Richmond Hill)
☎ 905 508-2665

Classes: evenings

www.culinaryarts.ca

If you have a passion for French sweets, look no further than Richmond Hill Culinary Arts Centre, where you'll learn the art of chocolate-making, how to turn out the perfect crêpe and the secrets behind delectable crème brûlée.

Strewn Winery

1339 Lakeshore Road, Niagara-on-the-Lake
☎ 905 468-8304

Classes: weekends

www.winecountrycooking.com

One of Ontario's most picturesque regions provides the perfect backdrop to learn all about French cuisine, wine sampling and the subtle art of pairing wine and food. This charming Niagara-on-the-Lake winery offers day classes on Saturdays and Sundays, as well as two-day weekend classes.

The Cookworks

99 Sudbury Street, Unit 8
☎ 416 537-6464

Classes: evenings

Subway: OSGOODE + streetcar

www.thecookworks.com

Je Mange, Je Bois, Je Fais L'Amour is the name of The Cookworks' French cooking class, which succintly summarizes three aspects of life the French enjoy celebrating — "I eat, I drink, I make love". *Bien sûr!*

a cultural adventure

information & entertainment

The French are passionate lovers of culture. While Toronto will never be Paris or Montreal, it is still possible to find many cultural activities for Francophiles in the city and around the Greater Toronto Area. French newspapers, bookstores, movies, film festivals, theatres, radio stations, gatherings, festivals of music and culture are not only great ways to meet other Francophones, but excellent venues and resources for Anglophones and Francophiles to get a taste of life *comme les français.*

Newspapers

L'Express

www.lexpress.to

L'Express is the most important French-language weekly in Toronto, covering international and local news, politics, job postings and, of course, culture and the arts. *L'Express* is available at La Maison de la Presse Internationale, Librairie Champlain and Indigo-Chapters for a nominal charge; however, you'll also find free copies in many locations across the city, such as Alliance française de Toronto, Glendon College and the Consulate General of France in Toronto.

Le Métropolitain

www.lemetropolitain.com

Le Métropolitain focuses on Francophone lifestyles in Toronto and the Greater Toronto Area. The publication is available free of charge in most locations where *L'Express* is distributed.

Books & Magazines

À bon verre bonne table

☎ 1 800 ONT-LCBO (info line)
www.lcbo.com/food_drink_fr

À Bon Verre Bonne Table is the French version of the LCBO's popular *Food & Drink* magazine. Each edition is packed with great recipes and suggestions for finding the right beverage to accompany a meal or to enjoy alone. You'll also find an eclectic group of recipes, cocktails and menus, articles about food, ideas for unusual place settings and centrepieces, the newest food gadgets and even the latest musical hits to accompany everything from picnics to parties. The magazines are published several times a year, and are distributed free of charge inside LCBO stores. Their popularity means they have a very short shelf life (this holds especially true of *À Bon Verre Bonne Table,* as each LCBO only receives a small quantity of the French edition) – so be sure to pick yours up early! (The next edition's publishing date can always be found in the current edition's masthead.) Home-delivery is available for a small charge, call the info line for further details.

Amazon.ca

www.amazon.ca

The Canadian branch of the world's biggest virtual bookstore carries a lot of classic and contemporary French fiction, as well as French titles in numerous other genres.

Archambault.ca

www.archambault.ca

This well-known Quebec-based site offers a diverse range of books in both French and English, including titles on the arts, biographies, comics, cooking, computers, children's literature, general fiction, health, reference materials, social sciences, travel. Not sure what to get? Archambault.ca features a list of recommended books that makes gift-giving and decision-making easy.

Indigo-Chapters

Various locations across the Greater

Toronto Area
www.chapters.indigo.ca

The Indigo-Chapters group is comprised of the following bookstores: **Chapters, Coles Books, Indigo** and **World's Biggest Bookstore** (20 Edward Street ☎ 416 977-7009; Monday –Saturday 9–10, Sunday 11–6). Most of the great classics of Camus, Molière and Voltaire's language can be found at this family of bookstores, as well as a selection of French-language magazines and newspapers.

La Maison de la Presse Internationale

102-104 Yorkville Avenue ☎ 416 928-2328
Monday–Friday 8:30–11, Saturday 8:30–midnight, Sunday 8:30–11
Subway: BAY or MUSEUM

Loads of great French books, magazines, newspapers and travel guides can be found at La Maison de la Presse Internationale, the Toronto location of the popular Montreal-based chain.

Librairie Champlain

468 Queen Street East ☎ 416 364-4345
Monday–Thursday 9–6, Friday 9–8, Saturday 9–5, closed Sunday
Subway: QUEEN + streetcar

Librairie Champlain is the largest source of French-language books and magazines in Toronto. You'll find classic literature, romance and mystery novels, children's educational and recreational books, cartoons, dictionaries, CDs and educational games, as well as magazines and newspapers from France, Quebec and Ontario. If, by

Did you know?

ALLIANCE FRANÇAISE de Toronto is a great place to learn French. You'll also be able to take advantage of the following services:

▸ **TOURISM IN FRANCE**

Guide books, atlases, maps, albums, CD-ROMs, magazines and more than 50 videotapes to help plan your next holiday to France.

▸ **LEARNING TOOLS**

Master the French language with over 30 videotapes, dictionaries, easy-reading books, audiotapes and CD-ROMs.

▸ **FRENCH AND FRANCOPHONE MUSIC**

Sample a variety of artists and genres on both CDs and tapes.

▸ **FRENCH AND FRANCOPHONE LITERATURE**

Explore a library of more than 1,800 books, ranging from classic to contemporary authors.

▸ **CONTEMPORARY FRENCH PRODUCTIONS**

Books, newspapers, magazines and approximately 100 videotapes focusing on science, the arts and current issues.

▸ **FRENCH FILMS**

Choose from more than 250 French blockbusters available for rent.

Further details are available at:
WWW.ALLIANCE-FRANCAISE.CA

some chance, you *can't* find what you're looking for on the shelves, simply stop by the special order desk and they will try to locate it for you.

Presse Internationale magazine super stores

Various locations across the Greater Toronto Area

www.presseinternationale.com

Presse Internationale carries a fantastic selection of French-language magazines and newspapers from around the world. With multiple locations and extended hours, Presse Internationale is tops for Toronto's Francophone readers. (Note: though similar in name, Presse Internationale is not the same as La Maison de la Presse Internationale.)

Québec Loisirs

☎ 1 800 361-2441
www.quebecloisirs.com

The Francophone's answer to Amazon.ca! Québec Loisirs is the Canadian branch of France's France Loisirs site (www.franceloisirs.com) and carries much the same content, without incurring the expense of overseas shipping costs. In addition, members are entitled to 20 to 40 per cent off purchases.

Renaud-Bray

☎ 1 888 746-2283
www.renaud-bray.com

Quebec-based Renaud-Bray's web site has a diverse selection of French books covering all genres.

Salon du Livre de Toronto

www.salondulivredetoronto.ca

Held annually every mid-October at the Metro Toronto Convention Centre (255 Front Street West), Salon du Livre de Toronto offers the largest selection of French books in Ontario. It's also a great forum to meet and talk to French authors and publishers through various scheduled seminars and book-signing sessions.

Taloua

☎ 416 934-0588
www.taloua.com
info@taloua.com

Welcome to the "multicultur-elle" world of *Taloua! Taloua* means "young women" in Agni, a dialect spoken in the Ivory Coast. This Toronto-based, French-language multicultural magazine for women boasts a contemporary style, an eclectic mix of cultures, a diverse range of subjects from contributors all over the world and a pool of talented up-and-coming photographers, graphic designers, illustrators and writers. In fact, *Taloua*'s only drawback is that it is published just twice a year! *Taloua* is available at Maison de la Presse Internationale, Chapters and Indigo. You can also subscribe online or order a copy by phone.

The Film Reference Library

2 Carlton Street East (Mezzanine level)
☎ 416 967-1517

Winter and summer hours are posted on the web site

Subway: COLLEGE (Carlton exit)

libraryservices@torfilmfest.ca
www.filmreferencelibrary.ca

Of the 17,000 or so books about film on the shelves of the Film Reference Library, about 1,200 are in French. Subjects covered include biographies of many pioneers in the world of film, theatre, acting, television, film history, technical aspects of film-making, cinematography and script writing. You'll also find a variety of French-language magazines covering the Francophone film industry such as *Trafic* (France), *24 images* (Quebec), *L'avant-scène cinéma* (France), *Cahiers du cinéma* (France), *Jeune cinéma* (France) and *Ciné bulles* (France), as well as numerous English-language magazines reviewing films from Latin American, Asia and Europe, including France.

Music

Amazon.ca

www.amazon.ca

Amazon stocks both the latest hits and older classics in Francophone music.

Archambault Musique

www.archambault.ca

Archambault Musique has a wide variety of music from Quebec, France and other French-speaking countries.

HMV

Various locations across the Greater Toronto Area

www.hmv.ca

Most HMV stores contain a small selection of the biggest artists in both French and Quebecois music. However, if there's a particular *chanteur* or chanteuse you're dying to hear, simply place a special order and HMV will try to find the title.

Librairie Champlain

468 Queen Street East ☎ 416 364-4345

Monday–Thursday 9–6, Friday 9–8, Saturday 9–5, closed Sunday

Subway: QUEEN + streetcar

The most popular French titles are available at Librairie Champlain.

Québec Loisirs

☎ 1 800 361-2441

www.quebecloisirs.com

From pop-rock to country and Christmas music to Francophone artists … you'll find it all at Québec Loisirs!

Renaud-Bray

☎ 1 888 746-2283

www.renaud-bray.com

This Quebec-based site carries all the latest and greatest French music.

Sam the Record Man

347 Yonge Street (North of Dundas Street) ☎ 416 646-2775

Monday–Thursday 9–10, Friday–Saturday 9–midnight, Sunday 11–7

Subway: DUNDAS

Sam the Record Man is tops for French music in Toronto – the second floor of this superstore contains one of the city's most impressive and extensive collections of music from France and Quebec. You'll find it all here, from golden oldies to the latest chart-topping hits; from Yves Montand and

Patrick Bruel to Gilles Vigneault and Garou. If you are looking for a particular title that is not stocked, ask the staff to place a special order.

Film Festivals

Cinéfranco – Toronto French Film Festival

☎ 416 928-6595

www.cinefranco.com

C'est vrai? One full week of French films, right here in Toronto? *Mais, oui!* Cinéfranco – The Toronto French Film Festival takes place annually during the end of March and beginning of April. All the films have subtitles, so there are no excuses for Anglophones to miss a wonderful week of great films.

Toronto International Film Festival – Festival des films étrangers

www.e.bell.ca/filmfest

Held at the beginning of September, the Toronto International Film Festival (Festival des films étrangers) marks the annual arrival of big movies and big movie stars in the city. Usually, quite a few French films of various genres are screened among the festival's dazzling and diverse repertoire.

Cinemas

Cumberland

159 Cumberland Street (corner of Avenue Road) ☎ 416 646-0444

Subway: BAY (Cumberland exit)

Carlton

20 Carlton Street (East of Yonge Street)
☎ 416 598-2309

Subway: COLLEGE

These two theatres show a fair number of superb French films throughout the year. Check your weekly paper for current listings.

Ciné Jeudi

150 John Street (National Film Board/Office National du Film)
☎ 416 973-3012

Subway: OSGOODE

www.alliance-francaise.ca

Now, Francophiles can experience the latest French and French-Canadian cinematographic hits on a big screen without having to wait for Cinéfranco or the Toronto International Film Festival! The Consulate General of France in Toronto, the National Film Board, Cinéfranco, the Bureau du Québec and Alliance française de Toronto have teamed up to create Ciné Jeudi – year-round presentations of French cinema in Toronto. Screenings take place in the viewing room located on the second floor of the National Film Board (Office National du Film) on the first Thursday of every month. For more information about upcoming films, visit Alliance française de Toronto's web site.

Cinemathèque Ontario

317 Dundas Street (Jackman Hall, Art Gallery of Ontario, McCaul Street entrance) ☎ 416 968-FILM (3456), extension 2

Subway: ST PATRICK

www.bell.ca/cinematheque

Cinematheque Ontario is a division of the Toronto International Film Festival Group (Festival des films étrangers) focusing on retrospectives and special series. Both well-known and obscure titles are screened from some of the biggest directors in French film – Cocteau, Deray, Godard, Malle, Renoir, Tati and Truffaut, to name but a few. Following the success of the now-defunct "Summer in France, Classics of French Cinema" program, Cinematheque Ontario has continued to spotlight French films during the months of July and August. (All films are sub-titled, so Anglophones can join in the fun, too.) *Bon film!*

The Film Reference Library

2 Carlton Street East (Mezzanine level)
☎ 416 967-1517

Winter and summer hours are posted on the web site

Subway: COLLEGE (Carlton exit)

libraryservices@torfilmfest.ca
www.filmreferencelibrary.ca

The Film Reference Library is a bountiful resource centre for the French *cinéphile* (film lover)! With over 8,000 Canadian and international films to choose from (more than 540 of which are French, all with English sub-titles), the library offers professionals, scholars and cinema buffs an exhaustive resource of cinematographic reference materials. Films can even be viewed on the premises, in one of two viewing rooms. There's even viewing equipment for European DVDs – a rare find in Toronto! The Film Reference Library is another division of the Toronto International Film Festival Group (Festival des films étrangers). Members can access all the library's services for free (details on their web site). If you need assistance, just ask one of the library's incredibly knowledgeable employees, who are resources in their own right and will not hesitate to help you in your search.

Video & DVD Rentals

▸ Queen Video

Various locations across the Greater Toronto Area

Monday–Sunday 11–11

▸ Revue Video

207 Danforth Avenue (near Broadview Avenue) ☎ 416 778-5776

Monday–Sunday 11–10

Subway: BROADVIEW

▸ Suspect Video

- 605 Markham Street (near Bloor & Bathurst Streets) ☎ 416 588-6674

  Subway: BATHURST

- 619 Queen Street West ☎ 416 504-7135

Subway: OSGOODE

Monday–Saturday 12–11, Sunday 12–10 (both locations)

▸ Very Video

- 1375 Yonge Street (South of St. Clair Avenue) ☎ 416 929-8379

  Monday-Thursday 10:30-10, Friday-Saturday 10:30-11, Sunday 10:30-10

  Subway: ST CLAIR

- 1689 Bayview Avenue (near Eglinton Avenue) ☎ 416 322-8379

  Monday-Saturday 10-6, Sunday 12-5

  Subway: EGLINTON + bus

Did you know?

Most video rental stores will gladly place an order for a particular French film if you know the exact title (an option to consider if you're looking for an older film!).

These independent video stores offer an amazing selection of movies from France and other French-language countries – most locations have several hundred titles to choose from! You'll find rare movies, just-released films and older classics from the French New Wave. To give you an idea of how extensive the selection is, Queen Video has approximately 600 French films for rent (about 500 are on video and 100 are on DVD). Suspect Video offers you up to 250 French titles, including films from Tunisia and French-speaking African countries, while Very Video has about 30 or so French films.

Video & DVD Sales

Amazon.ca

www.amazon.ca

This online superstore features the latest French blockbusters.

Archambault.ca

www.archambault.ca

From Louis de Funès to Vincent Perez and Clint Eastwood to Pierce Brosnan, you'll find it all at Archambault's online store. Archambault.ca features many French and translated films in both video and DVD formats.

Librairie Champlain

468 Queen Street East ☎ 416 364-4345

Monday–Thursday 9–6, Friday 9–8,
Saturday 9–5, closed Sunday

Subway: QUEEN + streetcar

Librairie Champlain sells numerous French films on video and DVD, as well as a selection of cartoons and movies for younger Francophiles.

Québec Loisirs

☎ 1 800 361-2441

www.quebecloisirs.com

Québec Loisirs offers an assortment of films and TV series in French. Not sure what to choose? Consult the 'Best Sellers' list for popular titles or choose from Québec Loisirs own list of favourites.

Renaud-Bray

☎ 1 888 746-2283

www.renaud-bray.com

Some of the best films French cinema has to offer are only a click away at Renaud-Bray's web site.

Sam the Record Man

347 Yonge Street (North of Dundas Street)
☎ 416 646-2775

Monday–Thursday 9–10, Friday–Saturday
9–midnight, Sunday 11–7

Subway: DUNDAS

Sam the Record Man has a good selection of French films on video and DVD. If you can't find what you're looking for, Sam's will be happy to place a special order.

Watching French Films at Home

TFO

Audience Relations
☎ 1 800 463-6886

Monday–Friday 9–5

The celebration of "the seventh art" takes place every night at 9 p.m. on TFO (Télévision Française d'Ontario, the French arm of TVO), where you'll discover films from France, Quebec and French Canada, Africa and Belgium (unfortunately for Anglophones, films are shown without English sub-titles). To keep up to date on films scheduled for the coming season, consult TFO's *Passeport Cinema* booklet, which includes information about each film aired (synopsis, schedule, critique, length, country of origin, year of production, producer, director and cast names). Call Audience Relations to have a free *Passeport* mailed to your home.

Art Galleries

Art Gallery of Ontario – AGO

317 Dundas Street ☎ 416 979-6648

Monday closed, Tuesday–Friday 11–6, Wednesday 11–8:30, Saturday–Sunday 10–5:30

Subway: ST PATRICK

www.ago.net

From Monet to Cézanne to Degas, the Art Gallery of Ontario is the ideal place to further your education in the world of fine arts ... *en français*. All descriptions for special exhibits and permanent collections, as well as audio guides, are available in French and English.

Glendon Gallerie

2275 Bayview Avenue ☎ 416 487-6859

Closed Sunday–Monday; Tuesday, Wednesday, Friday 12–3, Thursday 11–2, Saturday 1–4

Subway: LAWRENCE +bus

www.glendon.yorku.ca/gallery

The Glendon Gallery is a public art gallery located on the Glendon campus of York University. The gallery features monthly exhibitions, with emphasis on education and contemporary art. Literature in French and English, as well as guided tours and lectures by artists and curators, complement the program.

Royal Museum of Ontario – ROM

100 Queen's Park Crescent (corner of Bloor Street) ☎ 416 586-8000

Monday–Thursday 10–6, Friday 10–9:30, Saturday–Sunday 10–6

Subway: MUSEUM

www.rom.on.ca

At the Royal Ontario Museum, treasures from the past and present can be discovered in both French and in English. All the descriptions on the different pieces in the permanent, curated and special exhibits are available in both languages. Thematic guides for special exhibits are also available in French and bilingual guides are on staff to help with French group tours.

Theatre

Théâtre français de Toronto

26 Berkeley Street ☎ 416 534-6604
Subway: KING + streetcar
www.theatrefrancais.com

Created in 1967, Le Théâtre français de Toronto features a variety of quality productions for Francophone adults and children. Most plays are adapted from French, French-Canadian or international literature. Performances take place at the Canadian Stage Theatre.

Théatre La Tangente

☎ 416 485-1432
www.theatrelatangente.ca

Accolades for this Toronto-based theatre company have come from as far away as Quebec and Paris. Théâtre La Tangente presents only original creative works – no adaptations or translation pieces here. This interesting way of approaching theatre means only one new piece is produced every two years.

Radio

Radio-Canada – 860 AM

Radio-Canada (Ontario) is the local version of CBC's national French-language radio station, which broadcasts many different cultural, variety and entertainment shows.

Coopérative radiophonique de Toronto – 105.1 FM

Coopérative radiophonique de Toronto is the only French community radio station covering the Greater Toronto Area.

Television

RDI (Réseau d'Information)

This national and international news station presents breaking news much in the same style as CNN.

SRC (Société Radio-Canada)

La Société Radio-Canada's diverse programming includes French-language news, entertainment, information, sitcoms, soap operas and films.

TFO

www.tfo.org

TFO (Télévision Française d'Ontario) is the French arm of TVO. The station's cultural investment in Ontario's French community is reflected in their vast range of programming, which is mostly centred around the lives of Franco-Ontarians. TFO's local focus includes *Panorama and FranCœur,* the first Franco-Ontarian soap opera.

TVA (CHOT)

www.chot.ca

Montreal-based TVA television station showcases a broad range of entertainment and information based-shows.

TV5

www.tv5.org

Launched in 1989, TV5 is the only international French television station.

Programs vary from news to entertainment and movies from France, Quebec, Switzerland, Belgium, the Antilles and many French-speaking nations in Africa.

French Cultural Events in Toronto

Alliance française de Toronto

www.alliance-francaise.ca

Alliance française de Toronto's web site has a full page detailing Toronto's best French cultural and entertainment happenings.

Consulate General of France in Toronto

www.consulfrance-toronto.org

The Consulate General of France in Toronto's 'Cultural Highlights' section outlines all the city's upcoming French events.

Centre Francophone du Toronto Métropolitain

20 Lower Spadina Avenue (South of Front Street) ☎ 416 203-1220

Monday–Friday 8:30–4:30

Subway: UNION + streetcar

www.centrefranco.org

Visit Centre francophone du Toronto Métropolitain's *calendrier des évènement* (calendar of events) page to find out what's happening around the city. Note: this site is only in French.

Radio-Canada

www.radio-canada.ca/regions/ontario

This French-only site features a calendar of events put together by Claudette Gravel, host of *Enfin samedi.*

Did you know?

1. In between special exhibits, the ROM's general admission prices generally drop by about half. This is the perfect time to visit the permanent and curated exhibits.
2. Every Friday, the ROM offers free admission to the permanent and curated exhibits and a reduction on the price of special exhibits.
3. The ROM's web site (www.rom.on.ca) is available in French by selecting the button at the top of the home page – a great way to keep abreast of new and upcoming exhibits!
4. The ROM's information line offers the option to speak to a representative who can answer your questions in French.
5. The ROM's staff includes members who are bilingual, so you can always be assured of service in French.

Toronto-Franco

☎ 416 929-3769

www.toronto-franco.com

Finally – a web-based portal for Toronto's Francophone community! Since December 2003, the innovators at Toronto-Franco have created a convenient way for Francophones living in the city to access the information they

Did you know?

Radio-Canada, TV5 and TVA regularly feature a variety of French films. Consult your television guide for showtimes.

need, including local and international news stories, community service announcements and cultural information. Francophiles, take note – a full English version of this portal is also available. Although Toronto-Franco is a separate entity from *The French Side of Toronto* (www.franco-toronto.ca), the two organizations are accessible from each other's web sites through a link exchange.

Evening Entertainment & Social Gatherings

Franco Fun Wednesdays

☎ 416 596-8437

Jacques Charette, Coordinator
jacques.charette@sympatico.ca

This is an ideal opportunity for newcomers to Toronto to network and make new friends. Every Wednesday at 6 p.m., Francophones and Francophiles gather for drinks, laughter and conversation at a central Toronto bar or coffee house. For now, the meeting ground is The Bedford Academy pub (36 Prince Arthur Avenue, Bloor Street/Avenue Road area).

Franco Fun Dinners

☎ 416 596-8437

Jacques Charette, Coordinator
jacques.charette@sympatico.ca

One Thursday a month, Franco Fun Dinners holds a French evening at a local restaurant. This is a perfect way to both discover new restaurants and meet new faces. Prices for the meals are usually in the $25 range (including tax and tip), including the most anticipated event of the year – an annual lobster dinner in June!

Francophonique

☎ 416 763-8535

www.francophonique.com
info@francophonique.com

A networking system for French-speaking individuals in Toronto, Francophonique organizes many fun-filled brunches and ultra-cool social evenings. These events are also a great forum for Anglophones to meet Franco-Torontonians and practice *la langue de l'amour.*

Tam Tam Cyber Café

86 Nassau Street (inside Kensington Market) ☎ 416 603-0007

Subway: SPADINA + streetcar;
QUEEN'S PARK + streetcar

Just say *bonjour* as you walk in the door! A branch of the Centre des Jeunes Francophones de Toronto, Tam Tam Cyber Café opened its doors in March 2004. Like the area and its residents, the atmosphere here is very trendy and multicultural, but also very welcoming. The attentive staff will help you with whatever you need. Located few steps away from a youth hostel popular with French globetrotters, Tam Tam Cyber Café offers Internet access, photocopier and fax services at competitive prices.

Every Saturday, there is a French-style breakfast including baguettes and croissants. On weekdays, drop by for animated discussions with guest speakers, live music, art exhibits and more.

Zazou

315 King Street West (corner of John Street) ☎ 416 591-8600 or 416 591-3600

5 p.m. until the last customer has left

Subway: ST ANDREW

www.zazoulounge.com

Part of the Marcel's Bistro and Le Saint Tropez family, Zazou is a chic and sophisticated lounge that welcomes thirtysomething and fortysomething crowds in search of an oasis to unwind after a long day at the office. If you're looking for a comfortable setting, cool music and décor that lends itself to total relaxation, then drop by Zazou's for a drink.

Cultural Associations

Association France – Canada

☎ 416 485-5044

nadmoal@msn.com

Since 1948, Association France – Canada has promoted interaction between Canadians and new French immigrants. The organization sponsors numerous social activities including dinners, dancing, sporting events and Bastille Day celebrations. The annual membership fee is $25.

Association Morocaine de Toronto

☎ 416 494-7601

www.amdt.ca
martor@istar.ca

Another colourful aspect of French culture can be seen through the growing influence of the Moroccan community in Toronto. L'Association Marocaine de Toronto au Canada (The Moroccan Association of Toronto) is the umbrella under which approximately 350 members of this vibrant community gather for a variety of cultural, social and religious activities. This non-political association promotes and defends the interest of Moroccans living in Toronto, while recognizing and respecting ancestral traditions. It also advises and informs new Moroccan immigrants about the best ways to integrate and adapt to their new life.

Centre des Jeunes Francophones de Toronto

22 College Street, Suite 202
☎ 416 934-0588

Subway: COLLEGE

www.centredesjeunes.org

Born from the fusion of Regroupement des Jeunes Filles Francophones and Groupe Jeunesse Francophone de Toronto, the Centre des Jeunes Francophones de Toronto was founded in 1993 by a group of young women committed to improving their living conditions, and is recognized as a leading organization in Ontario's Francophone community. The Centre responds to the needs of young Francophones (ages 16 to 30) from diverse cultural background in the Greater Toronto Area. It offers a large variety of programs for Francophone youths to develop new skills, using a culturally-sensitive approach. Services include mentorship programs, internships (both local and international), counselling for new female immigrants who are victims of violence and a new cyber café in the heart of Kensington Market.

Club Richelieu de Toronto

☎ 416 299-3923

www.richelieu.org

Founded in Ottawa in 1944, Club Richelieu promotes French culture via social, artistic and humanitarian activities, including monthly dinners, which give members the opportunity to interact. An annual membership fee allows the club to maintain its charitable and educational mandates.

Le Cercle de l'Amitié Canadien de Toronto

1780 Meadowvale Road, Mississauga
☎ 905 542-1844

www.cercleamitie.ca
Liette Lacroix, Coordinator

Le Cercle de l'Amitié Canadien de Toronto (the Canadian Friendship Circle of Toronto) is a community and cultural centre that promotes French in Peel Region through a variety of monthly activites for children and adults alike. Most of its 400 members live in Mississauga and Brampton; however, this is not a prerequisite as many members are from other parts of the Greater Toronto Area.

Business Associations

Association des femmes d'affaires francophones

www.afafcanada.com

Angèle Desgagné, Ontario President
☎ 905 469-1889

Rita Holmes, Coordinator
☎ 905 822-3677

L'Association des femmes d'affaires francophones (Association of French-speaking Businesswomen) is a non-profit group that provides businesswomen across the Greater Toronto Area with a forum to network. Founded in 1983, the association has approximately 100 members divided into three groups – Toronto, Halton-Peel and Welland Regions.

Association Francophones des Entrepreneurs et des Professionnels (AFEP)

☎ 905 891-5989

www.afepcanada.com
Valérie Cité, Coordinator

L'Association Francophone des Entrepreneurs et des Professionnels (Association of French-speaking Entrepreneurs and Professionals) offers members a forum to exchange and influence the economic development of Francophones living in the Greater Toronto Area.

Club Canadien de Toronto

☎ 416 243-0662
www.clubcanadien.ca
Jean Martin, Coordinator

The members of the prestigious Club Canadien de Toronto include many high-profile Francophones in the private and public sectors across the Greater Toronto Area, including finance, politics and the arts. Founded in 1986, the club holds monthly lunch conferences featuring guest speakers presenting topics that are currently at the centre of national or international affairs.

French Chamber of Commerce of Canada (Toronto)

20 Queen Street West, Suite 2006
☎ 416 205-9820
ccfe@bellnet.ca
www.ccife.org/canada

The French Chamber of Commerce mandates economic development between France and Ontario. Members are part of an influential network of French-speaking businesspeople in Ontario and Canada. Every month, events like breakfast-and-learn sessions, conferences and guided tours of companies give members the opportunity to increase their business acumen and networking skills. The French Chamber of Commerce also sponsors many social events, such as cocktails, tennis tournaments, wine sampling and an annual ball.

Regroupement des gens d'Affaires Africains Canadiens

☎ 416 781-9780, extension 221
Rose Cathy Handy, President

Although there are many Francophone business associations in the Greater Toronto Area, none reflected the needs of the African community – until now. The creation of the Regroupement de gens d'Affaires Africains Canadiens (Group of Franco-African Canadian Business People) unites business people of African origin, giving them a voice and a forum to celebrate their achievements. It is an ideal setting to help Franco-African Canadians accelerate their economic development in their new homeland.

Artists Associations

BRAVO – Bureau des Regroupements des Artistes Visuels de l'Ontario

☎ 819 457-2502
www.francoculture.ca/bravo
bravo@franco.ca

The *raison d'être* for this group of 130 visual artists is to defend the individual and collective interests of Francophone artists living in Ontario. To accomplish this, BRAVO offers representation, promotion, distribution and marketing services for artwork created by its members. Another of the group's mandates is to create a communication network to overcome the isolation faced by so many independent Francophone artists.

the french side of toronto by neighbourhood

NEIGHBOURHOOD	BREADS, PÂTISSERIES & FRENCH SWEETS	CHOCOLATIERS	CHEESE SHOPS & CRÈME FRAÎCHE	DRIED MEATS, PÂTÉS & TERRINES
THE BEACH, EAST TORONTO & THE DANFORTH	Bonjour Brioche Zane	Belgian Chocolate Shop Sun Valley Fruits & Grocery	Alex Farm Sun Valley Fruits & Grocery	Alex Farm Meat on the Beach
BLOOR WEST VILLAGE & WEST TORONTO	Cheese Boutique Max Market Pâtisserie Saint Honoré	Bernard Callebaut Cheese Boutique Max Market	Cheese Boutique Max Market	Cheese Boutique Max Market Village Butcher
DOWNTOWN	Balzac's Coffee House Daniel et Daniel Mercatto St. Urbain Bagel Bakery Scheffler's	Chocolates & Creams Daniel et Daniel Domino Foods Mercatto Scheffler's The Bay The Pie Shoppe	Alex Farm Chris' Cheesemongers Olympic Cheese Mart Scheffler's	Alex Farm Caviar Direct Chris' Cheesemongers Cumbrae's Daniel et Daniel Olympic Cheese Mart Scheffler's White House Meats
KENSINGTON, BALDWIN ST. & COLLEGE ST.	Casa Açareana Magnolia	Chocolate Addict	Cheese Magic Global Cheese Mendel's Creamery	Global Cheese Mendel's Creamery
ENTERTAINMENT DISTRICT, KING ST. WEST & QUEEN ST. WEST	Clafouti Le Gourmand Senses	Clafouti Dufflet Pastries J.S. Bonbons Le Gourmand Senses		
AVENUE RD., DAVENPORT RD. & DUPONT AVE.	Dinah's Cupboard Holt Renfrew Pusateri's Whole Foods	Dinah's Cupboard Holt Renfrew J.S. Bonbons Leonidas Simone Marie Belgian Chocolate Teuscher Whole Foods	Alex Farm Dinah's Cupboard Pusateri's Whole Foods	Alex Farm Dinah's Cupboard Pusateri's Whole Foods

BUTCHERS	FISHMONGERS & OYSTER SPECIALISTS	SPICES	OTHER FRENCH SPECIALTIES	RESTAURANTS
Meat on the Beach Royal Beef	Bill's Lobsters	Strictly Bulk	Alex Farm Bonjour Brioche Zane	Bonjour Brioche Café Brussels
Bloor Meat Market Village Butcher	Big Fish Market Snappers Fish Market Village Butcher	Strictly Bulk	Cheese Boutique Max Market Village Butcher Pâtisserie Saint Honoré	La Petite France Merlot
Brown Brothers Meats Cumbrae's Di Liso's Fine Meats Greco Meat Packers Manos Meats Nick's Wholesale Meats Scheffler's St. Lawrence Upper Cut White House Meats	Caviar Direct Domenic's Fish Market Domino Foods Mike's Fish Market Seafront Fish Market	Domino Foods	Alex Farm Chris' Cheesemongers Daniel et Daniel Domino Foods Mercatto Scheffler's Great Cooks Olympic Cheese Mart	Agora Bistro 990 Bloor Street Diner Bouchon Café Moroc/ The Sultan's Tent Café Nicole Crêpes à Gogo Le Papillon Matignon Midi Bistro Provence
European Quality Meats Grace Meat Market	Coral Sea Fish Shop Global Cheese Mendel's Creamery Medeiros Fish Market New Seaway Sea Kings Seven Seas Fish	Casa Açareana House of Spices Perola's		Bodega Brasserie Aix Café Margaux Gamelle La Palette
	Oyster Boy Rodney's Oyster House		Clafouti Le Gourmand	Bloor Street Diner Crêpes Café Épicure Café Le Saint Tropez Le Sélect Bistro Marcel's Bistro Restaurant Jules
Pusateri's	Pusateri's		Alex Farm Dinah's Cupboard Holt Renfrew Pusateri's Sérénité Whole Foods	Arlequin Holt's Café Jacques Bistro La Brasserie.ca Le Paradis Le Trou Normand

the french side of toronto by neighbourhood

NEIGHBOURHOOD	BREADS, PÂTISSERIES & FRENCH SWEETS	CHOCOLATIERS	CHEESE SHOPS & CRÈME FRAÎCHE	DRIED MEATS, PÂTÉS & TERRINES
MIDTOWN & SUMMERHILL	All the Best Fine Foods Le Petit Gourmet Pain Perdu Patachou St. Urbain Bagel Bakery The Bagel House	Pain Perdu Sobey's	Alex Farm All the Best Fine Foods Sobey's	Alex Farm All the Best Fine Foods Patachou Sobey's The Butchers
BAYVIEW & MOUNT PLEASANT	Comptoir de Célestin La Cigogne Rahier The Bagel House	La Cigogne Rahier The Chocolate Messenger	Alex Farm	Alex Farm White House Meats
UPTOWN	Ace Bakery Pusateri's Senses	Pusateri's Senses Swiss-Master Chocolatier	Pusateri's	Pusateri's The Butcher Block Café
GREATER TORONTO	Arz Bakery Brandt Meat Packers Supermarket Pâtisserie d'Or St. Urbain Bagel Bakery	Arz Bakery Bernard Callebaut Brandt Meat Packers Supermarket Pâtisserie d'Or Truffle Treasures	Olympic Cheese Mart Quality Cheese	Brandt Meat Packers Supermarket Olympic Cheese Mart

BUTCHERS	FISHMONGERS & OYSTER SPECIALISTS	SPICES	OTHER FRENCH SPECIALTIES	RESTAURANTS
Nicola's Choice Meats Olliffe Sobey's The Butchers	Avenue Seafood Pisces Gourmet		Alex Farm All the Best Fine Foods Harvest Wagon Pain Perdu Patachou	Avant-Goût Boujadi Le Petit Gourmet Pastis Express Quartier
White House Meats	Caviar Centre Diana's Seafood Highland Farms Newport Fish Importers Pusateri's		Alex Farm Rahier	Célestin La Cigogne
Highland Farms Pusateri's The Butcher Block Café	Brandt Meat Packers Supermarket Lobster Island		Pusateri's	Auberge du Pommier Bloor Street Diner Chez Laurent La Maison Benoît Le Montmartre L'Escargot Bistro Monitz Pourquoi Pas
Brandt Meat Packers Supermarket European Quality Meats			Arz Bakery Brandt Meat Packers Supermarket Olympic Cheese Mart Pâtisserie d'Or Petit Gâteau	Bistro 1603 Bistro Matisse

index

A

À Bon Verre Bonne Table 122
Academy of Artisans 118
Ace Bakery 14
AGORA 90
Alex Farm Products 44, 50, 54, 71
Alliance Française de Toronto 123, 131
All the Best Fine Foods 14, 44, 50, 54, 71
Amazon.ca 122, 125, 128
Archambault.ca 122, 125, 128
Arlequin 90
Art Gallery of Ontario (AGO) 129
Arz Bakery 15, 30, 71
Association des femmes d'affaires francophones 134
Association France-Canada 133
Association Marocaine de Toronto 133
Association francophone des entrepreneurs et des professionnels (AFEP) 134
Auberge du Pommier 105
Avant-Goût 90
Avenue Seafood 62

B

BRAVO Bureau des regroupements des artistes visuels de l'Ontario 135
Balzac's Coffee House 15
Belgian Chocolate Shop 30
Big Fish Market 62
Bill's Lobster 62
Bistro 1603 105
Bistro 990 91
Bistro Matisse 92
Bloor Meat Market 52
Bloor Street Diner & Bistros 92, 107
Bodega 105 , 107
Bonjour Brioche 16, 71, 107
Bouchon 106
Boujadi 92
Brandt Meat Packers Supermarket 52, 54, 62, 72
Brasserie Aix 93, 107
Brown Brothers Meats 52

C

Café Brussels 106
Café la Gaffe 96
Café Margaux 93
Café Moroc 94
Café Nicole 94
Calphalon Culinary Center 118
Carlton Cinéma 126
Casa Açareana 16, 83
Caviar Centre 62
Caviar Direct 54, 62
Célestin 108
Centre des Jeunes Francophones de Toronto 133
Centre francophone du Toronto Métropolitain 131
Cheese Boutique 31, 50, 45, 77
Cheese Magic 45, 54
Chez Laurent 95
Chocolate Addict 31
Chocolates & Creams 31
Chocolates by Bernard Callebaut 31
Chris' Cheesemongers 45, 50, 54, 77
Ciné jeudi 126
Cinéfranco 126
Cinémathèque Ontario 126
Clafouti 16, 32, 72
Club canadien de Toronto 134
Club Richelieu de Toronto 134
Cook Gourmet 118
Cooking at the Harvest Kitchen 118
Coopérative radiophonique de Toronto – 105.1 FM 130
Comptoir de Célestin 18
Consulate General of France in Toronto 131
Coral Sea Fish Shop 64
Crêpes À Gogo 95
Crêpes Café 96
Cumberland Cinéma 126
Cumbrae's Naturally Raised Fine Meats 52, 54

D

Daniel et Daniel – Food Shop 19, 33, 54, 77
Di Liso's Fine Meats 53
Diana's Seafood 63, 77
Dinah's Cupboard 19, 46, 54
Dish Cooking Studio 118
Domenic's Fish Market 63, 77
Domino Foods 63, 83

E

Épicure Café 96, 107
European Quality Meats & Sausages 53

F

Franco Fun Wednesdays 132
Franco Fun Dinners 132
Francophonique 132
Fred's Bakery 19
French Chamber of Commerce of Canada (Toronto) 135

G

Glendon Gallery 129
Gamelle 108
George Brown College 118
Give it a Stir 119
Global Cheese 46, 54, 63
Grace Meat Markets 53
Great Cooks 78, 119
Greco Meat Packers Ltd. 53

H

Harvest Wagon 78
Highland Farms 53, 64, 70
HMV 125
Holt Renfrew – Epicure Shop 20, 33, 78
Holt's Café 97
House of Spices 83

I

Indigo-Chapters 122

J

J. S. Bonbons 33, 119
Jacques Bistro du Parc 97, 107
John & King Hot Dog Stand 103

K

K.I.S. Global Flavors 78
Kensington Market 70

L

LCBO 119
L'escargot Bistro 98
L'Express 122
La Brasserie.ca 99
La Cigogne 20, 34, 107
La Maison Benoît 99
La Maison de la Presse Internationale 123
La Maison du Chocolat 34
La Palette 99, 107
La Petite France 99
Le Cercle de l'Amitié Canadien de Toronto 134
Le Cordon Bleu Paris (Ottawa) 120
Le Gourmand 22, 34, 79
Le Métropolitain 122
Le Montmartre 113
Le Papillon 100
Le Paradis 100
Le Petit Gourmet 22, 100
Le Saint Tropez 101
Le Sélect Bistro 101, 107
Le Trou Normand 113
Leonidas 34
Librairie Champlain 123, 125, 128
Loblaws 46, 79, 120
Lobster Island 64

M

Magnolia Fine Foods 22
Manos Meats 56
Marcel's Bistro 114
Matignon 114
Max Market 46, 50, 54, 79
Meat on the Beach 55, 56
Medeiros Fish Market 64
Mendel's Creamery n' Appetizer 46, 55, 64
Mercatto 22, 80
Merlot 101
Midi Bistro 102
Mike's Fish Market 65
Monitz 102

N

New Seaway 64
Newport Fish Importers & Wholesalers 65
Nick's Wholesale Meats & Delicatessen 56
Nicola's Choice Meats 56

O

Olliffe 56
Olympic Cheese Mart 47, 50, 55, 80
Osler Fish Warehouse 65
Oyster Boy 65

P

Pain Perdu 23, 35, 80
Pastis Express 115
Patachou 23, 55, 80
Pâtisserie d'Or 24, 35, 81
Pâtisserie Saint Honoré 25, 81
Perola's 83
Petit Gâteau 81
Pisces Gourmet 65
Pourquoi Pas 103
Presse Internationale magazines super stores 124
Provence 107, 115
Pusateri's Fine Foods 25, 35, 47, 50, 55, 57, 66, 82

Q

Qualifirst Foods 82
Quality Cheese 48, 82
Quartier 103
Québec Loisirs 124, 125, 128
Queen Video 127

index

R

Radio-Canada – 860 AM 130, 131
Rahier 25, 82
RDI – Réseau d'information 130
Regroupement des gens d'affaires africains canadiens 135
Renaud-Bray 124, 125, 128
Restaurant Jules 104
Revue Video 127
Richmond Hill Culinary Arts Centre 120
Rodney's Oyster House 66
Royal Beef 57
Royal Ontario Museum (ROM) 129

S

St. Lawrence Market 70
St. Lawrence Upper Cut 57
St. Urbain Bagel Bakery 26
Salon du Livre de Toronto 124
Sam the Record Man 125, 128
Sea Kings 64
Seafront Fish Market 66
Senses 26, 35
Sérénité 84
Seven Seas Fish 64
Scheffler's Delicatessen & Cheese 48, 50, 55, 58, 82
Simone Marie Belgian Chocolate 36
Snappers Fish Market 66
Sobey's 48, 50, 55, 58
SRC – Société Radio-Canada 130
Strewn Winery 120
Strictly Bulk 83
Sun Valley Fruits & Grocery 49, 50
Suspect Video 127
Swiss-Master Chocolatier 36

T

TFO 129, 130
TV5 130
TVA (CHOT) 130
Taloua 124
Tam Tam Cyber Café 132
Teuscher Chocolates 36
The Bagel House 27
The Butcher Block Café 55, 58
The Butchers 55, 58
The Chocolate Messenger 41
The Cookworks 120
The Film Reference Library 124, 127
The Pie Shoppe 41
The Sultan's Tent 115
Théâtre français de Toronto 130
Théâtre La Tangente 130
Toronto-Franco 131
Toronto International Film Festival 126
Truffle Treasures 42

V

Village Butcher 55, 58, 66, 84
Very Video 127

W

White House Meats 55, 58
Whole Foods Market 27, 42, 49, 50, 55, 85

Z

Zane Pâtisserie & Boulangerie 28, 85
Zazou 133

Although we've come to the end of our journey, we hope you have enjoyed discovering the best spots in Toronto for French food and culture. We mostly hope you'll take it upon yourself to discover more of *The French Side of Toronto!*

Au revoir et à bientôt!

If you have any comments regarding the information in the guide, or would like to suggest any French merchants or organizations for a future edition, please feel free to contact us at: **contact@franco-toronto.ca**

Don't forget to visit **www.franco-toronto.ca** on a regular basis to keep up with the latest news on trips to France, as well as French food, wine and culture.

ORDER FORM

The French Side of Toronto • contact@franco-toronto.ca

☐ FRANCOPHONE ☐ ANGLOPHONE

☐ MR. ☐ MRS. ☐ MISS ☐ MS

NAME

ADDRESS

CITY POSTAL CODE

( )

TELEPHONE E-MAIL

QUANTITY ORDERED – CANADA:

_________ book(s) at $19.95 CDN/each = $ _______ CDN

Shipping costs for direct mailing: $4 CND per book x _____ copies = $ _______ CDN

7% GST = $ _______ CDN

TOTAL = $ _______ CDN

QUANTITY ORDERED – INTERNATIONAL & U.S.:

_________ book(s) at $14.95 USD/each = $ _______ USD

Shipping costs for direct mailing (INT'L): $11 USD per book x _____ copies = $ _______ USD

Shipping costs for direct mailing (U.S.): $6 USD per book x _____ copies = $ _______ USD

TOTAL = $ _______ USD

We are happy to offer discounts on quantities of 10 and up. Please e-mail us at **contact@franco-toronto.ca** to find out more about our discounts and shipping cost on larger orders.

Please send your completed order form and cheque, payable to the order of *Franco Toronto*, to: Franco Toronto
#61-494 Avenue Road
Toronto, ON CANADA M4V 2J5

Would you like to be on our mailing list?

☐ Please contact me via e–mail for future updates.

☐ I do not wish to be contacted in the future

franco **toronto**

Don't forget to visit our web site to download your FREE e-book Glossary of French Food *at* **www.franco-toronto.ca**

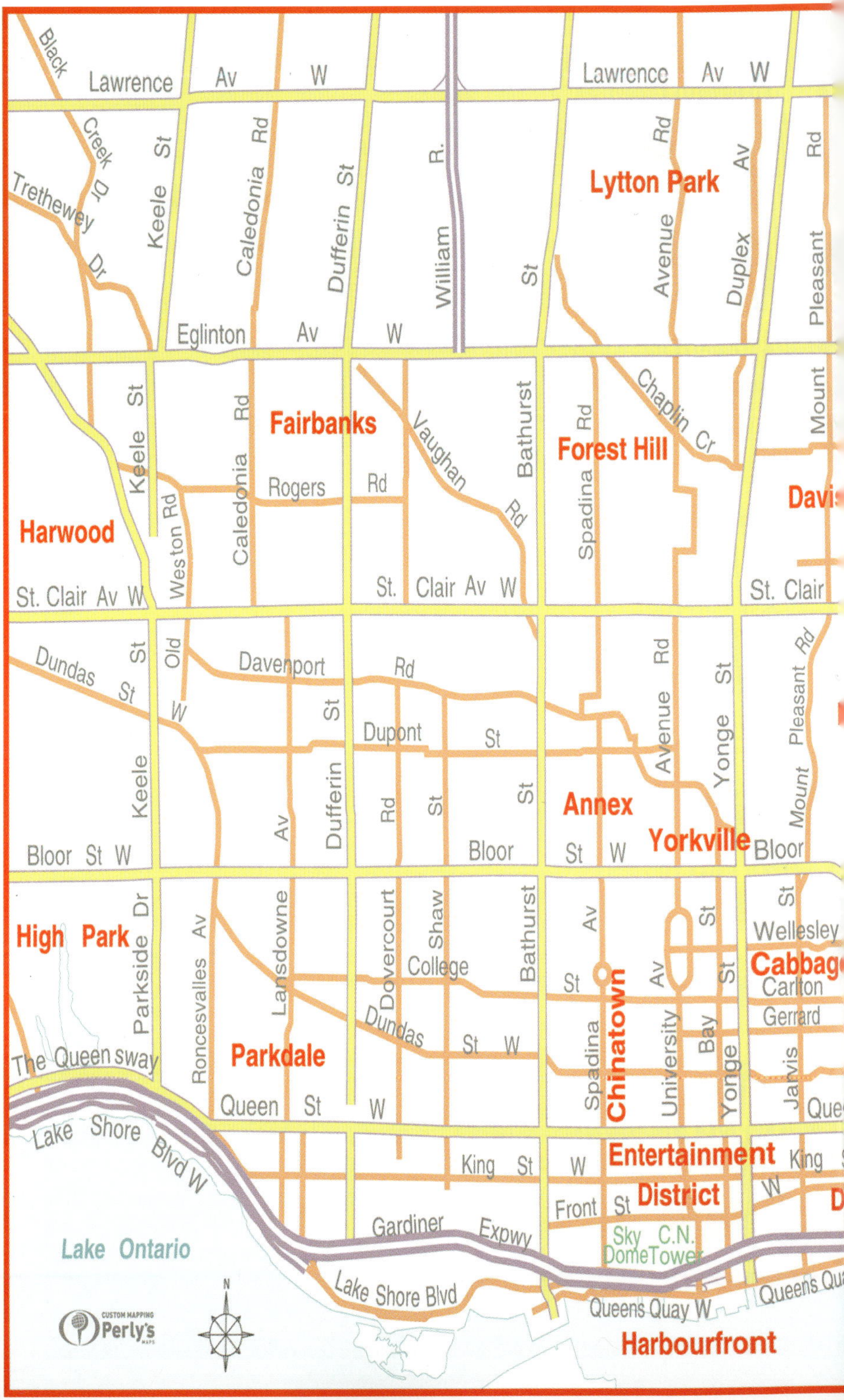

Lawrence Av W
Black Creek Dr
Trethewey Dr
Keele St
Caledonia Rd
Dufferin St
William R.
Bathurst St
Lytton Park
Avenue Rd
Duplex Av
Mount Pleasant Rd
Eglinton Av W
Fairbanks
Vaughan Rd
Forest Hill
Spadina Rd
Chaplin Cr
Davis
Rogers Rd
Weston Rd
Harwood
St. Clair Av W
Davenport Rd
Old Weston Rd
Dundas St W
Dupont St
Annex
Yorkville
Yonge St
Bloor St W
High Park
Parkside Dr
Roncesvalles Av
Lansdowne Av
Dovercourt Rd
Shaw St
College St
Chinatown
University Av
Bay St
Wellesley St
Cabbage
Carlton St
Gerrard
Jarvis St
Parkdale
The Queensway
Queen St W
Lake Shore Blvd W
King St W
Entertainment District
Front St
Gardiner Expwy
Sky Dome
C.N. Tower
Lake Ontario
Lake Shore Blvd
Queens Quay W
Harbourfront
N
CUSTOM MAPPING Perly's MAPS

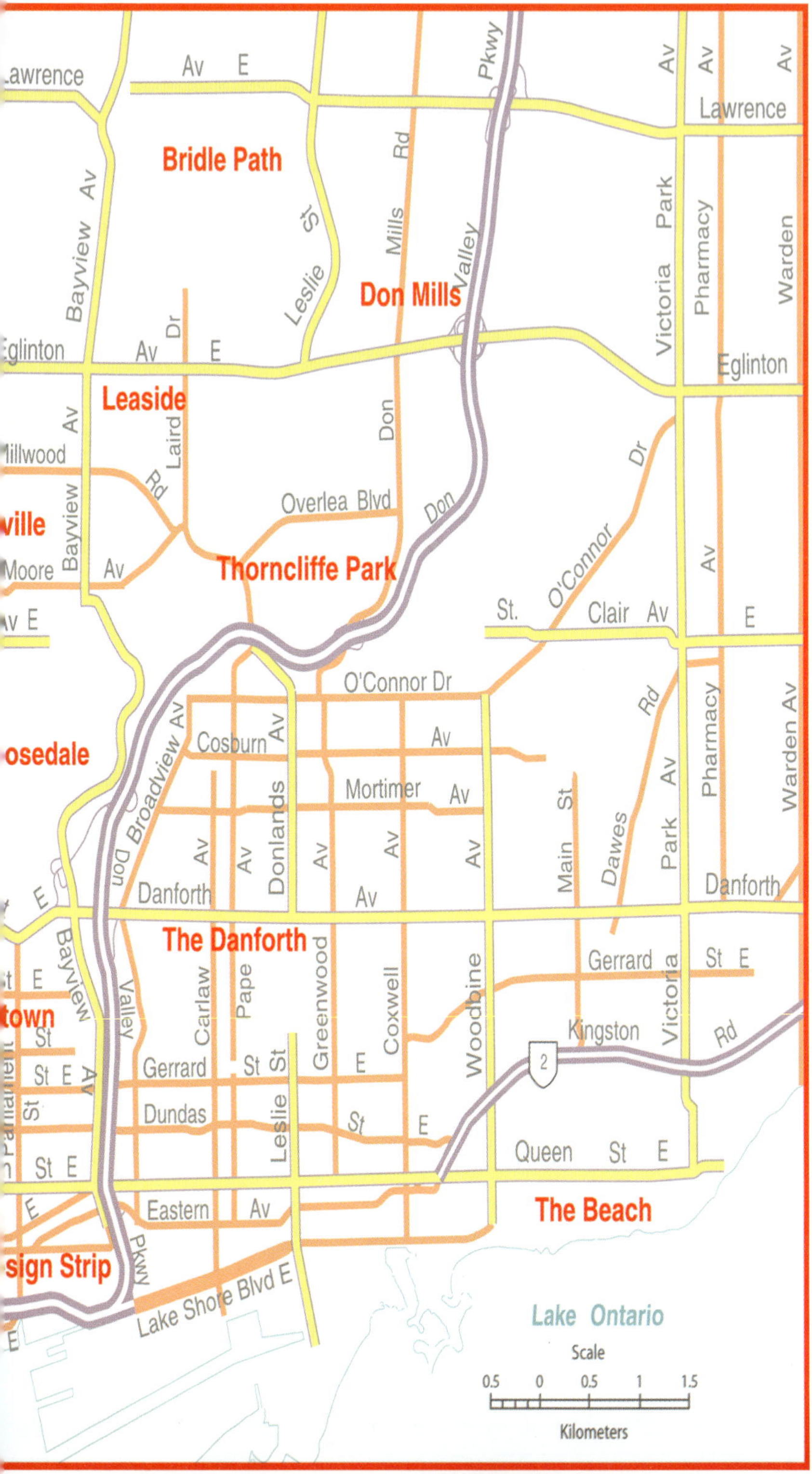
Bridle Path
Don Mills
Leaside
Thorncliffe Park
The Danforth
The Beach
Lake Ontario
Lawrence Av E
Eglinton Av E
Bayview Av
Leslie St
Don Mills Rd
Don Valley Pkwy
Victoria Park Av
Pharmacy Av
Warden Av
Laird Dr
Millwood Rd
Overlea Blvd
Moore Av
O'Connor Dr
St. Clair Av E
Cosburn Av
Mortimer Av
Broadview Av
Donlands Av
Danforth Av
Main St
Dawes Rd
Gerrard St E
Kingston Rd
Woodbine Av
Coxwell Av
Greenwood Av
Pape Av
Carlaw Av
Dundas St E
Queen St E
Eastern Av
Lake Shore Blvd E
Scale
0.5
0
0.5
1
1.5
Kilometers

Guide touristique
L'Ontario en français
Édition 2004
En Ontario,
le français c'est dans
notre nature.
Destination NORD de l'Ontario
1 877 OUI-6673 (684-6673)
www.destinationnord.com
ONTARIO
Destination NORD de l'Ontario
Pour recevoir votre guide,
faites le 1 877 684-6673
ou visitez le
www.destinationnord.com

vivre en français à toronto

Le guide incontournable sur l'art de vivre
à la française à Toronto – édition 2004

*franco*toronto

LES ÉDITIONS FRANCO TORONTO MEDIA & PUBLISHING

ISBN : 0-9733020-1-1

Vivre en français à Toronto/The French Side of Toronto est une propriété de Franco Toronto Media & Publishing.

Les informations publiées sont correctes à l'heure où nous écrivons ces lignes, mais peuvent bien évidemment changer entre le passage de nos rédacteurs et la sortie de notre guide; il est donc recommandé de vérifier auprès des établissements lorsqu'une exactitude totale est exigée. Nous prions nos lecteurs de nous excuser pour les erreurs qu'ils pourraient trouver dans les rubriques pratiques de ce guide.

Maison d'édition :	Franco Toronto Media & Publishing
Commandes :	contact@franco-toronto.ca
Espace publicitaire :	pub@franco-toronto.ca
Commande en gros :	Toutes les corporations, organisations, associations, institutions pédagogiques et tous les organismes à but non lucratif peuvent bénéficier d'une remise.
Imprimé au Canada par :	AGMV Marquis
Cartes de Toronto :	Perly's Maps, www.perlys.com

Consultez notre site Internet **www.franco-toronto.ca**

table des matières

Témoignages 9

Remerciements 10

L'équipe de *Vivre en français à Toronto* 10

Introduction 11

Aventures gastronomiques

OÙ FAIRE SES EMPLETTES

Pains, pâtisseries et sucreries 13

Chocolats 33

Fromages et crème fraîche 45

Viande, charcuterie, foie gras et terrines 55

Poissonneries et spécialistes des huîtres 65

Autres spécialités françaises 75

OÙ SE RESTAURER

Bistros 89

Repas gastronomiques 108

Brunchs 114

EN CUISINE AVEC LA FRANCOPHONIE

Écoles de cuisine 121

Aventures culturelles

INFORMATION ET DIVERTISSEMENT

Journaux 126

Livres et magazines 126

Musique 129

Films et vidéos 130

Beaux-arts 134

Théâtres 135

Radio et télévision 135

SE RETROUVER ENTRE FRANCOPHONES

Événements culturels francophones à Toronto 136

Soirées et rencontres branchées 137

Associations culturelles et sociales 138

Associations de professionnels 139

Associations pour les artistes 140

AUTRES RESSOURCES

Les bonnes adresses par quartier 142

Index 146

Voici quelques témoignages de nos lecteurs :

« *Si vous débarquez à Toronto armé d'un* Lonely Planet *(décidément trop lourd) et démuni des traditionnels bons plans du* Guide du routard *(oublié dans un café à l'aéroport de Roissy…), vous devriez comme moi apprécier à sa juste valeur* Vivre en français à Toronto *!* »

— CAMILLE LOMBARDOT, UNE BRETONNE (DE PLUS) À TORONTO

« Vivre en français à Toronto *est la clef magique qui livre les secrets inespérés d'un Toronto épicurien aux offrandes gastronomes et artistiques multiples. C'est un trésor de petites et grandes adresses pour tous ceux qui aiment chiner en français dans les recoins de Toronto. Un guide qui respire le savoir et le plaisir ! Un guide qui inspire le désir de la découverte !* »

— MARCELLE LEAN, CINÉFRANCO, TORONTO

« *Quelle surprise de découvrir que Toronto a tant de riches dimensions.* Vivre en français à Toronto *met bien en valeur l'importance de la gastronomie et de la culture française en Amérique du Nord. Voici enfin un guide en français qui m'invite vraiment à vouloir connaître cette ville cosmopolite. Bien joué !* »

— DÉSIRÉ ALAIN, PARIS

« *Un Toronto que je ne connaissais pas ! Merci* Vivre en français à Toronto *! Voilà enfin un guide unique et vraiment complet ! Trois fois bravo !* »

— PHILIPPE AUBRY, MONTRÉAL

« Vivre en français à Toronto *est une source sans pareille ! Quel travail ! Bravo !* »

— NANCY GIGUÈRE, MONTRÉAL

remerciements

Les personnes suivantes ont joué des rôles clés dans la poursuite de notre rêve et de notre vision. Nous les remercions pour leurs encouragements, conseils et efforts :

Dominic Canazzi, Thomas Chanzy, Alexandre Colliex, Tony di Pede, Randy Garrett, Marcelle Lean, Dan Mozersky, Lulu Phongmany, Christopher Tuner, Darren Weeks, Dan White.

Nous tenons également à témoigner notre reconnaissance à tous nos amis et proches.

L'équipe de *Vivre en français à Toronto*

Rédactrice en chef : Krizia de Verdier

Traduction : Krizia de Verdier

Révision et rédaction texte anglais/site Internet anglais : Fionna Boyle

Révision supports promotionnels : Nicholas Palmer

Révision et rédaction texte français/site Internet français : Aude Lemoine

Directrice artistique : Debi De Santis

Recherche : Krizia de Verdier, Fionna Boyle, Mark De Shaw, Derek Lowe, Franck Nanguy, Nicholas Palmer, Lulu Phongmany, Franco Taverna et Hilda Toh

Vérification des données : Faith Gill

Responsable de la mise en page pour la publicité : Steve Jenkinson

Site Internet : Helios Lab Design

Conseiller en édition : Dan Mozersky

Publicité : pub@franco-toronto.ca

Maison d'édition : Franco Toronto Media & Publishing

Consultez notre site Internet **www.franco-toronto.ca**

Note : Afin de faciliter la lecture du présent texte, nous avons employé le masculin comme genre neutre pour désigner aussi bien nos lectrices que nos lecteurs.

introduction

L'énergie multiculturelle de Toronto est contagieuse. La richesse de cette ville cosmopolite est extraordinaire du fait de la coexistence de Canadiens d'origines ethniques diverses. Ce guide est un hommage à l'énergie culturelle française qui se dégage de plus en plus de notre ville.

Contrairement à plusieurs autres groupes culturels, les francophones ne sont pas regroupés dans un quartier en particulier, à Toronto. Les établissements francophones sont en effet éparpillés à travers la ville et les banlieues avoisinantes. Voilà ce qui explique la difficulté pour certains d'entre nous à retrouver l'essentiel de cette culture riche et complexe.

La francophonie se découvre à Toronto par l'intermédiaire de la gastronomie, du vin et de la culture. Certes, tous les établissements dans ce guide n'offriront pas de service en français. Notre but ne se limitait pas à cibler uniquement les établissements où l'on parle français. Nous voulions mettre à l'honneur les établissements qui célèbrent la culture française à Toronto. Nous cherchions à permettre aux francophiles et francophones de retrouver facilement certains éléments clés de la culture française ici même, dans leur nouvelle ville d'adoption.

La longue recherche requise par ce guide reste la partie la plus électrisante du processus de création. Encore une fois, nous avons adoré discuter avec des passionnés de la bonne chair et de la bonne culture, tant les propriétaires d'une des nombreuses adresses de ce guide que les lecteurs satisfaits.

Nous avons accumulé les calories sans nous plaindre afin de partager avec vous toutes les bonnes adresses pour faire des emplettes ainsi que tous les bistros et restos qui offrent un bon menu français. Nous n'étions que trop heureux de nous sacrifier pour nos lecteurs. Nous avons également eu la chance de rencontrer plusieurs Franco-Torontois lors des différentes soirées culturelles très branchées qui réunissent les francophones d'origines diverses et les francophiles qui se retrouvent régulièrement pour discuter et parfois débattre.

Vous remarquerez que nos mésaventures culturelles et gastronomiques ont été méticuleusement recueillies dans cette seconde édition du guide. Dans cette nouvelle édition, nous avons par ailleurs découvert plusieurs adresses situées dans le grand Toronto. Ainsi, les habitants de Mississauga, Etobicoke, Richmond Hill et Brampton auront eux aussi la chance de découvrir plusieurs bonnes adresses franco-torontoises.

Vous découvrirez également de nouvelles sections, très pratiques et quelquefois insolites. Vous verrez que nous avons réussi à dénicher des produits que l'on croyait jusqu'ici impossibles à trouver dans une ville anglophone.

Notre philosophie demeure intacte, *Vivre en français à Toronto* est un guide qui vous permettra d'avoir sous la main les adresses des meilleurs rendez-vous de la francophonie à Toronto. Certaines adresses sont franco-françaises, d'autres ont une note québécoise et d'autres encore sont tout simplement des joyaux bien d'ici qui sauront satisfaire toutes

les envies des Français, francophones et francophiles vivant à Toronto. Elles ont été récoltées dans un seul but : vivre et revivre des expériences gastronomiques et culturelles françaises.

Au plaisir !

Krizia de Verdier
Rédactrice en chef

où faire ses emplettes

pains, pâtisseries et sucreries

On peut croire, à tort, qu'un francophone ou francophile vivant dans une ville anglophone ne serait pas bien gâté lorsqu'il s'agit de se ravitailler en produits français et francophones. Après tout, comment fait-on pour être heureux quand on doit vivre sans bon pain, sans viennoiserie, sans pâtisserie, sans sucreries ni chocolat ? Mais nous, Torontois, sommes particulièrement chanceux puisque l'on n'a pas besoin d'apprendre à se priver de nos produits français, franco-européens et québécois préférés.

Cette section vous prouvera qu'il n'y a plus de raison d'attendre un voyage en France ou au Québec pour satisfaire vos envies gastronomiques françaises. Vous allez vite vous rendre compte que c'est à cette première section que vous aurez sans aucun doute le plus recours, puisqu'elle vous permettra de bien manger (chez vous) à la française, ici à Toronto.

Bonne chasse !

Ace Bakery

1 Hafis Road (au sud de Lawrence Avenue et Keele Street) ☎ (416) 241-3600 (bureau général); (416) 241-8433 (Café Ace)

Lundi à vendredi 10h – 16h, samedi 10h – 15h, fermé dimanche (Café Ace)

Métro : LAWRENCE WEST + le bus

www.acebakery.com

DU BON PAIN Depuis 1993, c'est l'une des baguettes les plus populaires de Toronto. La baguette Ace est tellement populaire que la compagnie d'aviation Air France en a fait sa baguette officielle sur ses vols Toronto/Paris. La baguette Ace est croustillante à l'extérieur et bien moelleuse à l'intérieur. Vous pouvez vous rendre à la source de fabrication même ou encore vous la procurer dans plus de 700 magasins, restaurants et hôtels au Canada (Ontario et Québec) et aux États-Unis (Michigan et New York). En plus de confectionner d'excellents épis de blé et baguettes, Ace excelle dans l'art de préparer du pain de seigle, du pain aux fruits et aux noix, du pain complet et de la fougasse. Pendant la saison des fêtes, Ace fait preuve de créativité et présente des pains en forme d'oursons et d'énormes pétales de fleurs pour les fêtes de Noël, ou encore de mignons petits lapins pour Pâques. Soyez assuré que vous aurez chez Ace l'embarras du choix et le choix avec embarras. Comment choisir parmi tant de bonnes choses ?

All the Best Fine Foods

1099 Yonge Street (près du métro SUMMERHILL) ☎ (416) 928-3330

Lundi à mercredi 8h30 – 18h30, jeudi et vendredi 8h30 – 19h, samedi 8h30 – 18h, dimanche 10h – 17h

Métro : SUMMERHILL

www.allthebestfinefoods.com

Le saviez-vous ?

La baguette est sans aucun doute le symbole culinaire français le plus facilement reconnu. La baguette fut créée à la demande des consommateurs français à la veille de la Première Guerre mondiale. Selon certains experts gastronomiques français, au début du siècle dernier, le consommateur français n'avait le choix qu'entre deux formats de pain : la miche ronde et le pain long. Contrairement à la baguette contemporaine, le pain long avait une mie dense et peu délicate. Tout comme la baguette d'aujourd'hui, la croûte était croustillante. La plupart des consommateurs aimaient la croûte, mais étaient un peu moins séduits par la mie. Les boulangers de l'époque s'appliquèrent à répondre aux attentes de leurs clients. Le résultat est ce que l'on connaît aujourd'hui : une longue baguette bien mince à la croûte croustillante et la mie affinée. Légende ou réalité ? Pour en savoir plus sur l'origine de la baguette et sur le pain en général, il vous faudra visiter le Musée de la boulangerie Ismseng et la Maison du blé et du pain à Echallens, en Suisse romande. En attendant, nous vous proposons plusieurs adresses locales pour déguster la baguette et bien d'autres pains savoureux.

DE BONNES PÂTISSERIES All the Best Fine Foods vend des croissants au beurre, des amandines, des pains au chocolat, des tortillons et des danoises au citron en provenance des meilleures pâtisseries françaises de la ville.

DU BON PAIN Le boulanger d'All the Best Fine Foods prépare une série de pains façon artisanale. Le pain au levain et la baguette un peu rustique ne sont que deux des spécialités savoureuses parmi lesquelles vous aurez le choix ici. All the Best Fine Foods vend aussi des bagels de St. Urbain Bagel Bakery.

Arz Bakery

1909 Lawrence Avenue East (entre Warden Avenue et Pharmacy Avenue)
☎ (416) 755-5084

Lundi à samedi 8h – 21h, dimanche 8h – 19h30, les jours fériés 8h – 17h (Arz Bakery ne ferme jamais ses portes)

Métro : LAWRENCE + le bus

www.arzbakery.com

DE BONNES PÂTISSERIES Sur la carte de visite de cette pâtisserie libanaise, on lit : *French Cakes and Mediterranean Pastries.* Disons que ce n'est pas de la publicité mensongère. Armand Boyadjian est le chef pâtissier et le frère du propriétaire, Jack Boyadjian. D'origine libanaise, mais de formation française, le chef pâtissier dirige un groupe de pâtissiers qui ont tous fait leurs classes en France. L'équipe d'Arz comprend même un diplômé de l'école culinaire Lenôtre. Cette introduction aura assez clairement dévoilé, nous l'espérons, la qualité de la sélection de pâtisseries que vous trouverez chez Arz. Outre une vitrine pleine de pâtisseries françaises plus tentantes les unes que les autres, vous découvrirez aussi une vitrine tape-à-l'œil remplie de baklavas de style libanais. L'effet visuel des baklavas étalés sur de larges plaques est spectaculaire. Vous pouvez choisir une pâtisserie pour clore un bon repas à la maison ou vous pouvez vous asseoir et accompagner cette gourmandise d'un café serré au sein du petit café annexé au magasin.

DES SUCRERIES Il y a une grande vitrine de biscuits de styles libanais et français chez Arz. Nous avons reçu plusieurs demandes de la part de lecteurs qui tenaient à se procurer des dragées à Toronto. Arz Bakery vend les fameuses petites amandes enrobées de sucre et importe différents parfums de dragées de France et d'Espagne, ainsi que du massepain (sucrerie à base de pâte d'amandes) et des pâtes de fruits de Paris.

Balzac's Coffee House

55 Mills Street (à l'intérieur du Distillery District) ☎ (416) 207-1709

Lundi à samedi 7h – 20h, dimanche 8h – 20h

Métro : KING + le tram; PAPE + le bus

www.thedistillerydistrict.com

DE BONNES PÂTISSERIES Balzac's Coffee House est avant tout un café situé au cœur du récemment accessible « Distillery District », dans le sud-est de la ville. Heureusement que les propriétaires ont fait appel à deux spécialistes de la viennoiserie française à Toronto pour nous offrir de quoi accompagner notre café sur place ou à emporter. Portant l'emblème français, on retrouve

Clafouti et Daniel et Daniel. La liste de viennoiseries de Clafouti a le goût de croissants au beurre et croissants salés, chaussons aux pommes, pains au chocolat et amandines. Le maître traiteur Daniel et Daniel propose ses croissants, amandines, pains au chocolat, croissants au fromage et danoises aux fruits. Les viennoiseries signées Daniel et Daniel ne sont vendues que le lundi.

Bonjour Brioche

812 Queen Street East (un peu à l'est de Broadview) ☎ (416) 406-1250

Fermé lundi, mardi à vendredi 8h – 17h, samedi 8h – 16h, dimanche 8h – 15h

Métro : QUEEN + le tram

DE BONNES PÂTISSERIES Dès qu'on met les pieds à l'intérieur de ce petit miracle gastronomique, on est accueilli par les parfums alléchants des différentes pâtisseries et viennoiseries. Croissants, brioches, croissants aux amandes et brioches au sucre sont au garde-à-vous. La vedette est sans aucun doute la brioche royale – une brioche fourrée de crème pâtissière parfumée au citron et aux myrtilles (bleuets) ou aux framboises. Bonjour Brioche est une excellente adresse pour déguster une bonne tarte au citron à la française. Vous ne serez pas déçu par le gâteau au chocolat maison, préparé sans farine. Pendant que vous y êtes, essayez donc la tarte aux poires et aux amandes. Inoubliable ! Pour agrémenter vos soirées entre amis, pour les occasions spéciales ou encore pour célébrer certaines fêtes religieuses, vous pouvez commander tartes, gâteaux ou autres délices préférées. Chaque pâtisserie venant de chez Bonjour Brioche saura parfaitement clore de façon raffinée un bon dîner ou une célébration à la maison.

DU BON PAIN Bonjour la baguette ! La recette maison est un secret bien gardé… Pour cause, la baguette de Bonjour Brioche fond dans la bouche. Ceux qui aiment leur baguette un peu moins croustillante seront servis. Un peu de beurre et de confiture, voilà un petit coin de paradis qu'on peut s'offrir régulièrement. La baguette de Bonjour Brioche possède même le pouvoir de convertir les personnes qui redoutent la consommation de glucides en amateurs invétérés. Nul ne résiste à cette bonne baguette. On peut aussi acheter du pain complet ou multigrains chez Bonjour Brioche. Le week-end, du pain aux olives et au romarin est également en vente. Bonjour Brioche a tout récemment ajouté une petite nouveauté à son menu : une fougasse.

DES SUCRERIES Bonjour Brioche propose une belle sélection de biscuits maison, dont certains sont vendus en sachet et d'autres à l'unité. Au choix : petits sablés, tuiles, biscuits à la noix de coco et palmiers. C'est idéal pour satisfaire vos petites fringales sur le pouce !

Casa Açareana

235 Augusta Avenue (dans le marché Kensington) ☎ (416) 593-9717

Lundi à samedi 8h30 – 18h30, fermé dimanche

Métro : SPADINA + le tram;
QUEEN'S PARK + le tram

DES SUCRERIES Parmi le grand choix de bonbons très prisés des Torontois, vous

À la recherche des sucreries franco-européennes à Toronto !

Les sucreries, on aime se les offrir tout le temps ! Pendant longtemps, on a cru qu'il était impossible de retrouver à Toronto certaines de nos sucreries françaises préférées. Eh bien, notre détermination a porté ses fruits, puisque nous avons trouvé une longue liste d'adresses nous permettant d'acheter nos goûters préférés, ici même, à Toronto.

Nous avons déniché les grandes marques de sucreries franco-européennes suivantes pour vous ravitailler : bonbons *Barnier,* bonbons *La Vie de la Vosgienne,* pastilles *Vichy,* cachous *Lajaunie,* bonbons *Anis de L'abbaye de Flavigny,* sucettes *Pierrot Gourmand,* nougats aux amandes *Chabert et Guillot,* réglisses *Haribo,* biscuits *Mère Poulard,* caramels *Carambar,* biscuits *l'Or,* madeleines *Gaillard,* pâte de fruits de Provence et gâteaux *Brossard.*

Où trouver les sucreries franco-européennes à Toronto

1. All the Best Fine Foods
2. Arz Bakery
3. Brandt Meat Packers Supermarket
4. Cheese Boutique
5. Clafouti
6. Comptoir de Célestin
7. Daniel et Daniel
8. Dinah's Cupboard
9. La Cigogne
10. Le Gourmand
11. Max Market
12. Mercatto
13. Pâtisserie d'Or
14. Rahier
15. Scheffler's Delicatessen & Cheese

trouverez sur une étagère, à l'arrière du comptoir de caisse, les fameuses dragées. Celles de Casa Açareana sont importées du Portugal.

Clafouti

915 Queen Street West (à l'est de Strachan Avenue, en face du parc Trinity Bellwoods)
☎ (416) 603-1935

Fermé lundi, mardi à samedi 8h – 18h, dimanche 9h – 17h

Métro : OSGOODE + le tram

DE BONNES PÂTISSERIES Clafouti a ouvert ses portes début 2003 lors d'un hiver torontois des plus rudes. Les propriétaires ne s'attendaient pas au succès retentissant de leur petite pâtisserie. Après moins de six mois d'activité, le croissant de Clafouti a réussi à décrocher la mention du meilleur croissant de Toronto que décerne le journal *NOW.* Eh bien, *NOW* a tout à fait raison : en matière de croissant, Clafouti triomphe ! Le chef pâtissier Boris Dosne est un génie créatif. Lorsque nous sommes passés goûter ses fameux croissants, la queue était tellement longue qu'elle allait jusqu'à la porte d'entrée et les visages des clients rayonnaient à l'idée de dévorer l'un de ces sublimes croissants. Cet engouement explique pourquoi les

croissants disparaissent très vite chez Clafouti. Passé 11h, il ne reste plus grand-chose. Dès que les employés de cette pâtisserie placent les délices tant convoitées dans les vitrines, elles s'envolent. Non seulement la qualité du croissant de Clafouti est irréprochable, mais son originalité est aussi déroutante. Jusqu'à présent, on n'avait encore jamais entendu parler d'un croissant à la figue ou d'un croissant à la cannelle et au sucre brun à Toronto. Ces deux nouveautés font partie des croissants les plus demandés. On trouve aussi des pains au chocolat et des pains aux raisins succulents. Les brioches aux abricots, à la cerise et à la crème pâtissière ne déçoivent guère non plus. Clafouti excelle dans l'art de préparer tartelettes aux fruits et autres desserts

Le saviez-vous ?

« Entre la baguette et le camembert, au panthéon des gloires supposées du patrimoine gastronomique français se trouve le croissant. » *Le Monde,* 2003. Comme c'est bien dit ! Les Français ont peut-être perfectionné le croissant, mais son origine n'a rien de français. Le croissant désigne un petit pain en pâte feuilletée, abaissée en triangle, roulée et incurvée en forme de croissant de lune. L'origine de cette viennoiserie remonte à l'époque de la guerre entre l'Autriche et la Turquie, au moment où les Turcs s'apprêtaient à assiéger Vienne, la capitale, en 1683. Une nuit, les boulangers de Vienne entendirent le bruit des ennemis dans les sous-sols de leurs cuisines et ils donnèrent l'alarme, repoussant ainsi l'assaut ennemi. Les Ottomans furent vaincus grâce aux 25 000 hommes envoyés en renfort par Jean III Sobieski, roi de Pologne. Pour récompenser ces boulangers vigilants, le souverain leur accorda le privilège de fabriquer une pâtisserie qui immortaliserait l'événement. C'est ainsi que naquit le *Hörnchen,* « petite corne » en allemand, allusion au croissant qui orne l'étendard turc.

Une autre légende attribue l'invention du croissant à un certain Kolschitski, cafetier viennois d'origine polonaise. En récompense pour son courage pendant le siège turc, il aurait reçu des sacs de café pris à l'ennemi. Il aurait alors eu l'idée de servir ce café accompagné d'une viennoiserie en forme de croissant. C'est en 1770 que Marie-Antoinette, épouse de Louis XVI, introduisit le croissant à la cour de France, après un séjour passé en Autriche. Mais ce n'est qu'au début du siècle dernier, en 1920 pour être plus précis, que les boulangers parisiens créèrent le croissant feuilleté au beurre tel qu'on le connaît aujourd'hui. Le croissant est depuis devenu l'incarnation du bon goût et de l'authenticité française à l'étranger. Tout comme pour du bon pain, l'amateur de croissant peut se déplacer fort loin afin d'être assuré de la qualité de sa viennoiserie préférée. Un peu à l'exemple du bagel montréalais, plusieurs expatriés vivant à Toronto ont continué pendant longtemps à remplir leurs congélateurs de croissants en provenance des meilleures pâtisseries de Montréal. Heureusement que nous avons répertorié toutes les bonnes adresses de Toronto où acheter des croissants et bien d'autres viennoiseries !

tels que la tarte aux pommes caramélisées et au chocolat, la tarte au citron, le baba au rhum, la tarte à la noix de coco et aux pommes caramélisées, la tarte aux lychees et au caramel, sans oublier le fameux dominus (pommes caramélisées couronnées d'une mousse au chocolat). Autre surprise qui vous attend chez Clafouti : la galette des rois. Pendant les deux premières semaines de janvier, les commandes pour ce délice affluent. Une chose est sûre, que vous habitiez dans le coin ou pas, vous trouverez sans aucun doute toutes sortes d'excuses pour passer chez Clafouti.

DU BON PAIN Le pain, chez Clafouti, longe le mur de gauche et est placé dans de grosses caisses à vins en bois. C'est charmant et à la fois très invitant. Comme presque tout dans cette pâtisserie, les pains sont faits sur place. Au rendez-vous, le pain aux olives, la fougasse au romarin, la fougasse aux épinards, le pain muesli. Clafouti vend aussi les bagels de style montréalais de St. Urbain.

DES SUCRERIES Clafouti nous gâte déjà tellement qu'on aurait presque pu se passer de bonbons et autres sucreries. On a bien dit « presque »… La liste est longue et il ne tient qu'à vous de découvrir la liste complète. Pour ce qui est des biscuits en sachet, Clafouti vous surprendra agréablement avec ses biscuits au Grand Marnier, à la bergamote, à la noisette et à la vanille. En tout, vous aurez le choix entre huit parfums différents. Chose qu'on voit rarement à Toronto : des langues de chat maison. Clafouti vend enfin des madeleines et du quatre-quarts.

Comptoir de Célestin

623 Mount Pleasant Road (au nord de Manor Road) ☎ (416) 544-1733

Fermé lundi et mardi, mercredi à samedi 7h30 – 19h, dimanche 8h30 – 17h

Métro : EGLINTON + le bus

DE BONNES PÂTISSERIES Cette pâtisserie jouxte le nouveau restaurant Le Célestin. Les frères Martial et Pascal Ribreau sont les créateurs de ce concept de resto et comptoir de prêt-à-manger que peu ont adopté ici à Toronto, mais qui est très populaire en France. En matière de viennoiseries, le Comptoir propose les incontournables français : croissants, amandines, pains au chocolat, pains aux raisins, chaussons aux pommes, brioches, brioches Nantaire (brioche à la forme allongée), brioches Bostock et kouglofs. Entre nous, le croissant aux amandes invite au péché de gourmandise. Il est si bon qu'on ne peut se satisfaire d'un seul… Côté desserts, la liste est sans fin. Et ils sont plus alléchants les uns que les autres. On y retrouve certains classiques du grand Toronto (tartes aux fruits, tarte Tatin et tarte au citron), mais aussi des incontournables de la pâtisserie française, rarement disponibles à Toronto : le gland (crème pâtissière et kirsch), le paris-brest (crème pâtissière et crème de noisettes) et la religieuse (crème pâtissière et glaçage au café ou au chocolat). Il y a aussi des petits fours qu'on peut se procurer sur commande. Le diplomate est une autre spécialité française qu'on commence seulement à trouver en ville. Martial Ribreau le prépare avec les

ingrédients suivants : brioche, Grand Marnier, crème anglaise et fruits secs. Le millefeuille, très français et pas très évident à trouver à Toronto, est également disponible au Comptoir de Célestin, à condition de passer une commande spéciale.

DU BON PAIN La baguette de Célestin est la meilleure baguette artisanale que nous ayons mangée jusqu'à présent à Toronto. Elle est tout simplement sublime avec ou sans accompagnement. Le chef pâtissier Martial Ribreau vous propose également une savoureuse baguette au blé entier. Vous trouverez aussi une boule au miel et aux raisins, un pain au levain et un pain noir aux sept céréales au goût riche et intense. Ce qui est rare à Toronto, c'est la viennoise (baguette de style brioché). Chez Célestin, on trouve de la viennoise sucrée et de la demi-viennoise au chocolat. C'est le réveil idéal pour les week-ends !

DES SUCRERIES Contrairement à plusieurs autres pâtissiers de la ville, Martial Ribreau crée des macarons disponibles dans 12 parfums irrésistibles. Parmi nos parfums préférés figurent la framboise, la pistache et le chocolat.

Daniel et Daniel – Food Shop

248 Carlton Street (au coin de Parliament Street) ☎ (416) 968-9275

Lundi à samedi 7h30 – 18h, fermé dimanche

Métro : CASTLE FRANK + le bus; COLLEGE + le tram

www.danieletdaniel.ca

DE BONNES PÂTISSERIES Daniel et Daniel, c'est avant tout un maître traiteur – l'un des meilleurs de Toronto soit dit en passant. La boutique de Cabbagetown propose également une petite, mais savoureuse, sélection de viennoiseries d'inspiration française : croissants, amandines, pains au chocolat et croissants au fromage. Les tartes aux fruits et gâteaux sont délicieux et valent vraiment le coup. Chose surprenante, Daniel et Daniel est un des seuls pâtissiers en ville à vendre de la crème brûlée à emporter. Non seulement on peut déguster ce délice chez soi, mais on peut aussi déguster ce dessert dans un petit ramequin. Ce genre de tentation facile est très dangereux pour les gens qui raffolent de la crème brûlée. Laissez-vous aller, car tout est bon chez Daniel et Daniel !

Dinah's Cupboard

50 Cumberland Street ☎ (416) 921-8112

Lundi à vendredi 9h – 19h, samedi 9h – 18h, fermé dimanche (à l'exception du mois de décembre)

Métro : YONGE OU BAY

DE BONNES PÂTISSERIES Cette petite épicerie fine permet aux résidents du quartier de Yorkville de savourer les brioches et croissants venant de chez Patachou sans avoir à voyager bien loin.

Fred's Bakery

45 Brisbane Road, Unit # 13-14
☎ (416) 736-3733

**Cette boulangerie n'est pas ouverte au public*

DU BON PAIN Le duo d'artistes Andrea Damon-Gibson et Steve Gibson se cache derrière Fred's Bakery. Ce couple crée depuis 1995 une collection assez impressionnante de pains d'inspiration artisanale. Le plaisir réside vraiment dans la variété. La liste des plaisirs est longue chez Fred's – pain au levain, pain noir (un mélange de chocolat, espresso, mélasse et miel), pain aux raisins, pain aux noix, pain aux olives noires et vertes, pain aux graines anciennes et au miel sauvage, pain de seigle, trois types de fougasses (pommes de terre, romarin et tomates), baguette bien croustillante, pain au fromage, pain aux herbes et oignons et pain brioché. Le choix est tellement vaste qu'il faudra des semaines, voire des mois, avant de goûter à chacune de ces variétés de pain. Heureusement qu'il y a plusieurs points de vente dans la ville, ce qui vous permettra de vous en donner à cœur joie quand l'envie du bon pain vous prendra. Vous pouvez acheter l'une des confections signées Fred's chez les marchands suivants :
Big Carrot, All the Best Fine Foods, Pusateri's, Holt Renfrew, Max Market, Le Gourmand, Royal York Deli et IGA dans le quariter « the Beach ».

Holt Renfrew – Epicure Shop

50 Bloor Street West (au coin de Bay Street) ☎ (416) 922-2333

Lundi à mercredi 10h – 18h, jeudi et vendredi 10h – 20h, samedi 10h – 18h, dimanche 12h – 18h

Métro : YONGE ou BAY

DE BONNES PÂTISSERIES Si Holt Renfrew n'importe pas des produits de qualité supérieure, il s'organise pour s'associer avec des maîtres dans leurs domaines de prédilection. C'est ainsi qu'Holt Renfrew vend à sa clientèle très exigeante une sélection de croissants de Patachou.

DU BON PAIN Des milliers de Parisiens achètent le pain au levain naturel de Lionel Poîlane, tous les jours, à la boulangerie rue du Cherche-Midi. Pour nous Torontois, plus besoin d'attendre un voyage transatlantique pour savourer ce délice parisien. Grâce à Holt Renfrew, les francophones et francophiles d'ici peuvent eux aussi manger du pain Poîlane tous les jours. Holt Renfrew fait acheminer tous les deux jours par FedEx le pain le plus populaire de France et peut-être même du monde. Vous pouvez acheter le pain Poîlane en boule ou encore en quartier à l'Epicure Shop situé au sous-sol du magasin le plus chic de Toronto. La boule et même le quart de boule ne sont pas vendus au rabais, mais si l'envie vous prend et si la monnaie pèse lourd dans vos poches, c'est un plaisir qu'il faut satisfaire.

DES SUCRERIES Holt Renfrew importe les tentations françaises suivantes : des petits beurres, des palets bretons, des crêpes dentelées bretonnes, des bonbons aux marrons, des bonbons aux fruits, trois parfums différents de caramels, des dominos de nougat et les irrésistibles marrons glacés. Lors des fêtes de Noël, de la Saint-Valentin et de Pâques, Holt Renfrew importe plusieurs sucreries, destinées à célébrer l'occasion.

La Cigogne

(anciennement La Framboisine)

1626 Bayview Avenue (au sud d'Eglinton Avenue) ☎ (416) 487-1234

Lundi à vendredi 7h30 – 19h, samedi 8h – 19h, dimanche 8h – 17h30

Métro : **EGLINTON** + le bus

DE BONNES PÂTISSERIES Les habitants du Bayview Village ont de la chance : non seulement ils ont trouvé en Rahier l'une des meilleures pâtisseries de Toronto, mais ils sont également à quelques pas seulement de La Cigogne. Le nouveau propriétaire est le chef pâtissier Thierry Schmitt, Alsacien bardé de diplômes (on le voit au nombre de diplômes, médailles et trophées affichés sur le mur à l'entrée). La spécialité de la maison est la tarte flambée d'Alsace. Une fois que vous y aurez goûté, il faudra goûter les autres viennoiseries et pâtisseries. Ce n'est pas le choix qui manque – pain perdu (fait avec des pommes, des pêches, de la cannelle et de la brioche), éclair, opéra, mont blanc, crème brûlée, danoise, croissant, croissant aux amandes, croissant au chocolat, chausson aux pommes, palmier et bien d'autres encore.

Vous pouvez également commander des croquembouches et des petits fours. Pendant la saison des fêtes de Noël et Pâques, le chef Thierry Schmitt prépare d'alléchants desserts qui sauront régaler tous vos invités. Vous n'avez qu'à consulter le menu spécialement conçu pour célébrer l'occasion avant de passer votre commande. Le chef Thierry Schmitt confectionne même la galette des rois !

DU BON PAIN Vous trouverez sur place une baguette maison, ainsi que du pain au levain.

DES SUCRERIES Des madeleines, des langues de chat et des sablés aux noix vendus en sachet vous attendent en magasin.

Le Gourmand

152 Spadina Avenue (au sud de Queen Street) ☎ (416) 504-4494

Lundi à vendredi 7h – 21h, samedi 9h – 18h, dimanche 9h – 16h

Métro : **OSGOODE** + le tram;
SPADINA + le tram

DE BONNES PÂTISSERIES Le Gourmand n'a peut-être pas de chef pâtissier sur place, mais la petite variété de croissants et pâtisseries signés Rahier qu'il propose compense largement cette absence.

Le Petit Gourmet

1064 Yonge Street ☎ (416) 966-3811

Lundi à vendredi 7h30 – 19h, samedi 7h30 – 18h, fermé dimanche

Métro : **ROSEDALE**

DE BONNES PÂTISSERIES Depuis plus d'une vingtaine d'années, Christian Bonito s'affaire dans sa cuisine. La preuve en est que les viennoiseries disparaissent plutôt rapidement dans sa pâtisserie du quartier de Rosedale. La plupart des habitués n'hésitent pas à acheter une demi–douzaine de croissants à la fois. Aux choix, M. Bonito propose : croissants au beurre, croissants aux amandes, pains au chocolat, pains aux raisins, pains à la cannelle, chaussons aux pommes et chaussons aux

Le saviez-vous ?

Le « roi du pain » vend ses boules à plus de 600 points de vente à Paris et à plus de 300 restaurants dans la Ville lumière. Chaque jour, des avions partent de Paris le ventre gonflé de pain Poîlane, à destination des plus grandes villes du monde telles que Tokyo, New York et Chicago. La tradition Poîlane fut préservée même après la mort du « roi du pain ». Chaque boule est faite avec du levain naturel, de la farine française et du sel de mer. Jusqu'à présent, chaque boule a été formée à la main et cuite dans un four à bois. Cette façon artisanale de fabriquer le pain nous garantit qu'il n'y aura jamais deux boules qui se ressemblent. En fait, cette « imperfection » est la source même de la perfection du pain Poîlane.

fruits. Plus d'une quinzaine de gâteaux et tartes vous attendent. Vous reconnaîtrez sans aucun doute le gâteau basque que M. Bonito prépare également pour L'Escargot Bistro. La tarte au chocolat, aux poires et à la crème est fantastique. Autres desserts à ne pas manquer : le gâteau à la ganache et la tarte Tatin.

Magnolia Fine Foods

548 College Street, au coin d'Euclid Avenue ☎ (416) 920-9927

Lundi à vendredi 9h – 20h, samedi 9h – 18h, dimanche 10h – 18h

Métro : QUEEN'S PARK + le tram

DE BONNES PÂTISSERIES Cette petite épicerie fine de College Street West vend les fameux croissants signés Clafouti.

Mercatto

- 15 Toronto Street (à l'est de Yonge Street et au nord de King Street) ☎ (416) 366-4567

  Lundi à vendredi 7h – 18h, fermé samedi et dimanche

  Métro : KING

- 330 Bay Street (au nord d'Adelaïde Street) ☎ (416) 306-0467

  Lundi à vendredi 7h30 – 20h, fermé samedi et dimanche

  Métro : KING

DE BONNES PÂTISSERIES Mercatto est un petit bistro italien qui a un faible pour les produits français. Ses croissants viennent de la pâtisserie Clafouti. Faites vite, car les bons croissants qui viennent de chez Clafouti ont à peine le temps de refroidir une fois qu'ils sont placés sous les cloches. Mercatto vend des croissants au beurre et aux figues. Si vous travaillez au centre-ville et découvrez, après avoir goûté un croissant de Clafouti, que vous ne pouvez plus vous en passer, surtout ne nous en voulez pas, blâmez plutôt Boris Dosne, chef pâtissier chez Clafouti.

Pain Perdu

736 St Clair Avenue West (un peu à l'ouest de Christie Street) ☎ (416) 656-7246

Fermé lundi, mardi à vendredi 7h – 19h30, samedi 7h – 17h, dimanche 8h – 16h

Métro : ST CLAIR WEST + le tram

DE BONNES PÂTISSERIES On croyait que Pain Perdu était tout simplement un nom original. Il s'avère que les propriétaires (les frères Yannick et Christophe Folgoas) ont fait bien plus que donner un nom à leur pâtisserie, ils lui ont aussi donné un emblème – le pain perdu maison. Il est préparé dans la bonne tradition française et selon une vieille recette de famille, puisque c'est la baguette de la veille qu'on utilise. Pain Perdu offre un vaste choix de viennoiseries et autres pâtisseries françaises. La découverte chez Pain Perdu se fait par les sens, mais on vous livre quand même cette liste en avant-première : opéra, marquise, saint-honoré, paris-brest, religieuse, millefeuille, tartes aux fruits, croissants (nature, aux amandes et au chocolat), pain aux raisins et brioche sucrée. Les pâtisseries les plus demandées, selon les propriétaires, sont la tarte au citron et le gâteau basque. Nous devons admettre que leur gâteau basque est le meilleur que nous ayons goûté jusqu'à présent. Vous direz qu'il va de soi qu'un pâtissier basque (de la région de Saint-Jean-de-Luz) puisse maîtriser cette recette. Eh bien, dans ce cas-ci, c'est plus que réussi. Chose qu'on ne trouve pas partout, c'est la possibilité de choisir entre trois formats de tartes – petit, moyen et grand. Christophe Folgoas, chef pâtissier, nous dit qu'il innove sans cesse, donc il faut passer souvent pour découvrir les nouveautés. Parmi celles-ci figure le béret basque. Ce dessert au nom un peu intriguant est en fait une génoise au chocolat rehaussée d'une mousse au chocolat, arrosée d'un sirop au rhum et recouverte de pétales de chocolat. Avis aux amateurs de chocolat ! Détail qui a son importance : Pain Perdu prépare viennoiseries et desserts tout au long de la journée. Voilà enfin une des seules pâtisseries françaises en ville qui ne vend pas tout son stock avant 11h.

DU BON PAIN Une nouvelle pâtisserie française symbolise le changement en cours à l'ouest de Bathurst, rue St Clair. Les habitants du coin ont enfin accès à une bonne baguette et un bon pain au levain.

DES SUCRERIES Ça n'en finit plus chez Pain Perdu ! Il était déjà difficile de résister aux pâtisseries, maintenant ce sont les biscuits en sachet dont il faut se méfier... Aiguillettes à l'orange, petits sablés, fils aux amandes et palmiers sont disposés dans des petits paniers en osier et n'attendent que d'être dégustés. On trouve aussi des bonbons au nougat et au chocolat ainsi que deux parfums de pâtes de fruits : cassis et framboise.

Patachou

1095 Yonge Street (près du métro Summerhill) ☎ (416) 927-1105

Lundi à vendredi 8h30 – 19h, samedi 8h30 – 18h, fermé dimanche

Métro : **SUMMERHILL**

DE BONNES PÂTISSERIES Depuis 1978, cette boulangerie propose aux habitants de Rosedale les grands classiques de la viennoiserie et de la pâtisserie françaises. Vous y trouverez de nombreuses gourmandises telles que croissants, brioches, croissants aux amandes, pains au chocolat, brioches aux raisins et palmiers. Vous aurez en plus le choix parmi une très bonne sélection de petits

desserts et gâteaux. Le gâteau basque (parfumé d'un soupçon d'anis) et la tarte au citron ne font pas de vieux os sur les étalages, il est donc important d'aller faire ses courses tôt les samedis matins. Patachou prépare des spécialités saisonnières pour célébrer l'Épiphanie, la Saint-Valentin, Pâques, la fête des Mères et Noël. Les spécialités de saison les plus convoitées sont sans aucun doute les petits fours glacés. La petitesse de ces gâteries en fait un vrai péché par excès, puisqu'on peut en manger trois ou même quatre sans vraiment s'en rendre compte. Vous pouvez passer une commande spéciale pour tous vos plaisirs des fêtes afin de partager avec vos convives les charmes de la pâtisserie française. Si vous avez longtemps cherché des croûtes pour la préparation de vos bouchées à la reine, c'est ici que votre recherche prend fin. Une simple commande passée trois à cinq jours à l'avance vous garantit d'avoir ces belles timbales feuilletées. Patachou offre également une bonne variété de plats prêts-à-manger et prêts-à-emporter. Une terrasse à l'extérieur (pendant l'été) et plusieurs tables à l'intérieur permettent de s'attarder pour déguster tranquillement les pâtisseries, quiches, tartes salées, sandwichs et salades maison.

DES SUCRERIES Patachou vend d'excellents petits macarons sucrés aux trois parfums séduisants. Il vend également des feuilletés au fromage et au thym, des palmiers sucrés et des petits biscuits aux brisures de chocolat.

PÂTISSERIE D'OR

301 Robinson Street, Oakville (au sud de Lake Shore Road) ☎ (905) 815-8999

Fermé lundi et mardi, mercredi à vendredi 8h – 17h30, samedi 8h – 18h, dimanche 8h – 16h

DE BONNES PÂTISSERIES Le chef pâtissier Jean-Luc Soulabaille a ouvert depuis août 2000 sa propre pâtisserie à Oakville. Un simple coup d'œil et l'on comprend très vite que M. Soulabaille est de formation classique française (il a fait ses classes à Saint-Malo). Nombre de paniers regorgent de viennoiseries qui nous mettent l'eau à la bouche. Les délices proposées sont de dignes classiques et elles sont incroyablement savoureuses – croissants au beurre, pains aux raisins, croissants aux

Les pâtisseries et viennoiseries qui font craquer

1. La **brioche royale** de Bonjour Brioche
2. La **danoise aux pistaches** de Rahier
3. Le **bostock** de Patachou
4. Le **croissant aux amandes** du Comptoir Célestin
5. Le **croissant aux figues** et celui à la **cannelle** de Clafouti
6. Le **gâteau basque** de Pain Perdu
7. Le **pain au chocolat** de La Cigogne
8. Le **pain aux raisins** et les **danoises aux fruits** frais de Pâtisserie d'Or
9. Les **baklavas libanais** d'Arz Bakery
10. Les **financiers** de la pâtisserie Zane

Le saviez-vous ?

La dragée, c'est l'amande. L'amande est arrivée en France au Moyen-Âge, rapportée des guerres de croisades de Terre Sainte. Au temps du Moyen-Âge, l'amande était déjà enrobée de miel et elle était distribuée par les Romains lors des mariages et des naissances. Ce n'est qu'en 1220 qu'un pharmacien de Verdun eut l'idée de transformer l'amande en dragée, en recouvrant le fruit sec d'une couche de sucre et de miel mélangés. À l'époque, la dragée avait plutôt une vocation pharmaceutique. Elle était réputée vivifiante et pure. Les pharmaciens la recommandaient aux femmes enceintes et aux hommes (pour renforcer leur semence). Dès le XVIe siècle, les rois et reines de France ont tous leur drageoir de poche.

Aujourd'hui encore, Verdun demeure la référence pour la dragée française. C'est un confiseur de la rue des Lombards, à Verdun, qui élabore la dragée moderne en 1751, en lui fabriquant une enveloppe aussi lisse que celle de l'amande. Jusqu'au XIXe siècle, la dragée était fabriquée de façon artisanale. Ce n'est que vers la fin du dernier centenaire que l'on industrialise la fabrication de la dragée.

De nos jours, la dragée est associée aux étapes essentielles de la vie : mariages, baptêmes ou communions. Elle est surtout populaire dans certains pays européens tels que la France, l'Italie, la Grèce et le Portugal. En Amérique du Nord, elle s'installe dans les mœurs du fait de l'immigration européenne massive.

Vous pouvez bien entendu vous régaler de dragées en toute occasion. Vous trouverez dans cette section des magasins précis où acheter des dragées. Lors de nos recherches, nous avons notamment découvert que la dragée est monnaie courante dans les pâtisseries grecques, italiennes et portugaises de Toronto.

amandes et pains au chocolat. Pour sa préparation de danoises aux fruits, le chef Soulabaille n'utilise que des fruits frais de saison. Cette touche particulière n'est qu'une touche parmi les centaines d'autres qui le différencient de la concurrence. En matière de desserts, la liste est longue et appétissante. On trouve des spécialités françaises qui ne sont disponibles que dans un très petit nombre de pâtisseries du grand Toronto, telles que le paris-brest, l'éclair au chocolat, le croquembouche, le saint-honoré, la forêt-noire et le « vrai » millefeuille. Tous les desserts au chocolat sont préparés à base de chocolat suisse *Lindt* ou de chocolat belge *Callebaut.* Le chef Soulabaille a astucieusement réussi à marier sa formation classique franco-française à la tendance du marché et offre à ses clients plusieurs viennoiseries et pâtisseries de saison. Consultez la rubrique « produits surgelés » de ce guide pour connaître les trésors gastronomiques que nous avons découverts en vente dans le congélateur de cette pâtisserie. En résumé, le chef Soulabaille offre une

qualité irréprochable.

DU BON PAIN Le chef Soulabaille vous invite à goûter sa baguette classique. Elle est simple et très bonne.

DES SUCRERIES Les biscuits maison vous séduiront. Que ce soit le macaron, le palmier, la cigarette à la vanille ou le biscuit au beurre, vous ne pourrez pas être déçu par les créations du chef. Enfin, la madeleine est une autre confection maison dont vous ne pourrez plus vous passer.

Pâtisserie Saint Honoré

2945 Bloor Street West (au coin de Greenview Blvd., un peu à l'est de Royal York Road)

**il n'y a pas de numéro de téléphone pour cette pâtisserie*

Fermé dimanche et lundi, mardi à jeudi 8h – 19h, vendredi 8h – 21h, samedi 8h – 19h

Métro : ROYAL YORK

DE BONNES PÂTISSERIES Les résidents du Bloor West Village se régalent des pâtisseries et viennoiseries préparées par Jean-Jacques Carlier. La sélection classique est complète : croissants, croissants aux amandes, pains au chocolat, brioches aux raisins et danoises aux fruits. Pour ce qui est des croissants salés, ils sont fourrés au fromage ou au jambon et au fromage. Vous aurez également le choix entre plusieurs sélections adaptées aux goûts du marché comme le croissant à la feta et aux épinards par exemple. Les pâtisseries et gâteaux se font remarquer par leur quantité et par leur variété.

DU BON PAIN La Pâtisserie Saint Honoré permet aux habitants de l'ouest de la ville d'acheter une excellente baguette et plusieurs pains maison tout aussi savoureux.

Pusateri's Fine Foods

- 1539 Avenue Road (au nord de Lawrence Avenue) ☎ (416) 785-9100

  Lundi à mercredi 8h – 20h, jeudi et vendredi 8h – 21h, samedi et dimanche 8h – 19h

  Métro : LAWRENCE + le bus

- 57 Yorkville Avenue (au coin de Bay Street) ☎ (416) 785-9100

  Lundi à mercredi 10h – 20h, jeudi et vendredi 10h – 21h, samedi 8h – 20h, dimanche 10h – 19h

  Métro : BAY

  www.pusateris.com

DE BONNES PÂTISSERIES Pusateri's offre à sa clientèle de luxe les savoureux gâteaux, tartes et viennoiseries de Patachou, Clafouti et Rahier.

Rahier

1717 Bayview Avenue (au sud d'Eglinton Avenue) ☎ (416) 482-0917

Fermé lundi et mardi, mercredi à vendredi 8h – 17h, samedi 8h – 16h, dimanche 8h – 15h

Métro : EGLINTON + le bus

DE BONNES PÂTISSERIES Depuis 1996, la pâtisserie Rahier chatouille nos narines et satisfait nos envies avec ses alléchantes confections. Certains ont officieusement déclaré Rahier « la Rolls Royce » de la pâtisserie française à Toronto. Rahier est une bonne adresse en ville pour acheter petits gâteaux, tartelettes et mousses aux fruits de style français. Toutes les viennoiseries sont faites sur place. Vous remarquerez qu'ici, la viennoiserie règne. L'une de nos

préférées est la danoise aux pistaches. Pendant les fêtes de Noël, Rahier propose des sélections spéciales qui sauront terminer vos repas de festivités en beauté. Vous remarquerez que la bûche de Noël est en vedette. Il y a autre chose qui nous intéresse chez Rahier : certaines nouvelles pâtisseries ayant ouvert leurs portes fin 2002, début 2003 ont attribué leur courage d'aller de l'avant et d'offrir ainsi aux Torontois la possibilité de découvrir toujours plus la pâtisserie et la viennoiserie françaises au succès de Rahier. Grâce à ce dernier, de plus en plus de Torontois peuvent donc découvrir ce que nous, francophiles et francophones, savions déjà : en matière de pâtisserie, les Français dominent largement !

DU BON PAIN En vente sur place, une baguette maison ainsi qu'une petite variété de boules aux parfums suivants : multigrains, romarin, noix et raisins.

DES SUCRERIES Rahier a un choix exceptionnel de biscuits vendus à l'unité ou encore en sachet.

St. Urbain Bagel Bakery

Différentes adresses dans toute la ville

☎ (416) 787-6955 (numéro général d'information)

DU BON PAIN St. Urbain Bagel Bakery est un autre boulanger qui offre aux Torontois la possibilité de vivre une véritable expérience du bagel montréalais. Vous n'aurez donc plus vraiment d'excuse pour continuer à manger ces pains qui essaient de se faire passer pour des bagels… Donnez plutôt dans l'authenticité. Les bagels de St. Urbain Bagel Bakery sont aussi vendus chez Clafouti, My Market Bakery (172 Baldwin St., dans Kensington Market), Cheese Boutique et All the Best Fine Foods.

Senses

- 318 Wellington Street West (au coin de Blue Jay Way, à l'intérieur du SOHO Metropolitan Hotel) ☎ (416) 961-0055

  Lundi à dimanche 7h – 21h

  Métro : ST ANDREW + le tram
- 2901 Bayview Avenue (à l'intérieur de la Galerie Bayview/Bayview Village) ☎ (416) 227-9149

  Lundi à vendredi 8h – 21h, samedi 8h – 18h, dimanche 10h – 17h

  Métro : BAYVIEW sur la ligne Sheppard

  www.senses.ca

DE BONNES PÂTISSERIES Pâtisserie, traiteur et restaurant, Senses n'est pas un établissement purement français, mais ses pâtisseries sont de style français et elles sont incontestablement délicieuses. L'emplacement et le décor ont peut-être changé, pour autant la qualité des produits et la qualité du service sont les mêmes. Dans le domaine des pâtisseries et viennoiseries, on retrouve les incontournables français : assortiment de croissants, nombreuses tartelettes aux fruits et au chocolat, mousses aux fruits et gâteaux au chocolat. Vous pourrez également découvrir plusieurs créations typiquement locales qui valent vraiment la peine qu'on les déguste. Le gâteau aux marrons nous a particulièrement séduits. On dit que réussir, c'est bien choisir. Si c'est le cas, la réussite sera d'autant plus assurée chez Senses par une très grande sélection. Pour

Le saviez–vous ?

Le bagel a fait sa première apparition aux États-Unis en 1890. Bien que le bagel fasse partie de la gastronomie juive, il n'a jamais été considéré comme une denrée essentielle ou même de base dans la cuisine juive de l'Europe de l'Est ou même dans celle des Juifs de la Russie. Mais il est vrai que les immigrants juifs de l'Europe de l'Est en ont fait une partie intégrante de leur gastronomie.

L'histoire du bagel dans le Canada français remonte à près d'un siècle déjà. En 1919, Isadore Shlafman arrive au Canada et ouvre la première boulangerie de bagels à Montréal, dans une allée adjacente au boulevard Saint-Laurent, communément appelée « la Main ». C'est là que les Montréalais ont appris à connaître le bagel. C'est en 1949 qu'Isadore Shlafman ouvre sa boutique sur la rue Fairmount, où il installe un four à bagels.

Ceux qui n'ont jamais eu la chance de goûter à un bagel de style montréalais devront savoir que la particularité du bagel réside dans le fait que le pain est façonné à la main, passé à l'eau bouillante et cuit au four à bois. On ne trouve rien de comparable dans la famille des pains.

Pendant plusieurs années, les expatriés montréalais vivant à Toronto rapportaient de leurs week-ends à Montréal des sacs et des sacs de bagels qu'ils congelaient dans l'espoir de faire perdurer ce plaisir. Une chose était sûre, si un ami ou collègue de travail passait par Montréal, il fallait impérativement lui demander de passer par la rue Fairmount pour acheter une ou deux douzaines de bagels.

C'est vrai que le bagel n'est pas d'origine française, mais vous trouverez très peu de Québécois de souche française qui n'ont pas adopté cette importation juive dans leur quotidien.

Le temps où il fallait acheter des dizaines et des dizaines de bagels de Montréal pour les rapporter à Toronto est révolu. La liste suivante répertorie les endroits où dénicher ce délice juif montréalais, ici à Toronto.

N'oubliez pas qu'il y a bagel et bagel façon montréalaise. Il ne faut surtout pas confondre les deux. Maintenant, il ne vous reste qu'à choisir le parfum et la garniture de votre choix.

Où trouver les bagels de style montréalais à Toronto

1. All the Best Fine Foods
2. Cheese Boutique
3. Clafouti
4. My Market Bakery (marché Kensington)
5. Pusateri's
6. St. Urbain Bagel Bakery
7. The Bagel House

augmenter vos chances de succès, choisissez donc plus d'une pâtisserie…

Enfin, nous ajouterons que les prix des pâtisseries de Senses sont plus élevés que dans la plupart des autres pâtisseries françaises de la ville, mais ne laissez pas cette réalité vous empêcher de vous offrir une gourmandise de temps à autre.

DES SUCRERIES Les produits, chez Senses, sont tous aussi appétissants les uns que les autres. Pour satisfaire une petite envie de sucre, essayez les excellents biscuits maison. C'est une véritable explosion de saveur pour les papilles. Lors des fêtes de Noël, de la Saint-Valentin et de Pâques, Senses prépare des biscuits tout spécialement pour célébrer les festivités. Faites vite ! Si l'on prend l'exemple des confections de Noël, elles ne sont disponibles que pendant les deux dernières semaines de décembre.

THE BAGEL HOUSE

- 1548 Bayview Avenue (au sud d'Eglinton Avenue) ☎ (416) 481-8184

  Lundi à samedi 7h – 19h, dimanche 7h – 18h

  Métro : EGLINTON + le bus

- 1722 Avenue Road (au coin de Fairlawn Avenue) ☎ (416) 781-0032

  Lundi à samedi 6h30 – 19h, dimanche 6h30 – 18h30

  Métro : LAWRENCE + le bus

DU BON PAIN Jessie Sahdra est le propriétaire de ces « bagel shops » à Toronto. Ce boulanger expatrié, originaire de Montréal, a travaillé pendant plus de 17 ans dans la plupart des « bagel shops » du coin des bagels de Montréal (les rues Saint-Viateur et Fairmount). M. Sahdra instaure une authenticité dans la préparation des bagels qui manquait jusqu'à tout récemment. Le vrai bagel doit se distinguer du simple petit pain par sa texture, son goût et sa préparation. Les bagels de The Bagel House sont tels qu'ils devraient l'être – un peu collants, un peu sucrés, roulés à la main et parsemés de graines de sésame ou encore de graines de pavot. En magasin, vous retrouverez une douzaine de parfums, y compris un bagel allégé en sucre.

WHOLE FOODS MARKET

87 Avenue Road (au nord de Bloor Street) ☎ (416) 944-0500

Lundi à vendredi 9h – 22h, samedi 9h – 21h, dimanche 9h – 20h

Métro : BAY ou MUSEUM

www.wholefoodsmarket.com

DE BONNES PÂTISSERIES Whole Foods Market allège le fardeau de ses clients en leur offrant la possibilité d'acheter plusieurs pâtisseries en provenance de chez Patachou. Bien entendu, le choix est moindre, mais l'accessibilité compense le choix un peu plus limité. Nous avons dernièrement remarqué que Whole Foods Market vend des madeleines. Quelle bonne nouvelle !

DU BON PAIN Une belle variété de pains est cuite sur place, chez Whole Foods Market. Vous y aurez le choix entre des pains aux parfums classiques tels que le pain de campagne, le pain aux raisins et pacanes, le pain aux céréales, le pain aux olives et la baguette, mais vous pourrez aussi sortir de l'ordinaire avec le pain à l'ail rôti par exemple.

Zane Pâtisserie et Boulangerie

1852 Queen Street East (à l'ouest de Woodbine) ☎ (416) 690-2813

Fermé lundi, mardi à dimanche 7h30 – 17h30

Métro : QUEEN + le tram

DE BONNES PÂTISSERIES Les grands classiques de la viennoiserie sont à l'honneur : croissants au beurre, croissants aux amandes et pains au chocolat. Danoises au citron, aux abricots, aux myrtilles (bleuets) et aux noisettes font également partie des viennoiseries que vous pourrez déguster chez Zane. Toujours plus fort : le tortillon à la crème pâtissière et le carré à la crème pâtissière. Le chef pâtissier Mo Zane prépare également une douzaine de gâteaux et près d'une dizaine de tartes, tous plus délicieux les uns que les autres. Vous verrez que faire votre choix risque d'être un peu compliqué. Il y a autre chose d'intéressant chez Zane : les petits fours frais. Zane prépare des tartelettes aux fruits, des tartelettes au chocolat et à la framboise, des tartelettes au citron, des mini-éclairs et des mini-choux. Zane vend aussi des financiers (les cousins des madeleines). Ces petits gâteaux aux amandes et au beurre de noisette vont vous séduire. Il est vrai que des petits gâteaux de ce genre se préparent facilement à la maison, mais avouez qu'il serait bête de se casser la tête, quand on peut simplement faire un tour chez cette pâtisserie française de Queen Street East. D'autant plus que ces pâtisseries sont absolument succulentes.

DU BON PAIN C'est le lieu incontesté de l'empire de la baguette et du pain dans le quartier « the Beach ». Le chef pâtissier Mo Zane propose une bonne baguette, un pain multigrains, un pain aux noix épatant et un pain aux tomates séchées, romarin et olives noires. Le pain aux tomates séchées est particulièrement savoureux. Il se mange bien seul ou en accompagnement avec une bonne soupe ou une bonne salade.

DES SUCRERIES Lorsque nous avons rencontré Mo Zane, il nous a présenté ses excuses, car il était alors couvert de farine et de sucre. Nous, on aime bien la farine et le sucre… On aime même beaucoup ! Mo Zane mélange farine, sucre et bien d'autres ingrédients pour préparer des petits biscuits vendus par quinzaine en sachet. Au choix, on a : des tuiles à la noix de coco, des petits sablés, des nougatines, des pains turcs et des croques en chocolat.

où faire ses emplettes

chocolats

L'amour que nous, mortels, portons au chocolat n'a pas de nom. Le chocolat est toujours bon, en toute occasion, peu importe la saison. Comme pour tout ce qui touche à la gastronomie, les Français ont su faire de ce goûter, véritable élixir velouté, quelque chose d'irrésistible.

Les Français sont tellement passionnés de chocolat qu'ils ont eu la bonne idée de former une association de personnes qui partagent ce penchant. C'est ainsi que le Club des croqueurs de chocolat a vu le jour. Ce groupe parisien très privé du chocolat se rencontre pour déguster et débattre des bienfaits du chocolat.

Attention, en matière de chocolat, les Français ne détiennent pas l'exclusivité, puisqu'ils ont des concurrents assez féroces, la Suisse et la Belgique étant deux autres pays reconnus pour leur passion et leur travail acharné pour faire de la préparation du chocolat un art véritable.

Que ce soit dans le but de former votre propre « Club de croqueurs de chocolat » à Toronto ou pour déguster votre douceur préférée, cette section deviendra sans aucun doute votre section favorite !

Le vocabulaire du chocolat

Lors de nos recherches, nous avons réalisé que nous ne connaissions pas le lexique approprié pour qualifier les différents chocolats que nous aimons tant. Nous avons décidé de faire appel à un expert qui éclairerait notre lanterne. C'est ainsi que Mme Patricia Cohrs, de la boutique Belgian Chocolate Shop dans le quartier « the Beach », nous a fourni les bonnes définitions.

La truffe : On commence d'abord par former le cœur de la truffe. Une fois l'intérieur confectionné et ferme, on l'enrobe de chocolat liquide qu'on roule traditionnellement dans de la poudre de cacao. On peut aussi rouler la truffe dans la noix de coco râpée ou les amandes effilées.

La ganache : La ganache est un mélange de crème faite essentiellement à base de chocolat, soit en général $^2/_3$ de chocolat et $^1/_3$ de crème fraîche bouillante.

La praline : La praline est le nom donné à tout chocolat dont l'intérieur se compose de noisettes grillées ou caramélisées qui ont été broyées pour obtenir une pâte lisse qu'on mélange ensuite à du chocolat.

Arz Bakery

1909 Lawrence Avenue East (entre Warden Avenue et Pharmacy Avenue)
☎ (416) 755-5084

Lundi à samedi 8h – 21h, dimanche 8h – 19h30, les jours fériés 8h – 17h (Arz Bakery ne ferme jamais ses portes)

Métro : LAWRENCE + le bus

www.arzbakery.com

La vitrine de truffes et pralines importées de France ne déçoit pas.

Belgian Chocolate Shop

2455 Queen Street East (à l'ouest de Victoria Park Avenue) ☎ (416) 691-1424

Fermé lundi, mardi à vendredi 11h – 19h, samedi et dimanche 11h – 17h

Métro : QUEEN + le tram

www.belgianchocolateshop.ca

Nougatine d'amande croquante, poires pochées à la vodka, bergamote, crème au citron, caramel… Qu'ont tous ces parfums en commun ? Ils sont transformés en objets d'art chocolatés dans cette chocolaterie de l'est de Toronto. Depuis 1984, la charmante petite boutique du quartier « the Beach » ne cesse de satisfaire les amateurs, résidents du quartier ou non, en quête de chocolats raffinés. On sait d'emblée que les chocolatiers Eric Smets et Patricia Cohrs sont belges, car on remarque les deux horloges qui sont placées sur le mur à l'arrière de la vitrine. L'une de ces horloges est réglée à l'heure de Toronto et l'autre à l'heure de Bruxelles. Autre indice quant à la nationalité des chocolatiers : l'utilisation exclusive de chocolat importé de Belgique. Les truffes, pralines et ganaches sont préparées ici de façon très artisanale. Les ingrédients sont de grande qualité, la fraîcheur est assurée et l'on n'ajoute pas une goutte de conservateur.

Contrairement à plusieurs autres chocolats importés de Belgique, ceux-ci sont fabriqués sur place. Pour le consommateur, cela signifie pas de mise en entrepôt, pas de soute d'avion et pas de transport par camion. Les parfums sont fort classiques. Ceux qu'il faut à tout prix goûter sont les suivants : Grand Marnier, champagne et caramel.

Cheese Boutique

45 Ripley Avenue (au sud de South Kingsway et The Queensway)
☎ (416) 762-6292

Lundi à vendredi 8h – 21h, samedi 8h – 20h, dimanche 10h – 18h

Métro : **RUNNYMEDE** + le bus

www.cheeseboutique.com

En marketing, on nous dit souvent que tout réside dans le nom. Cheese Boutique est l'exception qui confirme la règle. Rien, dans le nom de ce magasin, ne laisse deviner une telle sélection de chocolats. Cheese Boutique est l'un des plus grands importateurs de chocolats de la francophonie à Toronto. Il y en a tellement qu'il a fallu en ranger sur la mezzanine, car le comptoir de devant ne suffisait plus. Non seulement on y trouve les grandes marques du chocolat, mais l'on peut aussi faire l'acquisition de plusieurs boîtes-cadeaux. Les boîtes-cadeaux de chocolats de la francophonie ne sont pas en vente dans beaucoup d'adresses de cette section. Ici, vous pourrez acheter les boîtes-cadeaux des chocolats de *la Maison du Praliné, Royal Lys, Poulain, Michel Cluizel, Valrhona* et *Maxim's.*

Chocolate Addict

185 Baldwin Street (Kensington Market)
☎ (416) 979-5809

Lundi à samedi 9h – 18h30, dimanche 10h – 18h

Métro : **SPADINA** + le tram;
QUEEN'S PARK + le tram

www.911chocolate.com

Nous avons déjà dit à quel point le marché Kensington cachait les meilleurs coins pour faire ses emplettes. Ce qu'on ne vous a pas encore dit, c'est que le marché Kensington cache aussi un petit chocolatier. Chocolate Addict offre aux « mordus » du chocolat une vingtaine de parfums de truffes faites à la main avec du chocolat belge. Parmi les parfums assez classiques de noix, alcool et fruits, on retrouve trois parfums hors du commun : Sambuca, lavande et basilic.

Chocolates & Creams

Queen's Quay Terminal, 207 Queen's Quay West ☎ (416) 368-6767

Lundi à dimanche 10h – 18h (l'hiver); lundi à vendredi 10h – 20h, samedi et dimanche 10h – 18h (l'été)

Métro : **UNION** + le tram

www.chocolatesandcreams.com

La boutique Chocolates & Creams est le seul importateur canadien des chocolats belges confectionnés à la main *Manon.* Les chocolats *Manon* sont bien connus en Europe pour la sélection raffinée de leurs ingrédients et le nombre de prix de qualité qui leur ont été décernés – en 1985, ces chocolats ont notamment remporté le prix d'excellence au concours international qui avait lieu à New York.

Chocolats pour tous les jours

Le chocolat est un plaisir qu'on devrait s'offrir tous les jours. Voilà pourquoi nous avons répertorié les chocolats qui s'adaptent au budget de chacun. Ainsi, cette rubrique regorge de bons chocolats de la francophonie. Les grandes maisons de chocolat sont bien représentées à Toronto : *Poulain, Côte D'or, Suchard, Swiss Delice, Alprose, Lindt, Michel Cluizel, Valrhona, Maxim's, Galler, Révillon, Jacques, Suchard, Mazet, Dolfin, Marquise d'Angélis, Petite Périgord Gold, Pierre Ledent* et *Sarments.*

OÙ TROUVER LES GRANDES MARQUES DE CHOCOLATS FRANCO-EUROPÉENS À TORONTO

1. Arz Bakery
2. Brandt Meat Packers Supermarket
3. Cheese Boutique
4. Chocolates & Creams
5. Comptoir de Célestin
6. Domino Foods Ltd.
7. Daniel et Daniel
8. La Cigogne
9. Le Gourmand
10. Leonidas
11. Loblaws
12. Max Market
13. Mercatto
14. Pâtisserie d'Or
15. Pusateri's Fine Foods
16. Rahier
17. Scheffler's Delicatessen & Cheese
18. Simone Marie Belgian Chocolate
19. Sobey's
20. Sun Valley Fruits & Grocery

Les chocolats Manon sont préparés de façon entièrement artisanale par Christian Vanderkerken. Les pralines sont fabriquées au fur et à mesure que les commandes arrivent puisqu'elles ne contiennent pas d'agent de conservation. La « durée de vie » d'une praline à la crème fraîche, par exemple, n'excède pas les sept jours. *Manon,* c'est avant tout une entreprise familiale, brevetée depuis 1953, qui exporte aujourd'hui plus de 25 tonnes de pralines par an. Vous aurez le choix entre plusieurs créations *Manon* à la boutique Chocolates & Creams. La plus intéressante et renversante reste sans doute le « bouchon » (qui fait partie de la collection des créations de Christian Vanderkerken). Chaque bouchon demande trois jours de préparation. Cette praline est fourrée d'une dizaine de farces sucrées. Une fois créé, le bouchon est trempé à la main dans du chocolat avant d'être recouvert d'or 24 carats. Quel sacré chocolat !

Chocolates by Bernard Callebaut

- 4242 Dundas Street West (à l'est de Royal York Road) ☎ (416) 234-0611

  Lundi à mercredi 9h30 – 19h, jeudi et vendredi 9h30 – 20h, samedi 9h30 – 18h, dimanche 12h – 17h

  Métro : ROYAL YORK + le bus
- 194 Lake Shore Road East, Oakville (près de Trafalgar Road) ☎ (905) 339-2100

  Lundi à jeudi 10h – 18h, vendredi 10h – 20h, samedi 10h – 18h, dimanche 12h – 17h

  www.bernardc.ca

Ici se marie la tradition d'une longue lignée de chocolatiers avec le moder-

nisme contemporain. M. Callebaut, ce chocolatier belge qui a élu domicile à Calgary, s'inspire de différentes cultures et religions pour nous surprendre en matière de chocolat. Ces tendances extraordinaires ne contraignent pas M. Callebault à pourchasser l'excellence absolue; il a dernièrement diminué la part de sucre utilisé dans la préparation de ses chocolats et il a augmenté la proportion de cacao. Cette équation ne signifie qu'une chose pour nous, les amoureux du chocolat : un chocolat nettement supérieur et nettement plus raffiné. Si vous recherchez un chocolat plus simple, vous trouverez aussi votre bonheur dans cette chocolaterie grâce aux truffes et aux ganaches. Vous pourrez également acheter une large gamme de chocolats à cuire (en barres, en pastilles et en poudre). Rappelons que M. Callebaut n'utilise aucun conservateur dans la préparation de ses produits. Conservateur ? Comme si on allait les laisser faire de vieux os, ces chocolats ! On a un petit secret à partager avec vous. Dans le congélateur se cache un goûter divin. Il s'agit d'une banane entière surgelée, trempée dans du chocolat *Bernard Callebaut !*

Clafouti

915 Queen Street West (à l'est de Strachan Avenue, en face du parc Trinity Bellwoods)
☎ (416) 603-1935

Fermé lundi, mardi à samedi 8h – 18h, dimanche 9h – 17h

Métro : OSGOODE + le tram

Clafouti fait uniquement dans le chocolat de tous les jours. Vous trouverez ici aussi le chocolat à boire *Poulain* et le chocolat pour fondue *Mazet.* N'oubliez pas que vous pouvez même commander sur place une bonne tasse de chocolat chaud *Poulain !*

Daniel et Daniel – Food Shop

248 Carlton Street (au coin de Parliament Street) ☎ (416) 968-9275

Lundi à samedi 7h30 – 18h, fermé dimanche

Métro : CASTLE FRANK + le bus;
COLLEGE + le tram

www.danieletdaniel.ca

Daniel et Daniel n'a que quelques parfums de truffes en magasin – noisette, chocolat blanc, noix de coco et noix. On y trouve aussi des truffes au champagne importées de France.

Holt Renfrew – Epicure Shop

50 Bloor Street West (au coin de Bay Street) ☎ (416) 922-2333

Lundi à mercredi 10h – 18h, jeudi et vendredi 10h – 20h, samedi 10h – 18h, dimanche 12h – 18h

Métro : YONGE ou BAY

Placés derrière une vitrine réfrigérée, les chocolats *Neuhaus* de Belgique et *Joseph Schmidt* nous guettent et nous font de l'œil. Holt Renfrew maîtrise l'art de la séduction silencieuse, il n'y a qu'à regarder le décor. Les chocolats *Neuhaus* sont importés de Belgique, tandis que les chocolats *Joseph Schmidt* sont importés des États-Unis, mais ils sont faits uniquement à partir de chocolat belge. Dans les deux cas, vous remarquerez que les parfums sont assez classiques. Les seuls qui sortent de l'ordinaire sont les suivants : le chocolat

Le saviez-vous ?

Une praline se déguste en une seule bouchée. C'est vraiment la seule façon de bien faire ressortir son goût. Vous voilà averti. N'essayez surtout plus de croquer plusieurs fois dans une praline pour en faire durer le plaisir, car tout ce que vous aurez réussi à faire, c'est à saboter partiellement l'expérience.

à l'orange et à l'écorce d'orange enrobée de chocolat noir et le chocolat à la cerise macérée dans de la liqueur d'armagnac et enrobée de chocolat noir. Lors des fêtes de Noël, de la Saint-Valentin et de Pâques, Holt Renfrew importe plusieurs boîtes-cadeaux de France et de Belgique, destinées à nous faire mieux célébrer l'événement. La sélection de chocolats pour tous les jours est assez limitée. Cela dit, les barres de chocolat *Neuhaus* valent la peine qu'on y pense en cas d'envie pressante de chocolat. Il y a aussi des amandes enrobées de chocolat de la maison *Fauchon.*

J. S. Bonbons

- 163 Dupont Street (au coin de Davenport Road) ☎ (416) 920-0274

  Fermé lundi, mardi à samedi 10h – 19h, dimanche 11h – 17h

  Métro : DUPONT
- 811 Queen Street West (à l'ouest de Bathurst Avenue) ☎ (416) 703-7731

  Fermé lundi, mardi à samedi 10h – 19h, dimanche 11h – 17h

  Métro : OSGOODE + le tram

  www.jsbonbons.com

Des truffes aux 26 parfums sous un même toit ! Si cette perspective ne vous séduit pas, c'est fichu ! Et si on vous dit que Jenn Stone, la créatrice qui se cache derrière J.S. Bonbons, peut aussi confectionner un sublime bol en chocolat pour accueillir votre sélection ? Épatant, n'est-ce pas ? Chez J.S. Bonbons, on se donne tout entier à la célébration de ce trésor noir d'Afrique. Les truffes sont en bonne compagnie ici, elles sont généralement alignées parmi de somptueux fruits trempés dans du chocolat. Cette jeune chocolatière n'utilise que du chocolat suisse ou belge pour ses confections. Ce qui place Jenn Stone en tête de peloton, c'est l'originalité et la qualité de ses chocolats. Vous trouverez quelques parfums classiques, mais, évidemment, ce sont les parfums moins classiques que nous vous conseillons. Les spécialités de la maison sont les infusions d'herbes et les infusions de thés. Les parfums de ces infusions vous surprendront : estragon et poivre noir, coriandre et citron vert, lavande, thé chai, bergamote et romarin. La liste peut sembler déroutante, mais le goût est tout simplement sublime et étonnamment subtil.

La Cigogne

(anciennement La Framboisine)

1626 Bayview Avenue (au sud d'Eglinton Avenue) ☎ (416) 487-1234

Lundi à vendredi 7h30 – 19h, samedi 8h – 19h, dimanche 8h – 17h

Métro : EGLINTON + le bus

Le chef Thierry Schmitt vous propose de superbes truffes maison. Vous pourrez choisir parmi une dizaine de par-

fums réalisés à base de chocolat français. Il ne faut surtout pas les rater pendant les fêtes de Noël, la Saint-Valentin, Pâques et la fête des Mères.

La Maison du Chocolat

Commande par avion du magasin de New York ☎ 1 800 988-5632

Lundi à samedi 10h – 19h, dimanche 12h – 18h

Oui, vous avez bien lu. On peut enfin acheter les chocolats de La Maison du Chocolat de ce côté-ci de l'Atlantique. Tous ceux qui ont eu le privilège de visiter les boutiques de Paris rue du Faubourg Saint-Honoré, rue François 1er et boulevard de la Madeleine savent à quel point les chocolats de cette maison sont sublimes. Que ce soit à Paris ou à New York, le simple fait de respirer ces parfums merveilleux suffit à nous enivrer. Bien que nous n'ayons pas encore la chance d'avoir une boutique de la célèbre enseigne La Maison du Chocolat à Toronto, nous avons tout de même la possibilité de nous offrir cette gourmandise affriolante. Il suffit de téléphoner pour passer commande à la boutique de New York. Attention le luxe se paie : la boîte de 77 joyaux coûte plus de 100 CAD.

Le Gourmand

152 Spadina Avenue (au sud de Queen Street) ☎ (416) 504-4494

Lundi à vendredi 7h – 21h, samedi 9h – 18h, dimanche 9h – 16h

Métro : OSGOODE + le tram;
SPADINA + le tram

Le Gourmand est un petit bistro-marchand situé en bordure du « Fashion District ». Voilà une des seules adresses où se procurer du chocolat à boire des marques françaises *Poulain* et *Monbana.* Sur place, vous aurez même la possibilité de déguster une tasse de chocolat *Poulain.*

Leonidas

- 50 Bloor Street West (au coin de Bay Street, à l'intérieur du centre Holt Renfrew) ☎ (416) 944-8822

  Lundi à jeudi 10h – 18h, vendredi 10h – 19h, samedi 10h – 18h, dimanche 12h – 17h

  Métro : YONGE ou BAY

- 176 Yonge Street, au sous-sol du magasin la Baie ☎ (416) 861-6486

  Lundi à vendredi 10h – 18h

  Métro : QUEEN

Leonidas est le plus grand fabricant de chocolats belges et il compte 2 000 boutiques dans le monde. La popularité de ses chocolats est sans aucun doute due au choix des ingrédients utilisés dans la préparation des pralines. Seuls du beurre frais, de la crème de lait, de la crème fraîche et du chocolat qui contient 100 % de beurre de cacao entrent dans la composition des pralines Leonidas. À cela, on ajoute des ingrédients qui proviennent des meilleures sources de production du monde, tels que des noisettes de Turquie, des cerises « Morello » du Périgord, des amandes d'Italie et des noix, pour n'en citer que quelques-uns. La vedette chez Leonidas, c'est la praline à la crème fraîche. Elle est incroyablement riche et onctueuse. Nous la préférons toute simple, dans sa version chocolat au lait et crème fraîche, mais vous pouvez aussi choisir d'autres parfums parmi la

gamme de douze pralines à la crème fraîche. Vous aurez également le choix du type de chocolat selon vos préférences : lait, noir ou blanc. Du fait de leur extrême fraîcheur et de l'absence d'agent conservateur, ces pralines ont une « durée de vie » de huit jours seulement. Nous sommes certains que cela ne devrait pas poser de problème au consommateur.

Pain Perdu

736 St Clair Avenue West (un peu à l'ouest de Christie Street) ☎ (416) 656-7246

Fermé lundi, mardi à vendredi 7h – 19h30, samedi 7h – 17h, dimanche 8h – 16h

Métro : ST CLAIR WEST + le tram

Des truffes, des truffes et encore des truffes. Voilà ce que nous propose le chef Folgoas en matière de gourmandises au chocolat. Au palmarès des parfums les plus populaires : chocolat noir et rhum, chocolat blanc et chocolat noir avec framboise.

Pâtisserie d'Or

301 Robinson Street (au sud de Lake Shore Road), Oakville ☎ (905) 815-8999

Fermé lundi et mardi, mercredi à vendredi 8h – 17h30, samedi 8h – 18h, dimanche 8h – 16h

Quelques savoureux chocolats suisses sont placés dans une vitrine à l'arrière de cette pâtisserie d'Oakville. Au menu des parfums, vous découvrirez les chocolats à l'orange, à la pistache, à la violette, aux pacanes, aux noisettes et à la noix de coco, ainsi que le chocolat blanc.

Pusateri's Fine Foods

1539 Avenue Road (au nord de Lawrence Avenue) ☎ (416) 785-9100

Lundi à mercredi 8h – 20h, jeudi et vendredi 8h – 21h, samedi et dimanche 8h – 19h

Métro : LAWRENCE + le bus

www.pusateris.com

Dans un recoin du magasin se cache une vitrine de truffes et ganaches de la maison *Neuhaus*.

Senses

- 318 Wellington Street West (à l'intérieur du SOHO Metropolitan Hotel, au coin de Blue Jay Way) ☎ (416) 961-0055

  Lundi à dimanche 7h – 21h

  Métro : ST ANDREW + le tram

- 2901 Bayview Avenue (à l'intérieur de la Galerie Bayview/Bayview Village) ☎ (416) 227-9149

  Lundi à vendredi 8h – 21h, samedi 8h – 18h, dimanche 9h – 17h

  Métro : BAYVIEW sur la ligne Sheppard

  www.senses.ca

Senses a fait appel au chocolatier Thomas Hass de Vancouver pour offrir à ses clients une expérience inoubliable. Le chocolatier de la côte ouest utilise exclusivement du chocolat français *Valrhona* pour la confection de ses truffes et pralines. On découvrira bien sûr des parfums classiques, mais aussi quelques surprises parmi lesquelles la truffe au champagne et à l'espresso, la truffe blanche à la vanille et au rhum, la truffe aux mûres et au miel.

Simone Marie Belgian Chocolate

126 Cumberland Street (au coin de Bellair

Street) ☎ (416) 968-7777

Lundi à samedi 10h30 – 18h30, fermé dimanche

Métro : BAY, sortie Cumberland

www.simonemarie.net

Depuis 1993, Mme Simone Marie s'est spécialisée dans l'importation de chocolats artisanaux belges. Vous découvrirez une sélection de truffes aux parfums d'alcools populaires tels que le champagne, le Cointreau et l'Amaretto. Vous aurez aussi la possibilité d'acheter des truffes fruitées à la crème d'orange, à la crème de citron, à la cannelle, à l'orange et à l'écorce d'orange, enrobée de chocolat noir. N'oubliez surtout pas de demander aux vendeurs quelle est la sélection du mois. En effet, chaque mois, la boutique met en vedette une nouveauté. La spécialité belge, adoptée par les Français et qu'il ne faut pas manquer, c'est le chocolat aromatisé à la liqueur. Eh bien oui, chez Simone Marie on peut acheter des chocolats *Bruyerre.* Cette maison, fondée en 1909, fabrique des chocolats fourrés à la liqueur (la vraie !).

Swiss-Master Chocolatier

2538 Bayview Avenue (au coin de York Mills Road, au nord de Post Road)
☎ (416) 444-8802

Lundi à samedi 10h – 18h, fermé dimanche

Métro : YORK MILLS + le bus

www.swissmaster.com

Les chocolats Swiss-Master viennent des Alpes suisses et remplissent cette petite boutique ainsi que sa boutique jumelle de Hong Kong. La propriétaire de cette boutique est à cheval sur la qualité et ce, depuis 1984; c'est l'une des raisons qui expliquent son refus catégorique du système de la franchise. Le chocolat chez les Läderach est une affaire de famille. Certes, puisque Mme Ingrid Läderach s'associe à l'un de ses oncles, qui vit en Suisse, pour nous faire découvrir un côté très raffiné du chocolat suisse. Les parfums sont très classiques puisque Mme Läderach n'adhère pas au courant de pensée de la fusion. Pour autant, ne croyez surtout pas que classique veuille dire prévisible. Il n'y a rien de prévisible dans certains

Où trouver les parfums de chocolat les plus exotiques

1. Chocolate Addict – **truffe à la lavande**
2. Chocolates by Callebaut – **ganache au chocolat amer à l'huile de lavande**
3. J.S. Bonbons – **truffe de chocolat aux parfums de masala chai, cannelle et safran** et **truffe de chocolat blanc au citron et au thym**
4. Simone Marie Belgian Chocolate – **truffe à la crème de violette,** enrobée de chocolat noir
5. Pâtisserie d'Or – **chocolat à la violette**
6. Teuscher – **truffe au jasmin**
7. The Belgian Chocolate Shop – **ganache aux poires pochées à la vodka**
8. The Chocolate Messenger – **praline au porto et praline au thé vert**
9. Truffle Treasures – **truffe au champagne Veuve Clicquot et aux fraises, truffe blanche à la mangue et au citron vert** et **truffe au gingembre macérée dans du cognac et enrobée de chocolat noir**

des chocolats que nous avons goûtés – truffe au Grand Marnier et à la crème fraîche, truffe au rhum et aux raisins, truffe au chocolat noir et à la liqueur de Grand Marnier (faite avec de la vraie liqueur de Grand Marnier !). Si vous avez quelque chose à exprimer de façon originale, optez donc pour les chocolats en forme de cœur qui portent les inscriptions suivantes : « I love you », « For you » et « Thank you ».

La spécialité de la maison la plus prisée est sans aucun doute la truffe pastel. Eh oui, ces petites boules de chocolat blanc et fruits frais colorées dans des tons pastel sont très populaires dans cette boutique. Lorsque la température se réchauffe à Toronto, régalez-vous de parfums d'orange, de fraise, de citron vert, de citron et de fruits de la passion. Les chocolats en forme d'insectes – abeilles et coccinelles – font toujours grand plaisir aux « bouts de choux ». Lors des fêtes de la Saint-Valentin, Noël et Pâques, le magasin se transforme en château de conte de fées plein à craquer sous le poids de figurines en chocolat aux parfums divers.

Teuscher Chocolates

55 Bloor Street West (au coin de Bay Street, à l'intérieur du centre Manulife)
☎ (416) 964-8200

Lundi à mercredi 10h – 18h, jeudi et vendredi 10h – 19h30, samedi 10h – 18h, fermé dimanche

Métro : YONGE ou BAY

Nombre d'épicuriens accordent à ces chocolats des éloges qui font envie. Le magazine de cuisine américain *Bon Appétit* déclare que les chocolats Teuscher sont « les plus merveilleuses créations chocolatées jamais réalisées ». Quel compliment ! Il y a plus de 65 ans que ce chocolatier suisse maîtrise l'art de séduire les palets. La fabrique de Zurich confectionne plus d'une centaine de parfums de chocolats en prenant soin de n'utiliser que les produits les plus raffinés. Les chocolats Teuscher qu'on retrouve à la boutique de Bloor West sont importés directement de Zurich chaque semaine. Vous aurez le choix entre plusieurs parfums classiques chez Teuscher, tels que l'orange, l'abricot, la crème de chocolat blanc, le citron, le nougat et le caramel. Si vous avez un petit penchant pour les cerises enrobées de chocolat, vous serez comblé, puisque Teuscher vend une cerise entière macérée dans du schnaps et enrobée de chocolat noir. Si vous étiez un inconditionnel de la *Cherry Blossom* lorsque vous étiez plus jeune, considérez que cette variété signée Teuscher est la version pour adultes de la *Cherry Blossom*. Teuscher réalise également certaines confections très originales. Au rendez-vous, des tranches d'oranges cristallisées puis trempées dans le chocolat au lait, le chocolat noir ou le chocolat blanc. Ce chocolatier cache aussi l'animalerie la plus délicieuse de la ville. Si vous voulez ajouter une note qui sorte de l'ordinaire à vos réceptions, prenez le temps de découvrir chiens, chats, abeilles, papillons et poissons en chocolat, disponibles chez Teuscher. Enfin, les vœux s'achètent chez ce chocolatier - une étoile filante ou deux en chocolat devraient faire l'affaire…

The Chocolate Messenger

1645 Bayview Avenue (au sud d'Eglinton Avenue) ☎ (416) 488-1414

Fermé dimanche et lundi, mardi à vendredi 10h – 18h, samedi 10h – 17h

Métro : **EGLINTON** + le bus

www.chocolatemessenger.com

Ce chocolatier d'origine suisse utilise le chocolat *Lindt* pour nous faire craquer. Les truffes et les pralines maison remplissent la vitrine. Les truffes à la crème fraîche sont les spécialités de la maison. Vous aurez le choix entre 20 parfums. Pour les pralines, de même, une vingtaine de parfums vous attendent, tous à base de beurre. Au sommaire des parfums les plus intéressants, voici ceux que nous avons retenus : vodka pêche, vodka orange, thé vert et porto. Nous devons aussi ajouter que ce chocolatier, comme tout chocolatier qui se respecte, n'ajoute aucun agent conservateur à ses préparations chocolatées. Lors des fêtes de la Saint-Valentin, Noël et Pâques, le magasin regorge de confections chocolatées et de boîtes de truffes. Pendant les fêtes de Noël, vous trouverez enfin des fruits confits et des marrons glacés en magasin.

The Pie Shoppe

93 Front Street East (St. Lawrence Market, au sous-sol) ☎ (416) 366-7957

Fermé dimanche et lundi, mardi à jeudi 8h – 18h, vendredi 8h – 19h, samedi 5h – 17h

Métro : **UNION**

Les truffes et pralines de The Chocolate Messenger y sont disponibles.

Truffle Treasures

178 Reach Industrial Park Road, unit # 10 (Reach Road et Highway 12), Port Perry ☎ (905) 982-0506/1 866 582-2773

Lundi à samedi 9h – 18h30

www.truffletreasures.com

Lara Vaarré a développé son art en étudiant avec un chocolatier chevronné qui avait 70 années d'expérience à son actif. Après avoir acquis les bases du métier, elle est allée parfaire son éducation à l'école de renommée internationale Lenôtre, à Paris. Aucun doute là-dessus, Lara Vaarré adore son métier. Ça se lit dans la passion qu'elle transmet et ça se goûte lorsque l'on croque dans ses truffes. Les parfums abondent, si bien qu'il devient difficile de choisir parmi la trentaine proposée. Il y a quatre façons de déguster les chocolats de Lara Vaarré : on peut aller directement à l'entrepôt de Port Perry, au nord d'Oshawa; certains magasins Fortino en ville les vendent; on peut les commander sur le site; enfin, si vous parcourez les foires gastronomiques de Toronto et du grand Toronto, vous serez presque assuré de tomber sur le point de vente de Truffle Treasures.

Whole Foods Market

87 Avenue Road (au nord de Bloor Street) ☎ (416) 944-0500

Lundi à vendredi 9h – 22h, samedi 9h – 21h, dimanche 9h – 20h

Métro : **BAY** ou **MUSEUM**

www.wholefoodsmarket.com

Les chocolats et le chocolat à cuire de la maison *Callebaut* y sont disponibles.

où faire ses emplettes

fromages et crème fraîche

Lorsqu'on pense à la France, on pense sans contredit à « la Sainte-Trinité » : du pain, du vin et du fromage. Il n'y a rien de plus français qu'une bonne baguette garnie de camembert et accompagnée d'un verre de vin. La Suisse est un autre pays francophone à la belle sélection de fromages. On ne doute pas qu'une bonne éducation au monde des fromages se fasse de l'autre côté de l'Atlantique. Vous serez néanmoins rassuré de savoir qu'on peut très bien parfaire son éducation ici aussi, à Toronto. Si vous êtes à la recherche de plaisirs fromagers, les adresses suivantes devraient pouvoir vous satisfaire.

Le saviez-vous ?

Un fromage AOC porte la garantie d'une longue tradition. L'AOC est la distinction légale la plus élevée que décerne l'Institut national des appellations d'origine (INAO). Un cahier des charges définit l'origine et la production de tous les produits AOC. Le consommateur a ainsi la garantie d'acheter un fromage qui provient d'une région bien précise en France, fabriqué à partir d'une méthode bien particulière avec un lait spécial. En d'autres termes, le fromage AOC est issu d'un produit qui, à sa source, n'a rien perdu de sa fabrication traditionnelle et même artisanale. Certains fromages d'appellation d'origine contrôlée sont fabriqués depuis plus de 2 000 ans. Le roquefort est le premier fromage AOC français. On le fabrique exclusivement avec du lait de brebis. Le cantal et la fourme d'Ambert sont deux autres fromages fabriqués de la même façon depuis plusieurs siècles. On dit qu'il y a plus de 2 000 sortes de brie ou variations de brie, mais il n'en existe que deux qui portent la mention AOC. Ces deux élus, qui ont retenu toute notre attention, nous inspirent beaucoup d'admiration.

Alex Farm Products

Différentes adresses dans toute la ville

☎ 1 877 488-7778 (numéro général d'information)

www.alexcheese.com

La France produit 150 à 200 fromages différents. Vous aurez l'impression de tous les retrouver chez Alex Farm, car cette boutique est celle qui importe le plus grand nombre de fromages français à Toronto. Parmi les fromages qu'on vous y propose : le vacherin Mont-d'Or de Badoz (AOC), le pouligny-saint-pierre, le coulommiers, le pont l'évêque, l'époisses de Bourgogne, le saint-andré, la fourme d'Ambert, le saint-agur, le rondin du Poitou, le brique de Jussac, le morbier, le fromage *Belle des Champs*, le grand pont l'évêque, le laguiole (AOC), le chaumes, l'etorki, l'abondance (AOC), le chaource (AOC), et le grain d'orge de Normandie. La gamme de fromages classiques est également impressionnante. Vous pouvez même acheter du p'tit Basque (fromage de brebis pur du Pays basque). Vous y trouverez également une bonne sélection de fromages suisses, parmi lesquels trois variétés d'emmenthal, du gruyère, trois types de fromage appenzeller et de la raclette.

All the Best Fine Foods

1099 Yonge Street (près du métro Summerhill) ☎ (416) 928-3330

Lundi à mercredi 8h30 – 18h30, jeudi et vendredi 8h30 – 19h, samedi 8h30 – 18h, dimanche 10h – 17h

Métro : SUMMERHILL

La sélection est très intéressante dans cette boutique du quartier Rosedale. Elle inclut des fromages français, québécois et suisses bien connus ainsi que quelques autres moins connus à Toronto. Entre autres, vous trouverez de l'époisses, du comté, du morbier, du camembert Jort, du livarot, du mothais,

du selles-sur-cher, du pouligny-saint-pierre et du brie, parmi les fromages les plus connus. Le fromage de chèvre chabichou du Poitou, le fougerus, le colombier, le fromage de Riblaire et l'édel de Cléron font partie de la liste des fromages moins connus. Vous trouverez également une bonne sélection de fromages crus du Québec tels que le saint-basile, le saint-félicien, le Lechevalier Mailloux, le pied de vent et l'ange cornu.

CHEESE BOUTIQUE

45 Ripley Avenue (au sud de South Kingsway et The Queensway)
☎ (416) 762-6292

Lundi à vendredi 8h – 21h, samedi 8h – 20h, dimanche 10h – 18h

Métro : **RUNNYMEDE** + le bus

www.cheeseboutique.com

Avouez que le nom est assez révélateur… et trompeur à la fois ! D'après nous, Cheese Boutique devrait adopter le nom suivant : *French* Cheese Boutique. En effet, puisqu'on y trouve une très bonne sélection de fromages de France (plus d'une centaine), du Québec (une trentaine) et de la Suisse (une dizaine). On a décidé de ne pas citer les grands noms du fromage en vente chez Cheese Boutique, puisqu'ils y sont tous. Vous trouverez même des fromages qu'on trouve difficilement ailleurs, comme l'explorateur. La plupart des autres importateurs s'approvisionnent en explorateur à l'époque des fêtes de Noël, mais le propriétaire de Cheese Boutique l'importe tout au long de l'année. Chose qu'on voit peu à Toronto : le nombre de fromages provenant de petits artisans fromagers québécois. Cheese Boutique en importe plusieurs. Ce qui nous a le plus surpris et ravis, c'est que chez Cheese Boutique, on importe plusieurs fromages de France qu'on affine ensuite sur place. Le propriétaire nous a fait goûter un petit bout d'explorateur venu de France et un petit bout d'explorateur affiné en boutique. Aucune comparaison !

CHEESE MAGIC

182 Baldwin Street (Kensington Market)
☎ (416) 593-9531

Lundi à samedi 8h30 – 19h, dimanche 9h – 18h

Métro : **SPADINA** + le tram;
QUEEN'S PARK + le tram

Cheese Magic ne propose pas un choix comparable à celui des deux géants du fromage de la francophonie du marché Kensington, mais sa sélection demeure tout à fait honorable. De la Suisse, on importe de l'appenzeller, du gruyère, de la raclette et de l'emmenthal. De la France, on importe du roquefort, du morbier, du bleu d'Auvergne, du port-salut et de la raclette française. Du Québec, on importe de l'oka, du saint-benoît bleu bénédictin, du brie et du chèvre.

CHRIS' CHEESEMONGERS

93 Front Street East (St. Lawrence Market)
☎ (416) 368-5273

Fermé dimanche et lundi, mardi à jeudi 8h – 18h, vendredi 8h – 19h, samedi 5h – 17h

Métro : **UNION**

Voici le petit cousin d'Alex Farm. Si Alex Farm se spécialise dans les

fromages en provenance de la France, Chris' Cheesemongers s'en donne à cœur joie dans les fromages en provenance du Québec. Leur liste en est presque étourdissante (une quinzaine de fromages français contre une soixantaine de fromages québécois). Vous trouverez une variété abondante côté Québec : chèvre noir, grand cru de Chaput, double brie aux herbes et double brie au poivre, pied de vent des Îles-de-la-Madeleine, capra et freddo, jeune cœur des Îles-de-la-Madeleine, mi-carême de l'Île aux Grues (un fromage très similaire au camembert de Normandie) et cendré de Warwick (la version québécoise du morbier). Vous remarquerez également quelques fromages français tels que le chaumes, le saint-paulin, le brie triple crème, le port-salut, le bresse bleu, le camembert de Normandie, le pont l'évêque, le boursault, le rouy et le vacherin Mont-d'Or, pour ne citer que ceux-là.

Dinah's Cupboard

50 Cumberland Street ☎ (416) 921-8112

Lundi à vendredi 9h – 19h, samedi 9h – 18h, fermé dimanche (à l'exception du mois de décembre)

Métro : YONGE ou BAY

Dinah's Cupboard importe une très petite quantité de fromages français; environ une demi-douzaine d'entre eux sont parmi les plus populaires.

Le saviez-vous ?

La France produit plus de 160 000 tonnes de camembert par an. Ça, c'est du fromage !

Global Cheese

76 Kensington Avenue ☎ (416) 593-9251

Lundi à vendredi 8h30 – 19h, samedi 8h – 18h, dimanche 9h – 17h

Métro : SPADINA + le tram;
QUEEN'S PARK + le tram

Global Cheese propose les fromages français suivants : morbier, saint-agur, truffier, fourme d'Ambert, champagne, chèvre, saint-andré, saint-paulin, pont l'évêque, bleu d'Auvergne et roquefort. Ces fromages font partie d'une liste totale d'environ quarante fromages français. Pour ce qui est des fromages du Québec, Global en importe une vingtaine, parmi lesquels le brie, le brie aux herbes, le brie aux poivres, l'oka, l'emmenthal du Québec et le camembert. Enfin, côté Suisse, la liste est plus courte. On a surtout accès aux plus connus : le gruyère et l'emmenthal. En plus, Global Cheese donne à ses clients la possibilité de goûter avant d'acheter. Pas moyen de se tromper !

Loblaws

Différentes adresses dans toute la ville

Si vous n'avez pas le temps de rendre visite à votre fromager préféré, vous pouvez toujours vous arrêter chez Loblaws. Le choix y est très satisfaisant pour un supermarché. Vous êtes sûr de trouver plus d'une vingtaine de classiques français, québécois et suisses. Le brie, le camembert, le *Boursin,* le *Caprice des Dieux,* l'emmenthal français, le coulommiers, le comté, le bleu d'Auvergne, l'oka, le bleu et le chèvre figurent, entre autres, sur la liste des fromages disponibles. Loblaws importe

également de la raclette et du gruyère de Suisse.

Max Market

2299 Bloor Street West (à l'ouest de Runnymede Road) ☎ (416) 766-6362

Lundi à mercredi 9h – 19h, jeudi 9h – 19h30, vendredi 9h – 20h, samedi 9h – 19h, dimanche 9h – 18h

Métro : RUNNYMEDE

On trouve chez Max Market une quantité raisonnable de fromages de France, du Québec et de Suisse. Au palmarès des grands noms figurent le morbier, la raclette de France et celle de Suisse, l'appenzeller, le bleu d'Auvergne, la fourme d'Ambert, le saint-agur, le roquefort, le chèvre de Riblaire, l'oka et le gruyère.

Mendel's Creamery n' Appetizer

72 Kensington Avenue ☎ (416) 597-1784

Lundi à vendredi 8h30 – 19h, samedi 7h30 – 18h, fermé dimanche

Métro : SPADINA + le tram;
QUEEN'S PARK + le tram

Mendel's Creamery n' Appetizer occupe une superficie bien moindre que son voisin, mais en matière de fromages de la francophonie, la taille du magasin n'a plus rien à voir. Selon la saison, Mendel's a en magasin jusqu'à 80 fromages français, une dizaine du Québec et une demi-douzaine de la Suisse. Sur la liste des fromages français, on a le morbier, le roquefort, le saint-paulin, le saint-andré, le fromage de chèvre de Corse et le bleu brie. Au palmarès québécois figurent l'oka, le camblu et le brie. Quant à la Suisse, ses couleurs sont bien représentées avec du gruyère, de la raclette, de l'emmenthal, de l'appenzeller et du vacherin Mont-d'Or.

Où trouver les fromages AOC à Toronto

1. Alex Farm Products
2. All the Best Fine Foods
3. Cheese Boutique
4. Chris' Cheesemongers
5. Global Cheese
6. Mendel's Creamery n' Appetizer (à Noël seulement)
7. Olympic Cheese Mart
8. Pusateri's Fine Foods
9. Scheffler's Delicatessen & Cheese
10. Whole Foods Market

Olympic Cheese Mart

- 93 Front St. East (St. Lawrence Market) sud ☎ (416) 363-7602

  Fermé dimanche et lundi, mardi à jeudi 8h – 18h, vendredi 8h – 19h, samedi 5h – 17h

  Métro : UNION

- 7780 Woodbine Avenue, Markham (au coin de la 14e Avenue) ☎ (905) 944-8676

  Lundi à mercredi 10h – 18h, jeudi et vendredi 10h – 19h, samedi 9h30 – 18h, fermé dimanche

Plus de 400 fromages y « dorment » sous le même toit. Les mordus de la fondue au fromage trouveront plusieurs types de raclette sans lait de vache et à faible teneur en sodium. En matière de fromages français, Olympic Cheese Mart propose plus de 100 variétés. On y retrouve les plus populaires, mais aussi certains moins bien connus, tels

Le saviez-vous ?

L'oka est l'un des fromages d'origine française les plus vieux du Canada. Il est arrivé au Canada (Nouvelle-France) en 1893, lorsque le frère Alphonse Juin immigra depuis l'abbaye de Port-du-Salut, en France. Le frère Alphonse entra dans l'ordre des moines cisterciens et s'installa près du lac des Deux Montagnes, au Québec. Déjà expert fromager, le frère Alphonse décida alors de mettre son savoir-faire en œuvre pour créer le fromage oka que l'on connaît. Bien entendu, l'oka n'est plus préparé aujourd'hui par les moines cisterciens de la Trappe d'Oka. Cependant, la recette de base et la méthode de préparation d'origine restent, à ce jour, inchangées. Tous les deux jours, l'oka est tourné et lavé à la main, tel qu'il y a plus d'un siècle. Ce souci de préserver la qualité à tout prix explique pourquoi l'oka est l'un des fromages que les Canadiens dégustent le plus souvent.

que le camembert au poivre, le gourmelin, l'époisses, le roquefort papillon, le comté, le beaufort et le *p'tit reblo.* Parmi les fromages les plus connus figurent le brie, le camembert, le brie en brioche, le saint-morgon, le saint-andré, la raclette et le chèvre. Olympic Cheese Mart est un autre marchand qui importe plusieurs variétés du Québec. Parmi celles-ci, on a le mouton noir, le saint-ambroise (un fromage à la bière), le frère Jacques, le moine, le douanier (façon morbier) et la mamirolle. Autres fromages intéressants en provenance du Québec : le Sir Laurier d'Arthabaska, les fromages de la région de Saint-Benoît, le cantonnier et les fromages de la région de Plessisville. Les fromages suisses sont bien représentés ici aussi : gruyère, emmenthal, raclette, vacherin fribourgeois, vacherin Mont-d'Or, maréchal, trois types d'appenzeller, Mont Vully, weinkäse (vieilli au vin) et tête de moine, pour n'en citer que quelques-uns. Olympic Cheese Mart importe également quelques fromages au lait cru.

PUSATERI'S FINE FOODS

- 1539 Avenue Road (au nord de Lawrence Avenue) ☎ (416) 785-9100

  Lundi à mercredi 8h – 20h, jeudi et vendredi 8h – 21h, samedi et dimanche 8h – 19h

  Métro : LAWRENCE + le bus

- 57 Yorkville Avenue (au coin de Bay Street) ☎ (416) 785-9100

  Lundi à mercredi 10h – 20h, jeudi et vendredi 10h – 21h, samedi 8h – 20h, dimanche 10h – 19h

  Métro : BAY

  www.pusateris.com

Comme vous pouvez l'imaginer, il y a chez Pusateri's un grand choix de fromages parmi les plus raffinés de la francophonie. En voici donc quelques exemples pour vous inciter à faire un tour au magasin et à y découvrir la gamme complète : roquefort, époisses, bleu d'Auvergne, saint-agur, etorki, tomme de Savoie, morbier, saint-albray et chaumes. Nous avons remarqué la présence de welsche, fromage affiné d'Alsace, de rebloch'art en provenance du Québec et de chimay, fromage belge.

Quality Cheese

111 Jevlan Drive, Vaughan (au coin de Highway 7 et Weston Road)
☎ (905) 265-9991

Lundi à vendredi 8h30 – 18h, samedi 8h30 – 17h, fermé dimanche

La famille Borog y fabrique des fromages de qualité « olympique ». Vous recherchez des fromages ayant remporté plusieurs médailles ? Dans la catégorie des fromages français, Quality Cheese vous propose un brie médaillé.

Scheffler's Delicatessen & Cheese

93 Front Street East (St. Lawrence Market)
☎ (416) 364-2806

Fermé dimanche et lundi, mardi à jeudi 8h – 18h, vendredi 8h – 19h, samedi 5h – 17h

Métro : UNION

Tout comme ses confrères du marché St. Lawrence, Scheffler's met à votre disposition un vaste choix de fromages du Québec et de France. Côté français, vous trouverez du saint-agur, du camembert, du saint-andré, de l'ermite, du chèvre, du fromage de brebis et du saint-paulin. De ce côté-ci de l'Atlantique, vous aurez le choix entre du camembert, du brie, du chèvre, de l'oka, du frère Jacques et du bleu bénédictin. En provenance de la Suisse enfin, il y a du gruyère et de l'emmenthal.

Sobey's

81 St. Clair Avenue East (un peu à l'est de Yonge Street) ☎ (416) 413-0594

Tous les jours, 24 heures sur 24

Métro : ST CLAIR

Sobey's est une franchise du grand Toronto et l'on retrouve ses magasins partout en ville. Cependant, le nouveau magasin du quartier de Yonge et St Clair a su s'adapter au goût un tantinet francophile du coin. Vous y découvrirez une petite sélection de fromages bien connus de la francophonie – saint-aubin, rustique de Normandie, morbier, *p'tit reblo,* saint-paulin, emmenthal, brie et camembert de France ou du Québec, oka et chèvre.

Sun Valley Fruits & Grocery

583 Danforth Avenue (à l'est de Pape Avenue) ☎ (416) 469-5227

Tous les jours, 8h – 21h

Métro : PAPE

Sun Valley est avant tout un expert de la feta grecque. Cependant, Sun Valley propose aussi les fromages les plus connus de la francophonie. Côté suisse, on a le gruyère et l'emmenthal. Pour les fromages français, le choix est un peu plus varié, avec une quinzaine de variétés de l'Hexagone représentées, parmi lesquelles le morbier, la tomme de montagne, la fourme d'Ambert, le saint-nectaire, le roquefort et le bleu d'Auvergne.

Whole Foods Market

87 Avenue Road (au nord de Bloor Street)
☎ (416) 944-0500

Lundi à vendredi 9h – 22h, samedi 9h – 21h, dimanche 9h – 20h

Métro : BAY OU MUSEUM

www.wholefoodsmarket.com

Cet empire de la nourriture biologique et de la qualité supérieure propose une

excellente sélection de fromages français et québécois rares à Toronto. De la France on importe la fourme d'Ambert, le comté, la tomme de Savoie, le chaumes, le saint-nectaire, le munster, le cantal, l'ossau-iratry-brebis Pyrénées, le crottin de chavignol, le pont l'évêque, le saint-aubin, le petit livarot de Normandie, l'explorateur de la fromagerie Petit-Morin, le chaource et le montagnou ! Whole Foods Market vend beaucoup de fromages d'appellation d'origine contrôlée (AOC). Whole Foods Market s'est donné pour mission d'initier les Torontois aux fromages recherchés du Québec. Et pour cause, puisque la sélection de la belle province ne cesse de s'agrandir. Sur place, vous pourrez choisir entre du maroilles, du geai bleu, de la tourelle de Richelieu, du pont couvert et du cantonnier au lait cru. Les fromagers proposent également deux types de fromages façon morbier – le douanier et le cendré de Warwick. Enfin, l'un des fromages les plus vieux du Québec, à savoir l'oka, sera au rendez-vous des amateurs. Les fromages qui vous étonneront le plus sont les fromages d'influence française du Nouveau-Brunswick. En effet, les producteurs de fromages y fabriquent des variétés à pâte dure assez succulentes. La gamme est restreinte, c'est pourquoi il faut tous les essayer ! Whole Foods Market importe le Sieur de Duplessis (au lait de brebis) et la tomme de champ doré. Pour ce qui est des fromages suisses, le choix ne se limite pas aux plus populaires que sont le gruyère, l'emmenthal et la raclette. Tandis que la plupart des fromagers de Toronto importent un seul type de gruyère, Whole Foods Market en importe trois. Ainsi, vous pouvez acheter du gruyère au lait cru, du gruyère haute altitude (préparé avec du lait de vache élevée en haute altitude) et du gruyère vieilli dans des grottes. De par sa fabrication, le gruyère qui a vieilli en grotte est un peu plus salé (ses petites taches blanchâtres sont les traces des cristaux de sel), a une texture un peu plus granuleuse et un goût plus prononcé, si on le compare aux deux autres. Whole Foods Market nous fait aussi découvrir des fromages suisses assez difficiles à trouver ailleurs à Toronto, tels que le vigneron, l'appenzeller et le mostkäse. Le mostkäse a une caractéristique peu commune puisqu'il est lavé dans le cidre de pomme afin d'être un peu plus alcoolisé. Le vaca prino est un autre fromage un peu moins connu que vous gagnerez à essayer. À noter, deux autres fromages suisses qui valent le coup qu'on s'y intéresse : le fromage aux graines de moutarde et celui aux olives.

Les vendeurs chez Whole Foods Market sont vraiment très qualifiés et ils n'hésitent pas à mettre leurs compétences au service de chaque client, tout le temps qu'il faut, afin que celui-ci puisse faire le bon choix. Contrairement à ce qu'on pourrait penser, les fromages vendus par Whole Foods Market sont assez abordables.

La crème fraîche

Elle n'est pas facile à dénicher cette crème fraîche ! À tous ceux qui désespéraient de pouvoir trouver de la véritable crème fraîche à la française à Toronto : votre patience est enfin récompensée, car nous avons repéré les bonnes adresses. Vous pourrez enfin ajouter ce délice crémeux et indispensable à la cuisine française, entre autres à vos desserts et soupes.

ALEX FARM PRODUCTS Cette boutique met fin à nos recherches de ce délice des dieux. On y trouve de la crème fraîche de Normandie en grande quantité.

ALL THE BEST FINE FOODS On vous propose ici une crème fraîche préparée sur place.

CHEESE BOUTIQUE On vend de la crème fraîche de France dans cette boutique.

CHRIS' CHEESEMONGERS Vous trouverez ici de la crème fraîche de Normandie.

MAX MARKET Voici une adresse, dans le Bloor West Village, où se procurer de la crème fraîche du Québec.

OLYMPIC CHEESE MART Voici une autre bonne enseigne du marché St. Lawrence où l'on vend de la crème fraîche du Québec.

PUSATERI'S FINE FOODS Vous trouverez, chez ce marchand de luxe, de la crème fraîche en provenance du Québec.

SCHEFFLER'S DELICATESSEN & CHEESE Vous pouvez y acheter de la crème fraîche du Québec ou de France.

SOBEY'S Plusieurs connaisseurs ont poussé ce marchand à avoir de la crème fraîche en magasin. La crème fraîche de Sobey's est un produit de l'Ontario.

SUN VALLEY FRUITS & GROCERY C'est l'adresse à connaître dans le quartier grec quand on est à la recherche de crème fraîche.

WHOLE FOODS MARKET Ce marchand chic met à la disposition des résidents de Yorkville et des quartiers avoisinants de la crème fraîche. Celle-ci est produite en Ontario et on la trouve dans le frigo des spécialités (« specialty cooler »). Ce frigo n'est pas évident à trouver dans le magasin, donc nous vous conseillons de demander un peu d'aide.

où faire ses emplettes

viande, charcuterie, terrines et foie gras

Parmi la sélection de base d'un boucher (veau, bœuf, agneau, porc et, dans bien des cas, volaille), les pièces de viande abondent et l'on peut toujours demander une coupe particulière. Ainsi, nous avons décidé de limiter nos descriptions aux spécialités de la maison. Nous y ajouterons une liste détaillée des viandes les plus prisées des francophones et francophiles. Vous n'aurez donc plus aucune difficulté à trouver les viandes qu'il vous faut pour préparer les meilleurs plats de France et de la francophonie.

Bloor Meat Market

2283 Bloor Street West (à l'ouest de Runnymede Road) ☎ (416) 767-2105

Fermé lundi, mardi à vendredi 9h30 – 18h30, samedi 8h30 – 18h, dimanche 10h – 17h

Métro : RUNNYMEDE

La spécialité de la maison, ce sont les viandes et kebabs marinés dans des préparations d'épices maison – une dizaine de marinades différentes. Même les poitrines de poulet ont droit à un traitement bien particulier : à la florentine, kiev ou encore cordon-bleu, pour ne citer que ces trois-là. Chez Bloor Meat Market, on trouve aussi du poulet de Cornouailles (petit poulet issu du croisement d'une poule et d'un poulet) surgelé et du bœuf pour les fondues. Notons que ce boucher prend le service à la clientèle très à cœur.

Brandt Meat Packers Supermarket

1878 Mattawa Avenue, Mississauga (près de Dundas Street et Dixie Road) ☎ (905) 279-4460

Fermé dimanche à mardi, mercredi 8h – 18h, jeudi et vendredi 8h – 19h, samedi 7h – 14h

Alors là, les Allemands font très fort ! Brandt Meat Packers comblera plus d'un francophile. Une très grande vitrine de viande révèle divers morceaux de bœuf, porc, volaille et veau. Au second coup d'œil, on remarque avec surprise les délices suivantes : saucisses de veau, reins de veau, tripes de bœuf, foies de veau, langues de veau, foies de poulet, boudins, cuisses de faisan, cuisses de faisan fumé et faisan fumé entier. Un grand congélateur, situé près du rayon des produits de beauté, dévoile d'autres surprises surgelées – oie, canard, poulet de Cornouailles, faisan, foie de veau et gras de porc.

Brown Brothers Meats

93 Front Street East (St. Lawrence Market) ☎ (416) 364-7469

Fermé dimanche et lundi, mardi à jeudi 8h – 18h, vendredi 8h – 19h, samedi 5h – 17h

Métro : UNION

Brown Brothers Meats vend les morceaux de viande qui conviennent aux cuisines francophones. Au sommaire : foie de veau, veau de lait, filet mignon (filet de bœuf premier choix, et non pas de porc, au Canada), viande pour la fondue chinoise ou bourguignonne et bœuf d'appellation AA et AAA d'Ontario.

Cumbrae's Naturally Raised Fine Meats

481 Church Street (au coin de Wellesley Street) ☎ (416) 923-5600

Lundi à vendredi 9h30 – 19h, samedi 9h – 18h, dimanche 11h – 17h

Métro : WELLESLEY

Cumbrae's Naturally Raised Fine Meats impressionne par le choix qu'il propose, son service, ses pièces de viande et la propreté qui y règne. Nous avons déniché de nombreuses viandes qui feront le plaisir des francophones et francophiles. Chez Cumbrae's, il y a plusieurs viandes marinées, du lapin, du canard, de la caille, des rognons, du boudin, du poussin, du pigeon, de l'oie, de la pintade et du faisan (il est préférable de passer une commande spéciale pour certaines viandes).

Sur place, on découvrira aussi du magret de canard, de la poitrine de canard fumée, du foie de poulet, du foie de veau et du confit de canard. Cumbrae's a également en magasin des viandes pour les fondues, de l'agneau du Québec et du cerf. Cumbrae's est l'une des rares adresses en ville où l'on peut acheter des merguez et du gras de canard.

Il y a une autre chose bien pratique : Cumbrae's Naturally Raised Fine Meats vend une très bonne sélection de viandes marinées et prêtes-à-cuire.

Di Liso's Fine Meats

93 Front Street East (St. Lawrence Market) ☎ (416) 601-9780

Fermé dimanche et lundi, mardi à jeudi 8h – 18h, vendredi 8h – 19h, samedi 5h – 17h

Métro : UNION

Vous trouverez chez ce boucher plusieurs morceaux de viande particulièrement adaptés à vos fondues chinoises ou bourguignonnes, ainsi que du filet mignon, du lapin et divers morceaux d'agneau.

European Quality Meats & Sausages

- 176 Baldwin Street (Kensington Market) ☎ (416) 596-8691
- Lundi à jeudi 8h – 18h30, vendredi 8h – 19h, samedi 7h – 18h30, fermé dimanche

  Métro : SPADINA + le tram; QUEEN'S PARK + le tram
- 16 Jutland Road, Etobicoke (près de Queensway et Kipling Avenue) ☎ (416) 251-6193

  Lundi à mercredi 8h – 18h, jeudi et vendredi 8h – 19h, samedi 8h – 18h, fermé dimanche

  Métro : KIPLING

Une spécialité règne ici : des prix très raisonnables. Dans la bonne tradition du marché Kensington, le service est sans façon et la foule afflue. Les pièces de viande sont simples – rien de très sophistiqué – mais elles s'adaptent à toutes les cuisines. Armez-vous de patience, car ici, on fonctionne avec un numéro pour servir les clients.

Grace Meat Market

644 College Street (au coin de Grace Street) ☎ (416) 534-7776

Lundi à mercredi 8h – 18h, jeudi et vendredi 8h – 19h, samedi 8h – 18h, dimanche 10h – 16h

Métro : QUEEN'S PARK + le tram

Ce boucher, situé dans le quartier italien, vous donne la possibilité d'acheter plusieurs viandes qui conviendront à ravir à la préparation de vos plats. Grace Meat Market vend du lapin, du poussin, de la pintade et du cerf sur commande spéciale. À part ça, vous trouverez de la dinde fumée, de la viande pour fondue, du filet mignon, du poulet de Cornouailles, de la caille surgelée, du veau de lait, des rognons, des saucisses d'agneau, du foie et des reins. Petit détail assez intéressant : ce boucher fait rôtir sur place poulets et saucisses à emporter.

Greco Meat Packers Limited

93 Front Street East (St. Lawrence Market) ☎ (416) 869-3251

Fermé dimanche et lundi, mardi à jeudi 8h – 18h, vendredi 8h – 19h, samedi 5h – 17h

Métro : UNION

Greco Meat Packers a en magasin une

Charcuterie, terrines et foie gras

Alex Farm Products Ce marchand importe de la mousse de foie gras truffée, de la mousse de foie gras au porto, de la mousse de canard, du confit de canard, des rillettes de canard et du magret de canard de France. Du Québec, il importe plusieurs très bons pâtés aux parfums plus extraordinaires les uns que les autres (environ une quinzaine). Chez Alex Farm, il y a aussi du foie gras de La Ferme Périgord, disponible en mousse, bloc, terrine, rillettes et pâté.

All the Best Fine Foods Cette épicerie fine vend des pâtés et terrines de La Ferme (Québec) ainsi que quelques sélections d'Ontario. Lors de notre dernier passage, nous avons noté les spécialités suivantes : pâté de caille aux poivrons verts, terrine de canard aux pistaches, mousse truffée, mousse de caille et truffes. Vous trouverez aussi du foie gras de La Ferme Périgord.

Brandt Meat Packers Supermarket Chez ce marchand allemand, une grande vitrine dévoile une sélection assez remarquable de viandes séchées et saucissons secs.

Caviar Direct Il n'y a pas que du caviar et du poisson fumé chez ce marchand. Caviar Direct vend aussi du foie gras du Québec qu'on peut acheter en bloc ou en plus petite portion. Il y a aussi un foie gras d'oie aux truffes français, vendu en bloc. Vos invités vous en diront des nouvelles !

Cheese Boutique Chez Cheese Boutique, blocs de foie gras français et blocs de foie gras québécois rivalisent. À vous de trancher. Cheese Boutique vend par ailleurs une mousse de foie gras du Québec au quart du prix du véritable foie gras français ou québécois. On y trouve également six pâtés de La Maison du Gibier, en provenance du Québec.

Chris' Cheesemongers Vous trouverez ici plusieurs pâtés et terrines de deux maisons québécoises fort réputées : L'Élevage Périgord et La Maison du Gibier. On y vend également une petite gamme de blocs de foie gras et de terrines importés de France. Enfin, vous pourrez vous régaler avec du magret et du confit de canard.

Cumbrae's Naturally Raised Fine Meats On trouve ici une bonne variété de pâtés et terrines en provenance du Québec. Au menu, vous aurez le choix entre du porc de Toulouse, du canard au poivre vert, du canard au poivre rose, du faisan aux pistaches, du pâté de campagne aux champignons sauvages et des rillettes de canard. Cumbrae's Naturally Raised Fine Meats vend du saucisson sec tel qu'on le trouve en France. Voici enfin une bonne adresse pour se procurer du foie gras.

Daniel et Daniel Les pâtés maison sont peu nombreux, mais comme on le sait, la qualité prime, plutôt que la quantité, dans cet établissement. Daniel et Daniel vous propose deux pâtés (campagne et poivre), ainsi que des rillettes de canard.

Dinah's Cupboard Cette charmante épicerie fine propose rillettes du Mans, rillettes de canard, terrine de lapin aux pistaches, terrine de faisan, mousse de truite fumée, terrine de sanglier aux abricots et foie gras ! En tout et pour tout, Dinah's a en magasin une douzaine de pâtés (selon la saison) qui proviennent du Québec ou qui sont faits sur place, en cuisine.

Global Cheese Voici une adresse où vous pourrez acheter du foie gras et du pâté importés du Québec et de France.

viande, charcuterie, terrines et foie gras

Max Market Ce marchand importe plus d'une quinzaine de pâtés et terrines du Québec. Au programme des réjouissances, on a : le pâté d'autruche au cassis, le pâté de caille, le pâté de porc aux truffes, le pâté au Grand Marnier, le pâté de canard aux pistaches.

Meat on the Beach Ce boucher vend du foie gras ainsi qu'une gamme originale de pâtés et terrines de France. Voici deux associations qui nous ont paru originales : le pâté de faisan aux raisins de Corinthe et la terrine de cerf au cognac. La terrine de lièvre que l'on trouve chez Meat on the Beach est assez rare à Toronto.

Mendel's Creamery n' Appetizer Mendel's importe du foie gras du Québec et de France. Les pâtés les plus en vogue sont le pâté au romarin et aux champignons, ainsi que le pâté au Grand Marnier, aux poivrons et au cognac.

Olympic Cheese Mart Cette fromagerie importe quelques foies gras de France. On y trouve aussi du pâté de campagne et du pâté au cognac du Québec. Il y a même des cretons (variété de rillettes de porc) de la belle province.

Patachou Cette pâtisserie vend du pâté de foie de volaille, du pâté de campagne ou un bloc de foie gras de canard.

Pusateri's Fine Foods Il y a dans cette épicerie fine une sacrée gamme de pâtés, terrines et foies gras. Le foie gras est disponible sous différentes formes : en bloc, en beurre, truffé, en mousse et en gelée. Le choix des pâtés et saucissons secs est tout aussi varié.

Scheffler's Delicatessen & Cheese Ce marchand importe du foie gras de France et du Québec. Il propose aussi une bonne dizaine de terrines, toutes en provenance du Québec. Scheffler's vend aussi du magret de canard, du canard tranché et du confit de canard importé de France. Enfin, il a chez Scheffler's plusieurs saucissons secs.

Sobey's Ce supermarché importe une bonne quantité de terrines du Québec. La sélection est d'une rareté impressionnante. En témoignent la terrine d'autruche et de porc aux raisins de Corinthe et la terrine de cinq gibiers (autruche, cerf, faisan, bison, sanglier) et porc aux airelles (canneberges). Sobey's vend également du foie gras du Québec.

The Butcher Block Café Ce boucher vend du foie gras du Québec.

The Butchers On vend ici une petite sélection de pâtés du Québec : faisan, canard aux pistaches, cerf et truite fumée. The Butchers vend aussi du foie gras.

Village Butcher Ce boucher vend des pâtés et de la mousse de foie gras.

White House Meats Ce boucher a en magasin une petite sélection de pâtés, ainsi que du foie gras frais et mi-cuit sous trois formes : mousse de foie gras, bloc de foie gras et foie gras de canard entier. La boutique de Bayview vend plusiers pâtés de foie du Québec. Sur place, vous trouverez également du foie gras de canard, du confit de canard, du magret et des cuisses de canard pour préparer vous-même votre confit.

Whole Foods Market Ce supermarché de luxe vend quelques variétés de pâtés de viande d'élevage et de gibier. Ces pâtés sans agents conservateurs viennent tous du Québec. On retrouve du pâté de caribou, du pâté de porc aux figues, du pâté de caille, du pâté de porc aux pistaches et, enfin, du pâté de canard et porc aux pistaches.

belle gamme de viandes de bœuf d'appellation AA et AAA d'Ontario et de bœuf « Black Angus ». Voici un autre marchand du marché St. Lawrence qui vend du foie de veau, du veau de lait et du veau nourri au grain. On y trouve aussi plusieurs morceaux d'agneau et de la viande pour fondue chinoise ou bourguignonne.

Highland Farms

4750 Dufferin Street (au Nord de Finch Avenue) ☎ (416) 736-6606

Lundi à samedi 7h – 22h, dimanche 8h – 20h

Métro : DOWNSVIEW + le bus

Le rayon boucherie de Highland Farms se démarque des autres grandes surfaces par sa quantité de viandes disponibles à la coupe. Sans compter qu'Highland Farms propose des viandes qu'on voit rarement dans les autres supermarchés, telles que du lapin, des tripes de bœuf et du foie de veau. Vous trouverez également du chapon, ainsi que plusieurs morceaux de veau et d'agneau.

Manos Meats

93 Front Street East (St. Lawrence Market) ☎ (416) 364-2652

Fermé dimanche et lundi, mardi à jeudi 8h – 18h, vendredi 8h – 19h, samedi 5h – 17h

Métro : UNION

La sélection est un peu limitée chez Manos Meats, mais on y trouve tout de même les éléments de base de la cuisine française : foie de veau, filet mignon et viande pour fondue bourguignonne ou chinoise.

Meat on the Beach

1860 Queen Street East (à l'ouest de Rainsford Road) ☎ (416) 690-1228

Lundi à jeudi 7h – 19h, vendredi 7h – 20h, samedi et dimanche 7h – 18h

Métro : QUEEN + le tram

Meat on the Beach a récemment déménagé. La nouvelle boutique offre le même niveau de qualité et de service qu'on connaissait. Les viandes qu'on utilise dans les meilleures recettes de la cuisine française ou francophone sont vendues ici. Il y a une bonne variété de volailles sauvages - canard, oie et pigeon. On y vend aussi de la dinde fumée, du boudin, de la pintade et du lapin (sur commande) pendant toute l'année. On peut s'approvisionner en faisan et en chapon pendant les fêtes de Noël. Contrairement à plusieurs bouchers qui n'ont qu'un ou deux abats en magasin, Meat on the Beach se distingue par son grand choix. On peut également choisir parmi une bonne quantité de morceaux d'agneau et un large éventail de saucisses maison, de viande pour fondue et de filet mignon. Aux amateurs de nouveauté, nous recommandons les viandes fourrées au lard. Enfin, notons que ce boucher vend les fameuses saucisses merguez et que toutes ses viandes sont nourries au grain.

Nick's Wholesale Meats & Delicatessen

93 Front Street East (St. Lawrence Market) ☎ (416) 362-5041

Fermé dimanche et lundi, mardi à jeudi 8h – 18h, vendredi 8h – 19h, samedi 5h – 17h

Métro : UNION

Si vous cherchez à composer un menu de brochettes, Nick's Wholesale Meats pourra certainement vous aider. En effet, ce boucher vend une gamme impressionnante de brochettes de porc, de bœuf et de poulet. Il vend également du filet mignon.

Nicola's Choice Meats

298 Eglinton Avenue West (au coin d'Avenue Road) ☎ (416) 485-4429

Lundi à vendredi 7h – 19h, samedi 7h – 17h, fermé dimanche

Métro : EGLINTON + le bus

La spécialité ici, c'est l'attention particulière qu'on accorde à l'achat des viandes : on les préfère médaillées. Ce boucher a reçu un prix de qualité et d'excellence de la « Royal Agricultural Winter Fair ». Parmi les viandes qui sauront plaire aux francophones, on a : le lapin, le boudin, le foie de veau, le mouton, la caille, le faisan, la viande pour fondue, l'oie et le canard. Chose assez rare, sur place on trouve des rognons d'agneau et beaucoup d'autres abats. Pour les spécialités françaises, il vaut mieux demander, car elles sont souvent conservées à l'arrière du magasin.

Olliffe

1097 Yonge Street (au sud du métro Summerhill) ☎ (416) 928-0296

Lundi à jeudi 8h30 – 18h30, vendredi 8h30 – 19h, samedi 8h30 – 18h, dimanche 10h – 17h

Métro : SUMMERHILL

Si connaître le prix avant d'acheter vous intéresse, il y a de bonnes chances pour qu'Olliffe ne puisse être votre boucher attitré. Les prix ne sont pas affichés (et pour cause…), la qualité répond aux « standards » d'exigence du quartier et les viandes sont bien coupées en même temps que quasiment dépourvues de gras. Vous pourrez acheter des merguez (livrées le jeudi), de la poitrine de canard, du lapin, du boudin, du foie de veau, de la caille (fraîche pendant l'hiver et surgelée le reste de l'année). Le faisan, le pigeon, le poulet de Cornouailles, le poussin et la pintade sont disponibles sur commande spéciale. Mais Olliffe a toujours en magasin du veau de lait. Il vend aussi de beaux morceaux de viande pour les fondues. Au temps des fêtes de Noël, Olliffe importe du foie gras de canard et d'oie de France et du Québec. Que ce soit pour une occasion spéciale ou pour vos courses hebdomadaires, Olliffe offre tout ce dont on peut rêver… à condition d'être prêt à payer le prix.

Pusateri's Fine Foods

- 1539 Avenue Road (au nord de Lawrence Avenue) ☎ (416) 785-9100

  Lundi à mercredi 8h – 20h, jeudi et vendredi 8h – 20h, samedi et dimanche 8h – 19h

  Métro : LAWRENCE + le bus

- 57 Yorkville Avenue (au coin de Bay Street) ☎ (416) 785-9100

  Lundi à mercredi 10h – 20h, jeudi et vendredi 10h – 21h, samedi 8h – 21h, dimanche 10h – 19h

  Métro : BAY

www.pusateris.com

Pusateri's rend la vie plus facile à sa clientèle en lui offrant un grand choix de viandes marinées et assaisonnées, telles que de la caille fourrée aux airelles

Où trouver des merguez ?

La plupart des marchands ci-dessous importent leurs merguez du Québec. Dans tous les cas, soyez assuré que vos saucisses marocaines seront rehaussées en saveur épicée.

1. Cumbrae's Naturally Raised Meats
2. Meat on the Beach
3. Olliffe
4. Scheffler's Delicatessen & Cheese
5. The Butchers
6. Village Butcher
7. White House Meats

(canneberges) et aux figues, de la caille méditerranéenne (caille enrobée de lard, fourrée au fromage de chèvre, aux piments et à la roquette) et du poulet de Cornouailles aux airelles. Ces viandes marinées sont incroyablement pratiques, car elles sont toutes prêtes en un tour de main et elles se cuisinent aussi bien au four, à la poêle ou grillées. Vous pourrez également acheter de la pintade et du magret de canard chez Pusateri's.

Royal Beef

1968 Danforth Avenue (à l'ouest de Woodbine Avenue) ☎ (416) 421-1029

Fermé lundi, mardi et mercredi 9h – 17h, jeudi et vendredi 9h – 19h, samedi 9h – 17h, dimanche 10h – 16h

Métro : WOODBINE

Attention, on ne badine pas ici. Les viandes sont coupées le jour même. Et pour être frais, c'est frais ! En plus, vous trouverez chez Royal Beef des escalopes de veau nourri à l'herbe et du poulet élevé en plein air. Au palmarès des préférences des francophones : lapin, faisan, boudin (sur commande spéciale), oie (à Noël), canard, pintade (sur commande spéciale), viande pour fondue, filet mignon, rognons, abats, caille et poulet de Cornouailles.

St. Lawrence Upper Cut

93 Front Street East (St. Lawrence Market) ☎ (416) 362-3142

Fermé dimanche et lundi, mardi à jeudi 8h – 18h, vendredi 8h – 19h, samedi 5h – 17h

Métro : UNION

St. Lawrence Upper Cut propose de beaux morceaux de filet mignon, du lapin, du veau de lait, du faisan et du poulet de Cornouailles. À notre grande surprise, St. Lawrence Upper Cut vend du pigeon. Enfin, voici une adresse en plus où dénicher de la viande pour fondue : il suffit de commander.

Scheffler's Delicatessen & Cheese

93 Front Street East (St. Lawrence Market) ☎ (416) 364-2806

Fermé dimanche et lundi, mardi à jeudi 8h – 18h, vendredi 8h – 19h, samedi 5h – 17h

Métro : UNION

Voici un rendez-vous dans le marché St. Lawrence pour les amateurs de merguez.

Sobey's

81 St. Clair Avenue East (un peu à l'est de Yonge Street) ☎ (416) 413-0594

Tous les jours, 24 heures sur 24

Métro : ST CLAIR

Si vous habitez dans le quartier de

Yonge et St Clair, Sobey's est l'adresse qu'il vous faut pour vos lapins, médaillons de cerf, cailles et poulets de Cornouailles. On nous a aussi laissés entendre qu'il devrait y avoir de plus en plus de gibier en magasin.

The Butcher Block Café

3251 Yonge Street (au nord de Lawrence Avenue) ☎ (416) 544-1729

Lundi 10h – 18h, mardi à vendredi 9h – 19h, samedi 8h – 18h, dimanche 11h – 18h

Métro : LAWRENCE

www.thefriendlybutcher.com

Les mordus de la grillade ne seront pas déçus. Sur place, on peut acheter le gril, la viande et les sauces dans un seul et même rayon. Le boucher peut même se déplacer à domicile, se faisant un plaisir de cuire votre viande à la perfection dans votre cour ou dans votre cuisine, histoire d'épater vos convives. Ce service fait partie du « service traiteur ». Les appellations AA et AAA du bœuf Angus noir canadien sont une autre spécialité chez ce boucher. Côté préférences des francophones et francophiles, on a du lapin, du veau de lait, de la caille, du poulet de Cornouailles, du filet mignon et de la viande pour fondue. Vous pourrez aussi acheter de la viande de cheval, du cerf, des abats et de la pintade en passant une commande spéciale.

The Butchers

2636 Yonge Street (au nord d'Eglinton Avenue) ☎ (416) 483-5777

Lundi à mercredi 9h – 18h, jeudi à vendredi 9h – 19h, samedi 9h – 18h, dimanche 9h – 17h

Métro : EGLINTON

The Butchers est un spécialiste de la viande biologique : on peut acheter du bœuf d'appellation AA et AAA d'Ontario, de l'agneau et du porc biologique. Ces viandes biologiques viennent de l'élevage de la ferme Beretta. The Butchers vend aussi une quantité remarquable de viandes qui sauront plaire aux francophones et francophiles : lapin, veau de lait, viande pour fondue, rognons, filet mignon, poulet de Cornouailles et cerf. Par ailleurs, on y trouve du confit de canard et du magret de canard. Les viandes qui suivent sont disponibles sur commande spéciale : faisan, pigeon, canard, oie, pintade, abats et caille. On peut même passer une commande pour la viande de cheval. Enfin, les amoureux du couscous trouveront ici de bonnes merguez !

Village Butcher

2914 Lake Shore Boulevard West (près d'Islington Avenue) ☎ (416) 503-9555

Fermé dimanche et lundi, mardi à vendredi 7h30 – 18h, samedi 7h30 – 17h

Métro : ISLINGTON + le bus

Village Butcher propose les viandes suivantes : lapin, veau de lait, foie de canard, caille, faisan, cerf, poulet de Cornouailles, bison, boudin, pigeon, foie et rognons. Vous pouvez aussi acheter d'autres types d'abats, il suffit de passer une commande spéciale. La viande de cheval et la pintade sont également disponibles sur commande. Chez Village Butcher, il y a aussi un filet mignon hors pair ainsi que de la viande pour fondue. La spécialité ici, c'est la saucisse maison – porc, veau,

dinde et agneau. Encore une chose qui a retenu notre attention chez ce marchand : la vente de poulet de culture biologique. Rupert, le boucher, nous dit aussi qu'il prépare des merguez maison sur commande. Son conseil : il est préférable de commander certaines viandes jusqu'à trois semaines à l'avance. Rupert les fera vieillir en magasin afin que vous puissiez les savourer aussi tendres que possible.

White House Meats

- 93 Front Street East (St. Lawrence Market) ☎ (416) 366-4465

  Fermé dimanche et lundi, mardi à jeudi 8h – 18h, vendredi 8h – 19h, samedi 5h – 17h

  Métro : UNION

- 1539 Bayview Avenue (au sud d'Eglinton Avenue) ☎ (416) 488-2004

  Fermé lundi, mardi à vendredi 9h – 19h (fermé à 18h pendant l'hiver), samedi 8h – 18h, dimanche 11h – 17h

  Métro : EGLINTON + le bus

Ce boucher remporte la Palme d'or en matière de service à la clientèle. Il n'y a pas à dire, ce duo fraternel a la passion du métier. Les habitués disent que la boutique est un paradis sur terre quand on est amateur de viande. Effectivement, nous avons été épatés par le choix qu'offre ce boucher. En magasin, on trouve plusieurs viandes qui sortent de l'ordinaire telles que les viandes d'autruche, de cerf et de bison. Côté viandes de la francophonie, une sélection impressionnante : morceaux d'agneau, saucisses de foie (à la boutique de Bayview), veau de lait, ris de veau, lapin et superbes morceaux de filet mignon. Quant à la viande pour fondue bourguignonne ou chinoise, là aussi, White House assure. Si vous passez commande à l'avance, vous serez assuré de déguster une fondue inoubliable. La variété de volailles ne laisse pas non plus à désirer : poussin, poulet de Cornouailles, oie, pintade, magret de canard, faisan frais ou surgelé et pigeon. Ce boucher vend aussi deux autres pièces rares à Toronto, à savoir la saucisse merguez et le boudin blanc ou noir (sur commande seulement). Enfin, chez White House Meats, vous pourrez acheter de la graisse de canard ainsi que des bouillons de bœuf, volaille et gibier faits maison.

où faire ses emplettes

poissonneries et spécialistes des huîtres

Pané, frit, poché, grillé, fumé ou en tartare, les façons d'apprêter le poisson sont nombreuses. Bien que les possibilités de préparation des fruits de mer semblent plus limitées, on raffole tout autant de ces coquillages succulents. Le poisson et les fruits de mer occupent une place importante dans la cuisine française et dans la plupart des cuisines francophones. Ainsi, nous savons à quel point un bon poissonnier est indispensable. Nous vous donnons donc rendez-vous dans tous les endroits qui suivent pour acheter toutes vos délices de la mer préférées.

Avenue Seafood

302 Eglinton Avenue West (au coin d'Avenue Road) ☎ (416) 481-2288

Lundi 12h – 19h, mardi à jeudi 9h15 – 19h, vendredi et samedi 9h – 19h, dimanche 12h – 18h

Métro : EGLINTON + le bus

Vous trouverez en magasin des pattes de crabes d'Alaska, du saumon de la côte ouest canadienne, de la truite et des queues de homards cubains. On y trouve aussi de la sardine (sur commande), du poulpe, du thon frais et plusieurs variétés de saumon.

Big Fish Market

765 The Queensway (à l'ouest de Royal York Road) ☎ (416) 259-1585

Fermé dimanche et lundi, mardi et mercredi 10h – 18h, jeudi et vendredi 10h – 20h, samedi 9h – 18h

Métro : ROYAL YORK + le bus

Big Fish Market vend une bonne sélection de poissons et fruits de mer « exotiques », tels que des pétoncles péruviens, du homard de la Nouvelle-Écosse, des huîtres de l'Île-du-Prince-Édouard, des moules à coquilles vertes de la Nouvelle-Zélande. La morue fraîche (cabillaud), le saumon fumé, la sardine surgelée ou fraîche, le thon frais et les écrevisses sont quelques autres exemples parmi tout ce que vous trouverez sur place. Ici, on importe généralement des variétés d'huîtres en provenance des États-Unis et de la côte est du Canada.

Bill's Lobsters

599 Gerrard Street East (à l'est de Broadview Avenue) ☎ (416) 778-0943

Lundi à samedi 9h30 – 18h

Métro : BROADVIEW + le tram

Le nom est assez révélateur… Mais chez Bill's Lobsters, on vend aussi, entre autres choses, des oursins de mer, des cuisses de grenouilles, des crevettes, de la truite et du crabe. Bill's Lobsters importe également des huîtres de la côte est et la côte ouest du Canada.

Brandt Meat Packers Supermarket

1878 Mattawa Avenue, Mississauga (près de Dundas Street et Dixie Road) ☎ (905) 279-4460

Fermé dimanche à mardi, mercredi 8h – 18h, jeudi et vendredi 8h – 19h, samedi 7h – 14h

La spécialité ici, c'est le poisson fumé et les filets de poisson en conserve et bocal. Brandt Meat Packers Supermarket a en magasin des filets de plusieurs variétés, qui vont de la sardine au maquereau. Il y a même des escargots en conserve ainsi que de l'anguille.

Caviar Centre

220 Duncan Mills Road (au coin de Don Mills Road) ☎ (416) 441-9788

Lundi à vendredi 11h – 18h, fermé samedi et dimanche. Possibilité d'ouverture le samedi sur demande.

Métro : SHEPPARD OU DON MILLS

www.caviarcentre.com

Pour tous les fous de ce délice russe, Caviar Centre propose du Beluga, de l'Osetra, du Sevruga. Il y a même du caviar de France !

Caviar Direct

93 Front Street East (St. Lawrence Market, au sous-sol) ☎ (416) 361-3422

Fermé dimanche et lundi, mardi à jeudi 8h – 18h, vendredi 8h – 19h, samedi 5h – 17h

Métro : UNION

www.caviarforsale.com

Voici un petit comptoir qui vaut son pesant d'or. Caviar Direct importe les grandes variétés de caviars – Beluga, Osetra et Sevruga. Il importe aussi certaines sélections « Black Label » perses. Caviar Direct vous propose également plusieurs variétés de poissons fumés, non seulement du saumon fumé d'Écosse et du Canada, mais aussi de la truite et du maquereau fumés.

Diana's Seafood

2101 Lawrence Avenue East (près de Warden Avenue) ☎ (416) 288-9286

Lundi 9h – 18h, mardi à vendredi 9h – 19h, samedi 9h – 18h, dimanche 10h – 17h

Métro : LAWRENCE + le bus;
KENNEDY + le bus

Diana's Seafood vend des huîtres de la côte est et de la côte ouest du Canada.

Domenic's Fish Market

93 Front Street East (St. Lawrence Market) ☎ (416) 368-1397

Fermé dimanche et lundi, mardi à jeudi 8h – 18h, vendredi 8h – 19h, samedi 5h – 17h

Métro : UNION

Ce marchand importe plusieurs poissons frais bien connus tels que le thon, le cabillaud, le poulpe, les palourdes, les huîtres et même la sardine fraîche. Domenic's Fish Market possède également un congélateur qui regorge de poissons et fruits de mer surgelés.

Domino Foods Ltd.

93 Front Street East (St. Lawrence Market, au sous-sol, tout au fond du marché) ☎ (416) 366-2178

Fermé dimanche et lundi, mardi à jeudi 8h – 18h, vendredi 8h – 19h, samedi 5h – 17h

Métro : UNION

Domino Foods n'est pas une poissonnerie, mais vous y trouverez plusieurs filets de poisson en conserve et en bocal.

Global Cheese

76 Kensington Avenue ☎ (416) 593-9251

Lundi à vendredi 8h30 – 19h, samedi 8h – 18h, dimanche 9h – 17h

Métro : SPADINA + le tram;
QUEEN'S PARK + le tram

Global importe quelques filets de poisson marinés. Au choix : filets de hareng, de truite et de maquereau.

Highland Farms

4750 Dufferin Street (au Nord de Finch Avenue) ☎ (416) 736-6606

Lundi à samedi 7h – 22h, dimanche 8h – 20h

Métro : DOWNSVIEW + le bus

Highland Farms vend plusieurs poissons fumés surgelés tels que le saumon, le thon, la truite, l'anguille, l'espadon et les sprats.

Kensington Market

Métro : SPADINA + le tram;
QUEEN'S PARK + le tram

▸ Coral Sea Fish Shop

198 Baldwin Street ☎ (416) 593-9656

Lundi à samedi 8h – 18h, fermé dimanche

▸ **Medeiros Fish Market**

168 Baldwin Street ☎ (416) 593-9738

Lundi à samedi 7h30 – 18h, fermé dimanche

▸ **New Seaway**

195 Baldwin Street ☎ (416) 593-5192

Lundi à dimanche 7h – 18h

▸ **Sea Kings**

189 Baldwin Street ☎ (416) 593-9949

Lundi à samedi 8h – 18h, dimanche 9h – 16h

▸ **Seven Seas Fish**

196 Baldwin Street ☎ (416) 593-9875

Lundi à dimanche 8h – 17h

Ces cinq adresses sont proches les unes des autres dans la rue Baldwin, au cœur du marché Kensington. Les marchands s'approvisionnent tous auprès du même distributeur, ainsi les prix et les produits proposés sont plus ou moins les mêmes. Attention, le samedi matin n'est peut-être pas le meilleur moment pour aller y faire ses courses. Les queues sont longues et le niveau d'adrénaline, parfois, monte ! Comme pour la plupart des magasins situés dans le marché Kensington, les prix sont incroyablement abordables et la qualité satisfaisante. La sélection est assez classique, mais on retrouve plusieurs des poissons et fruits de mer prisés des francophones – sardine fraîche ou surgelée, thon frais, morue fraîche (cabillaud), pétoncles, rouget, sole, crabe, moules, palourdes, huîtres, poulpe et plusieurs variétés de crevettes. La plupart des poissons sont vendus frais, cependant certains marchands ont un congélateur en magasin, ce qui vous permet de retrouver certains plaisirs de la mer même lorsque la saison est passée. La plupart des marchands vendent des poissons fumés et séchés. Sea Kings et Coral Sea Fish Shop vendent des oursins de mer pendant la saison des fêtes de Noël. Enfin, la plupart de ces poissonniers vendent de l'anguille pendant les mois d'hiver.

Lobster Island

27 Milliker Boulevard (à l'est de Kennedy Road) ☎ (416) 591-6488

Lundi à samedi 9h – 18h, dimanche 9h – 12h

Métro : FINCH + le bus

Lobster Island est un petit poissonnier qui se spécialise dans l'importation de fruits de mer. Vous êtes certain d'y découvrir un large choix parmi vos crustacés préférés. Ce marchand vous propose aussi des huîtres de la côte est et de la côte ouest du Canada.

Mendel's Creamery n' Appetizer

72 Kensington Avenue ☎ (416) 597-1784

Lundi à vendredi 8h30 – 19h, samedi 7h30 – 18h, fermé dimanche

Métro : SPADINA + le tram;
QUEEN'S PARK + le tram

Mendel's a une vitrine de filets de poisson marinés. Vous y découvriez des filets d'anchois, de maquereau à l'huile d'olive, des filets de maquereau fumés et des filets de hareng, ainsi que des huîtres fumées.

Mike's Fish Market

93 Front Street East (St. Lawrence Market) ☎ (416) 368-0876

Fermé dimanche et lundi, mardi à jeudi 8h – 18h, vendredi 8h – 19h, samedi 5h – 17h

Le saviez–vous ?

Comme pour le vin, un temps de repos s'impose pour la dégustation des huîtres. Ainsi, on recommande d'ouvrir les huîtres une demi-heure avant de les déguster. Il est également préférable de jeter la première eau, car les huîtres en sécréteront alors une nouvelle, plus parfumée.

Il est déconseillé de remettre des huîtres ouvertes au réfrigérateur. Mieux vaut les conserver sur un lit de glace. Lorsque les huîtres sont trop froides, elles perdent leur saveur.

Si vous préférez manger vos huîtres crues, faites ressortir leur saveur avec un peu de poivre blanc. D'après les puristes en la matière, il est préférable d'éviter le vinaigre aux échalotes et même le citron, qui dénaturent le goût des huîtres.

Contrairement à la tendance populaire, pour bien manger des huîtres, il faut les mâcher et non pas les gober. En les mâchant, on apprécie beaucoup plus les nuances qu'offre chacune de leurs variétés.

Le vin blanc est le meilleur nectar pour accompagner des huîtres.

Métro : UNION

Mike's Fish Market importe une variété de poissons et fruits de mer qui saura plaire aux francophones et francophiles. Au menu : moules, poulpe, thon frais, rouget, palourdes et huîtres. Mike's Fish Market importe aussi de la sardine fraîche tous les mois. Ce poissonnier propose également un bon choix de poissons et fruits de mer surgelés. Si vous cherchez la facilité pour un repas du soir, optez donc pour les poissons marinés, prêts à être dégustés.

Newport Fish Importers & Wholesalers

1140 Dupont Street (au coin de Dufferin Street) ☎ (416) 537-1278

Lundi à mercredi 7h – 17h, jeudi et vendredi 7h – 19h, samedi 7h – 16h, fermé dimanche

Métro : DUFFERIN + le bus

Si vous voulez acheter du poisson très frais chez Newport Fish Importers, n'y allez pas le lundi, car la cargaison n'arrive que le mardi matin. Cela dit, à compter du mardi, vous aurez le choix entre du poulpe, du cabillaud (morue fraîche), de la sardine fraîche, des crevettes (très généreuses par la taille), de l'anguille, du crabe, du thon frais et du rouget. Dans un récipient en plastique près des palourdes, des moules et des huîtres, nous avons trouvé des escargots. Et à Toronto, on n'en voit pas très souvent, puisque la plupart des poissonniers utilisent les escargots pour nettoyer leurs aquariums. De toute évidence, ces poissonniers n'en connaissent pas assez long sur la cuisine française... Il y a deux choses caractéristiques chez Newport : les filets de poisson frais d'une part et la vingtaine de congélateurs qui abritent tous les poissons et

fruits de mer qu'on peut imaginer d'autre part. Pour ce qui est des filets de poisson, on en importe plus d'une cinquantaine chez Newport. Quant à la liste de poissons surgelés, elle pourrait s'étendre sur deux chapitres, nous vous en donnons donc un petit aperçu : crevettes, filets de sole, pétoncles géants, homards et crabes. Vous trouverez également chez ce poissonnier du poisson salé et des palourdes en conserve.

Osler Fish Warehouse

16 Osler Street (au coin de Dupont Street) ☎ (416) 769-2010

Lundi 10h – 17h, mardi à vendredi 8h – 19h, samedi 8h – 17h, fermé dimanche

Métro : DUNDAS WEST

Osler est un expert des poissons et crustacés en provenance du Portugal. Mais il importe aussi les plaisirs de la mer suivants d'ailleurs, dans le monde : poulpe du Maroc, thon frais, sardine fraîche, cabillaud, morue salée, rouget, truite, anguille de mer et oursin de mer.

Oyster Boy

872 Queen Street West ☎ (416) 534-3432

Tous les jours, à partir de 17h

Métro : QUEEN + le tram

Selon la saison, Oyster Boy peut avoir en magasin jusqu'à six variétés d'huîtres.

Pisces Gourmet

1103 Yonge Street (au sud du métro Summerhill) ☎ (416) 921-8888

Lundi 9h30 – 18h30, mardi à jeudi 9h – 18h30, vendredi 9h – 19h, samedi 9h – 18h, fermé dimanche

Métro : SUMMERHILL

Pisces vend de très beaux morceaux de poisson. Le service est excellent et le prix reflète très bien la qualité des poissons. Aux francophones (et aux autres !), Pisces propose du cabillaud, de la truite, des palourdes, des huîtres (la chair est vendue sans les coquilles), du poulpe, de la truite fumée, du thon frais et de la sardine fraîche. Le sommet du plaisir chez Pisces, ce sont sans aucun doute les très belles brochettes de poisson marinées et prêtes-à-cuire. Si vous ne voulez pas vous fatiguer à préparer votre repas du soir, voici un très bon compromis, par ailleurs servi en quelques minutes seulement. Sur place, il y a aussi de la bouillabaisse qu'il suffit de réchauffer. En prime, un petit citron tout jaune est offert à chaque achat pour parfumer vos délices de la mer…

Pusateri's Fine Foods

- 1539 Avenue Road (au nord de Lawrence Avenue) ☎ (416) 785-9100

  Lundi à mercredi 8h – 20h, jeudi et vendredi 8h – 21h, samedi et dimanche 8h – 19h

  Métro : LAWRENCE + le bus

- 57 Yorkville Avenue (au coin de Bay Street) ☎ (416) 785-9100

  Lundi à mercredi 10h – 20h, jeudi et vendredi 10h – 21h, samedi 8h – 20h, dimanche 10h – 19h

  Métro : BAY

  www.pusateris.com

Au rayon des poissons frais de Pusateri's, vous pourrez acheter du thon, du cabillaud, du rouget, de la truite, des pétoncles, du poulpe et des crevettes géantes. Côté poissons surgelés, on vend du crabe d'Alaska, du homard, des écrevisses, des escargots, du cabillaud,

des crevettes et des pétoncles (au magasin d'Avenue Road). Plusieurs filets de poisson en conserve sont également disponibles. Enfin, Pusateri's vous propose du caviar : Beluga, Osetra et Sevruga d'Iran.

Rodney's Oyster House

469 King Street West (au coin de Spadina Avenue) ☎ (416) 363-8105

Lundi à samedi 11h30 – 1h (du matin), fermé dimanche

Métro : KING + le tram

www.rodneysoysterhouse.com

Rodney's importe la plus grande variété d'huîtres à son quartier général de King Street. En fait, il importe ses huîtres des quatre coins du monde – Europe, Japon, côtes est et ouest du Canada. Chez Rodney's, on trouve couramment jusqu'à une douzaine de variétés différentes. En règle générale, comptez 8 à 9 variétés l'été et jusqu'à 20 l'hiver. Eh non, on ne plaisante pas ! Rodney's vous accueille même jusqu'à une heure du matin pour l'achat de vos huîtres.

Seafront Fish Market

93 Front Street East (St. Lawrence Market) ☎ (416) 365-0086

Fermé dimanche et lundi, mardi à jeudi 8h – 18h, vendredi 8h – 19h, samedi 5h – 17h

Métro : UNION

Seafront Fish Market importe du thon frais, du cabillaud, du saumon, de la sardine fraîche, des pétoncles, des palourdes et des moules. Bien entendu, cette liste n'est qu'un bref aperçu de la sélection de ce poissonnier. Il a aussi un congélateur qui cache plusieurs poissons et fruits de mer surgelés.

Snappers Fish Market

263 Durie Street (au coin de Bloor Street West) ☎ (416) 767-4083

Lundi 10h – 18h, mardi à vendredi 10h – 18h30, samedi 9h – 18h, dimanche 12h – 17h

Métro : RUNNYMEDE

Ceux qui vivent dans le quartier de High Park sont enfin servis : un petit poissonnier local leur propose les incontournables de la mer. Au rendez-vous : thon frais, morue fraîche, sole, haddock, rouget et pétoncles. Dans le congélateur, il y a du crabe d'Alaska, des escargots, du poulpe, de la sardine et des queues de homard. Enfin, on trouvera plusieurs filets de poisson en conserve. Et pour les produits qui sortent un peu de l'ordinaire, on peut toujours passer une commande spéciale.

Les spécialistes des huîtres

Pour déguster des huîtres en toute saison et pour toutes les occasions, ces spécialistes des huîtres vous approvisionneront en ce qu'il y a de meilleur sur les côtes des océans d'ici et d'ailleurs. La plupart des poissonniers vendent des huîtres, mais les adresses que nous vous proposons ci-dessous font également la différence par rapport à la concurrence au niveau des diverses variétés d'huîtres disponibles.

1. Big Fish Market
2. Bill's Lobsters
3. Diana's Seafood
4. Lobster Island
5. Oyster Boy
6. Rodney's Oyster House

Village Butcher

2914 Lake Shore Boulevard West (près d'Islington Avenue) ☎ (416) 503-9555

Fermé dimanche et lundi, mardi à vendredi 7h30 – 18h, samedi 7h30 – 17h

Métro : ISLINGTON + le bus

C'est vrai que Village Butcher est avant tout un boucher… Cependant, vous découvrirez une petite sélection de poissons frais, acheminés chez ce boucher trois fois par semaine. La gamme est restreinte, mais n'oubliez pas, le mot d'ordre ici est « fraîcheur ». Vous pourrez ainsi acheter du saumon, du flétan, des pétoncles, des crevettes et du tilapia. Le tilapia est un poisson oriental qui se nourrit exclusivement d'algues. Il est vendu en filet et se prête particulièrement bien aux recettes façon meunière. On trouve aussi certains poissons de saison.

autres spécialités françaises

Cette section vous permettra de trouver encore davantage de spécialités françaises. Ces produits sont vendus frais, en conserve, en bocal ou même surgelés. L'important est qu'avec eux, vous avez accès à certains incontournables de la gastronomie française au cœur même de votre ville.

On peut préférer acheter des produits frais, le rythme effréné de nos vies ne nous le permet pas toujours pour autant. C'est pourquoi nous avons ajouté une rubrique « produits français surgelés » qui vous facilitera la tâche en cas de besoin.
Vous trouverez cette mention sous les adresses où l'on vend des produits surgelés.

Marchés

Highland Farms

☎ (416) 736-6606

Métro : DOWNSVIEW + le bus

C'est vrai que Highland Farms est avant tout un supermarché. Cependant, nous l'avons inscrit sous la section « marché » car Highland Farms offre la plus grande concentration de fruits et légumes au mètre carré. Des fruits et des légumes à en perdre la tête, plusieurs provenant de l'Ontario. Les semaines qui précèdent les fêtes de Noël, vous pouvez y trouver des betteraves jaunes ou encore des carottes rouges. Les mois d'été, vous avez le choix entre de multiples herbes fraîches et des jeunes pousses d'ail frais sont même en vente. Highland Farms est une très grande surface. Au fond du magasin, vous trouverez une vitrine de viande assez impressionnante ainsi qu'un choix d'olives à vous rendre fou si vous êtes un amoureux des olives. Vous remarquerez qu'Highland Farms possède aussi un rayon de fromages français et suisses pas négligeable. Le magasin importe surtout les variétés les plus connues. La boulangerie est remplie de plusieurs spécialités boulangères des quatre coins du monde. Chez Highland Farms vous découvrirez peut-être moins de produits de la francophonie que dans les marchés Kensington et St. Lawrence, mais les grands rayons de fruits, légumes et viandes compenseront largement.

Kensington Market

Métro : SPADINA + le tram;
QUEEN'S PARK + le tram

Baldwin Street et Spadina Avenue, c'est à cette intersection que prend forme ce « marché » de quartier abritant marchands de fruits et légumes, fromagers, commerces d'épices et graines en vrac, poissonneries et boucheries. Le marché Kensington a un double attrait : on peut y acheter tout ce qu'il faut pour préparer de nombreux plats de la cuisine française à des prix vraiment très raisonnables et l'on n'est qu'à quelques pas de l'exotisme du quartier chinois. Après tout, on ne peut se satisfaire du même type de cuisine tous les jours ! Il est facile et agréable de faire toutes ses emplettes au marché Kensington pendant les trois quarts de l'année. L'hiver, c'est une autre histoire. En effet, seuls les acheteurs les plus motivés s'aventurent au marché Kensington pendant les longs mois d'hiver rigoureux, car le marché est à ciel ouvert.

St. Lawrence Market

Métro : UNION

www.stlawrencemarket.com

Le marché St. Lawrence est vraiment un des joyaux de Toronto. Vous découvrirez toutes les délices de la francophonie sous un même toit. Quelle joie ! Les marchands permanents du marché St. Lawrence sont situés dans le bâtiment sud. Bouchers, fruitiers, légumiers, poissonniers et fromagers importent de vastes gammes de produits bien précieux pour la cuisine des francophones ou francophiles. La proximité des différents marchands, le fait que le marché soit couvert toute l'année et sa facilité d'accès font du marché St. Lawrence un excellent choix de destination pour faire ses courses. Le samedi, le bâtiment nord abrite le marché des fermiers : fruits et légumes frais de l'Ontario et produits de la ferme comme le miel, le sirop d'érable, les tartes et les fromages maison font le bonheur des nombreux acheteurs qui s'y déplacent le week-end.

Alex Farm Products

Différentes adresses dans toute la ville

☎ 1 877 488-7778 (numéro général d'information)

www.alexcheese.com

Alex Farm vend des huiles aux noix, aux truffes noires et blanches, aux amandes grillées et aux noisettes. Il vend aussi plusieurs parfums de vinaigre *Maille*. La fleur de sel nature ou aux herbes de Provence est vendue chez Alex Farm à un prix fort raisonnable. Enfin, le magasin dissimule quelques sauces (béarnaise et hollandaise) de la maison *Delouis fils*, importées de France.

All the Best Fine Foods

1099 Yonge Street (près du métro Summerhill) ☎ (416) 928-3330

Lundi à mercredi 8h30 – 18h30, jeudi et vendredi 8h30 – 19h, samedi 8h30 – 18h, dimanche 10h – 17h

Métro : SUMMERHILL

www.allthebestfinefoods.com

Vous trouverez, à cette adresse de Rosedale, les immanquables des spécialités françaises. Ainsi, nous avons découvert, sur les étagères d'All the Best Fine Foods, des trésors culinaires jamais vus à Toronto auparavant : de la purée de marrons, des cornichons, des marrons entiers en bocal, du miel de marron et du miel de lavande de Provence, ainsi que de l'huile de noisette, de l'huile d'olive de France, de l'huile de noix du Périgord, des chanterelles séchées, des olives niçoises, des olives de Nyons, des flageolets en conserve, de la moutarde de *Meaux Pommery*, de la fleur de sel de Guérande et des vinaigres des marques *Vilux* et *À l'Olivier*.

PRODUITS FRANÇAIS SURGELÉS Surprise, surprise ! Nous avons trouvé dans le congélateur de ce magasin une pâte feuilletée signée Rahier. Voici enfin une alternative aux pâtes surgelées qu'on trouve dans les supermarchés. C'est la solution idéale pour ceux qui peinaient avec leur pâte !

Arz Bakery

1909 Lawrence Avenue East (entre Warden Avenue et Pharmacy Avenue)

☎ (416) 755-5084

Lundi à samedi 8h – 21h, dimanche 8h – 19h30, les jours fériés 8h – 17h (Arz Bakery ne ferme jamais ses portes)

Métro : LAWRENCE + le bus

www.arzbakery.com

Arz Bakery est l'endroit idéal pour trouver certains ingrédients nécessaires aux plats libanais et à ceux du Moyen-Orient. Sur place, vous aurez le choix entre plusieurs sortes de boulgour (blé dur concassé) et de semoule de couscous. Chez Arz Bakery, vous pourrez acheter de la pâte d'harissa qui épicera vos plats. Nous avons par ailleurs remarqué une vitrine d'olives, ainsi que des olives sous vide en provenance de la Tunisie. Pas d'huiles d'olive importées de France, mais que d'autres pays fournisseurs : Liban, Italie, Espagne, Grèce ! Vous pourrez encore acheter de l'eau de rose et de l'eau de fleur d'oranger. Comme vous le savez, l'eau de fleur d'oranger est essentielle à la préparation des madeleines. Elle est aussi très difficile à trouver à Toronto, de même que les graines et les noix diverses qu'il y a chez Arz bakery. À cette adresse, nous vous promettons une expérience très agréable, un petit dépaysement qu'on peut s'offrir n'importe quand.

Bonjour Brioche

812 Queen Street East (un peu à l'est de Broadview) ☎ (416) 406-1250

Fermé lundi, mardi à vendredi 8h – 17h, samedi 8h – 16h, dimanche 8h – 15h

Métro : QUEEN + le tram

Si vous avez déjà eu la chance de déjeuner chez Bonjour Brioche, vous savez combien leur vinaigrette maison est savoureuse. Eh bien, vous pouvez continuer à savourer cette vinaigrette à la maison, en l'achetant dans son format prêt-à-emporter. Côté sucré, vous pouvez aussi ramener la confiture maison chez vous afin d'en tartiner généreusement votre baguette quand vous le voulez !

Brandt Meat Packers Supermarket

1878 Mattawa Avenue, Mississauga (près de Dundas Street et Dixie Road)
☎ (905) 279-4460

Fermé dimanche à mardi, mercredi 8h – 18h, jeudi et vendredi 8h – 19h, samedi 7h – 14h

Des marrons, des marrons et encore des marrons ! Ils sont vendus entiers, en purée et en tube dans ce magasin de Mississauga. Brandt Meat Packers Supermarket vend également plusieurs moutardes de France, une variété de champignons séchés et quelques champignons en conserve. Surprise ! Il y a aussi de la bouillabaisse en conserve et une grande quantité de choucroute en bocal. Les sirops *William* ainsi que des sirops de l'Europe de l'Est sont également en vente sur place. Ce supermarché allemand vous propose aussi du pain d'épice et des cerises griottes dénoyautées, en bocal dans un sirop léger, pour la préparation de vos desserts.

Clafouti

915 Queen Street West (à l'est de Strachan Avenue, en face du parc Trinity Bellwoods)
☎ (416) 603-1935

Fermé lundi, mardi à samedi 8h – 18h, dimanche 9h – 17h

Métro : OSGOODE + le tram

Des marrons entiers en conserve, des flageolets verts en conserve, des asperges blanches en bocal, quelques confitures de France et de Belgique, des sirops *William* et de la fleur de sel, voilà les spécialités que l'on peut acheter chez Clafouti. Pour le prêt-à-emporter français, Clafouti propose des croissants salés, des quiches, un croque-monsieur traditionnel et un autre végétarien, ainsi que plusieurs sandwichs sur baguette ou croissant. Nous avons par ailleurs un scoop à partager avec vous : on peut acheter des gaufres belges chez Clafouti ! Il n'y en a que le week-end. Et comme toutes les bonnes choses chez Clafouti, les gaufres partent très vite !

Cheese Boutique

45 Ripley Avenue (au sud de South Kingsway et The Queensway)
☎ (416) 762-6292

Lundi à vendredi 8h – 21h, samedi 8h – 20h, dimanche 10h – 18h

Métro : RUNNYMEDE + le bus

www.cheeseboutique.com

Cheese Boutique regorge de produits de la francophonie (et même de l'Europe entière). Les prix sont un peu plus élevés que ceux d'autres marchands, mais le choix est grand. En matière de

spécialités françaises, nous avons repéré les produits suivants : des sirops *William*, des flageolets en conserve, une douzaine de moutardes de France, plusieurs filets de poisson en conserve, des huiles AOC de Provence, des herbes de Provence, des truffes, des huiles de noix et de noisette, de la fleur de sel de Guérande, plusieurs vinaigres *Maille* et *Vilux*, des vinaigrettes *Maille* et des chanterelles fraîches.

Chris' Cheesemongers

93 Front Street East (St. Lawrence Market) ☎ (416) 368-5273

Fermé dimanche et lundi, mardi à jeudi 8h – 18h, vendredi 8h – 19h, samedi 5h – 17h

Métro : UNION

Chris' Cheesemongers vend des huiles de noix de l'huilerie *Lapalisse*, des truffes en bocal, quelques moutardes de France, de l'huile d'amande et du vinaigre de champagne importé de France.

Daniel et Daniel – Food Shop

248 Carlton Street (au coin de Parliament Street) ☎ (416) 968-9275

Lundi à samedi 7h30 – 18h, fermé dimanche

Métro : CASTLE FRANK + le bus; COLLEGE + le tram

www.danieletdaniel.ca

Chez Daniel et Daniel on découvre plusieurs produits qui valent le coup qu'on s'y attarde, tels que le confit de pétales de roses et celui aux pétales de violettes en bocal. Vous trouverez également des marrons cuits sous vide signés *Ponthier*, différentes marques de vinaigres de France et une grande sélection de sirops *William*.

Le saviez-vous ?

Les Bretons surnomment la fleur de sel le « caviar du sel ». La fleur de sel a un goût incomparable. Certains disent que ses cristaux sont de véritables spectres d'or blanc. Les amateurs iront jusqu'à prétendre que la fleur de sel est un « diamant de la mer ».

La fleur de sel est née de l'océan, du soleil et du vent. Ce trésor de la presqu'île de Guérande renferme des petits cristaux blancs qui se forment à la surface des œillets. Très rare et de qualité exceptionnelle, ce sel non raffiné est cueilli à la main à « fleur d'eau », à l'aide d'une louche en bois. Simplement égouttée au soleil, la fleur de sel révèle toute la saveur des mets, au grand bonheur de nos papilles.

La fleur de sel est idéale avec des légumes crus, des salades et des grillades. Mariée à d'autres épices ou aromates, la fleur de sel de Guérande est divine. Dès que vous l'aurez essayée, vous ne pourrez plus vous en passer pour assaisonner vos plats. Pour les fêtes, n'oubliez pas d'en saupoudrer vos toasts de foie gras... Vous pouvez même l'ajouter à la vanille, car elle convient à merveille aux pâtisseries.

autres spécialités françaises

Dinah's Cupboard

50 Cumberland Street ☎ (416) 921-8112

Lundi à vendredi 9h – 19h, samedi 9h – 18h, fermé dimanche (à l'exception du mois de décembre)

Métro : YONGE OU BAY

Chez Dinah's Cupboard vous pourrez acheter les spécialités françaises suivantes : des vinaigres de la maison *Vilux,* de la moutarde de *Meaux Pommery,* de la fleur de sel de Guérande, des truffes en bocal et de l'huile de truffe.

Domino Foods Ltd.

93 Front Street East (St. Lawrence Market, au sous-sol, tout au fond du marché) ☎ (416) 366-2178

Fermé dimanche et lundi, mardi à jeudi 8h – 18h, vendredi 8h – 19h, samedi 5h – 17h

Métro : UNION

Les apparences sont souvent trompeuses. Ce dicton s'applique très bien à ce magasin. Si, d'extérieur, il ne paie pas de mine, lorsqu'on y rentre, on découvre alors un vaste choix de produits français. C'est là que se trouve la gamme la plus complète de confitures *St. Dalfour* que nous ayons jamais vue. On a également découvert de la moutarde au cognac et de la moutarde à la violette (attention, l'originalité se paie), quelques vinaigres de vin français, du vinaigre de vin provenant de la région de Champagne, de la purée de marrons en conserve et sous vide, des truffes en pot ou en purée, de l'huile de vanille de Tahiti, de la fleur de sel et plusieurs parfums du sirop *William.* Le choix de champignons séchés nous a laissés bouche bée. Nous en avons compté 16, dont les champignons de Paris, les cèpes, les portobellos, les truffes blanches, les chanterelles et les morilles. Qu'est-ce qu'on vous disait déjà au sujet des apparences ?

Great Cooks

176 Yonge Street (au sous-sol de La Baie, Queen Street) ☎ (416) 861-4727

Lundi à vendredi 10h – 18h, samedi 10h – 17h, fermé dimanche

Métro : QUEEN

www.greatcooks.ca

Si vous en avez assez des soupes et des sandwichs peu savoureux à l'heure du déjeuner, voilà enfin une bien meilleure alternative. À ceux qui travaillent au centre-ville et qui désespéraient à l'idée de consommer de la « vraie » nourriture à midi, nous proposons Great Cooks. En effet, Great Cooks est avant tout une école de cuisine, mais tous les jours, les chefs de Great Cooks préparent d'incroyables plats. Les plats sont d'origines diverses. Quand ils sont d'origine française, ils mettent à l'honneur les

Les endroits où trouver de la fleur de sel

1. Alex Farm
2. All the Best Fine Foods
3. Cheese Boutique
4. Clafouti
5. Dinah's Cupboard
6. Domino Foods
7. Harvest Wagon
8. Holt Renfrew
9. Pusateri's
10. Scheffler's Delicatessen & Cheese
11. Whole Foods

créations du chef Jean-Pierre Challet, du restaurant Bouchon : tarte au chèvre et saumon poché par exemple. Tout a l'air bon et à vrai dire, tout est bon en effet. Le souci de la qualité est primordial ici et vos papilles le sentiront. En plus, les prix sont très raisonnables. Mais passé 14h, les vitrines sont vides !

Harvest Wagon

- 1133 Yonge Street (près du métro Summerhill) ☎ (416) 923-7542

  Lundi à mercredi 8h – 18h30, jeudi et vendredi 8h – 19h, samedi et dimanche 8h – 18h

  Métro : SUMMERHILL
- 546 Eglinton Avenue West ☎ (416) 487-0388

  Lundi à vendredi 8h – 19h, samedi et dimanche 8h – 18h

  Métro : EGLINTON + le bus

Les chanterelles et les morilles ne sont pas des champignons très courants à Toronto. On les voit rarement dans les marchés ou les grandes surfaces alimentaires. Harvest Wagon vous aidera à trouver des champignons qui sortent un peu de l'ordinaire. Vous constaterez aussi que Harvest Wagon a une très belle sélection d'herbes fraîches. Enfin, deux autres spécialités françaises vous y attendent : les flageolets en conserve et la fleur de sel.

Holt Renfrew – Epicure Shop

50 Bloor Street West (au coin de Bay Street) ☎ (416) 922-2333

Lundi à mercredi 10h – 18h, jeudi et vendredi 10h – 20h, samedi 10h – 18h, dimanche 12h – 18h

Métro : YONGE ou BAY

On va finir par croire que derrière cette marque canadienne du grand luxe se cache un francophile averti ! Holt Renfrew importe des spécialités de plusieurs marques de luxe françaises. Et vous découvrirez ainsi de chez Fauchon des marrons glacés, des vinaigres aux parfums divers, de la fleur de sel, des moutardes, des biscuits, des confitures et des thés. Fauchon fait rarement dans l'ordinaire, c'est ce qui explique les parfums de confiture d'une originalité surprenante – mangue et pêche, clémentine, poire à la gousse de vanille, pomme au calvados, cerise de Morello, melon de Cavaillon et abricot aux fleurs de jasmin. Vous pourrez également acheter de la pâte à tartiner aux noisettes Neuhaus. Enfin, Holt Renfrew importe le thé *Mariage Frères.* Sur place, un choix tout à fait satisfaisant vous fera découvrir ou redécouvrir cette grande maison du thé, fondée en 1854. Le livre de recettes *Mariage Frères, Éloge de la cuisine au thé,* est même en vente.

K.I.S. Global Flavors

☎ (905) 477-0024

www.kisglobalflavors.com

Le site de K.I.S. Global Flavors est une avalanche des meilleurs produits alimentaires haut de gamme. Cette compagnie importe des produits fins de France, de Suisse et d'Italie. Voici donc, entre vous et nous, un petit aperçu des produits français proposés sur le site : chocolats en forme d'olives de Provence, marrons glacés, fruits confits, oranges confites, citron au chocolat, calissons d'Aix-en-Provence, nougat,

truffes, gelée de fleur et miel de fleur de Provence. À noter qu'en quelques clics, vous pouvez offrir à la personne de votre choix un panier rempli de superbes produits français grâce au panier-cadeau.

Le Gourmand

152 Spadina Avenue (au sud de Queen Street) ☎ (416) 504-4494

Lundi à vendredi 7h – 21h, samedi 9h – 18h, dimanche 9h – 16h

Métro : **OSGOODE** + le tram; **SPADINA** + le tram

Le Gourmand vend de l'huile d'olive aux truffes blanches, de l'huile de pépins de raisin *Vilux,* de la moutarde de *Meaux Pommery,* de l'huile de noix et du vinaigre de la maison *Clovis.*

Loblaws

Différentes adresses dans toute la ville

Dans les rayons de ce grand nom de l'alimentation, vous trouverez les produits suivants : moutardes *Maille,* moutardes et vinaigres *Vilux* (incluant le vinaigre de cognac et celui de champagne) et moutardes de *Meaux Pommery.* Vous découvrirez aussi un nombre impressionnant de confitures *St. Dalfour* aux parfums peu courants à Toronto : figue royale, ananas et mangue, mirabelle, framboise noire, orange et gingembre.

PRODUITS FRANÇAIS SURGELÉS Loblaws vend plusieurs produits surgelés d'inspiration française. Il est vrai que ces produits ne sont pas aussi raffinés que ceux que l'on trouve chez les maîtres fabricants, mais plusieurs d'entre eux vous surprendront quand même. Sur place, vous découvrirez les produits surgelés de la marque « Le Choix du Président[MC]/President's Choice® » suivants : les croissants au beurre, les mini-éclairs au chocolat, les profiteroles, le cassoulet et la quiche lorraine.

Max Market

2299 Bloor Street West (à l'ouest de Runnymede Road) ☎ (416) 766-6362

Lundi à mercredi 9h – 19h, jeudi 9h – 19h30, vendredi 9h – 20h, samedi 9h – 19h, dimanche 9h – 18h

Métro : **RUNNYMEDE**

Max Market a une vitrine de prêt-à-emporter qui impressionne en matière de choix et de fraîcheur. Côté spécialités françaises, nous avons trouvé près d'une dizaine de variétés de crêpes fourrées, entre autres aux parfums suivants : fruits de mer, jambon-fromage, poulet et pistou, champignons et saumon. Il y a également chez Max Market une dizaine de parfums de vinaigres *Vilux.*

Mercatto

15 Toronto Street (à l'est de Yonge Street et au nord de King Street) ☎ (416) 366-4567

Lundi à vendredi 7h – 18h, fermé samedi et dimanche

Métro : **KING**

Huile de noix, huile d'olive de Provence et les fameuses herbes de Provence font partie des spécialités françaises que vous pourrez acheter ici.

Les endroits où trouver des flageolets

1. All the Best Fine Foods (en conserve)
2. Casa Açareana (secs)
3. Cheese Boutique (en conserve)
4. Clafouti (en conserve)
5. Harvest Wagon (en conserve)
6. Scheffler's Delicatessen & Cheese (en conserve)

Olympic Cheese Mart

- 93 Front Street East (St. Lawrence Market) ☎ (416) 363-7602

  Fermé dimanche et lundi, mardi à jeudi 8h – 18h, vendredi 8h – 19h, samedi 5h – 17h

  Métro : UNION
- 7780 Woodbine Avenue, Markham (au coin de la 14e Avenue) ☎ (905) 944-8676

  Lundi à mercredi 10h – 18h, jeudi et vendredi 10h – 19h, samedi 9h30 – 18h, fermé dimanche

Vous trouverez ici des truffes, des huiles d'olive de France, des vinaigres et vinaigrettes *Maille,* ainsi qu'un produit peu commun à Toronto : du vinaigre *Kressi* de Suisse. Il paraît que c'est *le* vinaigre qu'il faut pour faire la fameuse sauce hollandaise. Deux autres choses ont attiré notre attention : les girolles sont en vente chez ce marchand et un plateau de fromages français est disponible sur commande pour vos repas entre amis.

Pain Perdu

736 St. Clair Avenue West (un peu à l'ouest de Christie Street) ☎ (416) 656-7246

Fermé lundi, mardi à vendredi 7h – 19h30, samedi 7h – 17h, dimanche 8h – 16h

Métro : ST CLAIR WEST + le tram

Impossible de ne pas remarquer les bonnes quiches chez Pain Perdu ! En plus, elles rivalisent en saveur les unes avec les autres. La tarte aux oignons est, elle aussi, délicieuse. Le midi, les longues files de clients qui salivent n'en finissent pas. Il faut dire que le menu quiche/salade ou tarte/salade n'est pas seulement très bon, son prix défie aussi toute concurrence. Autres spécialités françaises : la mayonnaise, la vinaigrette et les confitures maison. La qualité du sirop d'érable dont on arrose le pain perdu est remarquable. On peut même acheter ce sirop biologique en provenance de la région du lac Érié.

Patachou

1095 Yonge Street (près du métro Summerhill) ☎ (416) 927-1105

Lundi à vendredi 8h30 – 19h, samedi 8h30 – 18h, fermé dimanche

Métro : SUMMERHILL

Patachou vend des huiles d'olive de France parfumées au piment, au basilic, aux herbes de Provence et au citron. On y trouve aussi des vinaigrettes et des confitures maison. En janvier 2004, Patachou a créé un menu prêt-à-emporter et un menu week-end.
Au menu des plats proposés pour le prêt-à-emporter : confit de canard sur lit de chou rouge et polenta, bœuf bourguignon, agneau navarin, champignons portobellos farcis de ratatouille

et chèvre, couscous façon israélienne et pissaladière. Avec le menu du week-end, on vous proposera plusieurs plats très appétissants et parfaits pour les repas en tête-à-tête à la maison ou pour les repas entre amis.

Pâtisserie d'Or

301 Robinson Street, Oakville (au sud de Lake Shore Road) ☎ (905) 815-8999

Fermé lundi et mardi, mercredi à vendredi 8h – 17h30, samedi 8h – 18h, dimanche 8h – 16h

La quiche à base de pâte feuilletée est la grande vedette de la maison. C'est sans aucun doute l'une des meilleures quiches que nous ayons jamais mangée.

PRODUITS FRANÇAIS SURGELÉS Le chef Jean-Luc Soulabaille ne le sait peut-être pas, mais il est en train de changer la tendance dans notre ville. En effet, les habitants du grand Toronto pourront déguster de délicieuses viennoiseries françaises préparées par un chef français chevronné quand bon leur semblera. Et comment le chef Jean-Luc Soulabaille a-t-il fait pour accomplir cet exploit ? Il a tout simplement installé un congélateur rempli de ses spécialités à l'entrée de sa pâtisserie. La sélection est bien variée – croissants au beurre, pains au chocolat, biscuits à la cuiller, petits pains, baguettes, danoises au raisin, vol-au-vent et la fameuse quiche maison. Une autre douceur à emporter : les pots de glace maison. Leurs parfums sont réalisés grâce à des ingrédients tels que du chocolat belge, des fruits frais, de la liqueur ou des noix grillées.
Au palmarès des parfums : cassis, framboise, citron, fraise, vanille, chocolat, caramel, café, pistache et pomme verte.

Pâtisserie Saint Honoré

2945 Bloor Street West (au coin de Greenview Blvd., un peu à l'est de Royal York Road)

**il n'y a pas de numéro de téléphone pour cette pâtisserie*

Fermé dimanche et lundi, mardi à jeudi 8h – 19h, vendredi 8h – 21h, samedi 8h – 19h

Métro : ROYAL YORK

Une dizaine de tables vous accueilleront pour apprécier sur place quelques-unes des spécialités de la maison : quiche, soupe à l'oignon, sandwich au pâté maison et pissaladière.

Petit Gâteau

2365 B Lake Shore Road, Oakville (à l'ouest de Bronte Road) ☎ (905) 847-1888

Fermé dimanche et lundi, mardi à samedi 9h – 18h

Cette pâtisserie permet de savourer une tourtière traditionnelle du Québec sans avoir à déployer tous les efforts requis par la longue préparation de ce plat.
À cette adresse, vous trouverez la tourtière traditionnelle de bœuf et de porc, mais vous pourrez aussi essayer quelques variations maison de ce plat – tourtière au saumon et tourtière au poulet. Il est préférable de passer votre commande à l'avance.

Pusateri's Fine Foods

- 1539 Avenue Road (au nord de Lawrence Avenue) ☎ (416) 785-9100

  Lundi à mercredi 8h – 20h, jeudi et vendredi 8h – 21h, samedi et dimanche 8h – 19h

  Métro : LAWRENCE + le bus

- 57 Yorkville Avenue (au coin de Bay Street) ☎ (416) 785-9100

  Lundi à mercredi 10h – 20h, jeudi et

Épices

Toute grande surface vend des épices en sachet. Mais le choix se limite souvent aux épices les plus populaires ici. Pour découvrir tout un monde d'épices, nous vous invitons à suivre le guide des adresses suivantes :

Casa Açareana

Kensington Market ☎ (416) 593-9717

Casa Açareana importe du chèvrefeuille, des feuilles de laurier, de la ciboulette, de la marjolaine, de la sauge, du thym et de l'estragon. Voici aussi une bonne adresse pour se procurer des herbes de Provence et même du safran d'Espagne à un prix tout à fait raisonnable. On y vend également des graines de moutarde jaunes et noires, de la lavande séchée, des flageolets secs et quatre types de lentilles. En outre, Casa Açareana importe de la vanille liquide pure et des fèves de vanille de Madagascar. Ce qui est rare à Toronto, mais qui ne l'est pas dans ce magasin, ce sont les baies de genièvre séchées (la traduction anglaise est *juniper berries*).

Domino Foods Ltd.

St. Lawrence Market ☎ (416) 366-2178

Pour acheter vos herbes en vrac au marché St. Lawrence, c'est chez Domino Foods qu'il faut que vous alliez! On y trouve du chèvrefeuille, du thym, de l'estragon, de la ciboulette, du romarin, de l'anis, de la marjolaine, de la sauge, du safran et des feuilles de laurier. Domino Foods vend aussi des herbes de Provence et des fèves de vanille.

House of Spices

Kensington Market ☎ (416) 593-9724

House of Spices importe une quantité extraordinaire d'épices du monde entier, souvent indispensables aux cuisines de la francophonie. Vous trouverez par exemple de l'estragon, du thym, des feuilles de laurier, des graines de moutarde jaunes et noires, des herbes de Provence et du safran. Vous pourrez aussi acheter des fèves de vanille de Madagascar et de la racine de réglisse. Enfin, House of Spices est une adresse où dénicher certains épices pour vos plats exotiques nord-africains, tels que la harissa, le zaatar et le razahanut.

Perola's

Kensington Market ☎ (416) 593-9728

Perola's est avant tout un marchand d'aliments pour les cuisines hispanique et brésilienne. Cependant, il mérite sa place dans ce guide de la gastronomie française ou francophone grâce à l'ingéniosité de son propriétaire. Ce dernier a en effet eu la brillante idée de sécher des bouquets d'herbes entiers. Vous trouverez des bouquets de romarin, sauge, sarriette et basilic chez Perola's.

Strictly Bulk

Différentes adresses dans toute la ville
☎ (416) 533-3242

Le choix est incomparable et les prix raisonnables. Tout est vendu en vrac. Vous y trouverez la plupart des herbes dont vous pouvez avoir besoin pour mijoter vos petits plats, ainsi que du safran et de l'essence de vanille pure.

vendredi 10h – 21h, samedi 8h – 20h, dimanche 10h – 19h

Métro : BAY

www.pusateris.com

Ce supermarché haut de gamme importe les spécialités suivantes : marrons glacés, truffes en bocal, marrons cuits sous vide, plusieurs huiles d'olive françaises de très haute qualité, fleur de sel, huile de noix et huile d'amande. Nous avons également trouvé des chanterelles fraîches (très peu de marchands en vendent). La longue vitrine et la section réfrigérée de plats prêts-à-emporter vous feront sûrement de l'œil, en même temps que gargouiller votre estomac. Les plats franco-français ne sont pas oubliés : gratin dauphinois et salade niçoise vous attendent chez Pusateri's.

PRODUITS FRANÇAIS SURGELÉS Vous trouverez ici des cèpes surgelés.

Qualifirst Foods

☎ (416) 244-1177

www.qualifirst.com

Qualifirst a commencé à distribuer des produits haut de gamme français dans l'Ouest canadien en 1957. Aujourd'hui, Qualifirst dessert tout le territoire canadien. Vous pouvez consulter son site Internet et passer une commande de produits français fins. Vous remarquerez que le choix est assez vaste, puisque ce distributeur passe des bonbons français aux truffes, puis des moutardes aux marrons. Profitez-en bien !

Rahier

1717 Bayview Avenue (au sud d'Eglinton Avenue) ☎ (416) 482-0917

Fermé lundi et mardi, mercredi à vendredi 8h – 17h, samedi 8h – 16h, dimanche 8h – 15h

Métro : EGLINTON + le bus

Rahier vous propose plusieurs variétés de quiches pour le week-end : chèvre et poivrons rouges, quiche lorraine, brocoli et cheddar, saumon fumé et asperges, aubergines et poireaux.

PRODUITS FRANÇAIS SURGELÉS Dans le congélateur de Rahier, vous trouverez les produits suivants : pâte feuilletée, sorbets et glaces maison, timbales feuilletées (type croûtes de bouchées à la reine), coulis de framboise, sauce au chocolat et quelques gâteaux.

Scheffler's Delicatessen & Cheese

93 Front Street East (St. Lawrence Market) ☎ (416) 364-2806

Fermé dimanche et lundi, mardi à jeudi 8h – 18h, vendredi 8h – 19h, samedi 5h – 17h

Métro : UNION

Le saviez-vous ?

Le marché St. Lawrence (qui a déjà 200 ans) a été reconnu comme étant l'un des marchés les plus raffinés du monde. Cette honorable mention lui a été attribuée par le magazine américain de cuisine *Food & Wine*, en avril 2004. Parmi la liste de 24 finalistes, on retrouve des marchés prestigieux dans les villes les plus chics de la planète : Paris, Milan et Tokyo.

Vous pouvez acheter chez Scheffler's beaucoup d'ingrédients essentiels à la cuisine française ou francophone tels que de la fleur de sel de Camargue, du safran, des flageolets, de la crème de marrons, des morilles en bocal, des truffes et des cornichons du Maroc et de France. On y trouve également une large gamme de vinaigres et vinaigrettes *Maille.*

Sérénité

87 Yorkville Avenue (au coin de Bellair Street) ☎ (416) 924-6398

Lundi à mercredi 10h – 18h, jeudi et vendredi 10h – 20h, samedi 10h – 18h, dimanche 12h – 18h

Métro : BAY

Les connaisseurs disent que le thé *Mariage Frères,* c'est le « caviar du thé »... Si c'est le cas, la boutique Sérénité dispose de plusieurs kilos de « caviar ». Cette boutique chic de Yorkville est le plus grand importateur de thé *Mariage Frères* au Canada, et peut-être même en Amérique du Nord. En plus d'une vaste sélection de thés *Mariage Frères,* la boutique Sérénité importe d'autres articles portant la griffe de la célèbre maison du thé : de la vaisselle, des confitures, des accessoires pour le thé, des bâtonnets de vanille pure, du sucre cristallisé et du thé glacé en sachet. *Mariage Frères* n'est qu'une des grandes marques françaises de l'alimentation qu'on retrouve dans cette charmante boutique au décor de Provence. Eh bien oui, si Sérénité importe le « caviar du thé », la boutique importe aussi le « prince des jardins » : *Prince Jardinier.* Derrière cette marque se cache un vrai prince français (Louis Albert de Broglie) qui avait un penchant marqué pour le jardinage et la récolte des fruits de son labeur. Parmi les mille et un articles *Prince Jardinier* figurent les confitures tant appréciées par la clientèle. La plus célèbre pour son goût et son originalité est sans aucun doute la confiture de tomate – tomate verte au citron, tomate verte aux noix, tomate rouge et orange confite et tomate rouge au gingembre. *Prince Jardinier* ne décevra pas non plus les amateurs de confiture de fruits. Découvrez les parfums extraordinaires suivants : la poire Louise Bonne d'Avranche du Potager du Roi, la rhubarbe et la fraise sauvage et l'orange amère à la cannelle.

Clément Bruno est la troisième grande marque française importée par Sérénité. Venez découvrir les surprises suivantes : huile de truffe, tapenade d'olives et de truffes, crème de cèpes, sauce tomate aux truffes, tomates confites aux truffes d'été et fondue de truffes blanches. Vous trouverez aussi quelques livres de cuisine et quelques ustensiles signés par ce maître de la truffe. Sérénité peut même vous approvisionner en truffes fraîches. Il suffit de passer une commande spéciale. Pour clore ce défilé de grandes marques de la gastronomie française, Sérénité vous propose les produits, livres de recettes, ustensiles et meubles de cuisine du grand chef Alain Ducasse.

Village Butcher

2914 Lake Shore Boulevard West (près d'Islington Avenue) ☎ (416) 503-9555

Fermé dimanche et lundi, mardi à vendredi 7h30 – 18h, samedi 7h30 – 17h

Métro : ISLINGTON + le bus

Si vous voulez régaler vos invités d'une traditionnelle tourtière québécoise pendant les fêtes de Noël, sachez que ce boucher en vend. Pensez à passer commande, car les fameuses tourtières partent extrêmement vite.

Whole Foods Market

87 Avenue Road (au nord de Bloor Street) ☎ (416) 944-0500

Lundi à vendredi 9h – 22h, samedi 9h – 21h, dimanche 9h – 20h

Métro : BAY ou MUSEUM

www.wholefoodsmarket.com

Whole Foods Market propose les produits français suivants : huile d'olive de Provence (AOC), huiles de Provence médaillées AOC (l'une d'or, l'autre d'argent), olives de Nyons, fleur de sel nature, fleur de sel aux herbes de Provence, moutarde *Meaux de Pommery* et sauces *Delouis fils* – hollandaise, béarnaise, mayonnaise à l'ail et mayonnaise césar. Enfin, une petite sélection de truffes en bocal ainsi que des champignons séchés (morilles, trompettes et cèpes) sont disponibles sur place.

Zane Pâtisserie et Boulangerie

1852 Queen Street East (à l'ouest de Woodbine) ☎ (416) 690-2813

Fermé lundi, mardi à dimanche 7h30 – 17h30

Métro : QUEEN + le tram

Tous les week-ends, Mo Zane prépare une demi-douzaine de quiches. Au palmarès des versions les plus demandées figurent la quiche végétarienne, la quiche au jambon et au lard et la quiche au saumon fumé.

bistros et restos

Certains Torontois ne sont pas toujours conscients de la chance qu'ils ont d'avoir accès à diverses fourchettes de prix en matière de cuisine française ou francophone. De même qu'à Montréal ou à Paris, ici on peut manger un petit bout dans un bistro de quartier pour une quarantaine de dollars pour un dîner, mais l'on peut aussi s'offrir une bonne table où l'addition dépassera largement les cent dollars. Très peu de villes nord-américaines offrent une telle amplitude de prix. Si vous avez déjà essayé de manger dans un restaurant français à New York, Los Angeles, Chicago ou même Vancouver, vous saurez à quel point cette expérience peut s'avérer un luxe. Les bistros, restos et restaurants haut de gamme de Toronto sont surprenants. Les chefs et les propriétaires sont dans le métier par amour, et ça se sent dans les plats ou dans le service offert. Nous avons savouré de délicieux repas tant dans des petits bistros qui comptent une dizaine de tables que dans les restaurants français les plus convoités de la ville. Chaque année à Toronto, la liste des chefs et propriétaires qui ravissent les papilles des francophiles et francophones à la recherche de bons petits plats de l'Hexagone s'allonge.

Alors, bon appétit !

le vin français de toronto à votre table !

L'histoire du vin français de Toronto débute avec M. Laurent Quetton (1771-1821). Cet exilé français royaliste lutta contre les Républicains pendant la Révolution française et réussit à s'enfuir en Angleterre vers la fin du XVIIIe siècle. Il prit le nom de St George tout simplement parce qu'il arriva en Angleterre le jour de la saint George, le 23 avril. À l'époque où Quetton arriva en Angleterre, le gouvernement britannique offrait aux exilés de France des « land grants » (parcelles de terrain) dans le Haut-Canada. C'est ainsi que Quetton St George s'est envolé vers les Amériques, en 1798, pour entreprendre une nouvelle vie. Il arriva d'abord à Québec, puis déménagea à Toronto en 1799.

Laurent Quetton St George se lança d'abord dans la traite des fourrures et établit des liens avec des tribus amérindiennes telles que les Objiboués. Il avait également plusieurs relations d'affaires avec des marchands de fourrures de New York et Montréal. Il devint lui-même marchand lorsqu'il déménagea à York et y ouvrit un magasin. Au temps où il vécut à York, Quetton St George ouvrit différents types de magasins dans plusieurs communautés avoisinantes telles que Queenston, Fort Érié et Dundas. Il fit du commerce de fourrures et vendit toutes sortes de biens, aussi bien locaux qu'importés d'Europe (Quetton St George importait des biens directement à Toronto, sans passer par Montréal. C'était une première à l'époque !)

Bien que résident cossu, Quetton St George ne fut jamais entièrement accepté par la haute société anglophone de York de l'époque. Ce détail ne l'empêcha pas de briller et de graver son nom dans l'histoire en tant qu'habile homme d'affaires. Il possédait en effet un talent hors pair pour la négociation. Son succès commercial colossal lui permit de se faire construire une imposante demeure, en 1809, à l'angle des rues King et Frederick : ce fut la première maison de briques de York (les briques furent importées des États-Unis).

Il fut l'ami du docteur William Warren Baldwin, qui a donné le nom de Quetton à l'un de ses fils et celui de St George à l'une des rues entourant sa maison de la rue Upper Spadina, en 1836. Cette rue St George traverse aujourd'hui l'université de Toronto. Mais les racines francophones de cette célèbre rue de Toronto sont mal connues.

Après le retour sur le trône du roi Louis XVIII, en 1815, Quetton retourna en France, où le roi le fit chevalier pour le récompenser de sa loyauté. Il acheta un important domaine « Le Château de l'Engarran », à Montpellier, grâce à sa fortune acquise dans le Haut-Canada (Toronto). Il décéda à l'âge de 50 ans. Son fils Henry retourna à Toronto en 1847 pour réclamer son patrimoine

canadien et commencer l'importation de vin du vignoble familial de Montpellier. Aujourd'hui encore, le vignoble acheté par Laurent Quetton St George produit du vin. Le Château de l'Engarran est situé sur des coteaux à l'ouest de Montpellier, dans le terroir de Saint-Georges d'Orques (la plus vieille appellation des Coteaux du Languedoc). Le Château de l'Engarran est classé monument historique et visité pendant les journées du patrimoine par des foules de curieux. Là, on découvre qu'on produit du vin au Château de l'Engarran depuis 1632, à savoir presque 200 ans avant le rachat du domaine par Laurent Quetton St George. Aujourd'hui, les vins produits au Château de l'Engarran sont des « vins de femmes ». Ce sont en effet les sœurs Constance Rerolle et Diane Losfelt qui gèrent aujourd'hui le vignoble (un métier peu commun pour des femmes). Ces dames du vin produisent plus de 200 000 bouteilles de vin par an, parmi lesquelles le vin que certains appellent le vin français de Toronto légué à la mémoire de Quetton St George : *Le Château de l'Engarran, Coteaux du Languedoc, Cuvée Quetton Saint-Georges.* Le titre de « vin français de Toronto » a été conféré au vin du château parce que c'est grâce à la fortune que Laurent Quetton St George a amassée à Toronto qu'il a pu s'offrir un tel domaine.

Ce vin rouge AOC est très coté dans le monde et il figure au palmarès des grands vins. On en parle dans des revues françaises, québécoises, allemandes et même américaines. Il impressionne à un point tel qu'il gagna la médaille d'or au Concours général agricole en 2001, en France.

Lisez les articles élogieux des chroniqueurs de vin sur la *Cuvée Quetton Saint-Georges :*

« … une réelle petite merveille… »,
Jérôme-Henri Dejardin (Québec)

« Parmi les 50 valeurs sûres »,
Terre de Vins (France)

« Domaine à découvrir », *Sud Vin,*
le catalogue des vins du Sud (France)

Si vous aimez les détails œnologiques, voici quelques lignes extraites du catalogue *Sud Vin* pour la cuvée 1998 : 75 % Syrah, 25 % Grenache. Sélection des meilleures parcelles constituant le cru Saint-Georges d'Orques. **ŒIL** : Robe très profonde, reflet violet et noir. **NEZ** : Le cassis domine, accompagné de tapenade, le bois est fin et élégant, harmonieusement fondu avec un beau vanille. **BOUCHE** : Pleine et charnue, structure ample sur des tanins présents mais enrobés, grande présence en bouche et grande longueur.

Au Canada, on peut acheter le vin à la Régie des alcools du Québec. Mais nous avons déjà entamé les démarches pour savoir dans quelle mesure la LCBO pourrait distribuer ce vin à Toronto. Quand vous lirez ces lignes, vous pourrez peut-être, nous l'espérons, siroter un bon verre de *Cuvée Quetton Saint-Georges* à la maison ou à la table d'un des restaurants de cuisine française à Toronto. À votre santé ! – *Ces faits historiques nous ont été fournis par M. Pierre Fortier de la Société d'histoire de Toronto.*

AGORA

(restaurant du Musée des beaux-arts de l'Ontario)

317 Dundas Street West ☎ (416) 979-6612

Fermé lundi et mardi, ouvert mercredi à dimanche pour le déjeuner seulement

Métro : ST PATRICK

AGORA vous offre une expérience exceptionnelle à l'heure du déjeuner. Ce splendide restaurant met en éveil plus d'un sens. En effet, la vue côté parc y est dans un premier temps époustouflante, ensuite la carte parmi laquelle vous pourrez choisir regorge de mets exquis et raffinés. Ce qui est intéressant chez AGORA, c'est que la carte s'adapte aux différentes grandes expositions du musée. Au moment où nous écrivons ces lignes, l'exposition de sculptures de l'artiste français Edgar Degas bat son plein. Pour célébrer cet artiste de génie, le chef, Anne Yarymowich, a créé un menu « Café Parisien » qui permet aux visiteurs d'explorer un éventail complet des charmes culinaires de la France. Au menu : huîtres, pâté à l'armagnac, confit de canard, steak frites, tarte Tatin accompagnée de glace au miel et à la lavande, tarte au citron sur un coulis de cassis et de mûres macérées dans le brandy. Bien sûr, ce menu n'aura duré que l'espace de quelques mois, mais nous pensons qu'un tel éloge à la gastronomie française méritait quand même qu'on le souligne.

– *menu bilingue*

Les meilleures caves à vins

1. Auberge du Pommier
2. Bistro 1603
3. Bistro 990
4. Bouchon
5. Brasserie Aix
6. Café Brussels
7. Café Margaux
8. Célestin
9. L'Escargot Bistro
10. La Brasserie.ca
11. La Petite France
12. Le Paradis
13. Le Trou Normand
14. Provence
15. Sélect Bistro

ARLEQUIN

134 Avenue Road (au coin de Davenport Road) ☎ (416) 964-8686

Lundi à samedi pour le déjeuner et le dîner, fermé dimanche

Métro : MUSEUM

La nouvelle direction, le nouveau décor et le nouveau chef propriétaire (Scott Saunderson) n'ont rien changé à l'essence même de ce bistro de quartier. Il reste un bistro sympathique, à l'ambiance chaleureuse. Arlequin propose un vaste menu, reflet d'une cuisine typique d'un bistro parisien. Ici, on vous sert de la bouillabaisse, du confit de canard, du gratin dauphinois, du cassoulet ou un steak frites avec de l'aïoli. Les viandes sont particulièrement bien apprêtées. Le menu permet de déguster un bon repas à prix moyen. La cuisson est toujours parfaite, à tel point que la viande fond dans la bouche. Quant au dessert, ne le ratez pas ! Laissez-vous séduire par la crème brûlée veloutée, l'exquis gâteau au chocolat ou encore la tarte au citron. La carte des vins est

également pleine de bonnes surprises. On y retrouve des sélections de France, notamment de Bourgogne et d'Alsace.

Avant-Goût

8 Birch Avenue (au coin de Yonge, près du métro Summerhill) ☎ (416) 975-9150

Mardi à vendredi pour le déjeuner, lundi à samedi pour le dîner, fermé dimanche

Métro : SUMMERHILL

Le chef et propriétaire, Kamal Hani, est d'origine marocaine et il s'est donné pour mission de bouleverser complètement l'expérience gastronomique des résidents de Rosedale. Avant-Goût propose, depuis l'été 2002, un vaste choix de plats d'influence française, mais aussi marocaine. À l'heure du déjeuner, voici à peu près ce qui figurera au menu : soupe du jour (qu'il faut absolument goûter tant elle est toujours très savoureuse), salade de confit de canard sur lentilles et mélange de feuilles vertes, ragoût de bœuf à la marocaine, koftas grillées servies avec un mélange de feuilles vertes, riz safrané avec jus d'ail et échalotes braisées. Au menu, le soir : canard fumé, ragoût marocain servi sur un lit de riz basmati, agneau à la marocaine et steak servi avec une sauce aux graines de moutarde. Quant au dessert, laissez-vous par exemple tenter par une très bonne crème brûlée. La carte des vins vous emporte dans plusieurs régions de vignobles, avec quelques bouteilles de vins blancs et de vins rouges français. Vous apprécierez de manger dans un décor un peu rétro. Avant-Goût... c'est le goût avant tout ! – *service en français*

Le saviez-vous ?

Après la parution de notre premier guide, nous avons reçu beaucoup de commentaires de la part de lecteurs franco-européens et québécois disant ne pas maîtriser suffisamment l'anglais pour pouvoir bien comprendre un menu. C'est vrai qu'il est parfois assez difficile de repérer un restaurant au service en français dans une ville anglophone. Nous avons donc décidé d'aiguiller un peu mieux nos lecteurs. Lorsque vous voyez la mention ***menu bilingue***, cela indique que le menu est disponible en français et en anglais à cette adresse. Avec la mention ***service en français***, vous saurez que le chef ou certains serveurs peuvent vous servir en français.

Bistro 990

990 Bay Street ☎ (416) 921-9990

Lundi à vendredi pour le déjeuner, lundi à dimanche pour le dîner

Métro : WELLESLEY

Bistro 990 possède un répertoire gastronomique classique de la cuisine française. Les ingrédients, la présentation et la préparation des plats reflètent tous la grande qualité ambiante. L'addition n'est pas mince chez Bistro 990, mais vous aurez peut-être la chance d'y voir des célébrités, notamment pendant le Festival des films étrangers. Si vous avez envie de vous faire plaisir et que les prix ne vous arrêtent pas, vous pourrez vous régaler avec les spécialités de la maison suivantes : saumon grillé par-

fumé au Grand Marnier, filet de thon à l'orientale, steak frites sauce au roquefort et filet mignon au stilton et porto. La carte des vins de Bistro 990 est impressionnante. La cave renferme environ 150 variétés de bouteilles, dont la moitié sont françaises. Parmi les vins français, 30 peuvent être consommés au verre. – *menu bilingue et service en français*

Bistro Matisse

1710 Lake Shore Road West, Mississauga (à l'intérieur du Clarkson Village, entre Port Credit et Oakville) ☎ (905) 822-2222

Fermé lundi, mardi à vendredi pour le déjeuner, mardi à dimanche pour le dîner

Le visage du grand Toronto a sans aucun doute changé avec l'ouverture du Bistro Matisse. Le chef et propriétaire, Jean Jacques Lemesle, sert depuis novembre 2002 des petits plats bien mijotés dans un coin de Toronto qui ne compte qu'un seul autre restaurant français. Le menu du soir vous présente une myriade de plats à prix raisonnables, tels que le suprême de poulet cordon-bleu, le foie de veau à la parisienne, les coquilles Saint-Jacques, le steak au poivre, le canard, la bouillabaisse et les merguez grillées servies avec du couscous. Le menu propose trois plats pour un peu plus d'une vingtaine de dollars. Nous avons entendu dire que le chef préparait aussi des andouillettes et du foie gras maison. Les desserts sont assez irrésistibles. Leur liste n'est pas très longue, mais elle change régulièrement, sauf dans le cas de la crème brûlée, qui figure toujours sur la carte. La liste des vins comporte quelques bouteilles de régions vinicoles françaises. On pourra également se rafraîchir avec diverses bières françaises. Vous reconnaîtrez peut-être la touche spéciale du chef Lemesle puisqu'il est l'ancien copropriétaire et chef du restaurant La Maison Benoît. – *menu bilingue et service en français*

Les restaurants qui ont une terrasse

1. Bloor Street Diner
2. Bodega
3. Café Margaux
4. Épicure Café
5. La Brasserie.ca
6. La Maison Benoît
7. La Palette
8. Le Saint Tropez
9. Le Trou Normand
10. Merlot
11. Pourquoi pas
12. Provence

Bloor Street Diner et Bistros

(La rôtisserie – L'express)

Différentes adresses dans toute la ville

www.eatertainment.com

Deux ambiances (bistro-resto) pour cet établissement proposant une large sélection de « classiques » à prix très raisonnables. Croque-monsieur, salade niçoise, soupe à l'oignon, quiche, moules marinière, steak frites, poulet rôti à l'aïoli de tomates séchées et foie de veau sont quelques exemples de ce qui figure sur la carte. Des plats de tous les jours qu'on peut s'offrir souvent !

Le menu est une bonne affaire et l'on ne résiste pas à la petite touche finale du Bloor Street Diner : une demi-baguette toute chaude.

Boujadi

999 Eglinton Avenue West
☎ (416) 440-0258

Fermé lundi et mardi, mercredi à dimanche pour le dîner

Métro : EGLINTON WEST

www.boujadi.com

Marhaba (« bienvenue ») à la cuisine marocaine ! Le chef et propriétaire, Charles Obadia, exécute depuis 1992 des recettes de plats traditionnels marocains que lui ont transmises ses aïeux. À l'opposé des cuisines « fusion » ou « nouveau genre », Boujadi vous propose trois plats de tajine, six plats de couscous et une demi-douzaine de plats végétariens. Au menu, vous retrouverez également le fameux thé vert à la menthe marocain ainsi qu'une limonade (façon nord-américaine) parfumée à l'eau de rose. La liste des desserts est limitée mais bien représentative de la cuisine marocaine. Il va de soi que le décor et la musique marocaine sont au rendez-vous pour créer une ambiance des plus animées. Si vous avez de la chance, vous dînerez lors d'une des soirées où les danseurs sont là (surtout le week-end). S'il vous est impossible de profiter de l'ambiance sur place, commandez donc les plats à emporter de Boujadi. – *service en français*

Brasserie Aix

584 College Street (près de Palmerston Boulevard) ☎ (416) 588-7377

Lundi à dimanche pour le dîner, dimanche ouvert pour le brunch

Métro : QUEEN'S PARK + le tram

www.brasserieaix.com

Située dans le quartier branché du « College strip », la Brasserie Aix offre une bonne sélection de plats français. En entrée, vous aurez le choix entre une brandade de morue, un tartare de saumon, des escargots et une salade de scarole ou des ris de veau. Pour ce qui est des plats principaux, attendez-vous à trouver les spécialités suivantes : coquelet rôti, coq au vin, foie de veau grillé, confit de canard et entrecôte grillée avec frites. Un plateau de fromages et un plateau de charcuterie sont également au menu. Les plats sont assez simples, mais leur présentation et les parfums qu'ils révèlent sont l'affaire d'une main experte. Un plat du jour est servi toute la semaine. Notez juste que ce restaurant n'est pas pour tout le monde. Amoureux des ambiances feutrées et dîners romantiques aux chandelles, abstenez-vous ! L'ambiance ici est très branchée et plutôt jeune. Le décor ultra moderne et la musique électronique forte en font plutôt un endroit « cool » pour sortir entre amis. Enfin, nous vous invitons à découvrir la belle cave à vins de la maison ! – *service en français*

Café Margaux

796 College Street (à l'ouest d'Ossington Avenue, au coin de Roxton Road)
☎ (416) 588-7490

Fermé lundi (ouverture le lundi pendant les mois d'avril à août), mardi à samedi pour le dîner, ouverture du lundi au vendredi pour le déjeuner pendant l'été

Le saviez-vous ?

Une enquête menée en mars 2004 par le magazine de cuisine *Elle à Table* dévoile les plats préférés des Français. La liste comprend quelques sélections qui vous surprendront. Parmi les préférences culinaires des Français figurent les moules marinière, la blanquette de veau et le pot-au-feu. Nous avons été particulièrement surpris par le choix des Français en matière de dessert : ils préfèrent la salade de fruits toute simple à tout autre dessert. C'est une révélation percutante pour tous les francophiles qui adorent les desserts français bien riches. Il va de soi que les Français préfèrent leur cuisine à toutes les autres (à la maison comme à l'étranger). L'enquête révèle que 77 % placent la cuisine française en tête de peloton. Côté cuisine internationale, les Français préfèrent le couscous (d'Afrique du Nord) et la pizza (celle des immigrants italiens). Heureusement pour eux, les Français ne seront pas déçus par la longue liste de restaurants torontois où l'on peut savourer leurs plats préférés ainsi qu'une variété de plats affectionnés des francophiles d'ici.

Métro : QUEEN'S PARK + le tram

Café Margaux a ouvert ses portes en octobre 2003. Ce petit bistro français s'inscrit dans la tradition des deux autres restaurants français situés sur College Street – ambiance incroyable, musique agréable, plats succulents, carte des vins remarquable et prix très abordables. Le propriétaire du Café Margaux a la restauration dans le sang puisque ses parents sont les anciens propriétaires de La Maison Benoît. À lui maintenant de faire ses preuves ! Et notre repas chez Café Margaux nous laisse penser que Pascal Barron y parviendra sans aucun problème. Le chef Rob Briden est un habitué de la cuisine française puisqu'il a travaillé chez Pastis et Quartier avant de rejoindre Café Margaux. À la carte, vous pouvez opter tantôt pour des plats classiques, tantôt pour des plats contemporains, mais quels qu'ils soient, ils sont tous vraiment bien préparés. Le menu du jour est l'occasion pour le propriétaire et le chef d'associer leurs débordements d'originalité. Et ça donne par exemple des raviolis de foie gras maison, servis avec des endives sautées, du vin de glace et du coing. Le mélange est subtil et comme velouté. La carte des desserts n'est pas très longue, mais les créations suivantes sont exquises : profiteroles à l'armagnac, assiette gourmande (sa composition varie), marquise au chocolat et crème brûlée. Vous pouvez aussi opter pour l'assiette de fromages (bleu d'Auvergne, chèvre et brie). La cave à vins de Café Margaux impressionne grandement. On dénombre 75 sortes de bouteilles de vin rouge, dont la plupart viennent de France. Les vins blancs sont au nombre d'une cinquantaine environ. Si la longue liste de vins vous dépasse, vous pouvez toujours consulter l'encyclopédie des vins qui se trouve sur le bar. – *menu bilingue et service en français*

Café Moroc

49 Front Street East (à l'ouest de Church Street) ☎ (416) 961-0601

Lundi à jeudi 11h30 – 23h, vendredi et samedi 11h30 – 1h, dimanche 16h – 22h

Métro : UNION

www.thesultanstent.com

Comme son nom l'indique, ce restaurant met le Maroc en vedette. Et comment ! Le décor est absolument splendide. Un vrai souci du détail a été apporté à la décoration pour vous transporter dans une médina. La céramique du mur d'entrée, les miroirs, la couleur riche du bois, les lanternes, les petites tables rondes couleur ébène, la teinte des murs, les affiches et les ventilateurs en bambou, tout, au Café Moroc, contribue au dépaysement. Le menu, bien évidemment, vous plonge plus avant en plein cœur du Maroc. On y retrouve des spécialités traditionnelles et contemporaines telles que la merguez sur baguette, le hamburger Moroc (un hamburger à l'agneau accompagné des frites Moroc) et la spécialité « Keskesu Casablanca » (tajine de couscous, légumes, fruits et noix). La carte des boissons est assez surprenante, car y figurent plusieurs cocktails signés Café Moroc que vous ne boirez qu'ici. Bien entendu, pensez à terminer votre repas avec le traditionnel thé marocain ! – *service en français*

Café Nicole

45 The Esplanade (entre Yonge Street et Church Street) ☎ (416) 367-8900

Lundi à dimanche pour le déjeuner et le dîner

Métro : UNION

Café Nicole est le restaurant situé à l'intérieur de l'hôtel Novotel, dans le centre-ville de Toronto. Les plats de Café Nicole sont savoureux, la cuisson est parfaite et le service est impeccable. Dans les sélections françaises, on retrouve les incontournables suivants : steak frites, carré d'agneau en croûte, magret de canard avec gratin dauphinois et filet de bœuf servi avec un ragoût de champignons sauvages et une sauce au porto. Le « menu théâtre » est très intéressant puisqu'il permet aux détenteurs de billets de théâtre de manger un excellent steak frites en très peu de temps. Pour clore un bon repas, offrez-vous l'un des desserts suivants : crème brûlée, crêpes ou gâteau au Grand Marnier. — *menu bilingue et service en français*

Chez Laurent

4965 Yonge Street (au nord de Sheppard Avenue) ☎ (416) 590-0909

Lundi à samedi pour le dîner, fermé dimanche

Métro : NORTH YORK CENTRE ou SHEPPARD

Chez Laurent est un restaurant sans prétention, situé dans une maisonnette qui donne davantage l'impression d'aller dîner chez des amis qu'au restaurant. L'atmosphère est fort conviviale. La famille Ferrari excelle dans la préparation de plats simples et revigorants. Le menu célèbre les classiques des cuisines française et italienne. Le concept de fusion ne s'applique pas ici. Qui dit français, dit français. Côté entrées, vous pourrez choisir des moules marinière, des escargots, une soupe à l'oignon ou une salade niçoise. Quant aux plats

Hors catégorie !

Café la Gaffe

24 Baldwin Street ☎ (416) 596-2397

Lundi à vendredi 12h – 23h, samedi 11h – 23h, dimanche 11h – 23h (fermé samedi et dimanche entre 14h et 16h)

Métro : ST PATRICK

Le Café la Gaffe n'est pas un café ou bistro français. En fait, le menu est assez éclectique et s'inspire de plusieurs cuisines. Cela dit, la crème brûlée qu'on retrouve sur le menu du Café la Gaffe est réalisée grâce à la recette originale de l'artiste Claude Monet. En fait, la recette provient du livre de recettes de l'artiste peintre (une reproduction du livre est dans les cuisines du Café la Gaffe). Cette recette date de 1885. Cette crème brûlée est non seulement bonne, elle a aussi une histoire et un passé incontestablement fascinants. Voilà un autre exemple du patrimoine culinaire français à son meilleur comme il existe à Toronto.

principaux, la maison vous propose du veau au citron, un suprême de poulet, du poulet chasseur et du poulet basquez. Trois préparations de steak sont également au menu. La liste des desserts est assez courte. La crème caramel et la crème brûlée restent des valeurs sûres. – *menu bilingue*

Crêpes à Gogo

244 Bloor Street West (sur le coin nord-est de Bedford Road, juste au nord de Bloor Street) ☎ (416) 922-6765

Lundi à samedi 10h30 – 20h (fermé lundi en hiver), dimanche 9h30 – 17h

Métro : ST GEORGE (sortie Bedford)

Crêpes à Gogo accueille, depuis mai 2003, francophiles et francophones à la recherche de la crêpe typiquement française. Ceux qui préfèrent leur crêpe collante et élastique adoreront aller chez Crêpes à Gogo. Plusieurs francophones les ont déclarées « meilleures crêpes de la ville ». Au palmarès des crêpes les plus demandées figurent « la campagnarde » (œufs, tomates, mozzarella, champignons, oignons rouges et persil) et « la Niçoise » (thon, fromage, basilic et tomates). Pour ce qui est des crêpes sucrées, goûtez la Nutella/banane, « la Juliatella » (confiture de framboise et Nutella) ou « la Big Ben » (mozzarella et confiture). Vous pouvez même avoir plus simple : sucre de canne et cannelle. Si vous n'avez pas envie de crêpes, vous aurez le choix parmi des sandwichs sur baguette. L'emplacement de la crêperie mérite qu'on l'éclaire. L'adresse donne sur Bloor Street, mais l'entrée de la crêperie donne sur Bedford Road. Tendez l'oreille et laissez-vous guider par la musique française qui s'échappe des haut-parleurs situés à l'extérieur de la crêperie. Un second point de repère est l'enseigne en bois de ce marchand de crêpes. Aucun doute là-dessus, le petit personnage coiffé d'un béret sur l'enseigne ne pouvait être que français. – *menu bilingue et service en français*

Crêpes Café

246 Queen Street West ☎ (416) 260-1611

Lundi à vendredi 9h – 22h, samedi 9h – 23h, dimanche 10h – 22h

Métro : OSGOODE

Qui dit balade à Paris, dit dégustation de crêpes préparées par les petits mar-

chands de crêpes ambulants. On retrouve ces derniers à tous les coins de rue à Paris. Longtemps, les Torontois n'ont pu goûter à ces fameuses crêpes. Mais voilà qu'est arrivé Crêpes Café, dans Queen Street West, en janvier 2003. Il n'y a pas que la dégustation qui plaît, voir comment on prépare votre crêpe est tout aussi agréable. Les variétés de crêpes sucrées et salées qu'on vous propose ont des parfums typiquement français ainsi que des parfums adaptés aux goûts locaux. Pour vous mettre en appétit, voici un échantillon des crêpes que vous pourrez déguster : œuf et fromage, poulet et champignons, emmenthal et sirop d'érable ou encore thon et mayonnaise. Côté crêpes sucrées, voilà ce qui vous attend : Nutella et banane, miel et noix, glace avec rhum, noix de coco et banane. Chez Crêpes Café, on peut manger sa crêpe sur place ou à la française – sur le pouce. Bien entendu, les variétés un peu plus élaborées peuvent se manger sur place ou à la maison. Si les crêpes ne font pas votre bonheur, vous pouvez opter pour l'un des sandwichs grillés ou sur baguette. Les sandwichs, préparés le jour même, ne sont disponibles qu'en quantité limitée, gage de leur fraîcheur.

Épicure Café

512 Queen Street West (à l'ouest de Spadina Avenue, au coin de Portland Street) ☎ (416) 504-8942

Lundi à vendredi pour le déjeuner, lundi à dimanche pour le dîner

Métro : OSGOODE + le tram

Il est vrai que dans ce restaurant à tendance méditerranéenne, les plats français et les plats italiens sont présentés sur le même menu, mais contrairement à d'autres établissements, le caractère distinct de chaque cuisine est préservé. Côté français, vous pourrez commander de l'agneau parfumé au romarin et au vin rouge, de la bouillabaisse provençale, du confit de canard, du foie de veau ou du thon provençal. Au cours d'une de nos dernières visites, le festival de moules battait son plein. Pas évident pour un francophile de dire non à un festival de moules. Épicure Café n'est pas un restaurant de luxe, mais c'est un endroit qui convient tout à fait à un repas qu'on veut sans prétention.

Holt's Café

50 Bloor Street West (au coin de Bay Street; au 2e étage) ☎ (416) 922-2333

Lundi à mercredi 10h – 18h, jeudi et vendredi 10h – 20h, samedi 10h – 18h, dimanche 12h – 18h

Métro : BLOOR ou BAY

Ce café de luxe situé au deuxième étage jouit d'un décor tout rénové. Le rendu est vraiment très moderne, très aéré et très chic. Contrairement à plusieurs restaurants au décor trop « ultra chic » qui misent avant tout sur les apparences pour séduire leur clientèle, Holt's Café séduit même les plus fins palets de la ville grâce à sa carte. Le menu, créé par le chef Corbin Tomaszeski, n'est autre que le pendant torontois d'un menu qu'on retrouve dans plusieurs bistros de Paris, au détail près que le chef Tomaszeski s'est inspiré d'un boulanger assez connu de la rue du Cherche-Midi à Paris : Poîlane. Eh oui, toutes les tartines du Holt's Café sont composées de pain Poîlane. Oui, oui, vous avez bien lu… du pain Poîlane. Le choix parmi douze

tartines environ saura satisfaire les clients les plus indécis. Une tarte au citron, un pain perdu à base de pain Poîlane ainsi qu'une crème brûlée au gingembre figurent sur la liste des desserts.

Jacques Bistro du Parc

126 A Cumberland Street ☎ (416) 961-1893

Lundi à samedi pour le déjeuner et le dîner, fermé dimanche

Métro : BAY

Ce tout petit bistro séduira les amoureux de la gastronomie. Jacques Sorin, chef et propriétaire, y prépare une sélection hors pair d'omelettes bien garnies pour le déjeuner. Le dîner se compose à la carte ou encore grâce au menu. Ni l'un ni l'autre ne vous décevra. En voici quelques exemples : carré d'agneau à la provençale, entrecôte au poivre vert, lapin aux petits oignons et vin blanc, ris de veau au calvados et terrine maison. Lorsque le plat de résistance est si bon, on a tendance à oublier de laisser une petite place pour le dessert… Jacques Sorin saura pourtant séduire les amateurs de sucré avec une île flottante, une mousse au chocolat, des profiteroles ou encore une multitude de tartes aux fruits frais. Jacques Bistro est le genre de restaurant où l'on revient régulièrement, car le rapport qualité-prix y est excellent et les plats sont toujours à la hauteur des espérances. En d'autres termes, cette adresse est une valeur sûre ! – *menu bilingue et service en français*

L'Escargot Bistro

3185 Yonge Street (au nord de Lawrence Avenue) ☎ (416) 485-8338

Lundi à samedi pour le dîner, fermé dimanche

Métro : LAWRENCE

www.lescargot.ca

L'Escargot Bistro est l'œuvre de Max Ballin. Ce propriétaire astucieux a su créer un décor et une atmosphère idéals pour s'arrêter et prendre le temps d'apprécier un bon petit repas français. Les plats sont simples, sans rien de superflu. En revanche, leurs parfums et saveurs sont envoûtants. On pourrait presque se satisfaire d'entrées chez l'Escargot Bistro, tant elles sont bonnes et variées. L'Escargot Bistro vous propose trois variations sur son thème : escargots bourguignons, fricassée d'escargots à la provençale et feuilleté d'escargots avec julienne de légumes et crème d'ail. Si vous vous arrêtez à une seule entrée, vous pourrez encore découvrir l'un des trois plats de poisson, la poitrine de poulet chasseur, l'une des deux variétés de steak frites, le filet de porc au sirop d'érable, le foie de veau, le carré d'agneau ou les médaillions de veau sauce au fromage bleu en plat de résistance. La liste des desserts est courte : crème brûlée, gâteau basque (une première pour un restaurant à Toronto) et poire pochée accompagnée d'une crème anglaise. Pas envie de sucre ? Régalez-vous avec une assiette de fromages. La cave à vins est majestueuse. Elle renferme plus de 1 000 bouteilles, dont plusieurs en provenance de France. Le choix est élaboré et plusieurs bouteilles à prix vraiment raisonnables vous sont proposées. Ce qui nous plaît aussi, c'est la chanteuse anglophone qui fredonne des airs du répertoire des grands chan-

sonniers français. Elle est au rendez-vous tous les deuxièmes dimanches du mois. – *menu bilingue et service en français*

La Brasserie.ca

162 Cumberland Street (Renaissance Court, près du Four Seasons Hotel)
☎ (416) 944-1504

Lundi à vendredi pour le déjeuner (fermé lundi pendant l'hiver), lundi à samedi pour le dîner, fermé dimanche

Métro : MUSEUM ou BAY

www.labrasserie.ca

La Brasserie.ca est une brasserie française bien typique où l'on peut manger un excellent repas en sirotant une bonne boisson. La Brasserie.ca sert une série de plats typiquement français : création du jour autour du poulet de Cornouailles signée le chef Philippe Cœurdassier, salade niçoise de thon frais, cassoulet toulousain, confit de canard, bœuf bourguignon, ris de veau, caille farcie et foie gras préparé spécialement par le chef. Vous découvrirez aussi un menu dédié aux fromages et vins français, le tout bien entendu accompagné d'une succulente baguette. Le décor, lui aussi, rend hommage à la France. Si vous y prêtez suffisamment attention, vous verrez que le grillage apposé aux murs rappelle la base de la Tour Eiffel. Chaque semaine, il y a une dégustation de bière, qu'un menu découverte accompagne. La cave de La Brasserie.ca est drôlement bien garnie en vins, bières et spiritueux. Tous les vendredis et samedis soirs, vous pouvez profiter du spectacle de musique jazz et rythm n' blues pour égayer vos repas. Vous aurez même droit à quelques performances d'artistes

francophones. – *menu bilingue et service en français*

La Maison Benoît

1921 Avenue Road (au nord de Brooke Avenue) ☎ (416) 782-9934

Lundi à samedi pour le déjeuner, lundi à dimanche pour le dîner

Métro : EGLINTON + le bus

La Maison Benoît est un restaurant situé dans le nord du quartier Forest Hill. Un menu typiquement français y est servi dans un décor invitant, chaleureux et à l'aspect « rétro ». Laissez-vous surprendre par la note singulière que le chef Jean-Luc Mole apporte aux plats les plus classiques – pétoncles accompagnés d'une sauce à l'anis, demi-canard rôti arrosé d'une sauce au porto et à l'orange, pâté maison au porto ou encore escargots au roquefort. Vous pour-

À la recherche des bonnes frites allumettes

1. Arlequin
2. Bloor Street Diner
3. Bouchon
4. Brasserie Aix
5. Café Brussels
6. Café Margaux
7. Café Moroc
8. La Maison Benoît
9. Le Paradis
10. Le Saint Tropez
11. Le Sélect Bistro
12. Marcel's Bistro
13. Matignon
14. Midi Bistro
15. Provence

rez également choisir le steak frites. N'oubliez pas les plats du jour de La Maison Benoît. Pour découvrir tous ces plats, on vous conseille de faire une réservation, le restaurant étant assez populaire dans le quartier...
– menu bilingue et service en français

La Palette

256 Augusta Avenue ☎ (416) 929-4900
Lundi à dimanche pour le dîner
Métro : **SPADINA** + le tram;
QUEEN'S PARK + le tram

Petit restaurant chaleureux et sans chichi, situé dans le quartier Kensington, La Palette vous propose un menu de plats classiques français, bien préparés et à des prix raisonnables. Le décor est simple (nappes colorées et affiches françaises sur les murs), la terrasse accueillante pendant la saison chaude et le service décontracté. C'est l'endroit idéal pour un bon repas en toute simplicité. Consultez la section « brunch » pour en savoir plus sur les plats alléchants qui figurent au menu.

Nouvelle tendance !

Selon le propriétaire du restaurant Café Margaux, Patrice Barron, on retrouvera la crème caramel au menu d'un nombre croissant de restaurants à Toronto. Rien ne remplace une bonne crème caramel bien préparée. C'est vrai que le flan que l'on retrouve chez les Portugais et les Hispaniques ressemble à la crème caramel, mais d'après nous, il n'est pas aussi raffiné et délicat que le célèbre dessert français.

On vous donne un indice : le mot *crêpes ! – service en français*

La Petite France

3317 Bloor Street West (à l'est d'Islington Avenue) ☎ (416) 234-8783
Lundi à vendredi pour le déjeuner, lundi à samedi pour le dîner, fermé dimanche, sauf pour les grands groupes
Métro : **ISLINGTON**

Les plats du chef Gilbert Letort sont simples, classiques et particulièrement savoureux. Le menu change tous les six mois et il s'adapte aux saisons. Par exemple, pendant les mois d'hiver, vous pourrez commander les plats suivants : bœuf bourguignon, blanquette de veau, cassoulet, rôti d'agneau à la marocaine et foie gras au porto. L'été, vous découvrirez la liste de mets suivante : tian d'escargots, timbales de truite fumée, confit de canard au rhum et aux raisins, carré d'agneau rôti à la menthe, cuisses de grenouilles et filet de sole meunière. Si vous ne trouvez pas votre bonheur à la carte, essayez donc le menu du dîner ou encore les plats du jour le lundi.
La carte des vins est particulièrement intéressante, avec une soixantaine de bouteilles proposées, la majorité étant des vins rouges français. Attention, pensez à garder une petite place pour le dessert. La crème brûlée à la vanille est renversante ! Parmi les autres desserts figurent la tarte aux pommes, les profiteroles, les crêpes, la galette bretonne et le gâteau Marjolaine. Les événements mensuels gastronomiques et les dégustations de vins ont particulièrement retenu notre attention. La Petite France célèbre les vins des différentes régions de France et d'ailleurs. Enfin, la fête du

14 juillet est une autre célébration à ne pas manquer dans ce restaurant. – *menu bilingue et service en français*

Le Papillon

16 Church Street ☎ (416) 363-3773

Fermé lundi, mardi à dimanche ouvert pour le déjeuner et le dîner

Métro : **UNION**

Un mélange de cuisines française, québécoise et bretonne donne le ton chez Le Papillon. Deux douzaines de crêpes bretonnes sont au menu : c'est la spécialité de la maison. En bref, Le Papillon vous propose une bonne cuisine servie dans un décor rustique. – *service en français*

Le Paradis

166 Bedford Road (juste au nord de Davenport Road) ☎ (416) 921-0995

Mardi à vendredi pour le déjeuner, lundi à dimanche pour le dîner

Métro : **MUSEUM** ou **ST GEORGE**

www.leparadis.com

Le Paradis est une adresse française où l'on peut à la fois manger et boire. Fidèle à la tradition des établissements de ce genre qui sont partout en France, on y mange exceptionnellement bien et l'on y boit presque encore mieux. Le mariage de différentes cuisines de la francophonie est assez subtil. La plupart des plats sont français, mais on retrouvera quand même quelques plats d'inspiration marocaine tels que le tajine, l'agneau à la marocaine, les merguez ou le couscous. Au menu, une longue liste d'incontournables français : blanquette au Sauvignon, bavette, entrecôte chasseur, lapin à la provençale, confit de canard, rognons de veau au porto. Le menu change régulièrement et Le Paradis prépare souvent des plats que convoite la clientèle régulière, accompagnés entre autres des célèbres flageolets. Le cassoulet est une autre spécialité qui fait des heureux chez Le Paradis. Il faut dire que la recette est vraiment bien au point. Ayant essayé plusieurs recettes et n'étant toujours pas satisfait du résultat, le propriétaire s'est un jour décidé à remonter à la source et, au cours d'un de ses voyages en France, il a demandé au chef d'un restaurant de Castelnaudary de lui envoyer du cassoulet surgelé qu'il avait mangé chez lui. C'est grâce à cette manœuvre que l'un des plats français les plus appréciés de cet établissement a vu le jour. Le Paradis est un des rares restaurants français de Toronto à ne pas servir de crème brûlée. En revanche, vous pourrez goûter à une succulente crème caramel (l'une des meilleures que nous ayons jamais mangées). La carte des vins se résume en un mot : franco-française. Les savoureux plats du terroir du Paradis seront merveilleusement rehaussés avec des vins français. Vous retrouverez des vins de plusieurs régions de vignobles français, dans les rouges comme dans les blancs, ainsi que quelques bières françaises. – *menu bilingue et service en français*

Le Petit Gourmet

1064 Yonge Street ☎ (416) 966-3811

Lundi à vendredi 7h30 – 19h, samedi 7h30 – 18h, fermé dimanche

Métro : **ROSEDALE**

Ce petit bistro du quartier Rosedale est

un bon endroit pour déguster un repas sans chichi. Quiches, poulet rôti au four, bœuf bourguignon, ragoût de veau, coq au vin et pâté au poulet font partie du menu régulier. Les plats du jour varient, mais les suggestions sont toujours aussi attirantes. Lorsque nous y étions dernièrement, M. Bonito, chef et propriétaire, proposait les plats suivants : canard aux pommes, gigot d'agneau et rôti de porc. Les plats sont simples et rappellent la cuisine « comme à la maison ». Enfin, un service traiteur est disponible. – *service en français*

Le Saint Tropez

315 King Street West (au coin de John Street) ☎ (416) 591-3600

Lundi à dimanche pour le déjeuner et le dîner

Métro : ST ANDREW

www.lesainttropez.com

Le Saint Tropez vous accueille dans une ambiance décontractée et sympathique. C'est souvent le rendez-vous des Français lors de célébrations nationales (14 juillet et coupe du monde de football par exemple). Au menu, vous aurez le choix entre plusieurs plats français, sur un petit air du Sud : saucisses de Toulouse, poêlée de crevettes et escalope de veau au porto avec champignons sauvages et herbes fraîches. Les desserts ne sont pas nécessairement du Sud, mais Le Saint Tropez n'oublie pas certaines des meilleures spécialités françaises, à savoir la crème brûlée, la tarte au citron et le millefeuille. La carte des vins nous a impressionnés et les régions françaises y sont bien représentées. Enfin, nous devons signaler que la chanteuse du Saint Tropez nous a séduits. Andrée Bernard est une chanteuse talentueuse qui maîtrise aussi bien le chant que le piano. Elle s'inspire de jazz, de folk et de blues pour envoûter les clients. Vous pouvez assister à l'une de ses représentations du mercredi au dimanche. Le lundi et le mardi, vous mangerez sur fond de jazz au Saint Tropez. – *menu bilingue et service en français*

Les restaurants où l'on peut manger des merguez

1. Bistro Matisse
2. Bouchon
3. Boujadi
4. Café Moroc
5. Le Paradis
6. Kiosque à hot-dogs au coin de King Street West et John Street
7. Monitz
8. Pourquoi pas
9. The Sultan's Tent

Le Sélect Bistro

328 Queen Street West ☎ (416) 596-6406

Lundi à vendredi pour le déjeuner, lundi à dimanche pour le dîner

Métro : OSGOODE

www.leselect.com

Voilà une véritable institution à Toronto, et ce, depuis plusieurs décennies ! Le décor du Sélect Bistro vous emmène rive gauche, à Paris. Le menu ? Il est franco-français bien sûr. Si vous voulez manger de la bonne cuisine du terroir comme de la bouillabaisse, du cassoulet, des escargots ou du foie gras, Le Sélect Bistro est l'adresse qu'il vous

faut ! Les viandes y sont cuites à la perfection. Le menu est d'un excellent rapport qualité-prix. Il peut s'avérer difficile de choisir le vin qui accompagnera votre repas, car Le Sélect Bistro vous donne à choisir parmi plus de 800 vins. Quelle cave ! Le choix des desserts donne un peu le tournis : on aimerait bien tout essayer... Ne manquez surtout pas la banane flambée. – *menu bilingue*

Merlot

2994 Bloor Street West ☎ (416) 236-0081

Lundi à vendredi pour le déjeuner, lundi à dimanche pour le dîner

Métro : ROYAL YORK

Le décor, le menu et les œuvres d'art au mur célèbrent bel et bien la France. Merlot est le second restaurant français qui accueille les résidents du Bloor West Village pour déguster de bons petits plats. Merlot sert des plats peu courants à Toronto, comme la choucroute à l'alsacienne. Vous remarquerez que la viande est particulièrement à l'honneur ici. Du steak frites à l'agneau, les variations se font sur le même thème : un bon morceau de viande bien cuit. Les prix sont très raisonnables et donnent ainsi la possibilité de goûter à des plats de viande un peu chers ailleurs, dans d'autres restaurants. Les desserts sont franchement épatants. La carte des vins à petits prix nous a impressionnés ! – *service en français*

Midi Bistro

168A McCaul Street (entre College Street et Dundas Street) ☎ (416) 977-2929

Lundi à vendredi pour le déjeuner, mardi à samedi pour le dîner, fermé dimanche

Métro : ST PATRICK

Midi Bistro est un tout petit restaurant qui vous emmène dans une belle aventure gastronomique. L'ambiance feutrée vous permettra de vous détendre et de savourer un repas des plus agréables. Le menu vous surprendra, tant par sa variété que par son total vraiment raisonnable. Dès l'arrivée, on réalise, en voyant la liste des entrées, que Midi Bistro se distingue par son originalité : Farçous « Claudine » (crêpes aux épinards, oignons et lardons), terrine de chèvre aux légumes, jambon de pays et fromage de chèvre chaud en témoignent. Bien entendu, en bon bistro qui se respecte, Midi Bistro sert aussi des moules. Quant à la sélection de bons petits plats bien mijotés, vous pourrez

Hors catégorie !

John & King Hot Dog Stand

Au coin de John Street et King Street West, en face du Princess of Wales Theatre

Ouvert presque toute l'année pour le déjeuner et le dîner, et même après 22h

Métro : ST ANDREW

Les merguez sur le pouce s'achètent dans le « Theatre District » ! Vous ne les trouverez pas sur le « menu » de ce kiosque à hot-dogs situé au coin de King Street West et John Street, mais si vous les commandez, on vous les préparera. Le propriétaire se nomme Moïse et il se fera un plaisir de vous servir en français. — *service en français*

Les déjeuners qui valent la peine d'être soulignés

Arlequin Si vous êtes à la recherche d'un endroit un peu plus intime pour vos déjeuners d'affaires, Arlequin est l'endroit qu'il vous faut.

Bistro 1603 Voici une adresse située dans le grand Toronto qui sert un bon déjeuner à la française.

Bistro Matisse Encore une autre adresse du grand Toronto où l'on sert un bon déjeuner à la française. Et les prix défient toute concurrence.

Bodega Parlez donc au propriétaire de son service traiteur. C'est une excellente façon de s'offrir un délicieux déjeuner d'affaires sans même quitter la salle de réunion. Avouez que ce serait une façon assez astucieuse d'impressionner vos clients.

Café Moroc et The Sultan's Tent Un déjeuner d'affaires dans un décor qui rappelle les médinas ? Pourquoi pas ! Venez déguster les spécialités marocaines du Café Moroc ou du restaurant The Sultan's Tent. Ces plats sauront sans aucun doute « épicer » vos négociations.

Holt's Café Des tartines de pain Poîlane pour le déjeuner, on n'y résiste pas. Et ça, Holt's Café l'a bien compris !

La Maison Benoît C'est vrai que ce restaurant est situé dans le nord de la ville, mais son accès facile par la voie rapide *(highway)* en fait un lieu idéal pour déguster un bon déjeuner.

Midi Bistro Ce charmant petit bistro français à l'ambiance agréable au déjeuner sert, entre autres, les professionnels des secteurs académiques et médicaux du quartier de University Avenue et St. Patrick Street.

Provence Et si vous alliez déjeuner dans l'un des restaurants les plus charmants de Toronto ? Faites dès maintenant votre prochaine réservation chez Provence.

choisir parmi : un saumon à la cannelle, sauce au citron vert qui vous surprendra, des moules frites, un confit de canard sauce légère à la moutarde *Pommery,* une fricassée de coquelet, sauce des vendanges, un faux-filet à la moelle et un agneau Dubonnet. La liste des desserts propose les choix suivants : une tarte Tatin, des profiteroles avec glace à la vanille, une crème brûlée et un gâteau tiède au chocolat (vous devrez patienter une vingtaine de minutes, mais « le jeu » en vaut vraiment la chandelle, croyez-nous). – *menu bilingue et service en français*

Monitz

352 Melrose Avenue (au coin d'Avenue Road) ☎ (416) 781-3764

Lundi à vendredi pour le déjeuner, lundi à dimanche pour le dîner

Métro : **EGLINTON** + le bus

Monitz est un bistro qui marie très judicieusement la cuisine française, la cuisine méditerranéenne et la cuisine nord-africaine. Cela ne s'arrête pas là puisque Monitz vous permet d'accompagner des plats de couscous avec harissa d'une originalité surprenante avec une sélection d'environ 40 vins, pour la plupart français. On ne vous dira que ceci : les plats de couscous avec harissa

ne sont pas les seules créations insolites. Les merguez ne figurent pas sur le menu, mais si vous en faites la demande, le chef se fera un plaisir de vous les préparer. Le tarif du menu est très intéressant, vraiment pas très cher. Pour ce qui est des desserts, on vous laisse découvrir par vous-même. – *menu bilingue et service en français*

Pourquoi pas

63 Sheppard Avenue West (à l'ouest de Yonge Street) ☎ (416) 226-9071

Lundi à vendredi pour le déjeuner et lundi à dimanche pour le dîner

Métro : **SHEPPARD**

www.toronto.com/pourquoipas

Pourquoi pas est situé dans une maison sur Sheppard Avenue, un peu à l'ouest de Yonge Street. Le décor a plutôt l'allure du salon d'une grand-tante que celle d'un restaurant. Le propriétaire d'origine égyptienne, Sherif Elkei, n'a pas bougé depuis 1975. Au menu, on vous propose des plats simples, intéressants et à des prix très raisonnables. L'ambiance vous met à l'aise, le personnel fait attention à vous et les plats sont savoureusement mijotés. Au palmarès des plats convoités par les habitués, on trouve les merguez, le cassoulet, le foie de veau à la bordelaise, les médaillons de porc au calvados, l'agneau à la marocaine, le canard à l'orange, les ris de veau et le filet mignon sauce béarnaise. Les plats de viande sont très bien préparés. Ces viandes fondent dans la bouche tant elles sont tendres. Crème caramel, saint-honoré et crêpes Suzette font parti de la courte liste des desserts. La carte des vins référence quelques vins de France. – *menu bilingue et service en français*

Quartier

2112 Yonge Street (entre Davisville Avenue et Eglinton Avenue) ☎ (416) 545-0505

Mardi à vendredi pour le déjeuner et lundi à samedi pour le dîner, fermé dimanche

Métro : **DAVISVILLE** ou **EGLINTON**

Quartier est un bistro typique de quartier qui associe les classiques de la cuisine française à d'autres courants gastronomiques internationaux. Ce restaurant est un endroit parfait pour un dîner simple et délicieux, à prix modéré et dans une ambiance détendue. Les spécialités du menu comprennent un lapin aux échalotes servi sur un lit de risotto aux truffes, un confit de canard aux pommes sardalaises, une poitrine de poulet aux morilles et un jarret d'agneau. Quartier maîtrise aussi la préparation des plats de poisson. Oh ! Et il va sans dire que le steak frites fait également partie des spécialités de la maison. Vous aurez droit à un menu « table d'hôte » pour le dîner du lundi soir. Si vous êtes plutôt d'un naturel patient, nous vous recommandons le velouté au chocolat en dessert (20 minutes d'attente quand même !). Mais vous pouvez également, selon vos préférences, terminer votre repas par une assiette de fromages. Nous l'avons trouvée épatante. La sélection des vins est assez française, surtout dans la catégorie des vins rouges. – *menu bilingue et service en français*

bistros et restos

Restaurant Jules

147 Spadina Avenue ☎ (416) 348-8886

Lundi à vendredi 11h30 – 21h, samedi 12h – 17 h, fermé dimanche, fermé samedi en juillet et en août

Métro : **SPADINA** + le tram;
OSGOODE + le tram

Le chef Eric Strippoli vous accueille chez Jules avec une bonne cuisine française à prix vraiment abordable. En bon bistro français, Jules vous propose une liste impressionnante de classiques simples et succulents : soupe gratinée à l'oignon, quiches, ratatouille et bavette. La mayonnaise et les croûtons sont même faits maison. Les plats de crêpes figurent au rang des meilleurs plats chez Jules. Les desserts ne vous décevront pas non plus. Au menu : tarte Tatin, crème brûlée et crêpes. – *menu bilingue et service en français*

Les bons endroits où trouver le dessert français préféré de la rédactrice en chef : la tarte au citron

1. Arlequin
2. Bonjour Brioche
3. Bouchon
4. Café Margaux
5. Clafouti
6. Daniel et Daniel
7. Gamelle
8. Holt's Café
9. La Cigogne
10. Le Paradis
11. Le Saint Tropez
12. Marcel's Bistro
13. Patachou
14. Pâtisserie d'Or
15. Rahier

repas gastronomiques

Auberge du Pommier

4150 Yonge Street (au nord de York Mills Road) ☎ (416) 222-2220

Lundi à vendredi pour le déjeuner, lundi à samedi pour le dîner, fermé dimanche

Métro : **YORK MILLS**

Année après année, l'Auberge du Pommier se voit attribuer le prix d'excellence, décerné par *Where Magazine*, du « *Most Memorable Meal Award* ». De façon générale, ce restaurant figure parmi les dix meilleurs de la ville. Les prix sont en conséquence plus élevés que la moyenne. Maisonnette ressemblant à une auberge de campagne française, on y propose une cuisine raffinée mélangeant les influences françaises et méditerranéennes aux tendances « nouvelle cuisine ». Pour terminer votre repas, choisissez parmi les desserts artistiques et savoureux ou une belle assiette de fromages. Il faudra aussi vous attarder sur la carte des vins. Le service est vraiment hors pair. Pas de fausse note dans cette Auberge du Pommier, que ce soit au niveau du service, des plats exceptionnels ou du décor particulièrement invitant. Nous vous recommandons d'aller dans ce restaurant, ne serait-ce qu'une fois par an. Sa découverte ou sa redécouverte ne vous décevra nullement. – *service en français*

Bistro 1603

1603 Clarkson Road, Mississauga
☎ (905) 822-5262

Mercredi à vendredi pour le déjeuner, lundi à samedi pour le dîner, fermé dimanche

taloua
femmes albinos: pourquoi sont-elles exclues?
dossier
la télé réalité frappe le Québec
juliette powell
un diamant aux mille facettes
femmes et cinéma: du baiser hollywoodien à la condition féminine
interview exclusif
les nubians
danielle carney
rend hommage à toutes les femmes du monde...
douala
new york
vancouver
rachel
vocation journalisme
LA TYRANNIE DE LA BEAUTÉ
THE BODY SHOP
ALICIA KEYS
musique
julie kim
art et culture
SHEILA COPPS
MANIPULATRICES OU VICTIMES
Beyoncé Knowles
L'afro
Jean
une force de la nature
dossier
le trafic sexuel au Canada:
Haily Berry
la lumière au bout du tunnel
www.taloua.com

Y'a pas deux matins pareils
AVEC YVES LAROUCHE
dès 6h
maintenant disponible aussi
au 90,3 FM
860 AM
Première Chaîne
Radio-Canada
90,3 FM
Chaîne culturelle
Radio-Canada
www.radio-canada.ca/toronto

Ce restaurant de Mississauga marie judicieusement la tradition des plats français aux ressources locales en matière d'ingrédients et crée de ce fait une expérience gastronomique surprenante. Bistro 1603 propose les spécialités suivantes : une bouillabaisse à tendance asiatique, un trio de poitrines de canard, du foie gras et du confit, un foie de veau et un steak frites maison. Il ne faut pas oublier les desserts. La crème brûlée et la mousse au chocolat et à la framboise accompagnée d'une boule de crème glacée au chocolat *Lindt* sont particulièrement savoureuses. Le menu impressionne déjà, mais c'est la carte des vins qui attire encore plus l'attention chez bistro 1603. Ce restaurant a obtenu deux prix du « *Wine Spectator Awards of Excellence* » en 2002 et 2003. Avec plus de 250 bouteilles en cave, vous pouvez comprendre pourquoi.
– *service en français*

Bodega *(anciennement La Bodega)*

30 Baldwin Street ☎ (416) 977-1287
Lundi à dimanche pour le déjeuner et le dîner
Métro : ST PATRICK
www.bodegarestaurant.com

Le nouveau propriétaire, le nouveau décor et la nouvelle ambiance n'ont rien changé à l'essence même de ce restaurant. Le « coup de neuf » a tout simplement amené une clientèle plus jeune qui sait apprécier les charmes d'un plat de cuisine française préparé par une main experte. Eh oui, chez Bodega on peut toujours s'attendre à manger de très bonnes spécialités françaises : bouillabaisse, terrine de foie gras, escargots et rognons servis dans une timbale feuilletée, foie de canard grillé, truite servie avec des lentilles et foie de canard. Le menu du jour est une excellente option pour une addition tout à fait raisonnable. Ne ratez pas les desserts dont la description suffit à mettre sérieusement l'eau à la bouche. Signalons notamment la crème brûlée, les profiteroles avec des figues accompagnées de glace au porto et de sauce tiède au chocolat et la mousse au chocolat blanc avec du Grand Marnier, servie avec un trio de sauces.

Bouchon

38 Wellington Street East ☎ (416) 862-2675
Mardi à vendredi pour le déjeuner, lundi à samedi pour le dîner, fermé dimanche
Métro : KING OU UNION
www.bouchon.ca

Jean-Pierre Challet, chef chez Bouchon, n'a pas peur des parfums rehaussés. Et la saveur est partout au rendez-vous sur le menu, puis dans votre assiette. Les plats proposés sont bien français, mais ils sont aussi exécutés avec un doigté expert et moderne – poutine de merguez et fromage saint-nectaire (avec des frites allumettes), foie gras et sauce aux airelles (canneberges) et à la rhubarbe sur lit d'asperges blanches, bœuf bourguignon, poutine de foie gras et fromage de chèvre, le tout servi dans un jus de canard. Vous remarquerez, à cette liste, que le chef, chez Bouchon, n'hésite pas à s'inspirer des cuisines de toute la francophonie. La carte des vins (à tendance plutôt française) accompagne harmonieusement les plats du restaurant. Quant aux

Brunch

Quoi de plus tentant que de traîner au lit un samedi ou un dimanche matin avant d'aller retrouver des amis pour un brunch ? D'accord, le brunch n'est pas vraiment une institution française, ce qui explique sans doute pourquoi peu de restaurants proposent un menu différent de leur menu régulier de la semaine. Malgré tout, les restaurants français suivants se sont adaptés à la demande locale et ont créé des menus pour les « lève-tard » du week-end.

Bloor Street Diner et **Bistros** Le menu du brunch est un peu plus cher que la moyenne, mais nous vous garantissons que ce qui y figure vous plaira.

Bodega Quel brunch ! Bodega offre un menu succinct, mais très alléchant. Au rendez-vous : pain perdu, œufs « Bénédicte » (œufs pochés servis sur muffins anglais avec sauce hollandaise) et omelette au saumon fumé. Si ces plats ne vous satisfont pas, vous pourrez choisir un plat dans le menu du déjeuner de la semaine.

Bonjour Brioche Le brunch est servi le samedi et le dimanche. Délicieuses quiches, omelettes et autres plats du jour viennent compléter la sélection de brioches et pâtisseries. Les plats du jour sont inscrits sur une grande ardoise, mais vous pouvez aussi commander des plats au menu du déjeuner.

Brasserie Aix Il est maintenant possible de passer chez Brasserie Aix le dimanche matin pour prendre le brunch. Au menu, des plats classiques qui revigorent le dimanche matin – steak œuf à cheval, œufs « Bénédicte », omelette du jour, pain perdu servi avec compote de fruits et œufs servis avec saumon fumé.

Épicure Café Épicure Café comprend très bien les besoins de sa clientèle, c'est pourquoi on y sert un brunch pendant une bonne partie de la journée jusqu'à l'après-midi, le week-end. Le menu ne sort pas vraiment de l'ordinaire, mais une grande variété de plats d'œufs et d'omelettes y figurent.

Jacques Bistro du Parc On ne sert de brunch que le samedi chez Jacques Bistro. Le menu est simple mais savoureux, avec différentes omelettes, des quiches et des salades.

La Cigogne Les habitants du Bayview Village profitent d'un bon brunch à la française à portée de chez eux. À La Cigogne, ils peuvent savourer des quiches aux parfums variés, des crêpes fourrées, des croque-madame et des omelettes. La Cigogne propose des crêpes en dessert ! N'oubliez surtout pas que la tarte flambée n'est servie que le week-end. Profitez-en lors de votre brunch.

La Palette Il est préférable d'arriver tôt, car ce petit restaurant de Kensington se remplit vite pour le brunch. L'attraction principale, ce sont les crêpes bien sûr ! Assez rare à Toronto, La Palette propose plusieurs crêpes fourrées ainsi que des omelettes, une salade basque ou niçoise et un steak frites œuf à cheval.

Le Sélect Bistro Il est ouvert le samedi et le dimanche pour le brunch et vous accueille avec les incontournables du brunch : omelettes, œufs « Bénédicte », pain perdu (*French toast* en anglais), œufs brouillés et saucisses, crêpe à la banane avec sirop d'érable.

Provence Le menu du brunch de Provence vous tend les bras le samedi et le dimanche. Le prix de ce menu incluant salade, œufs et crème brûlée est raisonnable. Des frites parfaitement cuites et bien assaisonnées accompagnent tous les plats qui figurent sur le menu du brunch.

desserts, leur liste est étourdissante. Les immanquables sont la tarte au citron et la crème brûlée. – *menu bilingue et service en français*

Café Brussels

124 Danforth Avenue ☎ (416) 465-7363
Fermé lundi, mardi à dimanche pour le dîner
Métro : BROADVIEW

Café Brussels est sans aucun doute un des secrets les mieux gardés de Toronto. Café Brussels vous reçoit dans un décor Art déco impressionnant. Le menu est axé sur la viande – agneau, steak frites, filet mignon, bœuf bourguignon. Et bien sûr, vous découvrirez chez Café Brussels un menu de 30 variétés de moules frites ! Pour couronner le tout, la portion de moules chez Café Brussels équivaut à 1 kg, ce à quoi l'on n'est pas habitué de ce côté-ci de l'Atlantique. La carte des vins est une autre très agréable surprise. En fait, cette dernière fut nominée pendant sept années consécutives parmi la célèbre liste des meilleurs vins « *Top restaurant wine list Award of Excellence* » du magazine *Wine Spectator.* Enfin, nous ajouterons que le service irréprochable de Café Brussels en fait dans l'ensemble une expérience gastronomique hors du commun. – *menu bilingue et service en français*

Célestin

623 Mount Pleasant Road
☎ (416) 544-9035
Fermé dimanche et lundi, mardi à samedi pour le dîner
Métro : EGLINTON + le bus

Le chef Pascal Ribreau (ancien chef du restaurant Provence) a peut-être instauré une nouvelle mode en ouvrant son nouveau restaurant dans l'immeuble d'une ancienne banque sur Mount Pleasant Road. Il y prépare une cuisine traditionnelle française, grâce à des ingrédients d'une qualité indiscutable et une créativité culinaire florissante. Dans ce restaurant, les palets les plus experts seront ravis, que ce soit avec les entrées ou les plats principaux, parmi lesquels le ragoût de pattes de porc, le lapin braisé, le boudin à l'ail, le magret de canard, la côte de porc et même l'agneau safrané accompagné de palourdes à la provençale. Faites attention, le pain maison est irrésistible. Pour les desserts, le chef Pascal Ribreau collabore avec son frère Martial pour nous mener jusqu'aux portes du paradis du sucre. La présentation du millefeuille vous laissera bouche bée. Vous n'êtes pas obligé de finir votre repas par un dessert, vous pouvez opter pour l'assiette de fromages. Célestin met à votre disposition une carte des vins tellement détaillée qu'elle fait environ 20 pages ! Évidemment, vous y retrouverez nombre de vignobles français. – *service en français*

Gamelle

468 College Street (au coin de Markham Street, à l'ouest de Bathurst Street)
☎ (416) 923-6254
Mardi à vendredi pour le déjeuner, lundi à samedi pour le dîner, fermé dimanche
Métro : OSGOODE + le tram
www.gamelle.com

Gamelle ressemble peut-être à un bistro de par sa petite taille, mais pourtant il

s'agit bien d'un restaurant. Dans une ambiance décontractée chic, Gamelle sert des plats d'une cuisine subtile et recherchée. On y mange du faisan, du canard fumé, du magret de canard, des escargots, un millefeuille de légumes, un steak au brandy ou encore du gigot d'agneau québécois. Les plats de poisson sont très bien apprêtés et assaisonnés. Le patron, Jean-Pierre Centeno, vient du Sud-Ouest de la France, alors bien sûr, il y a également du foie gras au menu ! Les vins sont majoritairement français. N'oubliez pas d'essayer les desserts ! Nous vous recommandons la tarte au citron, la crème brûlée et le gâteau au chocolat. – *service en français*

Le Montmartre

911 Sheppard Avenue West
☎ (416) 630-3804

Lundi à vendredi pour le déjeuner, lundi à samedi pour le dîner, fermé dimanche

Métro : DOWNSVIEW

www.toronto.com/lemontmartre

Si vous croyiez que tous les bons restos français se trouvaient au centre-ville, détrompez-vous. Depuis 1991, Le Montmartre accueille chaleureusement une clientèle régulière à l'affût de bons plats préparés avec soin. Ici, les viandes et les abats sont à l'honneur, avec notamment quelques classiques de la cuisine française tels que les cuisses de grenouilles, le canard à l'orange et les escargots à la bourguignonne. N'oubliez surtout pas de consulter le menu qui cache aussi de très bonnes choses. La carte des vins ne décoit pas non plus, que ce soit côté France ou côté international. Pour clore un savoureux repas, laissez-vous séduire par les profiteroles fourrées à la crème pâtissière ou à la crème glacée. Le Montmartre vaut sans conteste le détour. – *menu bilingue et service en français*

Le Trou Normand

90 Yorkville Avenue ☎ (416) 967-5956

Lundi à samedi pour le déjeuner et le dîner, fermé dimanche

Métro : BAY

www.letrounormand.com

Dans le quartier de Yorkville, ce restaurant sert une cuisine française authentique. Plusieurs plats sont d'inspiration normande, servis avec des pommes, de la crème ou des fruits de mer. Au palmarès des autres plats du terroir : médaillons de veau à la normande et assiette de coquilles Saint-Jacques, crevettes et homard servis avec une sauce au Grand Marnier. Le Trou Normand propose aussi plusieurs plats de foie gras, sans que les prix flambent pour autant. La liste des vins est longue et bien française et elle convient à tous les budgets – de 20 à 750 dollars ! Côté dessert, pour ne pas faire dans l'original, mais dans la valeur sûre, nous vous conseillons de commander la crème brûlée. – *menu bilingue*

Marcel's Bistro

315 King Street West (au coin de John Street) ☎ (416) 591-8600

Fermé dimanche et lundi, mardi à samedi pour le déjeuner et le dîner

Métro : ST ANDREW

www.marcels.com

Depuis 1984, Marcel's Bistro vous in-

vite dans une ambiance feutrée à choisir parmi un menu raffiné des plats servis de façon impeccable. Moules « Poulette », terrine de faisan, salade d'épinards aux pleurotes, pommes grillées et roquefort ou encore steak frites, noisettes d'agneau servies avec une mousseline de pommes de terre au pistou, filet de bœuf et son jus au cognac, servi avec un gratin auvergnat sont parmi les plats que vous pourrez déguster sur place. Tous les mois, Marcel's Bistro célèbre la gastronomie d'une région de France. Pour le dessert, les classiques sont à l'honneur : crème brûlée, profiteroles, gâteau à la mousse au chocolat noir et tarte au citron, entre autres. La carte des vins illustre l'excellence des vins français et n'oublie pas les apéritifs non plus (kir, pineau, pastis, etc.). – *menu bilingue et service en français*

Matignon

51 St. Nicholas Street ☎ (416) 921-9226

Lundi à vendredi pour le déjeuner, lundi à samedi pour le dîner, fermé dimanche (ouvert dimanche seulement pour les fonctions privées)

Métro : YONGE

www.matignon.ca

Matignon propose un excellent menu à prix très raisonnable et une carte bien variée. On y trouve des plats qui sortent de l'ordinaire, tels que le canard rôti servi sur un coulis de myrtilles, la pièce d'Angus (bœuf) au poivre noir flambée au cognac, le poulet au pistou ou le carré d'agneau à la moutarde, au miel et à la menthe. On peut également commander des plats plus traditionnels tels que le saumon « à la bonne femme », le steak frites, la truite au beurre blanc ou le foie de veau. La cave à vins est pleine de bons vins à petits prix. À ne pas manquer quand vous arrivez au dessert : la crème caramel au parfum d'orange. Matignon est situé dans une maison de briques, dans une rue résidentielle calme entre Yonge Street et Bay Street, au sud de Charles Street. Le restaurant comporte deux salles élégantes à l'ambiance tamisée, offre un service impeccable et est dirigé par un patron très affable : Mustapha Amrani. – *service en français*

Pastis Express

1158 Yonge Street (tout près du métro Summerhill) ☎ (416) 928-2212

Fermé dimanche et lundi, mardi à samedi pour le dîner

Les bons endroits où trouver le dessert français favori des Torontois : la crème brûlée

1. Auberge du Pommier
2. Bistro 1603
3. Bodega
4. Café la Gaffe
5. Café Margaux
6. Café Moroc/The Sultan's Tent
7. Célestin
8. Gamelle
9. Holt's Café
10. La Petite France
11. Le Saint Tropez
12. Marcel's Bistro
13. Midi Bistro
14. Pastis
15. Provence

Métro : SUMMERHILL

Tantôt bistro, tantôt resto, toujours bon. Pastis, qui se trouve dans le quartier chic de Rosedale, sert des plats hors du commun, tels que le foie gras poêlé aux poires caramélisées, que l'on peut savourer dans un décor chaleureux. Le chateaubriand pour deux est rare à Toronto et Pastis le prépare avec brio. Alors, que demande le peuple ? Notez que la crème brûlée est excellente. Mais si vous vous sentez particulièrement courageux, choisissez l'assiette gourmande en dessert : la fameuse crème brûlée y côtoie une pointe de gâteau au chocolat noir, une compote de framboises et une fine tuile. Hum, tout simplement délicieux ! Si le défi de l'assiette gourmande vous dépasse, essayez les profiteroles fourrées de glace au caramel, servies sur un coulis de framboise. La liste des vins n'est pas très longue, mais les choix sont judicieux. – *service en français*

PROVENCE

12 Amelia Street (au coin Parliament Street, près de Wellesley Street)
☎ (416) 924-9901

Lundi à dimanche pour le déjeuner et le dîner

Métro : COLLEGE + le tram;
CASTLE FRANK + le bus

www.provencerestaurant.com

Provence est à nos yeux le restaurant le plus charmant de Toronto. Situé dans le vieux quartier de Cabbagetown, au cœur d'une résidence reconvertie en restaurant, le menu de Provence est à la fois simple, classique et sophistiqué. Provence agrémente ses plats d'une touche de parfums riches et complexes dont le chef a le secret. Les serveurs sont attentifs et compétents. Les prix à la carte sont un peu au-dessus de la moyenne, mais les menus du déjeuner et du dîner permettent de déguster un bon repas à prix moindre. Les entrées sont assez recherchées : terrine de canard, escargots, huîtres et même du caviar Sevruga. Quant aux plats principaux, ils sont tout aussi soignés : bouillabaisse, canard et foie de veau font partie de la liste. Ce qui est assez original, c'est que Provence propose deux assiettes de fromages. La cerise sur le gâteau, c'est bien sûr le dessert : une crème brûlée au Grand Marnier. La carte des vins est très française et le choix est remarquable. Il est tellement exceptionnel que le restaurant a reçu le « *Wine Spectator Award of Excellence* » en 1999, 2000, 2001, 2002 et 2003. Que pouvons-nous dire de plus ? – *service en français*

THE SULTAN'S TENT

49 Front Street East (à l'ouest de Church Street) ☎ (416) 961-0601

Lundi à samedi pour le déjeuner, lundi à dimanche pour le dîner

Métro : UNION

www.thesultanstent.com

Comment être dépaysé à Toronto ? Pourquoi pas en réservant une table au restaurant The Sultan's Tent qui vous garantira une expérience inoubliable ? Le restaurant est situé à l'arrière du Café Moroc (mentionné dans la section précédente). Tout comme le Café, le décor de The Sultan's Tent est 100 % marocain. La différence ici, c'est que

l'on peut savourer des plats plus complexes dans un décor encore plus envoûtant qui ne manquera pas de vous séduire. Tout a en effet été conçu pour ravir tant le palet que les autres organes sensoriels. D'immenses divans vous permettent de vous installer à votre aise afin de décompresser sous des tentes de tissus aux couleurs chatoyantes. La lumière est tamisée et la musique marocaine fait vibrer. Le menu concourt également très bien à cette aventure magique qui vous emporte au cœur du Maroc. Nous sommes certains que vous serez séduit par les quatre plats proposés par The Sultan's Tent. De l'entrée au dessert, en passant par la théière de thé à la menthe marocaine, le tableau est complet. Vers 21h, toute la salle s'arrête : c'est le début du spectacle – des jeunes femmes fort séduisantes dansent au son de rythmes arabes.
– service en français

Nos desserts favoris

1. L'assiette gourmande de Café Margaux
2. L'assiette gourmande de Pastis
3. La crème caramel du Paradis
4. La tarte aux poires et à la pâte d'amandes de Bonjour Brioche
5. Le dominus et la tarte aux pommes caramélisées et au chocolat de Clafouti
6. Le gâteau au chocolat de chez Gamelle
7. Le gâteau aux marrons de Senses
8. Le millefeuille de Célestin
9. Les petits fours de Patachou
10. Les profiteroles à la crème glacée de Midi Bistro
11. Les profiteroles aux figues et à la glace au porto de Bodega
12. Les profiteroles de Jacques Bistro du Parc
13. Le pain perdu fait avec du pain Poîlane, des pêches et de la cannelle de Holt's Café
14. Toutes les tartes aux fruits de Bouchon
15. Toutes les tartes de Daniel et Daniel

en cuisine avec la francophonie

écoles de cuisine

Maintenant que vous disposez de toutes les adresses pour acheter les ingrédients de vos plats préférés de la francophonie, il est temps de mettre la main à la pâte et de peaufiner vos talents de cuisinier grâce aux écoles suivantes.

écoles de cuisine

Academy of Artisans

490 Eglinton Avenue West (à l'ouest d'Avenue Road) (tél.) (416) 322-9997

Cours : en soirée, pas de cours le week-end

Métro : EGLINTON + le bus

www.academyofartisans.com

Vous pourrez parfaire votre éducation en matière de cuisine française ou marocaine dans cette école de Forest Hill.

Calphalon Culinary Center

425 King Street West (au coin de Spadina Avenue) (tél.) (416) 847-2212

Cours : en soirée et le samedi

Métro : ST ANDREW

www.calphalonculinarycenter.com

On vous donnera ici des cours de base en cuisine, idéals pour les débutants ou pour perfectionner les connaissances que vous aviez déjà. Une fois que vous aurez maîtrisé les bases, vous pourrez vous lancer dans l'apprentissage des mystères de la cuisine française. Ensuite, on vous proposera un cours sur l'art de marier le vin et les plats avec finesse. Nous avons aussi remarqué que Calphalon animait un cours sur le mariage des bières belges avec les plats belges, ainsi qu'un cours grâce auquel vous apprendrez à préparer de merveilleuses crêpes.

Cooking at the Harvest Kitchen

134 Thomas Street, Oakville
(tél.) (416) 346-4236 (le bureau est situé à Toronto)

Cours : en soirée

www.epicureanexpeditions.com

Cette école propose un cours de cuisine française, mais seulement deux fois par an. En plus, les places sont limitées. Pour vous tenir au courant des activités, passez un coup de fil et demandez à recevoir le bulletin électronique mensuel.

Cook Gourmet

1204 Clarkson Road, Mississauga (près de QEW et Highway 10) (tél.) (905) 403-0059

Cours : en soirée

www.cookgourmet.ca

Voici une école située à Mississauga qui vous permettra d'élargir vos connaissances en cuisine française.

Dish Cooking Studio

390 Dupont Street (tél.) (416) 920-5559

Cours : en soirée et le samedi

Métro : DUPONT

www.dishcookingstudio.com

Dish Cooking Studio est une école sympathique où l'on peut appendre les rudiments de la cuisine française ou marocaine.

George Brown College

300 Adelaide Street East (tél.) (416) 415-5000

Cours : en soirée et le samedi matin

Métro : KING

www.gbrownc.on.ca

George Brown College propose plusieurs cours de cuisine française : cuisine classique, cuisine contemporaine, crêpes et cuisine du terroir. La série « *Wine and Dine at our Table* » vous permettra de

participer à une soirée d'apprentissage. Une fois la leçon terminée, c'est la dégustation qui commence ! Vous trouverez plus de détails sur ces cours sur le site, sous la rubrique « *Hospitality & Tourism* ».

Give it a Stir

1560 Yonge Street (Delisle Court)
☎ (416) 920-7447

Cours : le mardi soir

Métro : ST CLAIR

www.giveitastir.com

Give it a Stir est avant tout un magasin d'accessoires de cuisine. Cela dit, il y a à l'arrière de cette boutique une cuisine qui sert judicieusement de petite école culinaire. On y fait appel à Debbie Diamente pour vous permettre d'apprendre la cuisine marocaine. Mme Diamente donne également des cours privés de cuisine française ou marocaine. Voilà une idée sympathique pour votre prochaine soirée à thème.

Great Cooks

176 Yonge Street (au sous-sol de La Baie, Queen Street) ☎ (416) 861-4727

Cours : en soirée et le samedi mais pendant la saison hivernale pour ce jour

Métro : QUEEN

www.greatcooks.ca

Les propriétaires de cette école sont elles-mêmes des chefs. Esther Benaim et Maggie McKeown font appel aux plus grands noms de la cuisine francophone de Toronto pour vous emmener dans des aventures culinaires françaises et marocaines. Côté Maroc, c'est le chef Bouchra Sidali qui est aux fourneaux. Tandis que le chef Jean-Pierre Challet du restaurant Bouchon vient représenter l'art culinaire français, parfois même en français. C'est une première à Toronto ! Enfin, signalons que Great Cooks est l'une des premières écoles de cuisine privées à avoir ouvert ses portes à Toronto. – *cours de cuisine française dispensé en français*

J.S. Bonbons

163 Dupont Street (près de Davenport Road) ☎ (416) 920-0274

Cours : en soirée

Métro : DUPONT

www.jsbonbons.com

Si vous avez déjà lu la section des chocolats de ce guide, vous saurez que nous adorons les chocolats du chef pâtissier Jenn Stone. D'où notre joie d'apprendre qu'il était possible de prendre des cours avec elle sur l'art de confectionner des chocolats. Tout se passe à l'arrière de la boutique. La récompense reste bien entendu la dégustation…

LCBO

Partout en ville ☎ 1 800 668-5226

Cours : en soirée

www.lcbo.com

Vous pourrez suivre plusieurs cours de dégustation de vins avec la LCBO. « *Vins d'Alsace* », « *Les bières belges* » et « *Les blancs de la région de Bourgogne* » sont des exemples de cours proposés. Il est également possible de prendre des cours de cuisine française. M. Ektor Stroutzas, directeur des fromageries Alex Farms, donne aussi un cours sur

les fromages.

Le Cordon Bleu Paris

453 Laurier Avenue East, Ottawa
☎ 1 888 289-6302

Cours : en soirée ou le week-end, parfois à la journée

www.lcbottawa.edu

Il est vrai que lorsqu'on habite le grand Toronto, il est difficilement envisageable d'aller à Ottawa pour un cours de cuisine le temps d'une soirée. Mais si nous avons mis cette adresse dans le guide, c'est parce que cette école propose des cours d'une journée en semaine et même quelquefois le week-end. Voilà une bonne occasion pour s'évader, apprendre puis déguster les fruits de son labeur. Ici, la cuisine classique française est à l'honneur. Il y a aussi un cours intéressant sur le mariage du vin et des plats.

Loblaws

Partout en ville

Cours : en soirée et quelquefois le samedi

Dans plus d'une vingtaine de magasins Loblaws, il y a une école de cuisine. Elle est généralement située à l'étage supérieur. On vous y proposera des cours de cuisine sur différents thèmes tels que la préparation de la pâte feuilletée, la cuisine marocaine et la cuisine française. Vous aurez également la possibilité de participer à une dégustation d'huîtres et à un cours de cuisine française animé par le chef du restaurant Bouchon, Jean-Pierre Challet.

Richmond Hill Culinary Arts Centre

1550 16th Avenue, Richmond Hill
☎ (905) 508-2665

Cours : en soirée

www.culinaryarts.ca

Dans cette école de Richmond Hill, vous apprendrez l'art de confectionner des chocolats, de préparer des crêpes parfaites ou encore une savoureuse crème brûlée.

Strewn Winery

1339 Lake Shore Road,
Niagara-on-the-Lake ☎ (905) 468-8304

Cours : le week-end

www.winecountrycooking.com

Vous avez le choix entre les cours du samedi ou les cours du week-end entier pour apprendre les techniques de la cuisine française ou de la dégustation de vin, et même l'art de marier de bons vins à un bon repas. En plus, les cours ont lieu dans l'une des plus belles régions de l'Ontario.

The Cookworks

99 Sudbury Street, unit # 8
☎ (416) 537-6464

Cours : en soirée

Métro : OSGOODE + le tram

www.thecookworks.com

« Je mange, je bois, je fais l'amour » : voilà le titre du cours de cuisine française dispensé dans cette école de cuisine. Avouez que certaines des valeurs françaises sont ici bien résumées.

aventures culturelles

information et divertissement

Toronto ne sera jamais Paris ni Montréal, mais il est tout de même possible d'y avoir accès à un certain nombre de ressources culturelles en français. Journaux, librairies, cinémas, films, théâtres, stations de radio, festivals et soirées francophones permettent de s'informer et se divertir dans la langue de Molière. Ces événements et ressources culturelles sont également une très bonne occasion pour les anglophones de pratiquer leur français ou même de s'initier à la culture francophone.

Journaux

L'Express

www.lexpress.to

L'Express est l'hebdomadaire canadien-français le plus important à Toronto. Vous serez au courant de l'actualité internationale et locale, mais aussi politique, sociale et économique, sans oublier les événements culturels, les offres d'emploi et les petites annonces qui font également partie des rubriques. *L'Express* est disponible par abonnement et il est en vente à la Maison de la Presse Internationale, chez Champlain et Indigo. Il est disponible gratuitement dans certains lieux stratégiques tels que l'Alliance Française, le collège Glendon ou le Consulat Général de France.

Le Métropolitain

www.lemetropolitain.com

Le Métropolitain se consacre aux événements qui tournent autour de la vie des francophones du grand Toronto. Il est vendu en kiosque. Il est également disponible gratuitement dans les endroits où l'on trouve *L'Express.*

Livres et magazines

À Bon Verre, Bonne Table

Dans les magasins LCBO
☎ 1 800 ONT-LCBO
www.lcbo.com/food_drink_fr

Ce magazine sur la gastronomie, les vins et autres boissons alcoolisées est l'un des magazines préférés des francophones et francophiles torontois. Chaque numéro regorge de recettes, de suggestions en vins, bières et spiritueux, de conseils d'achat sur les derniers « tubes » musicaux et d'astuces bien utiles. Le magazine est distribué gratuitement dans les boutiques LCBO (société des alcools de l'Ontario). Mais faites vite, car il disparaît très rapidement. L'un des grands attraits de ce magazine, hormis le fait qu'il soit rédigé en français, c'est que les recettes qu'on vous y propose ont été créées à partir d'ingrédients disponibles ici. Si vous ne trouvez pas la version française dans le magasin LCBO le plus proche de chez vous, abonnez-vous pour une modique somme et recevez-le à la maison. Pour plus de renseignements, appelez la ligne d'information.

Amazon.ca

www.amazon.ca

Cette librairie virtuelle a un large catalogue de livres en français. Commander des livres sur le site d'Amazon est presque un jeu d'enfant. Vous serez étonné de voir à quel point Amazon vous présente une multitude de catégories pour trouver le livre français de votre choix.

Archambault.ca

www.archambault.ca

Archambault est un grand nom des produits culturels francophones au Québec. Nous le mentionnons dans notre guide parce que l'on peut avoir recours à son site pour effectuer ses achats, même si l'on vit à Toronto. Comme avec toutes les librairies virtuelles, il suffit de choisir et de cliquer pour commander.

Groupe Indigo-Chapters

Différentes adresses dans toute la ville
www.chapters.indigo.ca

Le Groupe Indigo-Chapters comprend les librairies suivantes : **Chapters, Coles Books, Indigo** et **World's Biggest Book Store** (20 Edward Street ☎ (416) 977-7009; lundi à samedi 9h – 22h, dimanche 11h – 18 h)

Indigo dispose d'une très petite sélection de livres en français, le choix se limitant surtout aux grands classiques. Côté magazines et journaux français, on retrouve les grands noms. Allez également faire un tour sur le site Internet et dans les autres librairies qui appartiennent au Groupe Indigo-Chapters, car vous y trouverez des journaux, des magazines et des livres en français.

La Maison de la Presse Internationale

102 – 104 Yorkville Avenue
☎ (416) 928-2328

Lundi à vendredi 8h – 23h, samedi 8h30 – 00h, dimanche 8h30 – 23h

Métro : BAY ou MUSEUM

Copie conforme des magasins montréalais, on retrouve dans cette maison de la presse des magazines et des journaux français et québécois, des guides touristiques et de nombreux livres français en tout genre.

Librairie Champlain

468 Queen Street East ☎ (416) 364-4345

Lundi à jeudi 9h – 18h, vendredi 9h – 20h, samedi 9h – 17h, fermé dimanche

Métro : QUEEN + le tram

Le saviez-vous ?

L'Alliance Française est un bon endroit où envoyer vos amis anglophones qui cherchent à apprendre le français; elle offre également les services de location et de prêt des ouvrages de référence suivants :

- **Matériel d'apprentissage**

Plus de 30 cassettes vidéo, dictionnaires, livres en français pour débutants, cassettes audio et CD-ROM

- **Musique française et francophone**

Les meilleurs chanteurs sur CD et cassettes

- **Littérature française et francophone**

Plus de 1 800 livres, des auteurs classiques aux contemporains, des romans policiers aux essais

- **Création française contemporaine**

Une centaine de cassettes vidéo sur la science, les arts, la société française d'aujourd'hui, des livres, des journaux et des magazines.

- **Films français**

Plus de 250 grands succès mondiaux du cinéma français y sont disponibles.

Pour plus de renseignements, consultez le site Internet :
WWW.ALLIANCE-FRANCAISE.CA

Voici la source à Toronto de livres français, académiques, littéraires ou autres. On y trouve tout : B.D., dictionnaires, livres de poche, nouvelles parutions, jeux éducatifs, grands classiques, romans à l'eau de rose, romans policiers, traductions de romans étrangers en français, etc. Vous pourrez aussi y acheter plusieurs journaux de langue française de Toronto, du Québec et de France. La librairie est à votre disposition si vous voulez passer des commandes spéciales.

Presse Internationale magazines super stores

Différentes adresses dans toute la ville
www.presseinternationale.com

À ne pas confondre avec La Maison de la Presse Internationale. Vous y trouverez plusieurs magazines et journaux français. Vous remarquerez aussi que la flexibilité des heures d'ouverture de cette chaîne permet de lire en français à n'importe quel moment de la journée.

Québec Loisirs

☎ 1 800 361-2441
www.quebecloisirs.com

Lorsqu'on devient membre de ce club, on bénéficie de 20 à 40 % de remise sur ses achats ! Québec Loisirs est le cousin canadien de France Loisirs. Si vous consultez les deux sites, vous remarquerez qu'ils se ressemblent. La différence pour nous, Torontois, réside dans les frais de transport. Quand on achète de ce côté-ci de l'Atlantique, on économise beaucoup.

Renaud-Bray

☎ 1 888 746-2283
www.renaud-bray.com

Voici un autre grand nom montréalais de la librairie qui permet aux Franco-Torontois d'avoir accès à une multitude de livres de diverses catégories grâce au site Internet. Vous n'avez qu'à consulter ce site pour découvrir votre prochain coup de cœur ! Vous pouvez également passer une commande par téléphone si vous ne vous sentez pas à l'aise à l'idée d'un paiement électronique sur Internet.

Salon du Livre de Toronto

www.salondulivredetoronto.ca

Ce grand salon annuel se tient en octobre au Palais des Congrès (Convention Centre, 255 Front St. West). Vous pourrez y rencontrer des auteurs et éditeurs de la francophonie et participer à des ateliers, séances de signature, débats, etc. Le Salon offre aussi le plus grand choix de livres français en Ontario et c'est donc l'occasion d'acheter des livres difficiles à obtenir autrement.

Taloua

☎ (416) 934-0588
info@taloua.com • www.taloua.com

Multicultur-elle ! C'est la vision de *Taloua,* seul magazine féminin et multiculturel en français à avoir vu le jour à Toronto (2002). *Taloua* signifie « jeune femme » en agni, dialecte parlé en Côte d'Ivoire. En feuilletant *Taloua,* on se sent « femme taloua » jusqu'au bout des ongles : engagée, ouverte sur le monde, libre et artiste ! Ce qu'on aime chez

Taloua, c'est le graphisme sensible, l'amalgame de cultures, la place faite aux jeunes talents (photographes, graphistes, illustrateurs, etc.), le traitement original des sujets, les journalistes qui sortent des sentiers battus, l'ouverture internationale (Toronto, Montréal, Paris, Douala, etc.). Ce qu'on regrette, c'est que le jeune magazine ne sorte pas plus souvent : deux fois par an. Vous le trouverez à la Maison de la Presse Internationale, dans la plupart des magasins Chapters ou Indigo, ou encore en vous abonnant (formulaire en ligne sur le site Internet ou par téléphone).

The Film Reference Library

2 Carlton Street East (au niveau de la mezzanine) ☎ (416) 967-1517

Les horaires d'hiver et d'été se trouvent sur le site Internet

Métro : COLLEGE (sortie Carlton)

libraryservices@torfilmfest.ca
www.filmreferencelibrary.ca

The Film Reference Library vous permet de feuilleter plus de 1 200 livres et une multitude de magazines en français (au passage, vous trouverez, toutes langues confondues, 17 000 livres sur le monde du cinéma). Bien entendu, le thème reste le cinéma. Vous trouverez des livres sur la biographie des pionniers du cinéma, le théâtre, le métier d'acteur, la télévision, l'histoire du film, les techniques cinématographiques, le scénario et bien d'autres sujets encore. Vous pourrez également consulter les magazines sur le monde du cinéma francophone suivants : *Trafic* (France), *24 images* (Québec), *L'Avant-Scène Cinéma* (France), *Cahiers du Cinéma* (France), *Jeune Cinéma* (France) et *Ciné Bulles* (France). Vous trouverez aussi plusieurs autres magazines en anglais sur les films de France, de Corée, d'Asie, d'Inde, de Suède, d'Amérique latine et d'Europe.

Musique

Amazon.ca

www.amazon.ca

Vous pourrez commander sur ce site les grands « tubes » du moment mais aussi vos chansons « rétro » préférées.

Archambault Musique

www.archambault.ca

Archambault Musique vend aussi les grands succès de la musique française, québécoise ou, plus généralement, francophone.

HMV

Différentes adresses dans toute la ville

www.hmv.ca

La plupart des magasins de cette chaîne nationale vendent des CD français. Ils ont une sélection honorable, principalement les grands noms de la chanson française. S'il y a des artistes en particulier qui vous font frémir et que vous n'arrivez pas à trouver leur dernier album dans les bacs, vous pouvez passer une commande spéciale.

Librairie Champlain

468 Queen Street East ☎ (416) 364-4345

Lundi à jeudi 9h – 18h, vendredi 9h – 20h, samedi 9h – 17h, fermé dimanche

Métro : QUEEN + le tram

Vous trouverez ici un très bon choix des plus grands « tubes » de la musique française.

Québec Loisirs

☎ 1 800 361-2441
www.quebecloisirs.com

Québec Loisirs répond aux besoins musicaux des francophones grâce à sa sélection d'albums sur Internet.

Renaud-Bray

☎ 1 888 746-2283
www.renaud-bray.com

Voici une autre enseigne québécoise qui vous permet, grâce à son magasin de disques virtuel, d'avoir accès à la musique que vous préférez.

Sam the Record Man

347 Yonge Street (au nord de Dundas Street) ☎ (416) 646-2775
Lundi à jeudi 9h – 22h, vendredi et samedi 9h – 00h, dimanche 11h – 19h
Métro : DUNDAS

Sam the Record Man est le « roi » à Toronto en matière de musique française. Le deuxième étage de ce très grand magasin de la musique cache la plus impressionnante sélection de musiques française et québécoise que nous ayons vue à Toronto. On y découvre les grands succès d'aujourd'hui et d'hier. Si, si, Sam the Record Man passe d'Yves Montand à Patrick Bruel pour ce qui est de la France, et de Gilles Vigneault à Garou côté Québec. Nous avons aussi été très surpris par la grande sélection de musiques africaines. En fait, le deuxième étage est une véritable caverne d'Ali Baba qui renferme des musiques exotiques des quatre coins du monde. Si vous ne trouvez pas certains albums bien précis, vous pouvez toujours les commander.

Films français – Festivals

Cinéfranco – Festival du film français à Toronto

☎ (416) 928-6595
www.cinefranco.com

Une semaine de films… en français ! Le festival a lieu tous les ans pendant la dernière semaine de mars et/ou la première semaine d'avril. Tous les amateurs, très fidèles, voient l'arrivée du festival comme une superbe occasion de satisfaire leur soif de culture francophone. Tous les films présentés sont sous–titrés en anglais, vous pourrez donc partager votre expérience cinéphile avec vos amis qui ne maîtrisent pas (encore) bien le français.

Toronto International Film Festival – Festival des films étrangers

www.e.bell.ca/filmfest

Le week-end de la fête du travail est marqué par l'arrivée à Toronto des grandes vedettes du cinéma international. Contrairement à Cinéfranco, le Festival des films étrangers ne cible pas une culture en particulier. Mais si l'on prend le temps de bien étudier les horaires des films, on peut certainement en trouver plusieurs en français qui pourraient même entrer dans l'histoire.

Cinémas

Cumberland

159 Cumberland Street (au coin d'Avenue Road) ☎ (416) 646-0444

Métro : BAY (sortie Cumberland)

Carlton

Rue Carlton, juste à l'est de Yonge Street ☎ (416) 598-2309

Métro : COLLEGE

Ces deux cinémas ont souvent un film français récent à l'affiche. Surveillez vos journaux pour en savoir plus.

Ciné Jeudi – Cinéma ONF de Toronto

150 John Street ☎ (416) 973–3012

Métro : OSGOODE

www.alliance-francaise.ca

Le Consulat Général de France à Toronto, l'Office national du film, Cinéfranco, le Bureau du Québec et l'Alliance Française ont entrepris un projet ambitieux : promouvoir le cinéma francophone à Toronto pendant toute l'année. Pour ce faire, vous avez droit à la projection mensuelle (le premier jeudi du mois) d'un des derniers succès du cinéma de la francophonie. Pour obtenir plus d'informations sur les films à venir, consultez le site de l'Alliance Française à Toronto.

Cinémathèque Ontario

Jackman Hall, Art Gallery of Ontario, entrée rue McCaul ☎ (416) 968-FILM (3456), poste 2

Métro : ST PATRICK

www.bell.ca/cinematheque

La Cinémathèque est une division du Festival des films étrangers (Toronto International Film Festival Group) et se spécialise dans les rétrospectives et les cycles spéciaux. On y présente souvent les films connus ou, au contraire, moins connus de grands metteurs en scène français : Truffaut, Tati, Malle, Cocteau, Deray, Renoir, Godard, etc. L'été, « on peut s'en mettre plein les mirettes » avec le cinéma français. Autrefois, la Cinémathèque Ontario présentait le cycle « Summer in France, Classics of French Cinema ». La programmation, en tant que telle, n'existe plus, mais une multitude de films français restent accessibles en juillet et en août. Voilà une bonne occasion de faire découvrir le septième art à la française à vos amis anglophones car tous les films sont sous-titrés. Bon film !

The Film Reference Library

2 Carlton Street East (au niveau de la mezzanine) ☎ (416) 967-1517

Les horaires d'hiver et d'été se trouvent sur le site Internet

Métro : COLLEGE (sortie Carlton)

libraryservices@torfilmfest.ca

www.filmreferencelibrary.ca

The Film Reference Library est une autre division du Festival des films étrangers (Toronto International Film Festival Group). Cette bibliothèque a pour mission d'offrir aux professionnels, aux académiciens et aux amoureux du cinéma d'importants ouvrages de référence sur le septième art. The Film Reference Library abrite des collections de films canadiens et internationaux. Les 8 000 films (et plus), dont 541 en français (ils sont tous sous-titrés en anglais), de The Film Reference

Library nous ont impressionnés. Vous pouvez regarder ces films sur place, grâce à deux salles mises à la disposition du public. The Film Reference Library est même équipée d'appareils permettant de regarder des cassettes vidéo et des DVD européens. Et ça, ça ne se trouve pas à tous les coins de rue à Toronto ! Vous remarquerez que les bibliothécaires et les employés de The Film Reference Library sont d'une aide précieuse à tout cinéphile. N'hésitez surtout pas à faire appel à eux. En devenant membre, vous aurez gratuitement accès à plusieurs services.

Cassettes vidéo et DVD à louer

Queen Video

Différentes adresses dans toute la ville

Revue Video

207 Danforth Avenue (près de Broadview Avenue) ☎ (416) 778-5776

Lundi à dimanche 11h – 22h

Métro : BROADVIEW

Lundi à dimanche 11h – 23h pour les deux boutiques

Suspect Video

- 605 Markham Street (Bloor Street et Bathurst Street) ☎ (416) 588-6674

  Métro : BATHURST

- 619 Queen Street West ☎ (416) 504-7135

  Métro : OSGOODE

Lundi à samedi 12h – 23h, dimanche 12h – 22h pour les deux boutiques

Very Video

1375 Yonge Street (au sud de St. Clair Avenue) ☎ (416) 929-8379

Le saviez-vous ?

La plupart des magasins vidéo qui louent des vidéos et DVD français peuvent aussi vous vendre les titres que vous recherchez. Si vous avez un film bien précis en tête et qu'il est toujours distribué, ces magasins pourront passer une commande spécialement pour vous. C'est la bonne solution pour les amateurs de classiques.

Lundi à jeudi 10h30 – 22h, vendredi et samedi 10h30 – 23h, dimanche 11h30 – 22h

Métro : ST CLAIR

- 1689 Bayview Av. (près d'Eglinton Avenue) ☎ (416) 322-8379

Lundi à samedi 10h – 18h, dimanche 12h – 17h

Métro : EGLINTON + le bus

Ces magasins indépendants de location de cassettes vidéo proposent un incroyable choix de plusieurs centaines de films français et de langue française : dernières nouveautés, films rares, classiques de la nouvelle vague, etc. On les trouve presque tous. Pour vous donner une idée de la multitude de films français disponibles, voici quelques chiffres : chez Queen Video, vous trouverez plus de 600 films, dont 500 en cassettes et une centaine en DVD. Suspect Video vous propose entre 100 et 200 films en français. Revue Video vous en propose 250 de la francophonie, y compris l'Afrique française et la Tunisie. Very Video vous en propose une bonne trentaine. Ça, c'est du cinéma !

Cassettes vidéo et DVD à acheter

Amazon.ca

www.amazon.ca

Le site Internet d'Amazon vous donne accès à une bonne quantité de films français.

Archambault.ca

www.archambault.ca

De Louis de Funès à Vincent Perez en passant par Pierce Brosnan, on les trouve tous sur le site d'Archambault. Reste à opter pour la vidéo ou le DVD.

Librairie Champlain

468 Queen Street East ☎ (416) 364-4345

Lundi à jeudi 9h – 18h, vendredi 9h – 20h, samedi 9h – 17h, fermé dimanche

Métro : QUEEN + le tram

La Librairie Champlain vend plusieurs films français en vidéo ou DVD, pour les petits et les grands.

Québec Loisirs

☎ 1 800 361-2441

www.quebecloisirs.com

Québec Loisirs vous permet de faire le plein de films français depuis chez vous.

Renaud-Bray

☎ 1 888 746-2283

www.renaud-bray.com

En quelques clics, faites acheminer chez vous les grands noms du cinéma de la francophonie.

Sam the Record Man

347 Yonge Street (au nord de Dundas Street) ☎ (416) 646-2775

Lundi à jeudi 9h – 22h, vendredi et samedi 9h – 00h, dimanche 11h – 19h

Métro : DUNDAS

Sam the Record Man vend une sélection tout à fait honorable de films français en vidéo et DVD. Cependant, si vous cherchez un film en particulier, vous n'avez qu'à le commander.

Films à regarder chez soi

TFO

Service de relations avec l'auditoire
☎ (416) 484-2645 et 1 800 463-6886

Lundi à vendredi 9h – 17h

La célébration du 7e art bat son plein tous les jours de la semaine à 21h, sur la chaîne de télévision francophone de l'Ontario. TFO vous propose de découvrir des films français, québécois, africains et belges. Vous pourrez aussi découvrir plusieurs films internationaux ayant été sous-titrés en français (malheureusement, les films français ne sont pas sous-titrés en anglais). Vous pouvez vous procurer le « passeport cinéma » qui vous donnera la description complète des films (date, durée, pays d'origine, année, noms des producteurs et des acteurs, critique, etc.). Il vous suffit de téléphoner au Service de relations avec l'auditoire pour en obtenir un exemplaire. On se fera un plaisir de vous l'envoyer gratuitement par la poste à votre domicile.

Beaux-arts

La Galerie Glendon

2275 Bayview Avenue ☎ (416) 487-6859

Fermé dimanche et lundi, de mardi à vendredi 12h – 15h sauf jeudi 11h – 14h, samedi 13h – 16h

Métro : LAWRENCE + le bus

www.glendon.yorku.ca/gallery

La Galerie Glendon est une galerie publique située sur le campus de l'université de Glendon. Elle est spécialisée dans l'art contemporain et offre un programme d'expositions mensuelles. Sa mission est d'ordre éducatif. La Galerie Glendon offre de la documentation en français et en anglais, ainsi que des visites guidées et des conférences données par des artistes et des commissaires d'expositions. Pour de plus amples renseignements, consultez son site Internet.

Musée des beaux-arts de l'Ontario (AGO – Art Gallery of Ontario)

317 Dundas Street ☎ (416) 979-6648

Fermé lundi, mardi à vendredi 11h – 18h, mercredi 11h – 20h30, samedi et dimanche 10h – 17h30

Métro : ST PATRICK

www.ago.net

De Monet à Cézanne en passant par Degas, le Musée des beaux-arts de l'Ontario vous propose des expositions permanentes bilingues. Les grandes expositions ainsi que les casques qui les accompagnent sont également en français et en anglais. Au Musée des beaux-arts de l'Ontario, vous vivez vraiment une expérience en français !

Musée royal de l'Ontario (ROM – Royal Museum of Ontario)

100 Queen's Park Crescent (au coin de Bloor Street) ☎ (416) 586-8000

Lundi à jeudi 10h – 18h, vendredi 10h – 21h30, samedi et dimanche 10h – 18h

Métro : MUSEUM

www.rom.on.ca

Le Musée royal de l'Ontario nous permet de découvrir les trésors historiques et contemporains de l'univers des beaux-arts en français. Au ROM, vous pourrez apprécier les œuvres permanentes des différentes galeries du musée, les expositions créées par le musée, ainsi que les expositions spéciales en français

Le saviez-vous ?

1. Hors grande exposition programmée, le prix d'admission est réduit de moitié. C'est le bon moment pour visiter les expositions permanentes et les expositions créées par le ROM.
2. Tous les vendredis, on peut visiter les collections permanentes ainsi que les expositions créées par le musée gratuitement. De plus, vous pourrez profiter d'une remise sur les expositions temporaires.
3. Vous trouverez une page en français sur le site Internet du ROM (bouton en haut de la page).
4. Un employé francophone peut répondre à vos questions au téléphone en français.
5. Il y a toujours du personnel bilingue à l'entrée du musée.

(des guides thématiques français sont disponibles pendant votre visite au musée lors des expositions spéciales). N'hésitez surtout pas à contacter le musée pour organiser votre prochaine visite guidée.

Théâtre

Théâtre français de Toronto

26 Berkeley Street ☎ (416) 534-6604
Métro : KING + le tram
www.theatrefrancais.com

Créé en 1967, le Théâtre français de Toronto présente des productions de qualité pour adultes et enfants, qu'il puise dans les répertoires canadien, français et plus généralement international. Les spectacles sont présentés au Canadian Stage Theatre, 26 rue Berkeley.

Théâtre La Tangente

☎ (416) 485-1432
www.theatrelatangente.ca

Le Théâtre La Tangente présente des pièces de création. En d'autres termes, les pièces de théâtre jouées à La Tangente sont originales et inédites. Ce côté insolite oblige le Théâtre La Tangente à ne présenter qu'une pièce tous les deux ans. Les pièces sont produites à Toronto et elles sont présentées à Toronto, au Québec et même en France.

Radio

Radio-Canada - 860 AM

Radio-Canada en Ontario est la station locale de cette radio nationale. Les programmes varient autour de thèmes de l'actualité, de la culture et du divertissement.

Coopérative radiophonique de Toronto – 105.1 FM

La Coopération radiophonique de Toronto est la radio communautaire des francophones.

Télévision

RDI (Réseau d'information)

Il s'agit d'une chaîne française d'information nationale et internationale.

SRC (Société Radio-Canada)

www.radio-canada.ca/regions/ontario

La Société Radio-Canada offre un éventail de programmes très divers avec des bulletins d'information, des émissions de variétés, des romans-feuilletons, des films et bien d'autres choses encore.

TFO

www.tfo.org

Chaîne de télévision franco-ontarienne, il y a sur TFO plusieurs émissions à vocation culturelle telles que l'émission « Panorama ». Le premier roman-feuilleton franco ontarien, « Fran-Cœur », passe même sur cette chaîne.

Le saviez-vous ?

La Société Radio-Canada, TV5 et TVA diffusent plusieurs films français chaque mois. Tous à votre programme télé pour connaître les horaires de ces films !

TVA (CHOT)

www.chot.ca

TVA est une autre chaîne montréalaise que l'on peut capter à Toronto, avec de nombreuses émissions de variétés et d'actualité.

TV5

www.tv5.org

TV5 est une chaîne de télévision internationale en français qui propose une programmation variée (journaux télévisés, reportages, divertissements), grâce au regroupement, depuis 1989, de programmes issus de chaînes françaises, belges, suisses et canadiennes.

Événements culturels francophones à Toronto

Alliance Française de Toronto

www.alliance-francaise.ca

Le site de l'Alliance Française a une page consacrée aux événements francophones qui se déroulent à Toronto.

Consulat Général de France à Toronto

www.consulfrance-toronto.org

Vous trouverez sur le site Internet du Consulat Général de France à Toronto, sous la rubrique « Pleins feux sur la culture », la liste de plusieurs événements culturels francophones.

Centre Francophone du Toronto Métropolitain

20 Lower Spadina Avenue
☎ (416) 203-1220
Métro : UNION + le tram
www.centrefranco.org

Pour être mis au parfum des événements francophones de Toronto et planifier votre prochaine sortie, consultez ce site Internet et la rubrique « Calendrier des événements ».

Radio-Canada

www.radio-canada.ca/regions/ontario

Pour savoir quoi faire, quoi voir et quoi visiter, allez jeter un œil au calendrier de Claudette Gravel « Enfin samedi », sur le site Internet de Radio-Canada.

Toronto-Franco

☎ (416) 929-3769
www.toronto-franco.com

Les francophones de Toronto ont leur propre portail en français ! Depuis décembre 2003, ce portail unique existe afin d'offrir un accès à l'information rapide et ciblé aux francophones. Vous y trouverez les nouvelles locales et internationales, ainsi que des informations sur les services et les événements communautaires qui intéressent la communauté francophone de Toronto. Notre site possède un lien vers ce portail d'information.

Soirées et rencontres branchées

Francophonique

www.francophonique.com

Réseau de regroupements entre francophones et francophiles, Francophonique organise des événements tels que des brunchs et des soirées branchées. C'est un forum de rencontres idéal pour les anglophones qui veulent pratiquer leur français.

Les Mercredis FrancoFun

☎ (416) 596-8437

Jacques Charrette (coordinateur)
jacques.charette@sympatico.ca

Chaque mercredi soir, à partir de 18h, des francophones et francophiles se retrouvent pour discuter et prendre un verre. Idéal pour les nouveaux arrivants qui souhaitent rencontrer d'autres francophones ou pour les anglophones qui veulent pratiquer leur français ! Le lieu de rencontre varie de temps en temps. Au moment où nous écrivons ces lignes, il s'agit du pub Bedford Academy, situé au 36 Prince Arthur Street (au nord-ouest de l'intersection entre Bloor Street et Avenue Road).

Les Soupers FrancoFun

☎ (416) 596-8437

Jacques Charrette (coordinateur)
jacques.charette@sympatico.ca

Un jeudi par mois, un dîner est organisé dans un restaurant. Événement populaire, ce dîner est l'occasion de découvrir un nouveau restaurant et de se retrouver entre francophones. Le prix est en général de 25 dollars, ce qui inclut le repas, les taxes et le service. Le dernier dîner de la saison, qui a lieu en juin, est le plus populaire, car c'est le dîner de homards !

Tam Tam Cyber Café

86 Nassau street ☎ (416) 603-0007

Métro : SPADINA + le tram;
QUEEN'S PARK + le tram

Dites « bonjour » en entrant ! Unique en son genre, Tam Tam Cyber Café a ouvert ses portes en mars 2004, à l'initiative du Centre des Jeunes Francophones de Toronto. Ce petit coin café accueille tous les internautes au cœur du marché Kensington. Situé à deux pas de l'auberge de jeunesse d'Augusta Street, réputée pour être fréquentée par bon nombre de Français, Tam Tam Cyber Café offre un accès Internet et des services d'impression à un bon prix. L'ambiance y est à l'image du quartier et de ses habitants : conviviale et un tantinet bohème. Tous les samedis matins, petits-déjeuners français autour de croissants chauds et tartines de baguette avec beurre et confiture; en semaine, soirées-causeries, concerts et expositions.

Zazou

315 King Street West (au coin de John Street) ☎ (416) 591-3600

Ouvert à partir de 17h, jusqu'au départ du dernier client !

Métro : ST ANDREW

www.zazoulounge.com

Zazou fait partie de la même famille que Marcel's Bistro et Le Saint Tropez. Ce bar chic et sophistiqué accueille les

jeunes adultes branchés de la ville. Si vous aimez les ambiances feutrées, la musique cool et un décor qui invite à la détente, passez prendre un verre chez Zazou. C'est l'endroit idéal pour se relaxer après une longue journée au bureau.

Associations culturelles et sociales

Association France-Canada

☎ (416) 485-5044
nadmoal@msn.com

Fondée à Toronto en 1948, l'Association France-Canada a pour but de créer des liens entre Français et Canadiens sur tous les plans. Cette association est accessible à tous pour la petite cotisation annuelle de 25 dollars et elle propose des activités telles que des soirées et des dîners dansants, des brunchs, des voyages et des excursions, des bals du 14 juillet et des sorties sportives (ski, vélo, tennis, etc.).

Association Marocaine de Toronto au Canada

☎ (416) 494-7601
martor@istar.ca • www.amdt.ca

Les riches couleurs de la francophonie se dévoilent de plus en plus grâce à la population marocaine de Toronto, toujours plus active dans notre ville. L'Association Marocaine de Toronto au Canada est l'organisme où cette communauté se regroupe à Toronto. En effet, cette association apolitique de Toronto compte 350 membres. Dans les grandes lignes, la mission de l'association peut se définir comme suit : promouvoir et défendre les intérêts des marocains de Toronto, conseiller et informer les nouveaux arrivants marocains à Toronto tout en les aidant à mieux s'intégrer dans leur ville d'accueil, favoriser l'épanouissement des membres des communautés de l'Association en leur proposant des activités culturelles et religieuses.

Centre des Jeunes Francophones de Toronto

22 College Street, bureau 202
☎ (416) 934-0588
Métro : COLLEGE
www.centredesjeunes.org

Au Centre des Jeunes Francophones de Toronto, ils savent ce que veut dire « expérience canadienne », la même qui fait défaut à tout jeune qui arrive à Toronto et entame un véritable parcours du combattant à la recherche d'un emploi. Organisme à but non lucratif, le Centre des Jeunes Francophones a été créé pour répondre aux besoins des jeunes francophones (16-30 ans) de tous horizons qui résident ou viennent d'arriver dans la région du grand Toronto. Fondé en 1993 par un groupe de jeunes francophones motivés et qui voulaient améliorer leurs conditions de vie, le Centre des Jeunes Francophones est un organisme incontournable au sein de la communauté franco-ontarienne. Né de la fusion du Regroupement des Jeunes Filles Francophones et du Groupe Jeunesse Francophone de Toronto, le Centre des Jeunes Francophones propose aujourd'hui une gamme d'activités aussi

variées qu'originales. Tout est bon pour l'intégration ! Programme de mentorat pour jeunes entrepreneurs, groupes de discussion destinés aux jeunes femmes immigrantes victimes de violences, projets de coopération internationale et, récemment, rien de moins que l'ouverture d'un cybercafé au cœur du marché Kensington !

Club Richelieu de Toronto

☎ (416) 299-3923
www.richelieu.org

Créé à Ottawa en 1944, le Club Richelieu est maintenant présent dans une douzaine de pays. Son principal objectif est de promouvoir le français par l'intermédiaire d'activités sociales, culturelles et humanitaires (principalement dirigées vers la jeunesse). La cotisation annuelle sert à soutenir des actions caritatives et éducatives.

Le Cercle de l'Amitié Canadien de Toronto

1780 Meadowvale Boulevard, Mississauga
☎ (905) 542-1844
Liette Lacroix (coordinatrice)
www.cercleamitie.ca

Le Cercle de l'Amitié est un centre communautaire et culturel qui a pour objectif de promouvoir la langue française dans la région de Peel. La grande majorité des 400 membres vivent à Mississauga et à Brampton. Cependant, le Cercle compte également de nombreux membres habitant Richmond Hill, Oakville et Toronto. Tous les mois, le Cercle de l'Amitié organise quantité d'événements pour les enfants et les adultes.

Associations de professionnels

Association des femmes d'affaires francophones

Rita Holmes (coordinatrice)
☎ (905) 822-3677
Angèle Desgagné (présidente pour la province) ☎ (905) 469-1889
www.afafcanada.com

L'Association des femmes d'affaires est une association à but non lucratif qui permet, depuis 1983, aux femmes d'affaires francophones de Toronto et du grand Toronto de se rencontrer mensuellement. L'Association a pour objectif principal le développement de réseaux de relations. L'Association compte une centaine de membres. Il y a deux regroupements : celui de Toronto et celui de la région de Halton-Peel. Un nouveau groupe sera créé en 2004 pour la région de Welland.

Association francophone des entrepreneurs et des professionnels (AFEP)

☎ (905) 891-5989
Valérie Cité (coordinatrice)
www.afepcanada.com

L'Association francophone des entrepreneurs et des professionnels (AFEP) a pour mission d'offrir aux entrepreneurs et professionnels francophones un espace d'échanges, de ressources, de compétences et d'influence, ainsi que de favoriser le développement économique francophone. Les avantages sont évidents pour tout entrepreneur francophone cherchant à faire des affaires

avec d'autres entrepreneurs francophones ou à influencer les instances décisionnelles et défendre les intérêts économiques des francophones.

Club canadien de Toronto

☎ (416) 243-0662
Jean Martin (coordinateur)
www.clubcanadien.ca

Depuis 1986, le Club canadien de Toronto rassemble les francophones et francophiles des domaines de la finance, de la politique et de la culture pour débattre de sujets déterminants. Ce club réunit les personnes clés autour d'un déjeuner d'affaires. Tous les mois, un conférencier est invité à présenter un sujet au cœur de l'actualité nationale et internationale. Grâce au statut des conférenciers et à celui des participants, les déjeuners d'affaires du Club canadien de Toronto illustrent l'influence qu'exercent les francophones à Toronto.

La Chambre de Commerce Française au Canada (Toronto)

20 Queen Street West, suite 2006
☎ (416) 205-9820
ccfe@bellnet.ca • www.ccife.org/canada

La mission de la division ontarienne de la Chambre de Commerce Française est de promouvoir les relations économiques entre la France et la région de l'Ontario. Les membres font partie d'un réseau de la communauté des professionnels français en Ontario et au Canada. Chaque mois, plusieurs événements sont mis en place pour permettre aux professionnels francophones de parfaire leurs connaissances du monde des affaires : déjeuners-conférences et visites d'entreprises en sont des exemples. Plusieurs événements à caractère social sont également organisés : cocktails, tournois de tennis, dégustations et bal annuel.

Regroupement des gens d'affaires africains canadiens

☎ (416) 781-9780, poste 221
Rose Cathy Handy (présidente)

La création d'un Regroupement de professionnels africains canadiens répond aux besoins exprimés par les communautés « ethnoculturelles » de la région de Toronto. Ce projet a donc vu le jour afin de regrouper les professionnels d'origine africaine et des Caraïbes en un réseau relationnel qui leur permet d'échanger, de s'informer, d'apprendre, de célébrer leurs réussites afin de contribuer à leur développement économique.

Associations pour les artistes

BRAVO – Bureau des regroupements des artistes visuels de l'Ontario

☎ (819) 457-2502
bravo@franco.ca
www.francoculture.ca/bravo

Ce groupe compte plus de 130 représentants des arts visuels de diverses disciplines, vivant en Ontario. La mission du groupe est simple : défendre les intérêts individuels et collectifs des artistes francophones de l'Ontario en offrant des services de représentation, promotion, diffusion et commerciali-

sation des arts visuels. Ce groupe a également pour raison d'être la mise sur pied d'une infrastructure et de réseaux de communication qui briseront l'isolement des artistes francophones.

les bonnes adresses par quartier

QUARTIERS	PAINS, PÂTISSERIES ET SUCRERIES	CHOCOLATS	FROMAGES ET CRÈME FRAÎCHE	CHARCUTERIE, PÂTÉS ET TERRINES
THE BEACH, L'EST DE TORONTO, DANFORTH AVE. ET BLOOR ST.	Bonjour Brioche Zane	Belgian Chocolate Shop Sun Valley Fruits & Grocery	Alex Farm Sun Valley Fruits & Grocery	Alex Farm Meat on the Beach
BLOOR WEST VILLAGE ET L'OUEST DE TORONTO	Cheese Boutique Max Market Pâtisserie Saint Honoré	Bernard Callebaut Cheese Boutique Max Market	Cheese Boutique Max Market	Cheese Boutique Max Market Village Butcher
CENTRE-VILLE (DOWNTOWN)	Balzac's Coffee House Daniel et Daniel Mercatto St. Urbain Bagel Bakery Scheffler's	Chocolates & Creams Daniel et Daniel Domino Foods Mercatto Scheffler's The Bay The Pie Shoppe	Alex Farm Chris' Cheesemongers Olympic Cheese Mart Scheffler's	Alex Farm Caviar Direct Chris' Cheesemongers Cumbrae's Daniel et Daniel Olympic Cheese Mart Scheffler's White House Meats
KENSINGTON, BALDWIN ST. ET COLLEGE ST.	Casa Açareana Magnolia	Chocolate Addict	Cheese Magic Global Cheese Mendel's Creamery	Global Cheese Mendel's Creamery
ENTERTAINMENT DISTRICT, KING ST. WEST ET QUEEN ST. WEST	Clafouti Le Gourmand Senses	Clafouti Dufflet Pastries J.S. Bonbons Le Gourmand Senses		
AVENUE RD., DAVENPORT RD. ET DUPONT AVE.	Dinah's Cupboard Holt Renfrew Pusateri's Whole Foods	Dinah's Cupboard Holt Renfrew J.S. Bonbons Leonidas Simone Marie Belgian Chocolate Teuscher Whole Foods	Alex Farm Dinah's Cupboard Pusateri's Whole Foods	Alex Farm Dinah's Cupboard Pusateri's Whole Foods

BOUCHERIES	POISSONS ET HUÎTRES	ÉPICES	AUTRES SPÉCIALITÉS FRANÇAISES	RESTAURANTS
Meat on the Beach Royal Beef	Bill's Lobsters	Strictly Bulk	Alex Farm Bonjour Brioche Zane	Bonjour Brioche Café Brussels
Bloor Meat Market Village Butcher	Big Fish Market Snappers Fish Market Village Butcher	Strictly Bulk	Cheese Boutique Max Market Village Butcher Pâtisserie Saint Honoré	La Petite France Merlot
Brown Brothers Meats Cumbrae's Di Liso's Fine Meats Greco Meat Packers Manos Meats Nick's Wholesale Meats Scheffler's St. Lawrence Upper Cut White House Meats	Caviar Direct Domenic's Fish Market Domino Foods Mike's Fish Market Seafront Fish Market	Domino Foods	Alex Farm Chris' Cheesemongers Daniel et Daniel Domino Foods Mercatto Scheffler's Great Cooks Olympic Cheese Mart	Agora Bistro 990 Bloor Street Diner Bouchon Café Moroc/ The Sultan's Tent Café Nicole Crêpes à Gogo Le Papillon Matignon Midi Bistro Provence
European Quality Meats Grace Meat Market	Coral Sea Fish Shop Global Cheese Mendel's Creamery Medeiros Fish Market New Seaway Sea Kings Seven Seas Fish	Casa Açareana House of Spices Perola's		Bodega Brasserie Aix Café Margaux Gamelle La Palette
	Oyster Boy Rodney's Oyster House		Clafouti Le Gourmand	Bloor Street Diner Crêpes Café Épicure Café Le Saint Tropez Le Sélect Bistro Marcel's Bistro Restaurant Jules
Pusateri's	Pusateri's		Alex Farm Dinah's Cupboard Holt Renfrew Pusateri's Sérénité Whole Foods	Arlequin Holt's Café Jacques Bistro La Brasserie.ca Le Paradis Le Trou Normand

les bonnes adresses par quartier

QUARTIERS	PAINS, PÂTISSERIES ET SUCRERIES	CHOCOLATS	FROMAGES ET CRÈME FRAÎCHE	CHARCUTERIE, PÂTÉS ET TERRINES
MIDTOWN ET SUMMERHILL	All the Best Fine Foods Le Petit Gourmet Pain Perdu Patachou St. Urbain Bagel Bakery The Bagel House	Pain Perdu Sobey's	Alex Farm All the Best Fine Foods Sobey's	Alex Farm All the Best Fine Foods Patachou Sobey's The Butchers
BAYVIEW ET MOUNT PLEASANT	Comptoir de Célestin La Cigogne Rahier The Bagel House	La Cigogne Rahier The Chocolate Messenger	Alex Farm	Alex Farm White House Meats
UPTOWN	Ace Bakery Pusateri's Senses	Pusateri's Senses Swiss-Master Chocolatier	Pusateri's	Pusateri's The Butcher Block Café
LE GRAND TORONTO	Arz Bakery Brandt Meat Packers Supermarket Pâtisserie d'Or St. Urbain Bagel Bakery	Arz Bakery Bernard Callebaut Brandt Meat Packers Supermarket Pâtisserie d'Or Truffle Treasures	Olympic Cheese Mart Quality Cheese	Brandt Meat Packers Supermarket Olympic Cheese Mart

BOUCHERIES	POISSONS ET HUÎTRES	ÉPICES	AUTRES SPÉCIALITÉS FRANÇAISES	RESTAURANTS
Nicola's Choice Meats Olliffe Sobey's The Butchers	Avenue Seafood Pisces Gourmet		Alex Farm All the Best Fine Foods Harvest Wagon Pain Perdu Patachou	Avant-Goût Boujadi Le Petit Gourmet Pastis Express Quartier
White House Meats	Caviar Centre Diana's Seafood Highland Farms Newport Fish Importers Pusateri's		Alex Farm Rahier	Célestin La Cigogne
Highland Farms Pusateri's The Butcher Block Café	Brandt Meat Packers Supermarket Lobster Island		Pusateri's	Auberge du Pommier Bloor Street Diner Chez Laurent La Maison Benoît Le Montmartre L'Escargot Bistro Monitz Pourquoi Pas
Brandt Meat Packers Supermarket European Quality Meats			Arz Bakery Brandt Meat Packers Supermarket Olympic Cheese Mart Pâtisserie d'Or Petit Gâteau	Bistro 1603 Bistro Matisse

index

A

À Bon Verre Bonne Table 126
Academy of Artisans 122
Ace Bakery 14
AGORA 92
Alex Farm Products 46, 53, 58, 77
Alliance Française de Toronto 127, 136
All the Best Fine Foods 14, 46, 53, 58, 77
Amazon.ca 126, 129, 133
Archambault.ca 126, 129, 133
Arlequin 92
Arz Bakery 15, 34, 77
Association des femmes d'affaires francophones 139
Association France-Canada 138
Association Marocaine de Toronto au Canada 138
Association francophone des entrepreneurs et des professionnels (AFEP) 139
Auberge du Pommier 108
Avant-Goût 93
Avenue Seafood 66

B

BRAVO Bureau des regroupements des artistes visuels de l'Ontario 140
Balzac's Coffee House 15
Belgian Chocolate Shop 34
Big Fish Market 66
Bill's Lobsters 66
Bistro 1603 108
Bistro 990 93
Bistro Matisse 94
Bloor Meat Market 56
Bloor Street Diner et Bistros 94, 114
Bodega 113, 114
Bonjour Brioche 16, 78, 114
Bouchon 113
Boujadi 95
Brandt Meat Packers Supermarket 56, 58, 66, 78
Brasserie Aix 95, 114
Brown Brothers Meats 56

C

Café Brussels 115
Café la Gaffe 98
Café Margaux 95
Café Moroc 97
Café Nicole 97
Calphalon Culinary Center 122
Carlton Cinéma 131
Casa Açareana 16, 85
Caviar Centre 66
Caviar Direct 58, 67
Célestin 115
Centre des Jeunes Francophones de Toronto 138
Centre francophone du Toronto Métropolitain 136
Cheese Boutique 35, 47, 53, 58, 78
Cheese Magic 47
Chez Laurent 97
Chocolate Addict 35
Chocolates & Creams 35
Chocolates by Bernard Callebaut 36
Chris' Cheesemongers 47, 53, 58, 79
Ciné jeudi 131
Cinéfranco 130
Cinémathèque Ontario 131
Clafouti 17, 37, 78
Club canadien de Toronto 140
Club Richelieu de Toronto 139
Cook Gourmet 122
Cooking at the Harvest Kitchen 122
Coopérative radiophonique de Toronto – 105.1 FM 135
Comptoir de Célestin 19
Consulat Général de France à Toronto 136
Coral Sea Fish Shop 67
Crêpes À Gogo 98
Crêpes Café 98
Cumberland Cinéma 131
Cumbrae's Naturally Raised Fine Meats 56, 58

D

Daniel et Daniel – Food Shop 20, 37, 58, 79
Di Liso's Fine Meats 57
Diana's Seafood 67
Dinah's Cupboard 20, 48, 58, 80
Dish Cooking Studio 122
Domenic's Fish Market 67
Domino Foods 67, 80, 85

E

Épicure Café 99, 114
European Quality Meats & Sausages 57

F

Festival des films étrangers 130
Francophonique 137
Fred's Bakery 20

index

G

Galerie Glendon 134
Gamelle 115
George Brown College 122
Give it a Stir 123
Global Cheese 48, 58, 67
Grace Meat Markets 57
Great Cooks 80, 123
Greco Meat Packers Ltd. 57

H

Harvest Wagon 81
Highland Farms 60, 67, 76
HMV 129
Holt Renfrew – Epicure Shop 21, 37, 81
Holt's Café 99
House of Spices 85

I

Indigo-Chapters 127

J

J. S. Bonbons 38, 123
Jacques Bistro du Parc 100, 114
John & King Hot Dog Stand 105

K

K.I.S. Global Flavors 81
Kensington Market 76

L

LCBO 123
L'escargot Bistro 100
L'Express 126
La Brasserie.ca 101
La Chambre de Commerce Française au Canada 140
La Cigogne 22, 38, 114
La Maison Benoît 101
La Maison de la Presse Internationale 127
La Maison du Chocolat 39
La Palette 102, 114
La Petite France 102
Le Cercle de l'Amitié Canadien de Toronto 139
Le Cordon Bleu Paris (Ottawa) 124
Le Gourmand 22, 39, 82
Le Métropolitain 126
Le Montmartre 116
Le Papillon 103
Le Paradis 103
Le Petit Gourmet 22, 103
Le Saint Tropez 104
Le Sélect Bistro 104, 114
Le Trou Normand 116
Les Mercredis Franco Fun 137
Les Soupers Franco Fun 137
Leonidas 39
Librairie Champlain 127, 129, 133
Loblaws 48, 82, 124
Lobster Island 68

M

Magnolia Fine Foods 23
Manos Meats 60
Marcel's Bistro 116
Matignon 117
Max Market 49, 53, 59, 82
Meat on the Beach 59, 60
Medeiros Fish Market 68
Mendel's Creamery n' Appetizer 49, 59, 68
Mercatto 23, 82
Merlot 105
Midi Bistro 105
Mike's Fish Market 68
Monitz 106
Musée des beaux-arts de l'Ontario 134
Musée royal de l'Ontario 134

N

New Seaway 68
Newport Fish Importers & Wholesalers 69
Nick's Wholesale Meats & Delicatessen 60
Nicola's Choice Meats 61

O

Olliffe 61
Olympic Cheese Mart 49, 53, 59, 83
Osler Fish Warehouse 70
Oyster Boy 70

P

Pain Perdu 23, 40, 83
Pastis Express 117
Patachou 24, 59, 83
Pâtisserie d'Or 25, 40, 84
Pâtisserie Saint Honoré 27, 84
Perola's 85
Petit Gâteau 84
Pisces Gourmet 70
Pourquoi Pas 107
Presse Internationale magazines super stores 128
Provence 114, 118
Pusateri's Fine Foods 27, 40, 50, 53, 59, 61, 70, 84

Q

Qualifirst Foods 86
Quality Cheese 51
Quartier 107
Québec Loisirs 128, 130, 133
Queen Video 132

index

R

Radio-Canada – 860 AM 135, 136
Rahier 27, 86
RDI – Réseau d'information 125
Regroupement des gens d'affaires africains canadiens 140
Renaud-Bray 128, 133
Restaurant Jules 108
Revue Video 132
Richmond Hill Culinary Arts Centre 124
Rodney's Oyster House 71
Royal Beef 62

S

St. Lawrence Market 76
St. Lawrence Upper Cut 62
St. Urbain Bagel Bakery 28
Salon du Livre de Toronto 128
Sam the Record Man 130, 133
Sea Kings 68
Seafront Fish Market 71
Senses 28, 40
Sérénité 87
Seven Seas Fish 68
Scheffler's Delicatessen & Cheese 51, 52, 59, 62, 86
Simone Marie Belgian Chocolate 40
Snappers Fish Market 71
Sobey's 51, 53, 59, 62
SRC – Société Radio–Canada 135
Strewn Winery 124
Strictly Bulk 85
Sun Valley Fruits & Grocery 51, 53
Suspect Video 132
Swiss-Master Chocolatier 41

T

TFO 133, 135
TV5 135
TVA (CHOT) 136
Taloua 128
Tam Tam Cyber Café 137
Teuscher Chocolates 42
The Bagel House 30
The Butcher Block Café 59, 63
The Butchers 59, 63
The Chocolate Messenger 43
The Cookworks 124
The Film Reference Library 129, 131
The Pie Shoppe 43
The Sultan's Tent 118
Théâtre français de Toronto 135
Théâtre La Tangente 135
Toronto-Franco 136
Truffle Treasures 43

V

Village Butcher 59, 63, 72, 87
Very Video 132

W

White House Meats 59, 64
Whole Foods Market 30, 43, 51, 53, 59, 88

Z

Zane Pâtisserie et Boulangerie 31, 88
Zazou 137

Nous voici à la fin de notre découverte. Nous espérons que vous avez aimé les aventures culturelles et gastronomiques dans lesquelles nous avons voulu vous emmener. Nous espérons surtout que vous continuerez à découvrir par vous-même, si vous ne l'avez déjà fait, le côté français de Toronto.

Au revoir et à bientôt !

Si vous avez des commentaires à nous adresser ou d'autres adresses francophones à nous transmettre, vous pouvez nous écrire à l'adresse électronique suivante : **contact@franco-toronto.ca**

Consultez régulièrement notre site Internet **www.franco-toronto.ca**

BON DE COMMANDE :

Vivre en français à Toronto • contact@franco-toronto.ca

☐ FRANCOPHONE ☐ ANGLOPHONE

☐ M. ☐ Mme ☐ Mlle

____
NOM

____
ADRESSE

____
VILLE CODE POSTAL

( ) ______________________________
TÉLÉPHONE EMAIL

QUANTITÉ COMMANDÉE – CANADA :

__________ livre(s) à 19,95 CAD/l'unité = __________ CAD

Frais de livraison pour
envoi par la poste : 4 CAD par livre x _____ exemplaire(s) = __________ CAD

7 % TPS = __________ CAD

TOTAL = __________ CAD

QUANTITÉ COMMANDÉE – INTERNATIONAL ET ÉTATS-UNIS :

__________ livre(s) à 14,95 USD/l'unité = __________ USD

Frais de livraison pour envoi par la poste (international) :
11 USD par livre x _____ exemplaire(s) = __________ USD

Frais de livraison pour envoi par la poste (États-Unis) :
6 USD par livre x _____ exemplaire(s) = __________ USD

TOTAL = __________ USD

Nous offrons des remises intéressantes sur les commandes de 10 exemplaires et plus. Veuillez nous contacter pour de plus amples renseignements sur nos prix et sur les frais de livraison pour les commandes de 10 exemplaires et plus : **contact@franco-toronto.ca**

Merci d'envoyer votre bon de commande et votre chèque à l'ordre de Franco Toronto à : **Franco Toronto**
#61—494 Avenue Road
Toronto ON CANADA M4V 2J5

Voulez-vous faire partie de notre base de données ?

☐ Veuillez me contacter via email pour des mises à jour.
☐ Veuillez ne pas me contacter pour des mises à jour.

franco **toronto**

N' oubliez pas de consulter notre site Internet à **www.franco-toronto.ca**